INSTITUTIONALIZING RIGHTS AND RELIGION

Modern statesmen and political theorists have long struggled to design institutions that will simultaneously respect individual freedom of religion, nurture religion's capacity to be a force for civic good and human rights, and tame religion's illiberal tendencies. Moving past the usual focus on personal, free expression of religion, this illuminating book – written by renowned scholars of law and religion from the United States, Britain, and Israel – considers how the institutional design of both religions and political regimes influences the relationship between religious practice and activity and human rights. The authors examine how the organization of religious communities affects human rights and investigate the scope of a just state's authority with respect to organized religion in the name of human rights. They explore the institutional challenges posed by, and possible responses to, the fraught relationship between religion and rights in the world today.

Leora Batnitzky is the Ronald O. Perelman Professor of Jewish Studies and Professor and Chair of the Department of Religion at Princeton University. Her publications include *Leo Strauss and Emmanuel Levinas: Philosophy and the Politics of Revelation* (2006) and *How Judaism Became a Religion: An Introduction to Modern Jewish Thought* (2011). She has been a visiting scholar at the Hebrew University of Jerusalem, the University of Tokyo, and New York University Law School.

Hanoch Dagan is the Stewart and Judy Colton Professor of Legal Theory and Innovation and former dean of the Tel Aviv University Faculty of Law, and a Senior Fellow at the Israel Democracy Institute. Dagan has written more than seventy articles in major law reviews and journals, as well as five books including, most recently, *Reconstructing American Legal Realism & Rethinking Private Law Theory* (2013) and *The Choice Theory of Contracts* (Cambridge, 2017, co-authored with Michael A. Heller).

Institutionalizing Rights and Religion

COMPETING SUPREMACIES

Edited by

Leora Batnitzky
Princeton University

Hanoch Dagan
Tel Aviv University

CAMBRIDGE
UNIVERSITY PRESS

CAMBRIDGE
UNIVERSITY PRESS

University Printing House, Cambridge CB2 8BS, United Kingdom
One Liberty Plaza, 20th Floor, New York, NY 10006, USA
477 Williamstown Road, Port Melbourne, VIC 3207, Australia
4843/24, 2nd Floor, Ansari Road, Daryaganj, Delhi – 110002, India
79 Anson Road, #06-04/06, Singapore 079906

Cambridge University Press is part of the University of Cambridge.

It furthers the University's mission by disseminating knowledge in the pursuit of education, learning, and research at the highest international levels of excellence.

www.cambridge.org
Information on this title: www.cambridge.org/9781107153714

DOI: 10.1017/9781316599969

First published 2017

A catalogue record for this publication is available from the British Library.

ISBN 978-1-107-15371-4 Hardback

Contents

Contributors

Ori Aronson is Assistant Professor in the Faculty of Law at Bar Ilan University.

Leora Batnitzky is Ronald O. Perelman Professor of Jewish Studies and Professor of Religion at Princeton University.

Yishai Blank is Associate Professor of Law in the Buchmann Faculty of Law at Tel Aviv University.

Mary Anne Case is Arnold I. Shure Professor of Law at University of Chicago Law School.

Hanoch Dagan is Stewart and Judy Colton Professor of Legal Theory and Innovation in the Faculty of Law at Tel Aviv University and Senior Fellow of the Israel Democracy Institute.

Peter G. Danchin is Professor of Law in the Frances K. Carey School of Law, University of Maryland.

Richard W. Garnett is Paul J. Schierl/Fort Howard Corporation Professor and Concurrent Professor of Political Science at the University of Notre Dame.

Roderick M. Hills Jr. is William T. Comfort III Professor of Law at New York University.

Michael Karayanni is Bruce W. Wayne Chair in International Law in the Faculty of Law at the Hebrew University of Jerusalem.

Cécile Laborde is Professor of Political Theory in the School of Public Policy at University College London.

Shahar Lifshitz is Professor in the Bar Ilan University Faculty of Law.

Amihai Radzyner is Associate Professor in the Bar Ilan University Faculty of Law.

Lawrence G. Sager is Alice Jane Drysdale Sheffield Regents Professor in the Austin School of Law at the University of Texas.

Haim Shapira is a senior lecturer in the Bar Ilan University Faculty of Law.

Yedidia Z. Stern is Vice President of the Israel Democracy Institute and Professor in the Bar Ilan University Faculty of Law.

Acknowledgments

The essays in this volume originated at a conference called "Religions, Rights, and Institutions," held at Princeton University in November 2014. The conference was co-sponsored by Princeton's Program in Law and Public Affairs and the Israel Democracy Institute, and we are especially grateful to Christopher Eisgruber and Kim Lane Schepple at Princeton and Yedidia Stern and Shahar Lifshitz of the Israel Democracy Institute for making such a productive collaboration possible. We also thank the administrative staff of Princeton's Program in Law and Public Affairs, Leslie Gerwin, Judith Rivkin, and Jennifer Bolton, for all their hard work that ensured the conference's success. Thanks are also due to Princeton's Center for Human Values for support in defraying editorial costs for this volume, as well as to Sally Freedman for her careful editing of the final manuscript.

Institutionalizing Rights and Religion: Introduction

Leora Batnitzky and Hanoch Dagan

THE TASK

Freedom of religion is a core human right, and a very complicated one. Its status as a core human right derives to some extent from its critical role in the historical development of human rights as we know them. But it is also a core human right thanks to its crucial significance to people's identity, which is revealed, in part, by its affinity with two other identitarian rights: the right to conscience and the right to culture. This connection raises difficult conceptual and normative questions concerning the value added (if any) of freedom of religion vis-à-vis these two rights and the putative justifications of freedom of religion. This book does not address these questions directly, but it is triggered by the complex cohabitation of these two aspects of the freedom of religion – by the way religion presents an intertwined individual and communal engagement.

Accordingly, our point of departure is freedom of religion's peculiar characterization as both deeply personal and essentially communal, and thus (at least typically) a highly institutionalized human right. The task of *Institutionalizing Rights and Religion* is to highlight the institutional challenges that are uniquely complex in the context of freedom of religion. We seek to shift the usual scholarly focus from the personal free expression of religion, to considering the significance of institutional design. Indeed, we believe that in order to understand freedom of religion, we must study how religions are structured as normative institutions and how state law regulates the way religious organizations are constituted and how they are able to function in a pluralistic society.

Our goal in this book, more specifically, is to highlight the significance of the institutional design of both religions and political regimes with respect to the relationship between religious practice and activity, and human rights. In the contemporary world, religious conviction, individual freedom, and institutional authority intersect in complex and volatile ways. Religiously motivated persons and organizations are sometimes among the most effective agents for securing human rights. But at other times and on other occasions, religion is the animating force behind terrifying and persistent threats to the rights of individuals. For several hundred years, modern statesmen and political theorists have struggled to design political and other institutions that will simultaneously respect the freedom of religion, nurture religion's capacity to be a force for civic good and human rights, and tame religion's illiberal tendencies.

Institutionalizing Rights and Religion seeks to reinvigorate this institutional study of the interaction of religion and human rights – a study that is particularly challenging, given that both religion and the state have institutionalized structures that claim authority over vital components of individual, family, and social life. This book examines how the internal organization (formal and informal) of religious communities affects the rights of members of these communities and the functioning of religion as a source of human rights. It investigates both the scope and limits of a just state's authority to compel changes in the internal aspects of organized religion, in the name of human rights. It explores how social and political institutions shape religious behavior and how they affect the human rights of members of religious communities and the society at large.

We do not of course purport to present a comprehensive discussion of these perennial multifaceted questions. All of the contributions that follow focus on rights rather than states' support of religions, which also entails an important institutional dimension; and most of these essays analyze the United States and Israel, both of which may be rather extreme test cases, since the former has a high level of separation of religion and state, while the latter has a high level of government involvement in religion. But we believe that the complexities of the issues discussed, as well as the particular – and particularly interesting – examples considered, already provide important insights that are of relevance beyond the particular contexts in which these issues and problems arise. Indeed, we think that they illuminate the institutional challenges posed by, and possible responses to, the fraught relationship between religion and rights in the world today.

Institutionalizing Rights and Religion is divided into two parts. The first part, "Secular Institutions and the Limits of Religious Recognition," considers what kinds of religions and religious institutionalization the secular state can and cannot tolerate. The second part, "The Challenges of Religious Institutions for the Secular State," turns to some of the ways in which religions and religious institutions put pressure on secular states to defend their own commitments to individual rights, tolerance, and democratic pluralism. Taken together, both parts resist the obvious and common temptation to treat the modern nation-state and religion as wholly separable enterprises. Instead, these essays show that religions, rights, and institutions not only influence, but also continually shape and form one another. This means that those concerned about the relation between religion and human rights need to attend to the complexity and diversity of religions, rights, and institutions in the modern world, rather than attempt to come up with a one-size-fits-all solution to these very real problems.

PART I: SECULAR INSTITUTIONS AND THE LIMITS OF RELIGIOUS RECOGNITION

Part I focuses on three interrelated issues: reasons for accommodating religious institutions, the limits of such accommodation, and the possibility of deflecting difficulties by delegating accommodation to geographical subunits. Chapter 1, "Religion in the Law: The Disaggregation Approach," by Cécile Laborde, raises the broad question of whether religion ought to be accommodated at all. Laborde engages two influential interpretive theories of freedom of religion in political theory: first, what she calls the *substitution approach*, which argues that freedom of religion can be adequately expressed by a substitute category, such as freedom of conscience; and second, what she calls the *proxy approach*, which argues that the notion of religion should be upheld in the law, albeit as a proxy for a range of different goods. After rejecting both of these strategies, Laborde defends a third alternative, which she calls the *disaggregation strategy*. This strategy suggests that different parts of the law should capture different dimensions of religion for the protection of different normative values. In Chapter 2, "The Puzzle of the Catholic Church," Lawrence Sager asks more specifically why the Catholic Church in the United States is entitled to insist that its priests be male without interference from the state. Sager considers four possible arguments for this accommodation, but argues that ultimately only the fourth one he describes warrants this accommodation. This is the claim that members of political communities have a right to be free from governmental intrusion into close and personal relationships, except in cases of harm or abuse.

Chapters 3 and 4 argue for a greater openness to religious accommodation in the United States and Israel, respectively. In "Religious Accommodations and – and Among – Civil Rights: Separation, Toleration, and Accommodation," Richard Garnett maintains that religion is special and therefore should be singled out for special treatment and respect in American laws, traditions, and practices. This means that while the tension between religious liberty and (other) civil rights is sometimes real, it is crucial to remember that the tension is *among* civil rights claims. Garnett argues that Americans have good reasons, anchored in a commitment to pluralism, for insisting that governments should not prevent, correct, or even discourage all instances of wrongful discrimination. Focusing on the Israeli context, in "Israeli Law and Jewish Law in Israel: A Zero-Sum Game?" Yedidia Stern argues that Jewish religious law (*halakha*) and Israeli civil law ought to contribute to each other and, in so doing, give the citizens of the Jewish and democratic state a legal system that suits the unique character of the Jewish nation-state. Stern maintains that an engagement between the *halakhic* authorities and secular legislators and judges is necessary, because the struggle between them ultimately affects the stability of Israeli democracy.

Chapters 5 and 6 argue for the limitations of religious accommodation in the United States and Israel, respectively. In "Why 'Live-and-Let-Live' Is Not a Viable Solution to the Difficult Problems of Religious Accommodation in the Age of Sexual Civil Rights," Mary Anne Case considers proposals over the past decade for accommodation of religious objectors in the context of state laws recognizing same-sex marriage in the United States. Case argues that the expansion of claims for accommodation does not solve, but rather compounds the problem of selective attention to only a subset of the laws and regulations to which religiously motivated actors might have a conscientious objection. Turning to the Israeli context, in "Control by Accommodation: Religious Jurisdiction Among the Palestinian-Arab Minority in Israel," Michael Karayanni argues that, while accommodation of religious minorities in non-Western states is generally considered in line with liberalism rather than in conflict with it, this is not the case in Israel. Karayanni argues that maintaining the *millet* system of religious courts has historically impeded relations between Jews and Arabs in Israel, and as long as the state of conflict between Israeli Jewish collective aspirations and Palestinian collective aspiration continues, there will be no genuine move toward the abolishment of the Israeli *millet* system.

Chapters 7 and 8 consider possibilities for deflecting some of the difficulties of religious accommodation by delegating accommodation to geographical subunits in the United States and Israel, respectively. In "Decentralizing Religious and Secular Accommodations," Roderick Hills argues that the decentralization of religious accommodations to subnational governments may be a way to extend equal concern and respect to rival and reasonable conceptions of religious liberty. Hills analyzes the American version of federalism, epitomized by the US Supreme Court's decisions in *Hobby Lobby* and *City of Boerne v. Flores*, as such a form of equal concern and respect. In "In Search of the Secular," Yishai Blank argues that secularism in Israel should be understood as an effort by a minority to confront and oppose the dominant and empowered state religion, and as such, it should be given protection. Blank contends that, in Israel, localities have been the only place where individuals and communities have been able to materialize a fuller idea of secularism, secularizing public spaces, disentangling their locality from religion and making belief in God one choice among others. Blank concludes by advocating for *islands of pluralism*, where individuals from different communities are exposed to each other, in spite of radical differences.

PART II: THE CHALLENGES OF RELIGIOUS INSTITUTIONS FOR THE SECULAR STATE

The second part of this book turns to distinct challenges posed by religious institutions regulating education, marriage, and religious conversion in Israel, the United Kingdom, and India. In Chapter 9, "The 'How Many?' Question? An Institutionalist's Guide to Pluralism," Ori Aronson considers adjudication and marriage registration in Israel's multiple religious communities, in order to theorize the institutional implications of normative pluralism and to identify workable, useful benchmarks, considerations, or heuristics for pluralist institutional design. Aronson identifies two fundamental paradigms of pluralist institutionalism: *mimetic pluralism*, in which the pluralist field is meant to accommodate an existing diversity of practices within the state apparatus; and *poietic pluralism*, in which the state engages in the design or fosters the development of new institutional alternatives.

Debates about state support of religious schools in England and Israel are the focus of Chapters 10 and 11. In Chapter 10, "Equality in Religious Schools: The *JFS* Case Reconsidered," Haim Shapira considers the *Jews' Free School* case in England and the *Emmanuel* case in Israel. Shapira argues that both cases represent the willingness of Supreme Courts to intervene in religious schools' policies in order to assure equality and prevent what they see as discrimination. Beyond the local difficulties involved in each ruling, both cases demonstrate the problematic nature of greater state involvement in religious schools and organizations. In Chapter 11, "Religious Freedom as a Technology of Modern Secular Governance," Peter Danchin also analyzes the recent decision of the UK Supreme Court in the *Jews' Free School* case. Danchin argues that once the antinomies generated by the paradoxes of religious freedom are made visible, it becomes clear that the right to religious liberty is not a single, stable principle existing outside culture, spatial geographies, or power, but instead is a contested, polyvalent concept existing and unfolding within historical political orders.

Chapters 12 and 13 focus on the challenges presented by state regulation of Jewish marriage and other religious matters in Israel. In Chapter 12, "Civil Regulation of Religious Marriage from the Perspectives of Pluralism, Human Rights, and Political Compromise," Shahar Lifshitz considers debates about the regulation of Jewish marriages in Israel from three points of view: a liberal-pluralistic perspective, a religious perspective that seeks to protect the right to religious marriage and divorce, and a national religious perspective that tries to accommodate both of these positions. Lifshitz argues that liberals must recognize non-liberal arguments for maintaining state regulation of religious marriage and divorce, while also demanding that the state offer its citizens a civil marriage or a parallel track called marriage and a means of divorce, irrespective of their religious faith. In Chapter 13, "The Impact of Supreme Court Rulings on the Halakhic Status of the Official Rabbinical Courts in Israel," Amihai Radzyner considers the complex relations between two rabbinical court systems in Israel: the official courts authorized by Israeli law to deal with matrimonial matters of Jews in Israel, and the dozens of private courts that primarily deal with civil arbitrations and have no legal powers. Radzyner focuses on the ruling of the Israeli Supreme Court, sitting as the High Court of Justice in the *Amir* case, that the rabbinical court must not litigate in areas that do not concern marriage and divorce, even if the parties have appointed it as an agreed-upon arbitrator to litigate their civil suit in order; he uses this case to show that basing the *halakhic* argument about the foundation of the court on Israeli law carries risks; when this status changes, so does the *halakhic* status of the court.

Finally, in Chapter 14, "Is Conversion a Human Right? A Comparative Look at Religious Zionism and Hindu Nationalism," Leora Batnitzky considers how ambivalence about religious conversion informs not just religious Zionism and Hindu nationalism, but also their secular predecessors and counterparts. Batnitzky argues that religious Zionists and Hindu nationalists utilize modern liberal commitments to the rule of law and to the priority of individual conscience as a means to support state regulation of religious conversion. She considers the implications of this analysis for thinking about whether religious conversion is a human right, as well as for what religious Zionist and Hindu nationalist anxieties about religious conversion might say about contemporary debates about religious freedom.

PART I

Secular Institutions and the Limits of Religious Recognition

1

Religion in the Law: The Disaggregation Approach

Cécile Laborde

Over the last few decades, sociologists, anthropologists, lawyers, and religious studies scholars have put the category of "religion" under intense critical scrutiny. This criticism has – belatedly, but vigorously – found echoes in the political theory of religious freedom. Prominent political philosophers have been asking questions such as: What justifies the special treatment of religion in the law? Do legal constructions of religious freedom adequately protect all forms of religious life? And is the special protection of religion an unfair privilege granted to religious believers?[1]

Liberal political philosophers reject two possible approaches to these questions from the outset. The first asserts that religion, because it is rooted in the duties we have to a transcendental being, expresses our essential nature as God-created creatures, and therefore deserves special deference and respect.[2] Liberal political

[1] RONALD DWORKIN, RELIGION WITHOUT GOD (2013); BRIAN LEITER, WHY TOLERATE RELIGION? (2013); CHARLES TAYLOR & JOCELYN MACLURE, SECULARISM AND FREEDOM OF CONSCIENCE (2011). On the political theory of the US Religion Clauses, see CHRISTOPHER EISGRUBER & LAWRENCE SAGER, RELIGIOUS FREEDOM AND THE CONSTITUTION (2007); ANDREW KOPPELMAN, *DEFENDING AMERICAN RELIGIOUS NEUTRALITY* (2013); Micah Schwartzman, *What If Religion Is Not Special?* 79 *U. Chi. L. Rev.* 1351–1427 (2012).

[2] Michael W. McConnell, *Why Protect Religious Freedom?* 123 *Yale L. J.* 770–92 (2013); Michael Stokes Paulsen, *Priority of God: A Theory of Religious Liberty*, 39 PEPPERDINE L. REV. 1159 (2013); Rafael Domingo, *Religion for Hedgehogs? An Argument against the Dworkinian Approach to Religious Freedom*, 1 OXFORD J. L. AND REL. 1–22 (2012).

Earlier versions of this text were presented in Ghent (Workshop "Law's Imagining of Religion," Sep. 2014), Princeton (Conference "Religions, Rights and Institutions," Nov. 2014), Oxford (Oxford Political Thought Conference, Jan. 2015), Brussels (ERC Public Lecture Series Human Rights and Politics, Feb. 2015), and London (RAPT Conference "Religion in Liberal Political Philosophy," University College London, June 2015). I am grateful to the organizers of and participants in these events for helpful feedback. For written comments, I am indebted to Aurélia Bardon, François Boucher, Emanuela Ceva, Chris Eisgruber, Lois Lee, Nick Martin, James Nickel, Onora O'Neil, Jean-Yves Pranchère, Enzo Rossi, Hans Ingvar Roth, Lawrence Sager, Winnifred Sullivan, and (especially) Andrew Koppelman and Daniel Statman. Research for this paper was supported by the European Research Council (ERC) Grant 283867, "Is Religion Special? Reformulating Secularism and Religion in Contemporary Political Theory." This text was published in *Law and Philosophy*, Sep. 2015.

philosophers, following John Rawls, start from the idea that a just political order should be responsive to a pluralism of ethical principles and ways of life.[3] It should not entrench any particular (here, theistic) conception of the good life as worthy of politico-legal protection. The second possible approach is that endorsed by most critical scholars of religion. It denounces not simply the notions of religion and freedom of religion, but the core ideals of normative liberalism (secularism, religious freedom, the separation between public and private, state sovereignty, and so forth) as ethnocentric, mystifying, and oppressive. The project of liberal political philosophy, by contrast, is a normative one. Its response to the defaults of particular laws and institutions is not to throw up its hands in despair and lament that religious freedom, or liberal justice, are "mission impossible."[4] It tries, rather, to articulate appropriate standards that can serve as benchmarks to evaluate (and reform) the existing state of affairs.

The political theorists' approach is normative in a further sense. It seeks to identify the core values that should be protected by the law. As a result, it eschews purely descriptive or semantic approaches to legal terms. When it considers freedom of religion, it is not concerned with defining what religion is – an elusive project at best, as critical scholars of religion have amply shown.[5] Rather, it rejects any essentialist or semantic approach, and is concerned with identifying the core values that the law can properly express.[6] This is important because not all values can, or indeed should, be expressed by the law. Just as we would not want the law to express the whole of the value of "the family," for example, so we would not want the law to capture the whole of the value of religion. At best, the law will put forward an interpretive notion of the family, or of religion. That a particular law or theory does not capture what religion really is, therefore, is not in itself a sufficient objection to it. What matters is that the law, or the theory, expresses and protects the correct underlying values. It is at this more fundamental level that interpretive approaches must be assessed and evaluated.

In what follows, I evaluate two influential interpretive theories of freedom of religion in political theory, before articulating and defending an alternative one. The first, which I call the *substitution approach*, argues that freedom of religion can be

[3] JOHN RAWLS, POLITICAL LIBERALISM (1996).

[4] Stanley Fish, *Mission Impossible: Setting the Just Boundaries between Church and State*, 97 *COLUM. L. REV.* 2255–2333 (1997); WINNIFRED FALLERS SULLIVAN, IMPOSSIBILITY OF RELIGIOUS FREEDOM (2005).

[5] WILFRED CANTWELL SMITH, MEANING AND END OF RELIGION (1990); WINNIFRED FALLERS SULLIVAN, PAYING THE WORDS EXTRA: RELIGIOUS DISCOURSE IN THE SUPREME COURT OF THE UNITED STATES (1994); TALAL ASAD, FORMATIONS OF THE SECULAR: CHRISTIANITY, ISLAM, MODERNITY (2003); JONATHAN Z. SMITH, RELATING RELIGION: ESSAYS IN THE STUDY OF RELIGIONS (2004); TOMOKO MAZUZAWA, INVENTION OF WORLD RELIGIONS (2005); TIM FITZGERALD, IDEOLOGY OF RELIGIOUS STUDIES (2005).

[6] Two interpretive theories of religious freedom are Timothy Macklem, *Faith as a Secular Value*, 45, Part 1, 1.65 *MCGILL L. J.* 1–64 (2000) and DWORKIN, RELIGION WITHOUT GOD.

adequately expressed by a substitute category: typically, freedom of conscience. The second, the *proxy approach*, argues that the notion of religion should be upheld in the law, albeit as a proxy for a range of different goods. After showing that neither approach adequately meets crucial desiderata for an inclusive theory of religious freedom, I set out my preferred approach – the *disaggregating approach* – and defend it against the alternatives.

THREE DESIDERATA/THREE CRITICISMS

Before describing the various approaches, I identify the desiderata that an inclusive theory of religious freedom must meet. I do so by surveying common criticisms of the existing law of religious freedom, from both critical and normative standpoints. They are all formulated against the implicit or explicit background of a theory of fairness as inclusiveness. Three different lines of critique have been developed: 1) religious freedom is construed too narrowly to protect a range of valuable religious practices adequately; 2) religious freedom is rooted in a sectarian view that religion itself is a special good; and 3) the privileges of religious freedom treat nonreligious citizens unfairly. Let me explain these in more detail.

1. *Too narrow*. A number of critical scholars have argued that the legal treatment of religion still bears the marks of the ethnocentric, Western, textualist, Protestant, and belief-based understandings of religion that have accompanied the rise of the modern, secular Euro-Atlantic state. As a result, religions that are more practice-, tradition-, or ritual-based have fared badly under the liberal law of religious freedom. There are many illustrations of this distortion. Mahmood and other writers influenced by Asad have argued that liberal law struggles to protect embodied practices of piety – paradigmatically, Islamic veiling practices.[7] Winnifred Sullivan has shown how the elitist, textualist, Protestant bias of US judges renders them incapable of capturing the popular, unruly, ritualized religiosity that she saw at work in certain funerary displays in a Florida cemetery.[8] Constitutional commentators have castigated a US Supreme Court decision that failed to see government logging plans through a Native American sacred territory as an infringement of religious freedom (*Lyng v. Northwest Indian Cemetery Protective Association*, 1988).[9]

This criticism is valid and important, provided it is clarified in two crucial ways. First, for reasons adduced earlier, it has to be presented as an interpretive

7 SABA MAHMOOD, POLITICS OF PIETY: THE ISLAMIC REVIVAL AND THE FEMINIST SUBJECT (2005).

8 SULLIVAN, IMPOSSIBILITY.

9 Lori Beaman, *Aboriginal Spirituality and the Legal Construction of Freedom of Religion*, 44 J. CHURCH AND STATE 135–49 (2002); TISA WENGER, WE HAVE A RELIGION: THE 1920S PUEBLO INDIAN DANCE CONTROVERSY AND AMERICAN RELIGIOUS FREEDOM 255–58 (2009); KENT GREENAWALT, RELIGION AND THE CONSTITUTION, PART 1: FREE EXERCISE 196–99 (1996).

not a semantic critique. In other words, the claim should not be that the existing law does not protect all that is religious, according to some ordinary-meaning, semantic understanding of the term. Rather, the claim is that the law fails to protect practices that exhibit those normative values – still to be specified – which are valuable in religion. Second, the critique must be formulated carefully. Some versions of it suggest that what is wrong with the liberal law of freedom of religion is that it protects only beliefs, and not practices.[10] If that is the claim, it is mistaken. While it is true that canonical liberal accounts of freedom of religion – from John Locke onward – distinguish (with good reason) between freedom of thought and belief on the one hand, and freedom of expression and practice on the other, this does not mean that the latter is left unprotected. That religious life has an essentially expressive dimension has been at the core of struggles over religious freedom for centuries. And the modern cases of religious exemptions from liberal laws have all concerned religious practices, not merely religious belief. This is true, for example, of Sabbatarian exemptions, conscientious objection to military service, and accommodation of religious dress in workplaces, to name just a few.

If that is correct, what does the *too narrow* critique amount to? In my view, it should be formulated as a more precise claim, as follows: the standard law of religious freedom tends to protect practices that are believed to be a matter of compulsory obligation. For example, Quaker pacifists see themselves as under a stringent duty to refuse to bear arms; Sabbatarians see themselves as obligated to honor the God-designed day of rest; and so forth. The *too narrow* critique here, then, is that a range of non-Christian or non-Protestant practices, when such practices do not directly express a belief in a divine injunction, is less likely to be protected by the liberal state. One example of such a narrow view of religious practice is the ruling of some European judges, in Islamic veiling cases, that because the *hijab* is not a compulsory requirement of the Muslim faith, it does not fall under the protection of religious freedom. Another example is the Florida burial displays studied by Sullivan. Insofar as much of religious activity is rooted in orthopraxy rather than orthodoxy, the *too narrow* critique is effective. An important desideratum of an inclusive theory of religious freedom is that it is not narrowly biased in favor of obligation-based belief and practices.

10 This criticism can, however, be validly applied to the European Court of Human Rights (ECHR) jurisprudence on freedom of religion. The Court has overemphasized the distinction between *forum internum* and *forum externum*, notably in order to deny religious freedom protections to "manifestations" of religious belief involving Islamic dress and symbols. See, e.g., Carolyn Evans, *"Islamic Headscarf" in the European Court of Human Rights*, 7 MELBOURNE J. INT'L L. (2006); Isabelle Rorive, *Religious Symbols in the Public Space: In Search of a European Answer*, 30 CARDOZO L. REV. 2673–74 (2008–09).

2. *Sectarian.* The critique here points in a different direction. It is that freedom of religion protects a sectarian good – a good whose value is not universally recognized: it is a relic from an earlier age, one that has little justification in contemporary pluralistic societies where religion is only one of the things that people value. Some political theorists, for example, point out that the liberal state should protect generic capacities or moral powers, such as people's ability to form, revise, and live by their conception of the good, whatever it might be.[11] The liberal state, then, should content itself with protecting generic rights and freedoms, such as thought, belief, expression, and association. It should not favor one specific way in which the good is pursued, namely, the religious life. To be properly inclusive of all its citizens, the liberal state should only appeal to values and ideals that everyone can, in principle, recognize and adhere to. For this to be the case, the relevant values have to be abstract rather than concrete, general rather than specific, ecumenical rather than sectarian.

3. *Unfair to nonreligious people.* This criticism follows from the previous one. One consequence of the sectarian privileging of religion in the law, it is argued, is that nonreligious citizens are unfairly treated by the law of religious freedom. This is particularly the case in the area of legal exemptions and accommodations. In modern, highly regulated states, citizens are subjected to a wide array of laws and regulations – ranging from health, safety, and educational requirements to nondiscrimination on grounds of gender or sexuality, or from parking and zoning regulations to regulation on dress and uniform. Yet typically, the law provides exemptions from these burdensome laws for religious citizens, but not for nonreligious citizens.

As egalitarian theorists of religious freedom have pointed out, this is unfair. It is unfair, in particular, if citizens with comparable beliefs are denied the protections enjoyed by religiously motivated citizens. Thus secular pacifists deserve the same level of protection as religious conscientious objectors – as the US Supreme Court recognized in celebrated Vietnam War cases (*United States v. Seeger*, 1965 and *Welsh v. United States*, 1970). And doctors refusing to abstain from life-endangering abortions in Catholic hospitals should be able to appeal to their conscience in the same way as Catholic doctors refusing to perform abortions.[12]

We have, then, three desiderata that an inclusive law of religious freedom must meet. It must not be (i) narrow, (ii) sectarian, or (iii) unfair to nonreligious people. An immediate objection arises. Can these desiderata be met simultaneously? On the face of it, it seems that they point in opposite directions: one cannot satisfy them all at the same time. Thus, if the law does not single out the seemingly sectarian

[11] RAWLS, POLITICAL LIBERALISM.

[12] TAYLOR & MACLURE, SECULARISM; EISGRUBER & SAGER, RELIGIOUS FREEDOM; Schwartzman, *What If Religion*; Schwartzman, *Religion as a Legal Proxy* (presented at APSA Annual Meeting, 2014; http://ssrn.com/abstract=2416254).

good of religion (ii), it is unlikely that it will be able to protect all valuable religious practices (i). In what follows, I argue that two existing strategies – the substitution strategy and the proxy strategy – are indeed vulnerable to this "trilemma," in that they fail to reconcile the three desiderata. Either they are nonsectarian but too narrow, or they accommodate all valuable religious practices but are sectarian in their valuing of religion itself. I then suggest that my proposed alternative – the disaggregation strategy – succeeds in meeting the three desiderata at once.

THE SUBSTITUTION STRATEGY

The substitution strategy is favored by prominent egalitarian theorists of religious freedom.[13] The general structure of the theory is clear enough. What grounds the respect that the state owes to persons *qua* persons is the human capacity for moral or spiritual agency, not for leading good lives with a determinate, perhaps religious content. Rawls, for example, argued that what the liberal state protects is a generic ability or moral power: people's capacity to form, revise, and live by their conception of the good. More recently, Ronald Dworkin has suggested that religious freedom is not *sui generis* and is only one implication of a right to ethical independence.[14]

But now egalitarian theorists of religious freedom face a problem. If religious freedom is broadened and dissolved into a general right of ethical independence, it will only ground a general right of moral freedom; it will not ground any special right of exemption. As Dworkin has argued, if the liberal state is to be neutral between different ways of pursuing the good (be it a life of religious piety, scholarly pursuit, or consumerist materialism), it becomes impossible to carve out a specific area of protection from the law. Yet while Dworkin is ready (at least on principle[15]) to bite this particular bullet, no other egalitarian theorist does so.[16] All seek to justify the principle of exemptions from the law. This means that they need to distinguish, among the vast range of commitments and conceptions of the good that people hold in pluralistic societies, those that deserve special protection. It is not sufficient to appeal to a "thin theory" of the good à la Rawls or Dworkin. Egalitarian theorists need a more substantive theory of the specific good that is protected by freedom of religion in accommodation cases. They need what Charles Taylor calls "strong

[13] TAYLOR & MACLURE, SECULARISM; Schwartzman, *What If Religion* and *Religion as a Legal Proxy*. See also MARTHA NUSSBAUM, LIBERTY OF CONSCIENCE: IN DEFENSE OF AMERICA'S TRADITION OF RELIGIOUS EQUALITY (2008).

[14] RONALD DWORKIN, JUSTICE FOR HEDGEHOGS, 376.

[15] But not consistently. See Cécile Laborde, *Dworkin's Religious Freedom without God*, 94 *B. U. L. Rev.* 1255–71 (2014).

[16] Taylor & McLure, Eisgruber & Sager, and Schwartzman all defend exemptions. Even explicitly anti-exemptionist theorists, such as Brian Barry (CULTURE AND EQUALITY, 2001) and Brian Leiter (WHY TOLERATE RELIGION?), make exceptions to their anti-exception stance.

evaluations": evaluations about better or worse; important or trivial conceptions of the good life; views that are not reducible to mere preferences, desires, and inclinations, but are rather the standards by which desires, preferences, and inclinations can be judged.[17]

Typically, egalitarian theorists find this good in the value of living by the demands of one's conscience. The good protected by freedom of conscience is the ability to act in accordance with one's perceived moral duties, which are seen as categorical.[18] Rawls, for example, justified the "lexical priority" of freedom of conscience by hypothesizing that the parties in the original position would under no condition agree to sacrifice the pursuit of their nonnegotiable, binding commitments. Maclure and Taylor argued that religious convictions ought to be legally protected as convictions of conscience, understood as "meaning-giving beliefs and commitments."[19] Convictions of conscience give a moral orientation to people's lives; they are the fundamental beliefs and commitments that make it possible for persons to have a moral identity and to make moral judgments. Egalitarian theorists, then, substitute conscience for religion – or, to put it differently, they identify acting conscientiously as the core moral value that is traditionally protected by freedom of religion. *Religion* is the semantic term, but *conscience* is the interpretive value. If that is the case, then, the law should protect freedom of conscience, instead of freedom of religion.

How does the substitution strategy fare in relation to our three desiderata? I argue that it meets (ii) and (iii) but fails to meet (i). The substitution strategy meets (ii), the nonsectarian requirement. This is because, as Paul Bou-Habib has argued, freedom of conscience is rooted in a good that many people, both religious and nonreligious, recognize as a valuable good. This is the good of living a life of integrity: a life where one's actions cohere with one's ideas about what is right for one to do. When people are forced to act against these convictions, they experience a loss of personal integrity, a feeling of self-alienation, a sense that their own actions violate the moral principles that define who they are.[20]

The substitution strategy also meets (iii): it is not unfair toward nonreligious citizens. Having identified the feature in virtue of which religious practices are protected, egalitarian theorists are able to extend protection to nonreligious practices that exhibit the same feature. So they are able to equalize relative comparable burdens. Eisgruber and Sager justify the draft exemptions granted

[17] CHARLES TAYLOR, SOURCES OF THE SELF: THE MAKING OF MODERN IDENTITY (1989).

[18] Paul Bou-Habib, A *Theory of Religious Accommodation*, 23 J. APPLIED PHILOSOPHY 109–26 (2006).

[19] MACLURE & TAYLOR, SECULARISM 75–76.

[20] Paul Bou-Habib, *Theory of Religious Accommodation*, in MACLURE & TAYLOR, SECULARISM 76–77; NUSSBAUM, LIBERTY OF CONSCIENCE 19–20, 53–55; CHANDRAN KUKATHAS, LIBERAL ARCHIPELAGO: A THEORY OF FREEDOM AND DIVERSITY 55 (2003).

to secular pacifists during the Vietnam War in this way.[21] MacLure and Taylor would treat secular and religiously motivated vegetarians equally,[22] while Schwartzman would grant secular doctors in Catholic hospitals the right to act as their conscience dictates in tricky abortion cases.[23] All these practices are relevantly similar and comparable because they are rooted in stringent obligations of conscience.

However, the substitution strategy fails to meet desideratum (i): it remains too narrowly tailored to a certain kind of obligation-based practice. As a result, it is vulnerable to the objection we set out previously, namely, that many valuable religious practices are not matters of obligation. Crucially, it does not mean that these practices thereby fail to express the core value that religious freedom expresses. Assuming – with Bou-Habib – that this core value is ethical integrity, it is obvious that many (though not all)[24] religious practices protect ethical integrity, even though they are not rooted in conscience.[25] Consider, for example, the following: the ingestion of peyote in Native American ceremonies, the wearing of *hijabs* by pious Muslim women, or funerary displays in Sullivan's cemetery. They are valuable religious practices: valuable because they allow individuals to live with integrity. But they may not be demands of conscience, strictly speaking.[26] Of course, there has been a tendency among legal practitioners to re-describe these practices in the language of conscientious obligation, so as to accommodate them under the label of freedom of religion. But this has been rightly castigated as a Protestantization of non-Protestant religion, and this re-description will not at any rate be relevant to all contested instances. Paradigmatic of these difficulties is, again, the *Lyng* case. However hard one tries, it is difficult to reconcile the intuition that the protection of sacred lands is a core dimension of Native American religious life (insofar as it allows members to live with integrity) with the egalitarian postulate that what

21 EISGRUBER & SAGER, RELIGIOUS FREEDOM, 113–14.

22 MACLURE & TAYLOR, SECULARISM.

23 Schwartzman, *Religion as Legal Proxy*.

24 Here I have in mind a range of activities of religious organizations – such as the hiring and firing of staff, the provision of public services, etc. There is a tendency to define all these activities as "religious" (cf. Hosanna-Tabor, 2012 and Burwell v. Hobby Lobby, 2014). In my view, the rights of religious associations should fall under the right of associations more generally. I make the case in Laborde, *Liberalism's Religion* (forthcoming), chapter 5.

25 Bou-Habib himself seems to concede that conscience cannot exhaust the value of integrity. He writes: "as well as depending on compliance with perceived duty, integrity may depend on one's attempting continuously (which is not to say incessantly) to discover what one's duties in fact are. It seems to me that religious conduct that aims at achieving communion with a divine will or ultimate reality may have a claim to accommodation under this heading. The ingestion of peyote in the sacramental worship of NAC is an example." Bou-Habib, *Theory*, 123).

26 Andrew Koppelman, *Conscience, Volitional Necessity, and Religious Exemptions*, 15 LEGAL THEORY 215, 222–23 (2009).

freedom of religion protects is the value of conscience. As we shall now see, the proxy strategy offers a solution to this particular problem.

THE PROXY STRATEGY

Following is the general structure of the proxy strategy, as recently articulated by Andrew Koppelman.[27] The proxy strategy accepts the general criticisms levelled against the concept of religion in the law, and endorses the shift from a semantic to an interpretive approach. In particular, Koppelman argues that there is no essence to religion, and that there is no directly identifiable good associated with religion that the law should aim to identify and protect. Therefore, the proxy strategy rejects the reductionist move of the substitution strategy and points out that whatever is protected under the label "religion" cannot be reduced to the value of conscience. Yet the fact that the term "religion" does not refer to one identifiable good, but rather to a loose cluster of different goods, does not mean that it is a useless legal term. On the contrary, the use of the term "religion" can be seen, in Wittgensteinian fashion, as a fairly stable linguistic practice exhibiting sufficient family resemblance to protect a broad range of activities. Inevitably, like all legal proxies, the term "religion" will be sometimes under-inclusive (when it fails to protect secular conscience) or over-inclusive (when it protects religious activities that do not express any particular good). But, Koppelman argues, it is still better than any other alternative. He draws an analogy with compulsory driving licenses. The aim of the law is to ensure safe driving, and it uses driving licenses as a proxy. Even though there is no guarantee that those holding a valid driving license, and only they, will be safe drivers, the proxy is still the best way to approximate safe driving.[28]

How well does the proxy strategy fare in relation to our three desiderata? I argue that it meets (i) but fails to meet (ii) and (iii).

First, because it sees religion as a set of loosely connected practices rather than as an essence, it is able to accommodate the critique that standard understandings of religion are too narrow. Koppelman argues, following Greenawalt, that in practice, courts have rarely found it difficult to identify what religious practices are. Some judges may hold a narrow, Protestantized view of the demands of religion, but this is a feature of their idiosyncratic training and bias, not of the polysemic and flexible notion of religion that has become prevalent in the law. On the family resemblance

[27] Andrew Koppelman, *Religion's Specialized Specialness*, U. CHI. L. REV. DIALOGUE, 71, 78 (2012); Andrew Koppelman, *Neutrality and the Religion Analogy* (2014, (http://papers.ssrn.com/sol3/papers.cfm?abstract_id=2454399). See also ANDREW KOPPELMAN, DEFENDING AMERICAN RELIGIOUS NEUTRALITY (2013).

[28] Koppelman, *Neutrality*, 12.

view, there is no reason why they should be biased in this way. On the contrary, a vague notion allows an ongoing conversation about the meaning of religion, and suggests the inclusion of unusual or minority religious beliefs and practices by analogical reasoning.[29] Thus practices that have no connection to a transcendental god or to individual conscience – from Buddhist rituals to Native American traditional practices – can be brought under the protection of freedom of religion. The *Lyng* case – the "blind spot" of the US First Amendment definition of religion – was wrongly decided only because judges took too narrow a view of what counts as a burden on religion.[30]

Second, however, it is not clear that the proxy strategy can escape the charge of being sectarian. This is not only (or necessarily) because it protects a good that is a good only for some but not for others. It is, more fundamentally, because it does not aspire to protect a clearly identifiable, valuable good (or bundle of goods): it is not clear what religion is a proxy for. Consider, in this context, the limits of Koppelman's analogy with the driving license. In this case, the law identifies a valuable aim – safe driving – and sets out a proxy to achieve it (however imperfectly). The structure of freedom of religion, however, is different. The problem is not that the proxy achieves the good imperfectly or indirectly (this, after all, is the point of proxies). The problem, rather, is that it is not clear that the law protects a good at all. If religion, in the ordinary-meaning semantic sense, is a complex bundle of things, not all of them good, then it is not clear that the legal protection of religion actually expresses any interpretive value at all.[31]

Third, the proxy strategy does not adequately protect nonreligious practices that, on the face of it, are as valuable as religious practices. Consider again the *Lyng* case. Koppelman's reading would suggest that as long as a practice can be called "religious," in the ordinary sense of the term, it will enjoy the protection of religious

[29] See also GREENAWALT, RELIGION AND THE CONSTITUTION, 139–42.

[30] Koppelman, *Neutrality*, 11.

[31] To clarify one possible misunderstanding: When I say that religion does not protect only "good" things, I do not refer to religious practices that, say, grievously infringe on the rights of others. When liberals talk about good and bad religion, they usually have in mind such cases. Religion is not religion, they claim, when it demands that abortion clinics or shopping centers be bombed, or that children be denied access to life-saving medicine. I disagree. Insofar as these actions are expressive of individuals' ethical integrity, they correctly express religious values. This does not mean to say, of course, that they should *ipso facto* be tolerated: in liberal societies, the pursuit of the good is constrained by the demands of the right. When I say that some religious activities are not "good," what I have in mind, instead, are practices that are claimed as exercises of religion by religious organizations, yet have only a tenuous connection to the normative value of ethical integrity. When religious organizations spend money, run businesses, hire staff, and provide secular services, it is not clear that they *ipso facto* express the value of ethical integrity. On the disaggregation theory I favor, as I suggest later, such activities are best protected under generic rights of freedom of association, with no special concern for the religious nature of the organizations. The good pursued here is associative freedom, not freedom of religion.

freedom. But, as critics have pointed out, the First Amendment's singling out of religion has led to a radical distortion of Native American practices. Aboriginal peoples typically see all their daily practices as suffused with their community way of life – not only praying, but also singing and dancing, as well as respecting sacred burial sites and food-gathering, hunting, and fishing. When the Pueblo Indians fought for recognition under the First Amendment, they were forced arbitrarily to separate their way of life into religious and nonreligious domains. One effect of the singling out of religion is arbitrarily to favor certain types of activities over more broadly defined "cultural" or "traditional" practices.[32] Such distortions are less likely to occur under constitutional settlements, such as the Canadian constitution, where religion is not *pro tanto* more valued than culture – insofar as both allow their members to live with integrity.[33] The worry here is that privileging religion over culture in the US Constitution is unfair to those with meaning-giving, integrity-protecting cultural commitments.

THE DISAGGREGATION STRATEGY

One possible way we could address the limitations of the two strategies surveyed previously is by combining them. Many scholars seem to veer toward this mixed position, which consists either in a dual-tracked "freedom of religion and conscience"[34] or a more radical protection of "people's sense of obligation and … core beliefs and identity."[35] These are promising strategies. However, in my view, they face a dilemma. Either they do not go far enough, and, by singling out freedom of religion as a specific kind of freedom, they reproduce the same difficulties as the proxy strategy. Or they succeed in providing a nonsectarian description of the plurality of values that underpin freedom of religion, but in that case they become indistinguishable from the disaggregation strategy. In what follows, therefore, I go straight to

32 WENGER, WE HAVE A RELIGION.

33 For a comparison, see Beaman, *Aboriginal Spirituality*. Beaman complains that "In Canada, where group rights and the correcting of systemic disadvantage are constitutionally possible, aboriginal claims are framed as treaty rights … resulting in the minimization or marginalization of issues concerning religious freedom." It may be the case that Aboriginal rights are not given sufficient weight, but the argument that this is because their "religious freedom" has been denied assumes what has to be demonstrated, namely, that the category of religious freedom is the most suitable to protect Aboriginal rights (p. 136).

34 Schwartzman, *Religion as Legal Proxy*. See also Koppelman's rejoinder: *Religion as a Bundle of Legal Proxies: Response to Micah Schwartzman*, 51 SAN DIEGO L. REV. (2014). As Schwartzman notes, the double protection of religion and conscience is in fact the actual law in many jurisdictions, including in the text of international conventions, such as the ECHR. For an early defense in the US context, see Rodney K. Smith, *Converting the Religious Equality Amendment into a Statute with a Little "Conscience,"* 3 *BYU* L. REV. 645–88 (1996).

35 Alan Patten, *Three Theories of Religious Liberty* (presented at APSA Annual Meeting 2014), 11.

sketching my own version of disaggregation, without ruling out the possibility that a radical mixed strategy, if suitably formulated, would be equally compelling.

The disaggregation strategy builds on an innovative proposal James Nickel made in a 2005 article titled "Who Needs Freedom of Religion?"[36] The gist of Nickel's argument is that freedom of religion does not need to be singled out by the law as a special freedom. Religious activities and practices can be adequately protected through generic liberal rights of belief, thought, expression, privacy, association, conscience, and so forth. This means that religious freedom is derivative, like scientific freedom or artistic freedom: it is implied and entailed by basic liberal freedoms, and justified on the same grounds. The fact that a liberty is derivative does not mean that it is less important.

While there is much to learn from Nickel's approach, it is, in my view, deficient in two ways. First, Nickel suggests that freedom of religion can be removed from the list of derivative rights. The disaggregation strategy, by contrast, makes no such claim: it merely aims to interpret the notion of religion in law (regardless of whether the category of freedom of religion is upheld or not). Second, Nickel does not specify in sufficient detail the different dimensions of religion that freedom of religion protects; nor does he explain how his reductionist approach to religion relates to other normative values such as equality, nondiscrimination, and non-establishment.[37]

The starting point of the disaggregation strategy is to suggest that different parts of the law should capture different dimensions of religion for the protection of different normative values. Consider the following, non-exhaustive list of legally relevant dimensions of religion.

1. Religion as conception of the good life
2. Religion as conscientious moral obligation
3. Religion as key feature of identity
4. Religion as mode of human association
5. Religion as vulnerability class
6. Religion as totalizing institution
7. Religion as inaccessible doctrine

This plurality of dimensions of religion has been obscured by the two strategies we have considered so far. The proxy strategy tends to bundle them all together and make them the normative basis of a special kind of freedom, "religious freedom." Yet it is unclear that freedom of religion is the right normative framework to capture all these dimensions. The substitution strategy, for its part, tends to collapse religion into conceptions of the good and conscience, and as a result has little to say about

36 James Nickel, *Who Needs Freedom of Religion?* 76 U. Colo. L. Rev. 941–64 (2005).
37 But see, for a more extensive treatment, James Nickel, Making Sense of Human Rights (2007).

the other dimensions. In what follows, I shall focus on dimensions 1–4, as they are directly relevant to the notion of freedom of religion which has concerned us here.[38]

Recall that, on the interpretive theory that I favor, it is not enough simply to say, "religion is X and Y." What is required is to identify the specific normative values that make X or Y legally relevant. Just saying that a practice or institution is multifaceted and internally complex, and irreducible to anything else (as is surely the case with religion), does not mean that it must be recognized as such in the law.[39] But, by parity of reasoning, nor does disaggregating the various empirical dimensions of religion in itself provide a reason for legal cognizance of any of them. So we need to know what kind of good is being protected in every case, and the good cannot be assumed to follow from the mere description of the empirical dimension of religion. With this in mind, let me briefly discuss the four first cases in turn.

1. *Religion as a conception of the good.* When religion is conceived as a conception of the good, it should be tracked by generic liberal freedoms, such as freedom of belief, thought, speech, and so forth. Freedom of religion, here, is simply derivative of a broader value, which itself justifies those generic freedoms – liberals usually refer to individual autonomy, or self-determination, or the capacity to pursue and develop the conception of the good that one in fact holds. The religious life, on this view, is one of the many ways for individuals to exercise their first "moral power," to use John Rawls's phrase. For many purposes of legal protection of religion, the content of religion does not need to be specified, because freedom of religion is merely derivative of this more general right of ethical independence – the right to form, develop, and pursue one's conception of what makes life good. Religious beliefs here have exactly the same status as any other belief, preference, commitment, or worldview. In a liberal state, there is a presumption that citizens should enjoy wide freedoms of thought, belief, and speech, and that the state should not be in the

38 Elsewhere I show that seeing religion as a vulnerable class is crucial to theories of equality and non-discrimination, whereas seeing religion as a totalizing institution and inaccessible doctrine helps account for the value of non-establishment and (minimal) secularism. See LABORDE, LIBERALISM'S RELIGION, chapters 4 and 6.

39 This is the problem with Michael McConnell's argument, which derives from the fact that religion is uniquely complex the conclusion that it should be specially protected. But this is a *non sequitur.* He writes: "Religion is a special phenomenon, in part, because it plays such a wide variety of roles in human life: it is an institution, but it is more than that; it is an ideology or worldview, but it is more than that; it is a set of personal loyalties and locus of community, akin to family ties, but it is more than that; it is an aspect of identity, but it is more than that; it provides answers to questions of ultimate reality, and offers a connection to the transcendent; but it is more than that. Religion cannot be reduced to a subset of any larger category. In any particular context, religion may appear to be analogous to some other aspect of human activity – to another institution, worldview, personal loyalty, basis of personal identity, or answer to ultimate and transcendent questions. However, there is no other human phenomenon that combines all of these aspects; if there were such a concept, it would probably be viewed as a religion." Michael W. McConnell, *Problem of Singling Out Religion*, 50 DE PAUL L. REV. 1, 42 (2000).

business of judging or evaluating what people are up to. Liberal neutrality rightly counsels a "religion-blind" tolerance or respect for all conceptions of the good.[40]

However, as I noted earlier, this presumption of freedom is not strong enough to generate a claim to be exempted from laws and regulations that apply to all. And yet, most liberals argue that exemptions are sometimes legitimate. So how can exemptions be justified? Consider the following examples. Freedom of expression entails that we are free to wear what we like on the street, from a clown hat to a Muslim *hijab*. But in workplaces where employees are required to be bareheaded, we need a principle that would justify exempting wearers of *hijab* but not of clown hats. In exemption and accommodations cases, therefore, the liberal default of neutrality about the good is not available, and Taylorian strong evaluations are required.[41] So what is the particular value that religious dress, but not eccentric hats, expresses? Egalitarian theorists of religious freedom, as we saw, located it in the value of conscientious action.

2. *Religion as conscientious obligation*. Special legal protection for religion as conscientious obligation, in turn, is justified by more specific appeal to the value of integrity. As we have seen, we have good reasons to think that integrity is a nonsectarian, ecumenical value. There is a specific harm caused by being prevented from doing what you feel is right, as opposed to what you would prefer to do, or what would make you happy.[42] But while ethical integrity – doing what you feel is right – is the correct interpretive value, it is not the case that it is exhibited only in conscientious action. Arguably, people act with integrity when they follow strongly valued practices, when they express "core beliefs and identity,"[43] to use Alan Patten's phrase, regardless of whether this is demanded by their conscience or not.

3. *Religion as key feature of identity*. Special legal protection for religion as key feature of identity, therefore, can also be justified by appeal to integrity. Political theorists have often resisted the argument that, for purposes of exemptions, religion should be interpreted not only as conscientious belief, but also as one form of meaning-giving cultural commitment.[44] Yet this suspicion is rooted in two mistaken assumptions. The first is that religion is essentially different from culture. This may well be the case – and it is easy to provide theological, sociological, anthropological, political, and phenomenological accounts of this difference. The question that

40 With the usual proviso that people should not infringe on the rights of others, etc.

41 See Cécile Laborde, *Protecting Religious Freedom in the Secular Age*, in POLITICS OF RELIGIOUS FREEDOM (ed. Winnifred Fallers Sullivan et al., 2015).

42 See also Chandran Kukathas, who writes that individuals have a basic human interest "in living in accordance with the demands of conscience. For among the worst fates that a person might have to ensure is *that he is unable to avoid acting against conscience* – that he be unable to do what he thinks is right." KUKATHAS, LIBERAL ARCHIPELAGO, 55.

43 Patten, *Three Theories*, 11.

44 See Avigail Eisenberg, *Religion as Identity* (presented at APSA Annual Meeting 2014).

preoccupies us, though, is not a semantic or descriptive, but rather an interpretive question. When we think of legal exemptions, the question we ask is: what kinds of commitment are so important to people that their integrity would be threatened were they prevented from acting on them? The onus is on critics to explain why certain kinds of cultural commitments would be less important to people than religious commitments.

The second mistaken assumption is that if the law aims to protect all integrity-promoting practices, whether religious, cultural, ethical, etc., it will protect everything and therefore nothing. There is something to this worry, but it is exaggerated. First, ethical integrity is defined so as to exclude the protection of trivial practices that hold only a marginal place in an individual's conception of the good or identity. One advantage of the approach is that it has the resources to accommodate the wearing of *hijabs*, as well as aboriginal practices, and to refuse accommodation to wearers of clown hats. There will inevitably be hard cases, but – I would argue – they are not intrinsically more troublesome than those generated by alternative approaches. Second, it is not clear that the proposed approach would be less easily administrable than existing legal practice. Judges, when dealing with freedom of religion and freedom of conscience cases, already apply complex tests of sincerity, centrality, meaningfulness, and so forth. They do so, usually, in order to define whether a practice is properly religious. The disaggregation approach, by contrast, bypasses the need to settle on the semantics of what is religious and what is not.[45] Third, the more specific fear of exemption proliferation can also be alleviated. We can assume that only individuals with integrity-upholding commitments will go to

[45] In private correspondence, Andrew Koppelman has put the following objection to me. "During Prohibition, the Volstead Act exempted sacramental wine. No attempt was made to examine individual Catholic priests and parishioners to determine the depth of their conviction. If 'religion' is not cognizable, it is hard to imagine how that could have been done … That is why proxies are indispensable." This is an important objection. In response, I would say two things. First, this is better understood as a right of collective exemption – a right held by the church as a whole, so on my theory it would fall under freedom of association (and the use of sacramental wine could be linked to a core purpose of the association). Second, even if construed on the model of individual exemption, the argument would be that the use of sacramental wine during church services is central to the integrity of the communicant. It is quite possible that the most effective way to account for this is to appeal directly to what we know about the importance of religion in general, and sacraments in particular. But this is different from saying that it is freedom of religion, as such, that is doing the work here. Consider the following analogy. Take the case of drug control. If doctors can show that they need to use illegal drugs, in a controlled environment, for important medical purposes, then doctors should get an exemption. By analogy, if a group can show that it uses drugs, in a controlled environment (i.e., without subverting the aims of the law that targets addiction, etc.), for central religious purposes, then this group should also get an exemption. We don't need freedom of religion to make this claim – even if "religion" is useful as an explanation of the activities of the group (just as "medical" is useful as an explanation of the activities of doctors, but they don't need to invoke medical freedom as a special right).

the trouble of requesting accommodations in the first place. Furthermore, because (on my theory, at least) ethical integrity does not carry the *pro tanto* weight conventionally accorded to claims of freedom of religion and conscience, it will only justify exemptions from a narrow range of laws and regulations (among which are most cases of exemptions from dress codes).[46]

4. *Religion as a mode of human association*. Consider the liberal freedoms that are broadly connected to this: freedom of association itself, freedom of expression and speech, freedom of peaceful assembly, economic freedom, political participation. Arguably, these freedoms do not flow – at least, not directly or exclusively – from the value of ethical integrity (so they do not justify the extension of individual rights of accommodation to corporate rights of exemption). Yet such freedoms are crucial to the vitality of churches and religious associations and to the diverse activities they take as central to the pursuit of their purposes. Some religions emphasize preaching and proselytizing; others, charity work; yet others, successful business activities. Some focus on the preservation of community ways of life; others on the visible display of signs of religious membership; yet others on personal ethics and conscience. If we take a broad view of the scope of religious activities, we can "avoid the misconception that we have to find all protections for religious activity within a phrase like 'the free exercise of religion' or 'freedom of thought, conscience and religion.'"[47] So the suggestion here is that even if we grant religious freedom, as such, lesser weight than existing approaches, we can still offer great scope for protection of religious practices and activities. The disaggregation strategy does not assume that all religious activities and practices must be protected in the name of freedom of religion. In particular, it rejects the tendency, within existing approaches, to capture the interpretive value of religion exclusively in terms of freedoms of belief, thought, or conscience.

CONCLUSION

The disaggregation strategy improves on both the substitution and proxy strategies, as I hope I have demonstrated. Unlike the proxy strategy, it does not single out freedom of religion as a special freedom protecting a loose cluster of activities and practices. Unlike the substitution strategy, it does not assume that all that freedom of religion protects should be protected under the label of freedom of conscience. As a result, the disaggregation strategy meets the three desiderata outlined at the start of this chapter. It is not narrow, because it protects a broad range of associational,

46 This argument does not follow from the conceptual strategy of disaggregation, but needs to be backed by a full theory of egalitarian justice. I develop an argument to this effect in LIBERALISM'S RELIGION, ms. in progress.

47 Nickel, *Who Needs Freedom*, 951.

expressive activities, including those religious activities that are not obligations of conscience. It is not sectarian, because it is rooted in the ecumenical value of ethical integrity and in the normative justifications for generic liberal rights such as speech and association. And it is not unfair to nonreligious citizens, because it respects their meaning-giving commitments, whether they are conventionally religious, cultural, or philosophical. The disaggregation approach, in a word, is religion-blind without being religion-insensitive, because it sees religion not as a specialized and self-contained area of human belief and activity, but as a richly diverse expression of life itself.

2

The Puzzle of the Catholic Church

Lawrence G. Sager

INTRODUCTION: RELIGIOUS FREEDOM AND THE PUZZLE OF THE CATHOLIC CHURCH

Religious faith creates outliers, and religious outliers flourish best when they are assured of equal membership and fair treatment by the community of which they are a part; when they are protected by the ability to dissent and to proselytize; when they are able to associate and worship with those who share their values and practices; and, finally, when their political community has a robust respect for individual liberties in general, making space at the margins in domains like the family. These are the necessary and sufficient conditions of religious freedom, and as such, they are requirements of a just state.[1]

For our purposes it is important to note what is not included in this complex and demanding view of religious freedom. Religious freedom does not entail the presumptive or *prima facie* right of religiously motivated persons to defy otherwise valid laws that prevent them from conforming their conduct to the dictates of their religion. There are two related and morally decisive reasons why no such right exists: first, there is no way to delineate what constitutes a religious motivation for these purposes, without creating an arbitrary orthodoxy of precisely the sort that religious freedom ought to deplore; and second, were we somehow able to surmount this obstacle, there would be no morally defensible reason for privileging religious commitments over other deep human concerns.

I will say more in support of the rejection of any special right of religious autonomy later, and have argued the point at greater length elsewhere.[2] But our primary

[1] For a defense and elaboration of this view of religious freedom, see Lawrence Sager, *In the Name of God*, 60 ST. LOUIS U. PUB. L. REV., forthcoming; CHRISTOPHER EISGRUBER & LAWRENCE SAGER, RELIGIOUS FREEDOM AND THE CONSTITUTION (2007).

[2] EISGRUBER & SAGER, RELIGIOUS FREEDOM.

Portions of this chapter appear in *Why Churches (and, Possibly, the Tarpon Bay Women's Blue Water Fishing Club) Can Discriminate*, in RISE OF CORPORATE RELIGIOUS LIBERTY (ed. Schwartzman et al., 2016).

concern here is with a widely shared view that seems at first blush to point in exactly the opposite conceptual direction. In its most particular and familiar form, it is captured by this proposition, which enjoys very broad (if not universal) assent: As a matter of political morality, the Catholic Church is entitled to insist that its priests be male without interference from the state. This right to discriminate in the choice of religious leaders seems appealing even in regimes of employment law that aggressively prohibit gender discrimination. It is far from clear why churches should have such a right, and the widely shared view that they do ought to be grist for checking our understanding of the appropriate shape and basis of religious freedom more generally.

RATIONALES FOR THE CHURCH'S RIGHT TO DISCRIMINATE

At least four explanations offer themselves for some form of a church's right to discriminate:

1. This is a specific case of a more general right to religious autonomy, pursuant to which, groups and individuals are free to act on deeply held religious convictions unless government has powerful reasons for restricting such action; and government would have no such justification here.
2. Religious institutions, of which churches are the most salient example, enjoy a distinct right to religious autonomy, pursuant to which they are free to act on the tenets of their faith unless government has powerful reasons for restricting such action; and a government would have no such justification here. A narrowed form of this explanation is limited to the internal affairs of religious institutions, including, for example, the decision of a church to hire only male clerics.
3. Government has a strong obligation of neutrality among religious faiths. In the name of this obligation, the state should refuse to decide any questions of theological substance that may arise in the course of resolving inheritance, property, or authority disputes between religious schisms. In the same vein, the state should decline to intervene in conflicts involving the employment of clerical leaders.
4. Members of political communities have a right to be free from governmental intrusion into close and personal relationships except in cases of harm or abuse. The relationship between a cleric and congregants is an instance of such a close and personal relationship, which is distinct because it plays out in a group institutional setting of commercial employment. The association among the congregants of the church community is another instance of a close and personal relationship, and carries with it entailments concerning

the choice of clerics. There is no harm or abuse of the choice-dissolving sort involved in a church's decision to hire only male clerics.

These are four (six, if we subdivide 2 and 4) very different claims, each of which brings together institutions, religion, and rights in a distinct way. They all implicate ideas that reach beyond the insistence of the Catholic Church that its priests be male. Among these there may be still other variations, but they are a good point of departure. In this chapter, I will argue that 1) is wrong in virtually every detail; that 2), on either variant, is in certain ways worse; that the initial promise of 3) unravels upon close reflection; and that 4), on either variant, offers a plausible moral foundation for the view that churches can discriminate in their choice of religious leaders. We will consider these propositions in turn.

Autonomy of the Religiously Motivated

The most direct explanation for the right of churches to discriminate builds on an idea that may seem immanent in the very idea of religious freedom: persons in the grip of religious convictions are entitled to be free of interference from the state unless the state has especially weighty reasons for frustrating their efforts to follow the dictates of their religion. Individual believers carry this entitlement – we can call it the right to religious autonomy – into group structures where their religious understandings are expressed, celebrated, reflected upon, acted upon, and otherwise advanced. The internal structure and external behavior of these groups are heir to the religious autonomy of their constituent members. On this view, the state's interest in prohibiting gender-based discrimination in employment is not sufficiently weighty to justify intrusion into the choice of clerics by the congregants of a church. There are important details that would need to be worked out to make this a complete argument on behalf of the right of the Catholic Church to discriminate. What makes a state interest weighty? Just how weighty does an interest have to be? Is the threshold of weightiness an absolute one, or is there a balance to be struck that is particular to the claim of religious autonomy and the state interest at stake? And why, overall, is it so clear that the state's interest in preventing gender discrimination in employment flunks the test? But, given the predicate of a robust right to religious autonomy, it seems plausible that the right of the Catholic Church to select only male priests could derive from such a right.

But the right of religious autonomy is a deeply flawed idea. It is fatally undermined both by the moral impossibility of defining religion for these purposes and by the absence of any moral justification for preferring religious commitments over other deep human concerns, however those commitments are delineated. Consider the problem as it confronted the Supreme Court of the United States. In two cases,[3] the Court considered the claims of young men who sought to qualify as conscientious objectors and be exempted from the military draft. Each of the young men was deeply committed to a set of values and precepts that forbade taking up arms against other human beings. None of them grounded his commitment in an organized religion or attributed his commitment to a deity of any sort.

The relevant statute seemed to speak directly to these cases, but in the negative:

> Nothing contained in this title shall be construed to require any person to be subject to combatant training and service in the armed forces of the United States who, by reason of religious training and belief, is conscientiously opposed to participation in war in any form. Religious training and belief in this connection means an individual's belief in a relation to a Supreme Being involving duties superior to those arising from any human relation, but does not include essentially political, sociological, or philosophical views or a merely personal moral code.[4]

Despite Congress's explicit exclusion of "essentially political, sociological, or philosophical views or a merely personal moral code," the Court found that the young men before them qualified as conscientious objectors. To do so, the Court had to read the statute in a remarkable way, concluding that what it required was "[a] sincere and meaningful belief which occupies in the life of its possessor a place parallel to that filled by the God of those admittedly qualifying for the exemption comes within the statutory definition."[5]

This heroic misreading of Section 6 (j) of the Universal Military Training and Service Act was motivated by an unwillingness to attribute to Congress a regime of conscientious objector status as unjust – and by implication, unconstitutional – as the one pretty clearly intended by Congress, which would have limited the privilege of military exemption to those opposed to war on grounds of an orthodox belief in a Supreme Being. The Court treated this as the thorny problem of how – nominally on Congress's behalf – it could define religion for purposes of the conscientious objection statute without creating unjust and unconstitutional distinctions among those who sincerely and deeply abhorred war and could not countenance participating in such slaughter.

But the problem, of course, runs deeper. Setting the conscientious objector statute aside, recognizing a right to autonomy reserved for the religiously motivated depends as a matter of concept and practice on the prior identification of what beliefs and commitments are religious and hence can found a claim to disregard legal rules that others are obliged to obey. This is a fundamental and treacherous

3 United States v. Seeger, 380 U.S. 163 (1965); Welsh v. United States, 398 U.S. 333 (1970).

4 50 App. U.S.C. § 456 (j).

5 Seeger, 380 U.S., 177.

problem. On any candidate view, religion is a capacious category and can include beliefs and commitments of all sorts, including those that center, for example, on deep prejudice and the intense pursuit of self-advantage. Familiar markers of religion, like a belief in a "supreme being," are patently incomplete in their scope and inexplicably leave out systems of belief and commitment that are widely viewed as religious. More important, without more, systems of belief and commitment that are excluded by such markers are as fully entitled to autonomous privilege as those that are embraced.

The problem is especially treacherous, because any attempt to define religion substantively will create an orthodoxy of a sort that is anathema to the freedom of individuals to shape their commitments, which lies at the heart of the appeal of religious liberty. This inevitable definitional orthodoxy is both deeply unfair and an affront to the impulse toward religious liberty that inspires the effort.

The difficulties the Supreme Court worked so hard to avoid in the conscientious object cases run deeper still: What the cases ultimately demonstrate is that there is no normatively sound reason for the state to prefer religious over nonreligious commitments, however the substantive content of the dichotomy is defined. Driving the outcome of these cases was a deep sense of the unfairness of the rejecting the claim of the young pacifists. That edge of injustice is not smoothed by the possibility that the deep judgments that drove their pacifist stances were not religious; on the contrary, the terms of the statute aside, it seems altogether irrelevant to the matter whether we consider their commitments religious or not.

If we match a variety of recognizably religious concerns with parallel concerns that lack a recognizably religious infrastructure, the injustice of the conscientious objector statute's preference for religion is evident. Consider these examples:

- Two women live across the street from each other in an American suburb; both want to run "soup kitchens" to feed the poor in their homes, and both are barred by a zoning ordinance that forbids restaurant-like enterprises in their neighborhood. One woman is driven not just by the guiding principle of her religious faith to minister to those less fortunate, but by a personal communication from her God to fulfill her mission by feeding the poor in her home. The other woman will not disclose what she regards as her religious affiliations; her strong desire to feed the poor comes from her sense that it is an abomination that adults and children should go hungry in a place and time of abundance. Suppose the zoning authorities were to permit only one of the women to proceed, on the grounds that her motives were (or were not) religious.
- It is determined that parents have a constitutional right to make important judgments about the education of their children: whether to educate them in private schools, as opposed to those run by the state; whether to take them out

of formal educational settings to acculturate them to community values at a certain stage of their education; and even whether, possibly, to educate them personally at home. But this constitutional right is reserved for those parents who have strong religious reasons for their nonconforming judgments.[6]

- Same-sex marriage in the eyes of the state is acknowledged to be a fundamental right, but limited to couples whose religious beliefs insist on such marriage.

In the conscientious objector cases, the Supreme Court evaded these seemingly intractable problems of scope and fairness by moving to a functional test, evaluating the role played by their pacifist beliefs in the lives of the young claimants. But as a general approach to the idea of religious autonomy, this would give anyone with a systematic and deep commitment to any life project or set of values, however evil or self-indulgent, a presumptive right to disobey laws that others are required to obey. Such a notion has little appeal as a precept of political morality.

Consider its application in the context that brings us here: An employer otherwise barred from discriminating on the basis of race or gender would have a claim that the prohibition was unjust, based simply on the fact that he or she harbored a deep and systematic aversion to members of the protected group, and, in particular, opposed and deplored their occupying positions of respect and responsibility in the world of commercial enterprise. It won't do to rescue the idea by suggesting that such an employer has a *prima facie* claim to autonomy, but the interest of the state in protecting vulnerable groups from private discrimination is sufficiently weighty to justify overriding that claim. For starters, this structure of argument does a poor job of reconstructing our impulse to reject this claim of passionate discrimination. More important, to serve the purpose of explaining the right of Catholic Church to discriminate in its selection of priests, the autonomy-of-the-deeply-committed would have to be sufficiently robust to override the state's interest in preventing discrimination.

These objections to the concept of religious autonomy are becoming familiar[7] and are decisive. The right of the Catholic Church to hire only male priests cannot find its normative foundation here.

External Autonomy of Religious Institutions

We have seen that religious institutions cannot acquire autonomy by inheritance from their members – at least not autonomy of the sort that could explain the Catholic Church's right to discriminate – because their members do not themselves

6 In the United States, this seemed to be the case for a time; see Wisconsin v. Yoder, 406 U.S. 205 (1972).

7 Sager, *In the Name*; EISGRUBER & SAGER, RELIGIOUS FREEDOM; RONALD DWORKIN, RELIGION WITHOUT GOD (2013).

enjoy that autonomy. There is, however, a *negative* inheritance at play: the problems of scope and fairness that rule out religious autonomy undermine religious institutional autonomy in turn. To define a religious institution, you need to define religion, and the problems of capacious scope, arbitrary orthodoxy, and self-defeating unfairness immediately crowd in.

Indeed, in one critical respect, the singling out of religious institutions for special advantage is worse than the effort to define and advantage religion itself. Let us assume for the moment that religious institutions, the most familiar examples of which we would call churches, enjoy a unique sphere of autonomy – a sphere that is not derived from the autonomy of their members, but belongs to them as institutions. Presumably, to qualify for this special institutional autonomy, these institutions must have some relatively formal and legible structure, secured by routine practice and probably by law. Now, many people who consider themselves religious or whom we would be tempted to consider as religious for these purposes do in fact study, express, and act upon their commitments (that is, practice their religion) through and in churches or other institutions that would qualify for our assumed religious institutional autonomy. But, crucially, many do not. If religious institutional autonomy gave to those whose religious commitments are facilitated or directed through churches prerogatives that they would not otherwise enjoy, then we would have an arbitrary, structural form of the problem of a self-defeating religious orthodoxy.

Suppose, for example, that only churches and church-sponsored groups were seen as having a right to operate soup kitchens to feed the needy in residential neighborhoods. Or suppose parents were seen to have the right to make some choices about the education of their children – say, the decision to remove them from high school two years earlier than the prescribed state curriculum – only if those choices were to be realized under the umbrella of church groups and/or church schools. Or suppose that conscientious objection to military service was seen as conferring a right to exemption from military service, but only when the impulse behind such objection was grounded in the doctrine of an organized religion. Rights of this kind would create an orthodoxy of institutionalized religious exercise of a singularly arbitrary and unjust sort. Granting religious groups license to pursue their projects while denying the same license to unaffiliated individuals or other, nonreligious groups can only exacerbate the unfairness of choosing among religions or privileging religion altogether. This is what could make the problems of religious institutional autonomy worse than those of religious autonomy *simplicitor*.

Internal Autonomy of Religious Institutions

The examples we have invoked – soup kitchens, schooling one's children, and exemption from military service – all involve the possibility that a religious institution could possess or facilitate autonomy with regard to events and circumstances outside of the institution. Suppose we consider instead the possibility that religious institutions – churches, for present purposes – have a degree of autonomy to manage their own, internal affairs. The Catholic Church's selection of priests, including decisions about the gender of those priests, could fall within the compass of that autonomy.

This claim from internal autonomy does not suffer from one of the features that make the claim from external church autonomy unacceptable. As we just saw, it is impossible to defend the proposition that churches and church members acting through or on behalf of churches should have the right to disregard laws that individuals acting on their own are obliged to obey. Such a right would arbitrarily distinguish among religious persons who choose (or are constrained by the nature of their beliefs and commitments) to act on their own, and those who can and do pursue their faith in and through churches and church-sponsored institutions. But this is not true of claims for internal church autonomy, for the simple and obvious reason that religious individuals pursuing their personal beliefs and commitments on their own have no needs or claims parallel to those of a religious institution for internal autonomy.

The turn to internal church autonomy answers the objection that an orthodoxy of organized religious believers is favored over believers whose commitments and profile of exercise do not lead them to organized faiths, since internal religious institutional autonomy is for them a functional *non sequitur.* But what about persons in other sorts of institutions, institutions that are not recognizably religious? There would seem to be a reprise here of the deep problems of scope and fairness that we took to be fatal to the idea of the autonomy of the religiously driven. To be sure, we are now considering the relatively narrow entitlement of a limited degree of internal organizational autonomy. Still, with regard to that entitlement, we will need to define religion and to justify extending internal autonomy to religious institutions but not to other organizations.

For present purposes, our interest in church autonomy is provoked by the question of why the Catholic Church is entitled to discriminate against women when it hires priests. So we can focus our questions about religious favoritism on the attribution to internal church autonomy, of this specific entailment, and work from there. The problems we face are obvious. Why should the Catholic Church and other religious institutions be entitled to discriminate in their selection of priests (or otherwise named clerics), while other organizations are obliged – morally and, potentially, legally – to conform their conduct to familiar and compelling norms of antidiscrimination? More troubling still, how can we identify religious organizations without undertaking the treacherous and self-defeating exercise of defining religion?

Internal church autonomy could be understood not as a variation on religious autonomy, but as a specific instance of a more general right of association. So understood, it would not be objectionable on these grounds. We take up the question of associational rights later; in the meantime, it is sufficient to observe that the notion of a distinct right of churches to internal autonomy seems every bit as much in need of rescue as was the autonomy of the religiously driven.

Keeping Government Out of Theological Disputes

There is one possible justification for the license of churches to discriminate in their choice of priests that turns on the worry that government will involve itself in theological disputes. Courts in the United States have adopted what has become known as the "hands-off" stance of the Court with regard to the resolution of certain internal disputes of religious organizations. The core notion of the hands-off doctrine is that courts need to steer clear of resolving disputes between religious schisms on grounds that could involve or be seen to involve matters of theological dogma. Where questions of authority, inheritance, ownership, or the like arise, courts cannot rule on questions of religious content even when they involve, say, not a question of which side represents the truth, or the true faith, but rather the freestanding question of what were the theological intentions of a particular testator. The concern is that any ruling in a controversy of this sort will put the government in the position of lending its power and support to one side of a theological dispute, and these are questions about which government has no legitimate concern.

This is a worry about discrimination and disparagement, a worry that in both direct and symbolic ways, the government will act in a manner inconsistent with the requirements of equal membership. At stake is not autonomy, but equality.

This concern, it might be argued, should extend to the imposition of antidiscrimination laws on churches with regard to selection of religious leaders. In one sense, the case for keeping the government out is more direct than it is in the traditional hands-off context. Here, the idea, essentially, would be that the process by which religious leaders are selected, the substantive principles or qualifications that govern their selection, and even the specific choice of leaders, are all extensions of a church's substantive identity – all part, in effect, of its theology. For the state to regulate the employment relationship between a church and its leaders, accordingly, is for the state to set itself in direct and unduckable conflict with the church's theology.

Put this way, the hands-off rationale for discrimination in the selection of religious leaders is odd and a bit tangled. The problem is this. Suppose for the moment we set aside the hands-off doctrine and its side-taking/disparagement rationale and ask, as a bottom line, whether churches have an autonomy right with regard to the employment of their leaders. If the answer is yes, then the hands-off doctrine in this context is an unnecessary, second-order claim. If, on the other hand, the answer is no, it is odd in the extreme not to protect the church's decisions directly but to do so indirectly in service of something like the hands-off doctrine.

True, there might well be a clash between a theological commitment to male priests and an employment law forbidding gender discrimination in employment. But the right of churches to prevail in such a clash is precisely what we are trying to find a justification for. The widely shared view that some form of the ministerial exemption is an important element of political justice does not travel through a set of risks that would attach to an otherwise valid regime of state regulation. Rather, it seems wrong as a matter of first-order principle to tell the Catholic Church that it must hire women priests.

Beyond Religious Autonomy: Right of Close Association

The problem with these first efforts to found the right of the Catholic Church to discriminate against women priests is that they depend on our capacity both to define religion and to justify selectively benefiting those activities and commitments upon which we have conferred that designation. What is needed is an explanation for our embrace of the Church's right that does not depend on drawing and privileging the boundaries of religion. We have such an explanation readily at hand: the right of close association.[8]

Individuals in a free society enjoy important rights of autonomy. Some of these rights are by their nature public. Freedom of expression is the example that comes quickly to mind. The public nature of free expression is not incidental, of course; at the core of this right is the freedom to address anyone who will listen. Other rights to autonomy are distinctly personal. They can involve acts of which it can be said that they are none of the state's business. They are personal and private. When rights of this sort are called out by name – and they are frequently assumed and respected rather than championed and contested – they are sometimes described as the right to privacy – in part, perhaps, because moral limitations on the gaze of the state often overlap with moral limitations on its regulatory reach.

Both the public right of free expression and the private right of privacy have distinct, associational dimensions. People often ban together in an effort to discuss, debate, and, important, amplify their messages. Groups may not be absolutely essential to free expression, but they are enormously important, and it is difficult to

[8] "The right of intimate association" would be both apt and more familiar, but it suffers from the ambiguous reach of "intimate" – to simply that which is close and personal, on one hand, and to the domain of sexuality, on the other. Many but by no means all close human associations involve sexuality; those relevant to our analysis do not.

imagine a commitment to free expression that did not embrace rights of assembly and expressive association.

The right to privacy is if anything more exquisitely bound to association. There are some solipsistic personal acts, to be sure, but most personal acts excite claims of autonomy or privacy precisely because they involve relationships between or among individuals. Some of these personal relationships are formal and durable, like marriage and the family. But some are more glancing, like the persons one chooses to invite to dinner, take walks with, or bond with in joint activities. In between are a set of characteristic relationships that are deeply important to human flourishing and often deeply private. Prominent among these are the relationships between friends, between advisor and advisee, between mentor and mentee, and among members of durable and bounded groups. The typical structure of these relationships is not one in which the state likely would be tempted or even able to impose rules along the lines of prohibiting discrimination even on paradigmatically disfavored grounds like race or gender. But if we were to imagine a fantastic world where antidiscrimination audit and prescription invaded important friendships or guidance relationships, we would, I hope, recoil.

From this observation, two closely related claims for the right of a church to discriminate in its choice of leaders follow. Both are variations on what we can call the right of close association. The first focuses directly on the relationship between a religious leader and congregants; the second on the group associational rights of the members of an organized church, from which, in turn, autonomy in the choice of leaders derives. In the first, the close association at stake can be thought of as the dyadic relationship between a single congregant and the priest. The church is a more or less public, formal setting in which many iterations of this protected relationship occur. In the second, the church group is itself the locus of close associational rights, which include the right to choose the association's leaders.

Organized religions like the Catholic Church are structured with regard to their religious leaders in a way that opens them to public scrutiny and could open the door to state regulation. Priests and their counterparts are formally employed and have a set of enforceable legal rights, including stipulated compensation, and ongoing, stable, and publicly recognized leadership roles. They function, however, in close relationship to their congregants, acting as religious guides, moral advisors, sources of consolation, role models, best friends, and mentors.[9]

The setting in which clergy play this amalgam of roles makes the close associational interests at stake particularly high. For many members of organized religions, the ability to engage in worship under the guidance of religious leaders is as important as, say, as books to Daniel Seeger, or discussion to a moral philosopher.

[9] EISGRUBER & SAGER, RELIGIOUS FREEDOM, 63–64.

Practicing Catholics and members of other organized faiths routinely embrace the active religious leadership of their clergy. Ritual, guidance, interpretation of text and practice, the broad and fine strokes of belief – all emanate from the church's chosen leaders. The congregant–clergy relationship is not only close, it is sustained and substantive.

On this account, the moral spark of the right of the Catholic Church to discriminate in its choice of priests is the dyadic variant of the right of close association, projected into the unusual context of organized religion where religious leaders play an intensely personal, substantively rich role with regard to congregants. The right of close association is not a right distinct to religion. Everyone could lay claim to it in some familiar settings. If it assumes an apparently distinct form in the congregant/clergy context, that is because group-sized, formal employment structures do not typically provide the ground for intimate dyadic association. But if there were a non-religious group that organized and conducted itself as organized religions typically organize and conduct themselves, the member–leader relationship should enjoy the umbrella of the right of close association.

Suppose a group, the Secularists, meets on Thursday nights to share art, music, presentations about world events, and sustained discussions about "leading the good life – a life open to the good things and guided by the ethics of good behavior." The important feature of the situation from our standpoint is that the Secularists have leaders called Guides. Without belaboring the details, Secularist Guides are formally employed by the Secularist Association and function in many of the ways that clergy typically function. They conduct events on Thursday nights, offer insights and guidance on wholesale (group presentations) and retail (individual counseling) levels, join members to celebrate joyous occasions and commiserate sad ones, and so forth.

But – you surely saw this coming – the Secularist Association has openly discriminatory policies with regard to the selection of Guides. To maintain the parallel with the Catholic Church, we'll say that Guides must be men. The Secularists should enjoy a group/leader right of close association on the same grounds that we have discussed. It is the relational structure of organized religion, not its theological or otherwise substantive orientation, that generates its immunity from public norms of employment with regard to clergy.

The right of close association could enter the picture in a second – possibly more familiar – way, through the associational rights of organized religious groups *qua* groups. Here, it is the relationship among members of a group and their common enterprise that evokes the right. Groups that are sustained by members with common values and purposes, and that in turn sustain the well-being and development of those members in light of their shared values and purposes, offer the opportunity for close bonds of the sort that a free society should both encourage and grant the license of privacy to. The "club" is in this sense an extension of the individual to the group, a provision of an environment in which the individual can find her own way with the benefit of her chosen "family" of like-minded way-seekers.

Close association groups, on this account, are entitled to be free from state regulation in matters of membership and discrimination. And many antidiscrimination laws make explicit exceptions for clubs, presumably on exactly this moral impulse. It would seem to follow that close associations are likewise entitled to discriminate in their choice of leaders. The argument is not that the group can be discriminatorily composed and that the group can choose leaders from among its own membership. Rather, the point is that the same, shared-values-and-purposes concerns that would support the group in restricting its membership on what otherwise would be legally disfavored grounds should likewise support a comparably discriminatory choice of leadership.

Organized religions present paradigm instances of groups that depend in this way on close association. For many members of organized faiths, collective worship is at the heart of their religious practice, and their group enterprise is essential to their spiritual beliefs, development, and fulfillment. For some, in turn, it is important – perhaps crucial – that their fellow religionists be like-minded and appropriately situated to pursue the collective spiritual enterprise. And, in the same vein, some religions may incline to the practice that is the focus of our inquiry, that of discriminating in their choice of leaders.

The group-centered right of close association, like the dyadic version of the right, offers a justification for the right of the Catholic Church to discriminate in its choice of priests. And like the dyadic version, the group-centered right is in principle available outside the realm of religion. The Secularists club is an obvious candidate; so would be clubs of the sort likely to be exempted from extant regimes of antidiscrimination law.

CONCLUSION: PUZZLE SOLVED?

This is the moment for critical second thoughts – not in service of recantation, but rather caution.

We have, I think, found a satisfactory moral basis for the widely shared view that the Catholic Church is entitled to discriminate in its selection of priests. Or, more precisely, for the view that the Catholic Church is entitled to be free from governmental interference if and as it continues in its practice of discriminating in that selection. Nothing we have said could be offered as a defense of the Church's discriminatory practices against the challenge (from within or without the Church) that the broader society's good reasons for deploring gender discrimination apply and the Church should reform its anachronistic and unjust practice. But, on this account, the dyadic and group variations on the right of close association support the view that the state should leave the question of persistence or reform to the Catholic Church.

Even with regard to the right of the Church to be free from state interference in this regard, there are important questions left to be considered. One line of inquiry concerns the hierarchical, global structure of the Catholic Church, with the exclusion of women from positions of religious leadership running all the way up to the selection of the pope. The argument for close associational right fits the Church comfortably at the level of the congregation, but less so as we work our way up through the expansive hierarchy of the Church. How are we to understand the view – if we are prepared to hold to it – that the right to discriminate extends to the global leadership of the Catholic Church? There are several possibilities: We could simply limit our view of the Church's immunity from antidiscrimination laws to lower levels of its hierarchy; we could look to other – presumably related – moral claims that travel better up the Catholic hierarchy;[10] or we could adopt a view of the Church's right to discriminate in its choice of leadership that was in some sense parasitic on the right of close association at the congregational level.

I am not prepared to lay the question to rest in this chapter, but I will offer some preliminary thoughts. Of these three possibilities, I am most immediately drawn to the third. The claim on behalf of the Catholic hierarchy would likely include this proposition: The Catholic hierarchy is crucial to the associational experience of Catholic believers at the congregational level, with regard both to the dyadic relationship between priest and congregant, and the group associational relationship. On this account, associational rights are not inevitably dependent on matters of systematic substance, but when they are, hierarchical infrastructures that are directly in service of the substance-infused associational relationships may enjoy some of the same immunities as those relationships themselves. For these purposes, the Catholic hierarchy would be seen as being in service of the congregational experience. Authority may flow from top to bottom, as expected, but associational value on this account flows from bottom to top.

Another question about our understanding of the associational rights of the Catholic Church concerns its extent and entailments. Were we drawn to religious autonomy *simplicitor*, or to the autonomy of religious institutions as the rationale for the Catholic Church's shield from legally imposed antidiscrimination principles, the Church would have broad license to discriminate in its internal operations, and religiously motivated institutions (and ultimately, we can assume, individuals)

[10] This problem was brought to my attention by Nelson Tebbe. His solution is to see the right of the Catholic Church to discriminate with regard to its global hierarchy as dependent on the Church's *expressive* associational rights; he explores this at length in his forthcoming book, RELIGIOUS FREEDOM IN AN EGALITARIAN AGE (Harvard University Press).

would have *prima facie* claims to immunity from a broad range of laws that interfere with their religious commitments. But we have, with abundantly good reason, rejected those rationales. The question for us is, what are the implications of the associational rationales for the Church's license to discriminate?

The dyadic associational rationale, in the setting of the Church itself, extends to a limited number of religious leaders who occupy the role in the lives of their congregants that we have sketched in service of the claim of a protected dyadic relationship. It may extend, as well – on the conceptually tentative hypothesis that discrimination with regard to the Catholic hierarchy is in some salient way in service of dyadic association at the congregational level – to figures in the Catholic hierarchy whose selection and identities are properly understood to be in service of the priest–congregation relationship. The dyadic associational rationale is not limited to religious groups, but it is unclear in what other settings the state might be tempted to interfere with close dyadic relationships. When we imagine secular groups that parallel the structure of religious congregations, like our Secularist Association, the right of close dyadic association surely attaches. But we had to strain to imagine such a group. It is an open question whether other, more common settings may emerge that are plausible candidates for state regulation but involve close dyadic relationships that ought to qualify for the same immunity as we are inclined to extend to the Catholic Church and its priests.

The group associational rationale is much more open-ended in its potential application, and for that reason, more than a little nervous making. There are related dangers of both bad faith and ill-definition. Clubs can be a bit like islands of otherwise normal life where the rules of even-handed inclusion are suspended. The worry is this: If, say, restaurants, bars, hotels, theaters, golf courses, and the like could simply adopt thin trappings of clubbishness – as I imagine the gambling clubs of London do – public space could be significantly remade in service of the impulse to create or sustain patterns of discrimination. It would be an open secret that, behind the closed doors of these clubs, things were pretty much like the outside world, save only that members of disfavored groups were excluded. The group-centered variant on the right of close association is, for this reason, on somewhat more fragile ground, despite its more familiar form. My doubts do not run to the point of rejecting the group version of the right to close association altogether, but they do argue for strict metrics of close association. There are many potential parameters of clubbishness: size, exclusiveness, guests, traditional public accommodation services like room and board, purposes, purpose-related activities vs. non-purpose-related activities, the closeness and intensity of group functions and individual interaction, the paid vs. volunteer status of various positions, and so forth.

For our present purposes, most churches, including the Catholic Church, are plausible claimants for group rights of close association, even under strict criteria of eligibility for treatment as a close association. But while we have found in both the dyadic and group versions of close associational rights plausible moral footing for the right of the Church to choose male-only priests, the group variant brings with it a set of concerns about limits, and those limits could shape the right in a fashion that might in the end be uncongenial to the right of the Church to discriminate.

In all, it seems best to end on a somewhat tentative note. To be sure, religious autonomy on an individual or institutional basis is a failed moral principle and cannot explain the right of the Catholic Church to discriminate in its choice of priests. In contrast, the dyadic and group forms of the right of close association both provide plausible moral foundations for the license of the Church. But important concerns remain: The large, hierarchical structure of the Catholic Church does not easily find support in the right of close association, especially in its dyadic form; group associational rights call out for limits toward which we have only gestured in this chapter; and the Catholic Church has to answer to women as to the injustice of their exclusion from the priesthood, not merely to the state.

3

Religious Accommodations and – and Among – Civil Rights: Separation, Toleration, and Accommodation

Richard W. Garnett

I

Americans recently marked and celebrated the fiftieth anniversary of the passage of the Civil Rights Act of 1964.[1] During the past half-century, a wide variety of antidiscrimination laws, civil rights protections, and equal-access rules has been enacted by the full range of authorities and jurisdictions, from small towns to the United Nations.[2] These measures, in addition to a broad array of policies and programs having to do with education, voting rights, social welfare, and economic opportunity, have in many ways helped to make more real what might otherwise have remained only an ideal of equal citizenship.[3] As President Obama remarked on the anniversary of the Act, it "brought us closer to making real the declaration at the heart of our founding – that we are all created equal."[4] We continue to disagree, reasonably even

1 Civil Rights Act of 1964, Pub. L. No. 88–352, 78 Stat. 241 (1964).

2 See generally BRUCE ACKERMAN, WE THE PEOPLE: THE CIVIL RIGHTS REVOLUTION 3(2014), for a recent scholarly reflection on the civil rights revolution and its implications for the American Constitution.

3 See Kenneth L. Karst, *Supreme Court 1976 Term: Foreword: Equal Citizenship Under the Fourteenth Amendment*, 91 *HARV. L. REV.* 1, 6 (1977): "A society devoted to the idea of equal citizenship, then, will repudiate those inequalities that impose the stigma of caste and thus 'belie the principle that people are of equal ultimate worth,'" quoting ROBERT E. RODES JR., LEGAL ENTERPRISE 163 (1976).

4 President Barack Obama, Statement by the President on the 50th Anniversary of the Civil Rights Act of 1964 (July 2, 2014), www.whitehouse.gov/the-press-office/2014/07/02/statement-president-50th-anniversary-civil-rights-act-1964.

Earlier versions of this text were presented in Ghent (Workshop "Law's Imagining of Religion," Sep. 2014), Princeton (Conference "Religions, Rights and Institutions," Nov. 2014), Oxford (Oxford Political Thought conference, Jan. 2015), Brussels (ERC Public Lecture Series Human Rights and Politics, Feb. 2015), and London (RAPT Conference "Religion in Liberal Political Philosophy," University College London, June 2015). I am grateful to the organizers of and participants in these events for helpful feedback. For written comments, I am indebted to Aurélia Bardon, François Boucher, Emanuela Ceva, Chris Eisgruber, Lois Lee, Nick Martin, James Nickel, Onora O'Neil, Jean-Yves Pranchère, Enzo Rossi, Hans Ingvar Roth, Lawrence Sager, Winnifred Sullivan, and (especially) Andrew Koppelman and Daniel Statman. Research for this chapter was supported by the European Research Council (ERC) Grant 283867, "Is Religion Special? Reformulating Secularism and Religion in Contemporary Political Theory." A version of this text was published in *Law and Philosophy*, Sep. 2015.

if strongly, about the precise content of this ideal, the best ways to implement it, and its coherence.[5] Even if the idea of equality is not entirely empty,[6] it is certainly more easily and more often admired than understood.[7] This is not surprising and does not detract from its being a shared ideal. In any event, and in the president's words, "the journey continues."[8]

It is a premise of the chapters in this volume that we are, and have been for some time, living in an "age of civil rights." The developments mentioned in the previous paragraph provide a strong foundation for this premise. As we remember and reflect upon it, we might also recall that, not that long ago, we marked and celebrated another anniversary, the sixtieth anniversary of the Universal Declaration of Human Rights of 1948.[9] The Declaration – which, like the Civil Rights Act, both reflected and advanced a revolution in our laws and views – identified the right to freedom of religion as a fundamental right, grounded in the inherent dignity that every person bears, because he or she is a person, and in equal measure. This right to religious freedom includes the "freedom, either individually or in community with others and in public or private, to manifest … religion or belief in worship, observance, practice and teaching."[10] That is, at the heart of what Michael Perry calls the "morality of human rights" is the claim – the commitment, really – that every human person is "inviolable." One manifestation or implication of this inviolability is the right to religious freedom.[11]

Now, it is not entirely clear – it is and will be reasonably contested – what this right includes and entails, what it permits, and what it rules out. As I take it, it involves more than a particular person's right to believe (or not) in God, to pray (or not) in private, and to worship and engage in ritual or liturgical practices (or not) in distinctively religious gatherings. The Declaration on Human Rights is clear on this point, and certainly there is a long tradition in the United States of regarding religious freedom or liberty as attaching not only to matters of

5 See generally STEVEN D. SMITH, GETTING OVER EQUALITY: A CRITICAL DIAGNOSIS OF RELIGIOUS FREEDOM IN AMERICA (2001).

6 See Peter Westen, *Empty Idea of Equality*, 95 HARV. L. REV. 537 (1982).

7 See generally JOHN E. COONS & PATRICK M. BRENNAN, BY NATURE EQUAL: ANATOMY OF A WESTERN INSIGHT (1999).

8 Obama, Statement by the President.

9 See generally MARY ANN GLENDON, A WORLD MADE NEW: ELEANOR ROOSEVELT AND THE UNIVERSAL DECLARATION OF HUMAN RIGHTS (2001).

10 Universal Declaration of Human Rights, G.A. Res. 217 (III) Am, UN Doc. A/RES/217(III) (Dec. 10, 1948), Art. 18.

11 MICHAEL J. PERRY, POLITICAL MORALITY OF LIBERAL DEMOCRACY 15–18 (2010). As Perry notes, the Universal Declaration is, along with the International Covenant on Civil and Political Rights and the International Covenant on Economic, Social and Cultural Rights, part of the International Bill of Rights. The former covenant "largely repeats the capacious guarantee of religious rights and liberties first announced in the [Universal Declaration]." JOHN WITTE JR. & JOEL A. NICHOLS, RELIGION AND THE AMERICAN CONSTITUTIONAL EXPERIMENT 271 (2011).

private profession or interior confession, but also to "the duty which we owe to our Creator, and the manner of discharging it."[12] "Religion," said Justice William Douglas in his *Wisconsin v. Yoder* opinion, "is an individual experience."[13] The opinion was a partial dissent, and this statement is partially correct. However, it does not tell the entire story. Many religious experiences are those of monks, mystics, and prophets, and of salesmen, coaches, teachers, and cops. But many are also of peoples, tribes, communities, and congregations. As Douglas's colleague, Justice William Brennan, insisted in *Corporation of the Presiding Bishop v. Amos*, "For many individuals, religious activity derives meaning in large measure from participation in a larger religious community. Such a community represents an ongoing tradition of shared beliefs, an organic entity not reducible to a mere aggregation of individuals."[14]

Religion is famously difficult (some would say impossible) to define. The distinctions among religion, culture, tradition, identity, and politics are much more contested than clear.[15] We can say, though, that the idea that religion is or involves only or even primarily an interior, individual experience is relatively new on the scene. In any event, religion in our experience and understanding involves more than the commitments, values, beliefs, professions, and practices of particular persons. It also involves and is exercised both by and through communities, families, associations, societies, authorities, assemblies, and institutions.[16]

Among the questions that remain is what freedom of religion includes – specifically, whether it includes a right to reasonable accommodation in cases when the application of general laws would impose a substantial and avoidable

[12] VA. DECLARATION OF RIGHTS § 16 (1776). See also MICHAEL W. MCCONNELL ET AL., RELIGION AND THE CONSTITUTION 125 (2011): "Each of the state constitutions first defined the scope of the free exercise right in terms of the conscience of the individual believer and the actions that flow from that conscience. None of the provisions confined the protection to beliefs and opinions … nor to expression of beliefs and opinions"; WITTE, RELIGION AND THE AMERICAN, 45 (noting that for most eighteenth-century writers, religious practices were inseparable from religious beliefs).

[13] Wisconsin v. Yoder, 406 U.S. 205, 243 (1972) (Douglas, J., dissenting).

[14] Corp. of Presiding Bishop v. Amos, 483 U.S. 327, 342 (1987) (Brennan, J., concurring).

[15] See, all discussing the challenges in defining religion, e.g., ROBERT N. BELLAH, RELIGION IN HUMAN EVOLUTION: FROM THE PALEOLITHIC TO THE AXIAL AGE xiv (2011); WILLIAM T. CAVANAUGH, MYTH OF RELIGIOUS VIOLENCE: SECULAR IDEOLOGY AND THE ROOTS OF MODERN CONFLICT 33 (2009); WINNIFRED FALLERS SULLIVAN, IMPOSSIBILITY OF RELIGIOUS FREEDOM 89–137 (2005); BRENT NONGBRI, BEFORE RELIGION: A HISTORY OF A MODERN CONCEPT 15–22 (2013); Andrew Koppelman, *Corruption of Religion and the Establishment Clause*, 50 *WM. & MARY L. REV.* 1831, 1920 (2009); Eduardo Peñalver, *Concept of Religion*, 107 *YALE L. J.* 791, 793–94 (1997); *Note, Toward a Constitutional Definition of Religion*, 91 HARV. L. REV. 1056, 1060 (1978).

[16] I have tried to develop this point elsewhere. See Richard W. Garnett, *Church, State, and the Practice of Love*, 52 *VILL. L. REV.* 281 (2007); *"Freedom of the Church": (Towards) an Exposition, Translation, and Defense*, 21 J. CONTEMP. SOC. ISSUES 33 (2013); and *Religion and Group Rights: Are Churches (Just) Like the Boy Scouts?* 22 ST. JOHN'S J. LEGAL COMMENT. 515 (2007).

burden.[17] Others include, for example, whether religious practices, objections, and motivations do or should have a stronger claim for accommodation than other conscientious or deeply held ones;[18] whether the Free Exercise Clause authorizes judges to accommodate religion by requiring exemptions from generally applicable laws, or instead invites politically accountable actors to do so;[19] and whether and to what extent the Establishment Clause or principles of political morality constrain attempts by judicial or political actors to remove substantial burdens from religious exercise.[20] Especially in the wake of the *Hobby Lobby*[21] and *Elane Photography* cases,[22] scholars, judges, and practitioners alike will continue to wrestle with the specific technical and doctrinal challenges involved in the operation of a religious accommodation regime like the one set out in the Religious Freedom Restoration Act[23] and similar statutes. What (for that regime's purposes anyway) is religion or religious exercise or the exercise of religion? Are these laws' protections fully available to for-profit business corporations and in the economic and commercial spheres? What constitutes a substantial burden on religious exercise, and to what extent should judges and other government officials defer to a religious believer's claim that such a burden exists? What criteria should courts employ when determining whether a government interest is compelling? Is the political or financial feasibility of an alternative means of furthering that compelling government interest relevant to the question whether the means at issue is the least restrictive one? And so on.[24]

[17] As Witte observes, the 1966 International Covenant on Civil and Political Rights – again, part of the International Bill of Rights – provides that the "[f]reedom to manifest one's religion or beliefs may be subject only to such limitations as are prescribed by law and are necessary to protect public safety, order, health, or morals or the fundamental rights and freedoms of others." WITTE, RELIGION AND THE AMERICAN, 271. See also John Witte Jr. & M. Christian Green, *Religious Freedom, Democracy, and International Human Rights*, 23 EMORY INT'L L. REV. 583, 606 (2009) (arguing that religious freedom is necessary for democracy).

[18] Compare, e.g., Michael McConnell, *Accommodation of Religion*, 1985 SUP. CT. REV. 1, 27 (1985) ("The purpose of accommodation is furthered when the broadest scope of religiously motivated actions is permitted, within the constraints of countervailing governmental interests."), with, e.g., William P. Marshall, *In Defense of* Smith *and Free Exercise Revisionism*, 58 U. CHIC. L. REV. 308, 321 (1991) (arguing that the contention that religious belief is uniquely entitled to exemption because it involves a duty to God, a transcendent sovereign, is neither persuasive nor fully accurate).

[19] Compare, e.g., Douglas Laycock, *Remnants of Free Exercise*, 1990 SUP. CT. REV. 1 (1990) with, e.g., William K. Kelley, *Primacy of Political Actors in Accommodation of Religion*, 22 U. HAW. L. REV. 403, 422 (2000).

[20] Compare, e.g., Carl. H. Esbeck, *Religion and the First Amendment: Some Causes of the Recent Confusion*, 42 WM. & MARY L. REV. 883 (2001) with, e.g., Ira C. Lupu, *Trouble with Accommodation*, 60 GEO. WASH. L. REV. 743 (1992).

[21] Burwell v. Hobby Lobby Stores, Inc., 134 S. Ct. 2751 (2014).

[22] Elane Photography, LLC v. Willock, 284 P.3d 428 (N. M. Ct. App. 2012)

[23] Religious Freedom Restoration Act of 1993, 42 U.S.C. §§ 2000bb–2000bb-4.

[24] See generally Thomas C. Berg, *What Hath Congress Wrought? An Interpretive Guide to the Religious Freedom Restoration Act*, 39 VILL. L. REV. 1 (1994); Christopher C. Lund, *Religious Liberty after* Gonzales: *A Look at State RFRAs*, 55 S.D. L. REV. 466 (2010).

As we consider and answer these questions, we should keep in view the fact that religious freedom is one of those civil rights – a fundamental human right, grounded on the "inherent dignity and … equal and inalienable rights of all members of the human family"[25] – the increased appreciation of which is plausibly said to characterize our age.[26]

II

The topic of religious accommodation in the age of civil rights invites and prompts at least two lines of inquiry. Proceeding along the first, and in keeping with the claims proposed in the preceding section, we might ask and argue about whether our religious accommodation practices are all that they should be in our age of civil rights. Are accommodations and exemptions being extended prudently but generously, in as many cases and to as many persons and entities as possible, in a sincere effort to welcome religious minorities, objectors, and dissenters as fully as we can into what Justice Harlan called "the dignity and glory of American citizenship"?[27] What barriers exist to the promotion and achievement of civil rights goals through religious accommodations, and how might these barriers be overcome?[28] Are civil rights laws being designed and enforced in ways that guard against unintended or unjustified disregard for or sacrifices of the civil (and human) right to religious liberty in the pursuit or protection of others?

Michael McDonnell noted that "[i]n a society that is pervasively regulated, as ours now is"[29] – and in a society that is religiously pluralistic and divided on serious moral questions, as ours now is[30] – "there are many more occasions for conflict between the government and religious actors."[31] Such conflicts, clashes, and tensions are real, and, like the civil rights enterprise itself, they are difficult and pressing. Still, the demands of the age of civil rights are seen as including a commitment to the inclusion and protection of the religious believers and groups involved in these conflicts, and a determination to respect their place in the *civitas*

25 Universal Declaration of Human Rights, Art. 18, pmbl. See also Pope Paul VI, *Declaration on Religious Freedom (Dignitatis Humanae) on the Right of the Person and of Communities to Social and Civil Freedom in Matters Religious* § 2 (Dec. 7, 1965): "[T]he right to religious freedom has its foundation in the very dignity of the human person."

26 See Abner S. Greene, *Religious Freedom and (Other) Civil Liberties: Is There a Middle Ground?* 9 *Harv. L. & Pol'y Rev.* 161 (2015).

27 Plessy v. Ferguson, 163 U.S. 537, 555 (1896) (Harlan, J., dissenting).

28 Cf. Richard W. Garnett, *Political (and Other) Safeguards of Religious Freedom*, 32 Cardozo L. Rev. 1815, 1817 (2011).

29 MCCONNELL ET AL., RELIGION AND THE CONSTITUTION, 121.

30 Cf. ROBERT D. PUTNAM & DAVID E. CAMPBELL, AMERICAN GRACE: HOW RELIGION DIVIDES AND UNITES US 495 (2012).

31 MCCONNELL ET AL., RELIGION AND THE CONSTITUTION, 121.

rather than insist on boundaries and loyalties and conditions that exclude or "shut [them] out."[32]

There is at least one other way to approach the topic. A second avenue of inquiry presumes that the dynamic at issue is (as a *USA Today* headline recently put it) "[r]eligious liberty vs. civil rights,"[33] rather than "religious freedom and, and among, civil rights."[34] This dynamic played out in the failed effort to enact the Religious Liberty Protection Act (RLPA) in the late 1990s, after the Supreme Court ruled that the 1993 Religious Freedom Restoration Act (RFRA), as applied to state and local governments, exceeded the power of Congress.[35] As Douglas Laycock and others have recounted, the broad coalition that produced unanimous and near-unanimous votes in Congress for RFRA broke down for RLPA after civil rights advocacy groups insisted on a "global exception for any civil rights claim … the bill died in party-line acrimony."[36] The same dynamic is also at work in the current and roiling arguments about whether and to what extent religious employers should be accommodated in the Affordable Care Act's preventive services mandate or exempted from anti-discrimination laws requiring recognition of same-sex marriages or the provision of services in connection with marriage or commitment ceremonies of same-sex couples.[37] This approach tends to produce a narrative in which religious liberty claims and claimants are difficulties to be managed, obstacles to be negotiated, or even enemies to be defeated.[38]

There is no way or need to deny that some religious liberty claims and policies are in tension, and even in conflict, with other civil rights claims and policies. True, it is sometimes declared that such conflict does not, or does not really, exist – that

32 Cf. Nomi Maya Stolzenberg, "He Drew a Circle That Shut Me Out": Assimilation, Indoctrination, and the Paradox of a Liberal Education, 106 HARV. L. REV. 581 (1993).

33 Richard Wolf, *Religious Liberty vs. Civil Rights: A Balancing Act*, USA TODAY, Feb. 28, 2014; www.usatoday.com/story/news/nation/2014/02/27/arizona-religion-gays-lesbians-supreme-court/5872879.

34 This dynamic was the theme, for example, of an eight-part *New York Times* series, *In God's Name*, that ran several years ago on the ways (many presented as troubling) that governments accommodate religious entities by exempting them from otherwise applicable laws. See, e.g., Diana B. Henriquez, *Where Faith Abides, Employees Have Few Rights*, N. Y. TIMES, Oct. 6, 2006, B5; www.nytimes.com/ref/business/churchstate.html.

35 City of Boerne v. Flores, 521 U.S. 507, 511 (1997).

36 Douglas Laycock, *Sex, Atheism, and the Free Exercise of Religion*, 88 U. DET. MERCY L. REV. 407, 412–13 (2011).

37 See, e.g., Douglas NeJaime, *Marriage Inequality: Same-Sex Relationships, Religious Exemptions, and the Production of Sexual Orientation Discrimination*, 100 CALIF. L. REV. 1169 (2012); Elizabeth Sepper, *Doctoring Discrimination in the Same-Sex Marriage Debates*, 89 IND. L. J. 703 (2014). See generally DOUGLAS LAYCOCK ET AL. EDS., SAME-SEX MARRIAGE AND RELIGIOUS LIBERTY: EMERGING CONFLICTS (2008).

38 See, e.g., Douglas Laycock, *Religious Liberty and the Culture Wars*, 3 U. ILL. L. REV. 839 (2014); Steven D. Smith, *Die and Let Live? The Asymmetry of Accommodation* (Aug. 2014) (research paper) (http://papers.ssrn.com/sol3/papers.cfm?abstract_id=2484801).

it presents a false choice – but such declarations generally involve an attempt to dissolve or evaporate the conflict by imposing a contested definition or boundary on "real" religious liberty.[39] If religious liberty does not include a right to discriminate, then obviously there is very little conflict between religious liberty and anti-discrimination laws. But in fact, religious liberty does sometimes include a right to discriminate, and in ways that would otherwise violate civil rights laws.[40] The tension between religious liberty and (other) civil rights is sometimes real, but this fact is unremarkable and should be unsurprising. Certainly, religious freedom is not the only civil right the exercise of which sometimes bumps up against the exercise of others.

Although this tension cannot plausibly be defined away or declared illusory, it is still crucial to remember that the tension is *among* civil rights claims. In order to appreciate this point, one need not believe that religious freedom is importantly basic, prior, fundamental, and "infrastructural"[41] – that it is a necessary condition for the meaningful enjoyment and reliable protection of other human and civil rights.[42] The RFRA is a civil rights act. And like many others, it recognizes a presumptive right to accommodation and embodies a promise of equal regard as a means of achieving equal access, participation, membership, and citizenship.[43] So, when we discuss the feasibility or justifiability or wisdom of religious accommodations, we are not discussing something external or alien or hostile to the character of our age or to the enterprise of civil rights under and through law. We are, instead, taking up a question and a challenge inherent in that enterprise.

Many scholars and others believe and contend that singling out religious or religiously motivated activities, beliefs, and commitments, as such, for protection or accommodation is unwarranted and even unjust. Religion, in other words, is

39 See, e.g., Joshua Dorner, *Religious Liberty for Some or Religious Liberty for All?* CENTER FOR AM. PROGRESS, Dec. 12, 2013 (www.americanprogress.org/issues/civil-liberties/report/2013/12/12/80968/religious-liberty-for-some-or-religious-liberty-for-all); S. Alan Ray, *How Religion and Rights Align on Campus*, CHRON. HIGHER EDUC., Aug. 15, 2014, A56.

40 See, e.g., Hosanna-Tabor Evangelical Lutheran Church & Sch. v. EEOC, 565 U.S. 1, 15 (2012) (holding that there is a ministerial exception grounded in the Religion Clauses of the First Amendment). See Richard W. Garnett, *Religious Freedom and the Nondiscrimination Norm*, in LEGAL RESPONSES TO RELIGIOUS PRACTICES IN THE UNITED STATES: ACCOMMODATION AND ITS LIMITS 194 (ed. Austin Sarat, 2012).

41 See, e.g., Garnett, *Freedom of the Church*; Richard W. Garnett, *Do Churches Matter? Towards an Institutional Understanding of the Religion Clauses*, 53 VILL. L. REV. 273 (2008).

42 See Daniel Philpott, *Explaining the Political Ambivalence of Religion*, 101 AM. POL. SCI. REV. 505 (2007), for a compelling account of the ways that religious freedom and "consensual differentiation" between religious and political authority help to promote democratization and development.

43 Cf., e.g., Vikram David Amar & Alan Brownstein, *Reasonable Accommodations Under the ADA*, 5 GREEN BAG 2D 361 (2002).

not special.[44] On this view, any accommodations or exemptions from general laws that are specific to religion would be defensible, if at all, only on prudential or pragmatic grounds. I believe, though, that religion *is* special – indeed, as my former colleague John Garvey once put it, that "religion is a good thing"[45] – and that this is one reason why it and religious freedom may be, are, and should be singled out for special treatment and special respect in our constitutions, laws, traditions, and practices.[46] The fact that we are in an age of civil rights – like the facts that our political communities are increasingly diverse in values and beliefs, and our governments' regulatory aims and activities have expanded – gives rise to new challenges and arguably complicates the enterprise of appropriately protecting religious freedom among and along with other civil and human rights. It is not, however, a reason or an occasion for abandoning or downgrading that enterprise.

My impression of both the current academic and political debates is that this second approach to the topic – that is, the one that approaches religious authorities, religious teachings, and religious believers' claims or requests for accommodations as obstacles to the civil rights enterprise – is, or is becoming, the prevailing one. As a general matter, religious exemptions and accommodations are increasingly seen as departures from the rule of law, as special and unjustified benefits for powerful interests, as threats to the progress made in the cause of racial justice, or as dangerous or at least disingenuous ploys by those hostile to abortion rights or legal recognition of same-sex marriage. It is, as many have observed, extremely unlikely that the RFRA would be enacted today, let alone enacted with near-unanimous and bipartisan support, and, in fact, the *Hobby Lobby* ruling has prompted some calls to modify or even repeal the RFRA.[47] As Paul Horwitz has noted, the reaction to *Hobby Lobby* may signal and speed "the collapse of a national consensus on a key element of religious liberty: accommodation."[48] What Steven Smith has described as "secular egalitarianism" seems to be increasingly influential, and "there are reasons," as he warns, "to doubt the capacity or willingness of secular egalitarianism to cherish religious

44 Micah Schwartzman, *What if Religion Is Not Special?* 79 U. CHI. L. REV. 1351 (2012).

45 John H. Garvey, *An Anti-liberal Argument for Religious Freedom*, 7 J. CONTEMP. LEGAL ISSUES 275, 283 (1996). See also Steven D. Smith, *Rise and Fall of Religious Freedom in Constitutional Discourse*, 140 U. PA. L. REV. 149, 149 (1991).

46 See generally Michael W. McConnell, *Problem of Singling Out Religion*, 50 DEPAUL L. REV. 1, 3 (2000) (arguing "that 'singling out religion' for special constitutional protection is fully consistent with our constitutional tradition").

47 See, e.g., *Congress Should Narrow the Religious Freedom Restoration Act*, WASH. POST (June 30, 2014); www.washingtonpost.com/opinions/congress-should-narrow-the-religious-freedom-restoration-act/2014/06/30/096af01a-009b-11e4-8572-4b1b969b6322_story.html.

48 Paul Horwitz, *Hobby Lobby Is Only the Beginning*, N. Y. TIMES (Jul. 1, 2014); www.nytimes.com/2014/07/02/opinion/for-the-supreme-court-hobby-lobby-is-only-the-beginning.html. See also Paul Horwitz, *The* Hobby Lobby *Moment*, 128 HARV. L. REV. 154 (2014).

freedom."[49] In a similar vein, Douglas Laycock reported almost twenty years ago that "[m]any secularists see little reason to accommodate an incomprehensible superstition that has lingered beyond its time, and many modernist believers see no reason why anyone's religious belief should affect the pursuit of public policy."[50]

If Horwitz is correct – and I am inclined to think that he is – about the "collapse of a … consensus" on the importance of accommodation and exemptions as means of respecting religious freedom while negotiating and navigating our country's pluralism and diversity, then the responses of those who celebrate our age of civil rights should be concern and regret. This collapse is a setback and not a step forward for the civil rights project, correctly understood. When political authorities are unwilling, or lose the will, to acknowledge and respect the priority of our "first freedom,"[51] other human rights are vulnerable. The civil rights enterprise ought to aim for the enriching of civil society through the practice of what John Inazu calls a "confident pluralism"[52] – a practice that includes a generous policy of religious accommodation.

III

The shared goal of chapters in this volume is not to definitively resolve or define out of existence the tensions and conflicts we observe in American cases like *Hobby Lobby*, *Elane Photography*, *Hosanna-Tabor*, or *Christian Legal Society v. Martinez*.[53] It is – or at least it should be – to help and to challenge authors and readers alike to more fully and sympathetically understand all that is at stake in these and similar cases.

My own thinking about religious accommodation in the age of civil rights is pluralistic in at least two ways.[54] First, it accepts as given, unavoidable, permanent, and human the fact that people, associations, institutions, and communities reasonably disagree about things that matter.[55] Pluralism is not (or need not be) relativism. Still,

49 Steven D. Smith, *Religious Freedom and Its Enemies, or Why the* Smith *Decision May Be a Greater Loss Now Than It Was Then*, 32 CARDOZO L. REV. 2033, 2052 (2011).

50 Douglas Laycock, *Continuity and Change in the Threat to Religious Liberty: Reformation Era and the Late Twentieth Century*, 80 MINN. L. REV. 1047, 1098 (1996).

51 See Michael W. McConnell, *Why Is Religious Liberty the "First Freedom"?* 21 CARDOZO L. REV. 1243, 1243 (2000). James Madison, in his Memorial and Remonstrance Against Religious Assessments (1785), memorably contended that the "duty" to "render to the Creator … homage" is "precedent both in order of time and in degree of obligation, to the claims of Civil Society" (p. 1246).

52 John D. Inazu, *Confident Pluralism*, 88 S. CAL. L. REV. 587 (2015).

53 Christian Legal Soc'y v. Martinez, 561 U.S. 661 (2010).

54 "Pluralism," in political and legal theory, is – to put it mildly – a complicated and rich subject, and I do not make any attempt here to treat it in depth. Two thoughtful and recent studies are JACOB T. LEVY, RATIONALISM, PLURALISM, AND FREEDOM (2014) and VICTOR M. MUÑIZ-FRATICELLI, STRUCTURE OF PLURALISM (2014). Parts of what follows from this point are taken from Garnett, *Religious Freedom*.

55 Inazu presents a more developed account of pluralism in this sense; see Inazu, *Confident Pluralism*.

we and our governments should acknowledge and accept our limited competence and prerogative to resolve or dissolve our moral disagreements. We and our governments should resign ourselves – comforted, perhaps, by the "spirit of liberty" as described by Judge Learned Hand[56] – to the "crooked timber" of free society.[57] There are "many reasonable … worldviews that are compatible with good citizenship, and it is neither necessary nor desirable to attempt to forge agreement."[58] It is not necessary – in fact, it is self-defeating – for liberalism to insist on liberalism "all the way down."[59] The "logic of congruence"[60] is antithetical to the civil rights enterprise as I understand it.

My approach to the topic is also pluralistic in another, related sense.[61] It proceeds from what Mark DeWolfe Howe described as,

> the conviction that government must recognize that it is not the sole possessor of sovereignty, and that private groups within the community are entitled to lead their own free lives and exercise within the area of their competence an authority so effective as to justify labeling it a sovereign authority. To make this assertion is to suggest that private groups have liberties similar to those of individuals and that those liberties, as such, are to be secured by law from governmental infringement.[62]

We can debate the extent to which it is helpful to use the term "sovereign" to describe non-state authorities,[63] but to embrace pluralism is to acknowledge the reality of these authorities, to deny that non-state authority exists, and is exercised only by state concession,[64] to "refuse […] to limit the domain of law to the law of the

56 In his May 21, 1944, speech in New York City's Central Park, Hand said that "[t]he spirit of liberty is the spirit which is not too sure that it is right." Judge Learned Hand, Speech at New York City's "I Am an American Day" (May 21, 1994) (www.providenceforum.org/spiritoflibertyspeech).

57 See ISAIAH BERLIN, CROOKED TIMBER OF HUMANITY (ed. Henry Hardy, 2013).

58 Michael W. McConnell, *New Establishmentarianism*, 75 CHI.-KENT L. REV. 453, 454 (2000).

59 See Larry Alexander, *Illiberalism All the Way Down: Illiberal Groups and Two Conceptions of Liberalism*, 12 J. CONTEMP. LEGAL ISSUES 625 (2002).

60 See, e.g., Nancy L. Rosenblum, *Democratic Character and Community: The Logic of Congruence?* 2 J. POL. PHIL. 67 (1994).

61 For more on this second sense, see Garnett, *Freedom of the Church*, 39 (2013): "[C]onstitutionalism relies, both in theory and in fact, not only on the separation and limitation of the powers of the political authority, but also on the existence and the health of authorities and associations outside, and meaningfully independent of, that political authority, or 'the state.'"

62 Mark DeWolfe Howe, *Foreword: Political Theory and the Nature of Liberty*, 67 HARV. L. REV. 91, 91 (1953).

63 Compare ABNER S. GREENE, AGAINST OBLIGATION: MULTIPLE SOURCES OF AUTHORITY IN A LIBERAL DEMOCRACY 2, 139 (2012) (developing an idea of "permeable sovereignty"), with Andrew Koppelman, *"Freedom of the Church" and the Authority of the State*, 21 J. CONTEMP. LEGAL ISSUES 145, 146 (2013) (arguing that special treatment of religion is not appropriately conceptualized as "freedom of the church" because the church is not a separate sphere of authority over which a state has no jurisdiction).

64 Cf. Koppelman, *"Freedom of the Church,"* 164: "[T]le law decides which things are more important than the law. Constitutional law constrains the state, but it is still law, not something outside the law."

state,"[65] and to accept that "[w]ithin society, as distinct from the state, there is room for the independent exercise of an authority which is not that of the state."[66]

I have proposed that religious institutions, communities, and groups are non-state authorities that play important structural and infrastructural roles in the social and legal orders.[67] They help to clear out and preserve the civil society space for the exercise of religion, as well as the enjoyment of other rights, liberties, and freedoms. They contain and check power. In addition, they are among the conditions – part of the infrastructure – that make the exercise of religious (and other) freedoms possible. Jack Balkin has made this point with respect to the "infrastructure of free expression,"[68] noting that freedom of expression requires "more than mere absence of government censorship or prohibition to thrive; [it] also require[s] institutions, practices and technological structures that foster and promote [it]."[69] That is, freedom of expression is not only enjoyed by and through, but also depends on, the existence and flourishing of what Paul Horwitz calls "First Amendment Institutions."[70] In my view, religious freedom also has and requires an infrastructure, and this infrastructure, in turn, requires pluralism. Like free expression, religious freedom is not exercised only by individuals. Like free expression, its exercise requires more than an individual with something to say. Like free expression, it involves more than protecting a solitary conscience. The freedom of religion is not only lived and experienced through institutions, it is also protected, nourished, and facilitated by them. This is true as a matter of fact and as a matter of American constitutional law.

Conversations about religious accommodations in the age of civil rights, and, more specifically, our laws and policies having to do with the reach, application, and content of antidiscrimination laws and values, should be animated by a commitment to pluralism in both of these senses. It does not have to be, and should not be, a feature of this age that we ignore or downplay important questions about both the principled and the practical limits on the reach, application, and content of civil rights laws. When we design antidiscrimination and other civil rights laws, and when we use mechanisms such as conditional spending and access to public spaces and program funds to promote antidiscrimination and civil rights values, we should pay more attention than we

65 Perry Dane, *Maps of Sovereignty: A Meditation*, 12 *Cardozo L. Rev.* 959, 963–64 (1991).

66 John Courtney Murray, We Hold These Truths: Catholic Reflections on the American Experience 78 (1964).

67 See, e.g., Richard W. Garnett, *Religious Liberty, Church Autonomy, and the Structure of Freedom*, in Christianity and Human Rights: An Introduction 267 (ed. John Witte Jr. & Frank S. Alexander, 2010); Garnett, *Do Churches Matter*, 274.

68 See Jack M. Balkin, *Two Ideas for Access to Knowledge: Infrastructure of Free Expression and Margins of Appreciation* (http://balkin.blogspot.com/2007/04/two-ideas-for-access-to-knowledge.html).

69 Jack M. Balkin, *Infrastructure of Religious Freedom*, Balkinization (http://balkin.blogspot.com/2007/05/infrastructure-of-religious-freedom.html).

70 Paul Horwitz, First Amendment Institutions (2013).

sometimes do to the reasons why discrimination is wrong, when it is wrong. We should consider carefully whether, how, and to what extent, consistent with pluralism in both of the senses sketched previously, governments like ours may or should prohibit or discourage discrimination.[71] It is clearly part of the civil rights enterprise to identify wrongful discrimination and to take regulatory and other steps to prevent, remedy, discourage, and denounce it. At the same time, it is not the case that discrimination is always or necessarily wrong, nor is it always the case that governments should or may regulate or discourage it, even when it is. After all, we discriminate – we draw lines, identify limits, include and exclude, make judgments, and act on the basis of preferences – all the time, and often for good or at least tolerable reasons.[72]

Even in the age of civil rights, there is no reason for governments like ours to ban, regulate, or disapprove discrimination that is not (all things considered) wrong. Of course, we do and will continue to disagree about what it is that makes discrimination wrong. My own view is that the reason discrimination is wrong, when it is wrong, has to do with what I take to be the fact that every person is created, sustained, and loved by God and has been bestowed an equal dignity that should not be violated. This is as true for all of us as it is for some, and it directs and constrains how we ought and ought not to treat each other and how our governments may and may not treat us.[73] In any event, we have good reasons, sounding in pluralism, for insisting that governments should not prevent, correct, or even discourage all instances of wrongful discrimination. Some wrongs and bad acts are beyond a constitutionally and morally limited government's power to correct. Some are too difficult or costly to identify, let alone regulate. Others are, put simply, none of the government's business.[74] A government committed to the civil rights enterprise should oppose, discourage, or prohibit wrongful discrimination – conduct that wrongly excludes persons from or pushes persons to the margins of the full life of the political community – when doing so is within its constitutionally limited powers, is consistent with pluralism, and makes sense, all things considered.

Sometimes, then, a political community that is committed to religious freedom and, and among, civil rights will protect a right to discriminate.[75] Sometimes, as with the Civil Rights Act or the Fourteenth Amendment, it will regulate or prohibit

[71] I develop these suggestions in more detail in Garnett, *Religious Freedom*, from which some of what follows is taken or adapted.

[72] See Larry Alexander, *What Makes Wrongful Discrimination Wrong? Biases, Preferences, Stereotypes, and Proxies*, 141 U. PA. L. REV. 149, 151 (1992): "All of us well-socialized Westerners know that discrimination against other human beings is wrong. Yet we also realize, if we think about it at all, that we discriminate against others routinely and inevitably."

[73] Cf. Michael J. Perry, *Morality of Human Rights: A Nonreligious Ground?* 54 EMORY L. J. 97 (2005).

[74] Cf. Koppelman, *Corruption of Religion*, 1891: "[T]he constitutional prohibition against laws respecting an establishment of religion must at least mean that in this country it is no part of the business of government to compose official prayers for any group."

[75] See, e.g., Hosanna-Tabor Evangelical Lutheran Church & Sch. v. EEOC, 565 U.S. 1 (2012).

that right. Sometimes, a community will discourage or disincentivize its exercise.[76] Sometimes it will disapprove but tolerate it. And, sometimes, the political community should be entirely unbothered and uninterested. Reading the times correctly is challenging, and I do not expect that there is a neat and tidy formula that could determine reliably and uncontroversially the appropriate response (or non-response) in every situation. We will disagree over what counts as a harm and therefore about whether pluralism actually provides a good reason for tolerating or enduring harms caused by or associated with religious exercise. We cannot avoid trade-offs, compromises, sacrifices, and perhaps even "tragedy."[77] In my view, the much criticized but nevertheless crucial public–private distinction will and should do significant work.[78] So might Abraham Kuyper's "pillars,"[79] Walzer's "spheres of justice,"[80] Greene's "permeable sovereignties,"[81] and "subsidiarity" as it is understood in Catholic social thought.[82] Still, at the end of the day, something like the following framework might be helpful when thinking about particular cases or responding to particular conflicts.

In a first category, there will be some cases (not very many, but some) where the issue is not really whether a religious institution or religiously motivated action should be accommodated through an exemption from an otherwise valid, generally applicable nondiscrimination or civil rights law. It is, instead, whether the secular political authority has the power to regulate, prohibit, or punish the action or decision in question, even assuming it is or resembles the kind of wrongful discrimination with which that authority should be concerned. *Hosanna-Tabor*, I think, is such a case. The question in these cases is best seen as one of legitimate authority or jurisdiction.[83] These are cases sounding more in separation, autonomy, entanglement,

76 See, e.g., Title IX of the Civil Rights Act of 1964, Pub. L. No. 88–532, §§ 901–02, 78 Stat. 266 (1964). See generally COREY BRETTSCHNEIDER, WHEN THE STATE SPEAKS, WHAT SHOULD IT SAY? (2012). But see INAZU, *Confident Pluralism*. Inazu notes, for example, that "while not every government funding decision is constitutionally problematic or in tension with a confident pluralism, some may be. We might be especially concerned when government imposes ideological constraints on generally available funding offered in settings that welcome and encourage a diversity of viewpoints and ideas" (p. 608).

77 MARC O. DEGIROLAMI, TRAGEDY OF RELIGIOUS FREEDOM (2013).

78 See Inazu, *Confident Pluralism*, 9, citing Lillian BeVier & John Harrison, *State Action Principle and Its Critics*, 96 VA. L. REV. 1767 (2010).

79 See, e.g., Paul Horwitz, *Churches as First Amendment Institutions: Of Sovereignty and Spheres*, 44 HARV. C.R.-C. L. L. REV. 79 (2009); Nicholas Wolterstorff, *Abraham Kuyper on the Limited Authority of Church and State*, 7 GEO. J. L. & PUB. POL'Y 105 (2009).

80 MICHAEL WALZER, SPHERES OF JUSTICE: A DEFENSE OF PLURALISM AND EQUALITY (1983).

81 GREENE, AGAINST OBLIGATION, 2.

82 See, e.g., F. Russell Hittinger, *Social Pluralism and Subsidarity in Catholic Doctrine*, in CHRISTIANITY AND CIVIL SOCIETY: CATHOLIC AND NEO-CALVINIST PERSPECTIVES 16 (ed. Jeanne Heffernan, 2008); Michael P. Moreland, *Practical Reason and Subsidiarity: Response to Robert K. Vischer, Conscience and the Common Good*, 49 J. CATH. L. STUD. 293, 319 (2010).

83 See, e.g., Steven D. Smith, *"Jurisdictional" Conception of Church Autonomy* (on file with author); Steven D. Smith, *God and Caesar: Religious Freedom and the Two Jurisdictions* (on file with author).

and disability than in accommodation or toleration. The reasons for insisting that a secular, constitutional government lacks the power to answer certain questions or respond to certain decisions – even wrongful ones – are not undermined by the goals and values of the civil rights enterprise and are not inimical to that enterprise's success, properly understood.

The next category is also probably best viewed not as a place for accommodation and exemption, but instead for neutrality and toleration. I am thinking here of cases involving conditional spending, public forums, access to public lands and even public contracting. This admittedly large category would include a case like *Christian Legal Society*, or the question presented in cases about whether to allow the Boy Scouts to use public lands notwithstanding their policy (perhaps former policy) of excluding gay men from service as troop leaders, or the ongoing controversy about whether public universities should de-recognize Christian student groups that reject all-comers policies.[84] Even in the age of civil rights, it makes sense – as Inazu has explained[85] – for governments not to leverage too heavy-handedly their ownership of property and their management of forums, in order to penalize or discourage non-state groups, associations, and societies whose internal practices and policies do not mirror those that we (correctly) expect of government agencies.[86] True, governments will sometimes have good reasons not to subsidize, support, or promote practices, including expression, that they conclude are harmful, but the viewpoint neutrality often required by the First Amendment seems an appropriately humble aspiration.

A third category, and one whose coverage and boundaries will be very sharply contested, is where we really are negotiating a conflict between religious exercise and a civil rights law or policy that targets activities or decisions that are presumptively wrongful and that are within the power (and the practical competence) of the government to regulate or prohibit. It is here, in this category, that the questions being confronted are questions of accommodation, compromise, and concession. Our government has the power to regulate or ban drugs it determines to be dangerous, but it decides (or not) to accommodate religious believers and communities who use that drug in their religious worship.[87] At least some of our governments have the power to regulate land use and building construction, but they decide to accommodate religious interests that are substantially and unnecessarily burdened by such

But see Koppelman, *"Freedom of the Church,"* 146 (noting that the Church is not a separate sphere of authority over which the state has no jurisdiction); Richard Schragger & Micah Schwartzman, *Against Religious Institutionalism*, 99 VA. L. REV. 917, 919 (2013) (arguing that religious organizations do not have a special form of sovereignty).

84 See John Inazu, *Perverse Effects of the "All Comers" Requirement*, LIBERTY LAW FORUM (Sep. 15, 2014); www.libertylawsite.org/2014/09/15/the-perverse-effects-of-the-all-comers-requirement.

85 Inazu, *Confident Pluralism*.

86 But see BRETTSCHNEIDER, WHEN THE STATE SPEAKS.

87 See, e.g., Gonzales v. O Centro Espirita Beneficente Uniao do Vegetal, 546 U.S. 418 (2006).

regulations.[88] Our government has the power to enact and collect taxes of various kinds, but it decides (or not) to exempt parsonages or property owned by churches. This category reflects the fact that, as Michael McConnell put it, "between the accommodations compelled by the Free Exercise Clause" – at least some of which, discussed earlier, might not really be accommodations at all – "and the benefits to religion prohibited by the Establishment Clause there exists a class of permissible government actions toward religion, which have as their purpose and effect the facilitation of religious liberty."[89] Identifying these permissible and all-things-considered warranted actions is, again, difficult, and there are tests and standards we might design and employ for this purpose.

The key point is that this effort is not only consistent with what should be our aspirations for the age of civil rights; it also honors and reflects those aspirations. The generous and sympathetic accommodation of religion is a crucial part of, not an obstacle to, the practice and promotion of civil rights.

88 See Religious Land Use and Institutionalized Persons Act of 2000, 42 U.S.C. § 2000cc (2013).
89 McConnell, *Accommodation of Religion*, 3.

4

Israeli Law and Jewish Law in Israel: A Zero Sum Game?

Yedidia Z. Stern

INTRODUCTION

The most significant event in the life of the Jewish people in the past century, and perhaps in the last few thousand years, was the establishment of the State of Israel. Its Declaration of Independence describes it as "a Jewish state," a phrase that would become part of Israel's constitutional definition as "a Jewish democratic state."

But what is a Jewish state, and how does it differ from an ordinary democratic state? There is no ready-made answer to the riddle of Israel's Jewish identity. The literature dealing with nation-states is not sensitive to the uniqueness of Judaism, which weaves together religion, nationality, and culture. Nor does the Jewish literary canon offer answers. The long years of exile, during which most works on Jewish law were written, silenced Jewish thought on the subject. Given the lack of historical experience in the management of a Jewish state, tracing our contemporaries' inquiries into the meaning of Israel's Jewishness in various contexts is a fascinating quest. The legal system is a central stage for this drama.

Jewish religion is a legal religion. A believing Jew is asked to accept a normative religious code – known as *halakha* – that aspires to regulate all aspects of human existence: the individual's relations with other individuals, with the society at large, with her God, and even with himself. The halakhic way of life preserved Jews, who were spread throughout the globe for 2,000 years without a territorial or political center, as one people. Halakha has now become less important for most Jews, but still serves as the central criterion for determining a Jew's measure of religiosity.

With the establishment of the State of Israel, halakha was pushed to the margins of national life. A religious person can observe halakhic commands individually or in a communal framework, but Israel, despite its definition as a Jewish state, has not adopted halakha as the law of the state. With the establishment of Israel in

Article translated from the Hebrew by Batya Stein.

1948, Israeli statutes absorbed the laws of the British Mandate that were in force in Palestine at the time and has replaced them with original Israeli laws over the years.

Israeli Jewish citizens who observe religious commandments, then, assume a dual normative commitment: to Israeli law, the product of a secular-liberal parliament, and to religious law, the product of rabbinic decisions made over centuries. Since these two normative systems, the religious and the civic one, aspire to be total in their scope, many areas of friction emerge between them and between the two establishments that enforce them: rabbis on the one hand, and legislators and judges on the other.

Here I describe how these two establishments relate to one another. A picture of mutual alienation emerges that reflects a deep cultural dispute between two Jewish visions. I will suggest some thoughts about a possible amendment supporting the mutual recognition of civic law and religious law. These suggestions could turn the current situation from a zero sum game, wherein each system hopes to gain from the other's loss, into a positive sum game that would work for the benefit of Israel's public domain.

ISRAELI LAW AND JEWISH LAW: A STORY OF MUTUAL ALIENATION

Jewish society in Israel exists in a cultural duality. It forges its life by mining the rich lodes of two great cultures: the Western-liberal and the traditional-Jewish. Most Jews in Israel – secular, traditional, religious, and even some ultra-Orthodox (*haredi*) – are influenced, at various levels of internalization and awareness, by the cultural baggage of both these legacies, which serve as elements in their identity, shaping their behavior and their ways of life. Hence, one could plausibly have expected the normative systems regulating the lives of Jews in Israel – state law[1] (Israeli law) on one hand, and religious halakha[2] (Jewish law[3]) on the other – to reflect, each in its own way, the cultural duality noted previously. Is this expectation fulfilled?

[1] Obviously, state law regulates the life of all the citizens, including about 20 percent of Israeli citizens who are not Jews. Should this fact deny all legitimacy to any aspiration to have state law express Jewish values or cultural preferences? Here I assume that the answer to this question is negative, without discussing the matter in detail. Whatever the case, Israel's choice to define itself as "a Jewish democratic state" rather than "the state of all its citizens" raises the possibility of state law expressing particularistic Jewish preferences.

[2] Given the demographic dominance of Orthodox Judaism in Israel (which itself covers a broad range of approaches), its control of the state rabbinic establishment, and its vast political power, I use the term *halakha* in this chapter in its Orthodox denotation. As other Jewish religious movements become stronger in Israel in the future, there will be room for reformulating the arguments presented later according to their halakhic outlooks.

[3] My use of the term "Jewish law" as an alternative to "religious law" is not precise, since Jewish law need not be religious. Nevertheless, I choose this term because the dominant proposal for promoting any aspect of particularistic Jewish law in the current Israeli reality is based, in the consciousness of its supporters, on religious halakha.

Israeli Law

For many years, both before and after the establishment of the State of Israel, there were calls to include in the new state's statutes norms drawn from Jewish law, either through specific substantive laws or through the regulation of an entire legal area. There were also demands to use Jewish law and principles drawn from the Jewish heritage as a source in the interpretation of Israeli law.[4] These demands, voiced by politicians[5] and religious intellectuals, remained unanswered. Despite some exceptions,[6] the general picture that emerges from Israeli statutes and from the case law of the civil courts is one of alienation from Jewish law and from classic Jewish value preferences.

The most prominent and radical expression of Israeli law's obliviousness to Jewish legal tradition is the draft of the Civil Law 5771-2011, which has been under discussion in Israel in recent years. This is an ambitious legislative endeavor that seeks to unify in one law (with about 1,000 provisions) the arrangements currently in force in most branches of Israeli civil law. The proposed civil code was prepared by a committee headed by former president of the Supreme Court Aharon Barak, which was engaged in this effort for more than twenty years. This code, if legislated, will replace a series of existing statutes with one coherent whole.[7]

An examination of the proposed code reveals that it lacks any significant connection with classic sources of Jewish law. It disregards the wisdom and experience stored in the Jewish library, whose shelves are packed with the thought of many generations of rabbis on key issues of civil law. This reality frustrates the hope of one of the most brilliant Supreme Court justices in the founders' generation, Moshe Silberg, who wrote with the establishment of Israel in 1948:

> It is somewhat absurd that, when coming to renew national life in the homeland, we should ignore the spiritual sector that, for two thousand years, has been at the

4 Foundations of Law Statute, 5740–1980, 34 LSI 181 (1948–89) (Isr.), states that, in cases of legal lacunae, the court will decide "in light of the principles of freedom, justice, equity and peace of Israel's heritage."

5 For example, the platform of the National Religious Party in elections for the 15th Knesset states that one of the party's goals is "to promote original legislation, based on Torah law and Jewish tradition."

6 For a specific substantive law that incorporates religious law into state law, see Law of Guards, 5727–1967, SH No. 496 p. 52 (Isr.) or the Law on the Duty to Rescue, 5758–1998, SH No. 1670 p. 245 (Isr.). For the regulation of an entire legal branch – personal status – according to halakha, see Section 2 of the Rabbinical Courts Jurisdiction (Marriage and Divorce) Law, 5713–1953, SH No. 134 p. 165 (Isr.).

7 Aharon Barak, *Independence of the New Civic Codification: Risks and Prospects* (Hebrew), 7 *Hebrew U. L. Rev.* [Mishpatim] 15 (1977). The rationale of the bill states that it "seeks to regulate fully and completely legal relationships in the realms of civil law, without leaving any realms deliberately unregulated."

> very center of the nation's interest and concern. And we will have no other alternative but to return to Jewish law.[8]

Not only has the Israeli legislator forsaken Jewish law, but so have Israeli courts. Even when specific judges (typically religious ones) show interest in including a value or a halakhic norm in their verdicts, they often find themselves in a minority in the judicial panel. Hence, even the limited number of decisions that do mention traditional Jewish law do so in the context of a *dictum* or as comparative law. Therefore, one can hardly question the determination of an Israeli Supreme Court judge that the influence of traditional Jewish law on the case law "has been marginal and, rather than setting principles, it spread a scent."[9]

Jewish Law

It is plausible to expect that contemporary halakhists will realize the enormous significance of renewing a Jewish public domain after seventy generations of coerced exile and will strive to shape it in ways responsive to this change. But this expectation is yet to be fulfilled. Despite almost seventy years of Israeli independence, halakhists seldom deal with issues related to what might be called "Zionist halakha." A prominent instance of the halakhic failure to take into account the meaning of sovereignty is the halakhists' reservations (to say the least) about Israeli law.

Almost all halakhists hold that Israeli courts lack religious legitimacy for a variety of reasons: the judges are unqualified from a halakhic perspective (for example, they are women, or not Jewish, or lack expertise in Jewish law); the procedures of Israeli law are halakhically inadmissible (for example, they accept the testimony of women or minors or witnesses who are deemed untrustworthy for other reasons); and the differences between substantive Israeli law and Jewish law.[10] Each one of these issues and all of them together are obstacles in the way of granting halakhic recognition to Israeli courts from a religious perspective. But are these obstacles insurmountable? Could halakhic activism, had contemporary halakhists endorsed it, have reached a different result without rejecting the ethos of Jewish law and the positive case law of previous generations? Elsewhere I have presented a series of arguments enabling recognition of Israeli courts from the perspective of Jewish law.[11] As of today, the accepted halakhic view has not endorsed this course and has chosen to place Israeli

[8] Moshe Silberg, *On the Redaction of a Hebrew Codex* (Hebrew), 4 HAPRAKLIT 262 (1948).

[9] Mishael Cheshin, *Jewish Legacy and the Law of the State*, in CIVIL RIGHTS IN ISRAEL: AN ANTHOLOGY HONORING HAIM COHEN 47, 50 (ed. Ruth Gavison; Hebrew, 1982).

[10] Haim Shapira, *Halakhic Status of Courts in the State of Israel: Halakhah and Zionism*, in ZIONIST HALAKHAH (ed. Yedidia Stern & Yair Sheleg; Hebrew, forthcoming).

[11] Yedidia Z. Stern, *On the Attitude of Halakhah to the Israeli Legal System*, in RELIGION AND POLITICS IN JEWISH THOUGHT: ESSAYS IN HONOR OF AVIEZER RAVITZY 897 (ed. Benjamin Brown et al., Hebrew, 2012).

courts in the halakhic category of "Gentile courts," a rubric that forbids turning to them.

What are Gentile courts? In the long years of exile, halakhists were resolutely opposed to Jews resorting to non-Jewish courts that implemented the laws of the countries where Jews lived. The reasons for this opposition were professional, religious, and national.[12] Behind the professional opposition was the suspicion that, in some cases, non-Jewish judges failed to meet proper standards of quality or fairness due to hatred of Jews or a culture of corruption or lack of expertise. Rather than being an a priori, in-principle rejection of non-Jewish judges, this opposition rested on purported cumulative experience. Religious opposition to Gentile courts focused on the connection between the foreign legal system and its religious background. When the foreign legal system did not symbolize any religious preference, opposition to it reflected a fear that Jews turning en masse to Gentile courts would lead to prolonged neglect of Jewish law and hence to its decay over the years. National opposition tended to stress the potential injury to the social solidarity of community members. The choice of one party in a dispute between Jews to entrust the decision on their disagreement to Gentile courts was perceived as having delivered the other Jewish side to the hostile attack of a foreign ruler.

Obviously, the validity of these reasons should be considered against the backdrop of the times, when Jews throughout the world lived in isolated communities in surroundings not always tolerant of them. Unsurprisingly, then, Maimonides (1135–1204) stated: "Anyone who sits in judgment in front of Gentile judges and in their courts, even if their laws are like the laws of Israel, indeed such a person is wicked, and it is as if he cursed and swore and raised a hand against the Torah of Moses our teacher."[13]

But is the halakhic decision to declare non-Jewish legal systems in the Diaspora invalid meant to apply to the courts of the Jewish democratic state? Most contemporary halakhists say yes. Thus, one of the most important haredi rabbis in the past generation, Ovadia Yosef (1920–2013), who was also a Chief Rabbi of Israel, was conclusive on this matter: "You know my view of the Supreme Court … Anyone who turns to the courts, to the secular courts that do not rule according to Torah law … raises a hand against the Torah of Moses our teacher; it is as if he cursed and swore [against God]; and he has no share in the world to come."[14]

The picture that emerges is thus one of mutual alienation between Israeli law and Jewish law in our generation. Israeli law ignores Jewish law as a product lacking any value for the sovereign life of contemporary Jews. For their part, halakhists strongly

[12] This classification relies on YITZHAK BRAND, NON-JEWISH COURTS IN THE JEWISH STATE (Hebrew, 2010).

[13] MAIMONIDES, MISHNE TORAH, Laws of Sanhedrin 26:7 (n.d.).

[14] Yair Ettinger, *Ovadia Yosef: Whoever Turns to Civil Courts Has No Share in the World to Come*, HAARETS (June 20, 2010).

reject the legitimacy of Israeli law and view it, as it were, as a foreign law that constitutes a threat to Jewish law.

ISRAELI LAW AND JEWISH LAW: A ZERO SUM GAME

Why do Israeli legislators and judges choose to minimize the possibility of Jewish law influencing state law? Why do halakhists choose to ignore the crucial distinction between the reality of Jewish life in exile in a hostile environment and the reality in the State of Israel, where most judges are Jews and the public domain is distinctly Jewish? What are the cultural disputes that have led the leaders of both legal systems – the Israeli and the Jewish one – to adopt an extreme view of total alienation?

Israeli Law

From the end of the eighteenth century, the cultural content of Jewish society has been affected by the movement of Jewish Enlightenment (Haskalah). This movement challenged rabbinic leadership, opposed the limitation of Judaism to the dimensions of halakhic religion, and aspired to improve the lives of Jews by striving for their integration into Western culture. Beside a Jewish emphasis, whose crucial component was the revival of the Hebrew language, Haskalah supporters endorsed humanistic thought and rationality as key components of the renewed Jewish culture. Large segments of the Jewish people underwent a process of secularization involving two central dimensions. The first was liberation from a rigorous way of life centering on observance of the commandments and on Torah study as an ideal. The second was the opening of Judaism to an external culture "that strives to replace worldly contents and assets of Torah Judaism … with contents and assets from another culture"[15] (including, as will be shown, the replacement of Jewish law with another law). The counter-reaction of the rabbis took the form of self-enclosure, isolation, and raising the walls of religion around the communities that remained loyal to them. These were the seeds of the Jewish *Kulturkampf* that persists to this day in the State of Israel.[16]

The national movement of the Jews – Zionism – grappled from the start with the place of religion in national life. The religious held that religion is the organizing principle and the source of the Jewish people's national existence, whereas the secularists rebelled against tradition and held that national existence should be set on foundations other than religion and independently from it.[17]

[15] ELIEZER SCHWEID, JUDAISM AND SECULAR CULTURE 18 (ed. Meir Ayali; Hebrew, 1981).

[16] SHMUEL FEINER, JEWISH ENLIGHTENMENT 13 (trans. Chaya Naor, 2004).

[17] See EHUD LUZ, PARALLELS MEET: RELIGION AND NATIONALISM IN THE EARLY ZIONIST MOVEMENT 32 (trans. Len J. Schramm, 1988); Jacob Katz, *Zionism and Jewish Identity*, in JEWISH NATIONALISM: ESSAYS AND STUDIES 73 (Hebrew, 1979).

Positions denying the centrality of religion in renewed Jewish life assumed various forms. Extremists sought to contrast Jewish culture in the Land of Israel with Jewish culture in exile. They called for "the negation of exile," for liberation from the "grief of heritage," and viewed all these as conditions for normalizing the existence of Jews in their land. Thus, Micha Josef Berdyczewski called for the Jews' return to their pre-exilic past and asked that his contemporaries be "the last Jews" and "the first Hebrews."[18] Others held a more moderate view, seeking to blend traditional Jewish culture and secular European culture. The dominant voice expressing this view was that of Ahad ha-Am, who formulated the vision of a "spiritual center."[19] He questioned the simplistic view of political Zionism, stating that the ingathering of exiles and the creation of a political structure for the Jewish people would solve "the Jewish problem." Ahad ha-Am understood the crucial significance of culture in constituting personal and collective identity, and therefore sought to translate religious contents into national contents and the ancestral religious commitment into a new national spirit. A. D. Gordon also viewed political Zionism of the Herzl variety, as well as socialist and Marxist Zionism, as a form of assimilation, given their alienation from the spiritual content of Judaism. In his view, the national renaissance movement was a religious movement. It was not a return to exilic Orthodox religion, but a religious renewal centering on the transition from halakha to Scripture, from observance of the commandments to the religion of labor.[20] Within secular Zionist thought, participants in the dispute concerning the new culture required for the Jewish people (supporters of the spiritual center, political Zionism, socialist Zionism, and so forth) agreed on one issue: Zionism was meant to enable the normalization of the Jewish people and their return to history. Thus, in the mid-twentieth century, Israel was established – its character state-centered, its worldview secular, and its orientation modern and futuristic. This organizational setting was dramatically different from the Exile Judaism of previous eras – its character communal, its worldview religious, and its orientation devoted to the memory of the past. The dominant and charismatic leader of the new state, David Ben-Gurion, held that ensuring the success of the Zionist project required fostering a new Jewish identity: Israeli. A "new Jew" must be created – courageous, pioneering, independent, sovereign – to replace the Jew of the Exile, who was perceived as decadent, weak, dependent, and too spiritual. Ben-Gurion and his contemporaries sought to make a revolution, "a holy rebellion" against Exile Judaism, and for this purpose they consciously renounced any association with the Jewish cultural output of the Exile. In the service of the Zionist revolution, most Jewish contents were

[18] Avner Holzman, *Old Jews, New Hebrews*, in LITERATURE AND LIFE: ESSAYS ON MICHA JOSEF BERDYCZEWSKI (Hebrew, 2003).

[19] RINA HEVLIN, COPING WITH JEWISH IDENTITY: A STUDY OF AHAD HA-AM'S THOUGHT (Hebrew, 2001).

[20] SCHWEID, JUDAISM, ch. 6.

erased from the consciousness of the founders' generation – above all, halakha and its talmudic sources, as well as philosophy, poetry, mysticism, and other treasures. Ben-Gurion sought to found Jewish-Israeli identity on the historical narrative of the Bible,[21] which confirmed the association of Judaism and the Land of Israel, the historical homeland. He tried to skip from King David to David Ben-Gurion, and everything in the middle – the formative Jewish experience of 2,000 years – was for him irrelevant.

The cultural and intellectual history of Israeli law exceeds the scope of this chapter, and I will confine myself to a brief description. At the beginning of the twentieth century, the Movement for the Revival of Hebrew Law strove to introduce content from Jewish law into the legal system of the future, secular State of Israel.[22] The movement's leaders were secular, and their motivation was cultural and national rather than religious. They did not view halakhic norms as holy, but as an expression of the Jewish people's unique spirit and identity. The revival of Hebrew law was for them part of their Zionist activism. Beginning in 1909, judicial tribunals called Hebrew Justices of the Peace, which sought to apply national Jewish law according to their understanding, began to operate in the Land of Israel. Their supporters stressed the link between the nation's law and its soul, and they consequently held that recourse to colonial British law equaled legal assimilation.[23] Over the years, they dealt with thousands of cases in various fields. Efforts in this direction, however, were short-lived and a target for attack from two flanks. On one side were religious jurists and the rabbinic establishment, who saw them as a desecration and felt that any "adjustment" of halakha or its acceptance on a national basis was invalid. What was required was the endorsement of halakha in its entirety as state law, because this was the law binding on Jews for theological reasons. On the other, vital side were the political leaders of the Zionist public institutions,[24] who saw in the communal religious courts and in their national connection to Jewish culture a form of return to exile, worthy of condemnation.

Ultimately, the Movement for the Revival of Hebrew Law declined in the 1940s, even before the establishment of the State of Israel. Henceforth, most (but not all) jurists who voluntarily engaged in the revival of traditional Jewish law, either as state law or as communal law, were religious.

21 Anita Shapira, *Ben-Gurion and the Bible: The Creation of a Historical Narrative?* 14 ALPAYIM 207 (Hebrew, 1997).

22 Asaf Lahovsky, *Hebrew Law and Zionist Ideology in Eretz Israel during the Mandate*, in MULTICULTURALISM IN A DEMOCRATIC AND JEWISH STATE 633 (ed. Menachem Mautner et al.; Hebrew, 1998).

23 PALTIEL DICKSTEIN, HISTORY OF THE HEBREW JUSTICE OF THE PEACE: TRENDS, ACTIONS AND ACHIEVEMENTS (Hebrew, 1964).

24 Ronen Shamir, *Lex Moriandi: On the Death of Israeli Law* (Hebrew), in MAUTNER, MULTICULTURALISM, 589.

Before and after the establishment of Israel, attempts were made to make traditional Jewish law part of Israeli law, but to no avail.[25] When Israel was established, the British Mandatory law that had regulated life in Palestine until 1948 became the law. Over the years, Israeli legislators replaced Mandate laws with Israeli laws that were usually Western-liberal in their orientation. American political theory and legal thought have been extremely influential. By contrast, "the place of Jewish law in Israeli law is modest, and actually – minuscule. The legal system of the State of Israel is, fundamentally, still distinctly Anglo-American."[26]

Jewish Law

The accepted halakhic view rejects the legitimacy of the Israeli legal system and places it in the category of Gentile courts. The extremely wide acceptance of this view is astonishing. The position a halakhist endorses concerning the halakhic legitimacy of the State itself could be assumed to be an influential, if not critical, factor in the decision on the halakhic status of the judiciary. And yet, even halakhists holding a Zionist worldview and those ascribing religious significance to the State of Israel refuse to recognize Israeli courts as halakhically valid. Furthermore, even modern Orthodox halakhists who identify with the liberal values promoted by Israeli courts share the harsh reservations regarding Israeli courts. Nor do we find differences between halakhists with an Ashkenazi background (a tradition that was forced to grapple with the Haskalah and thus tended to isolationism) and those with a Sephardi background (who tend to be more tolerant and open). Even rabbis officiating in the Israeli judiciary (serving as judges in rabbinic courts established by virtue of Israeli law) and in the executive (serving as rabbis on behalf of the Israeli Chief Rabbinate) take the halakhic position that civil courts are Gentile courts. Insofar as alienation from the Israeli legal system is concerned, then, a broad – and rare – consensus prevails among contemporary halakhists[27]

What is behind this broad common denominator in the opposition to the courts? I offer two explanations – one focusing on the content of Jewish law and the other on the rabbinic establishment that implements it.

[25] Ron Harris, *Absent-Minded Misses and Historical Opportunities: Jewish Law, Israeli Law and the Establishment*, in ON BOTH SIDES OF THE BRIDGE: RELIGION AND STATE IN THE EARLY YEARS OF ISRAEL 21 (ed. Mordechai Bar-On & Zvi Zameret; Hebrew, 2002).

[26] Aharon Kirschenbaum, *Foundations of Law 1980: Today and Tomorrow* (Hebrew), 11 TEL AVIV U. L. REV. 117, 117–20 (1985).

[27] In the years immediately before and after the establishment of the State of Israel, Zionist rabbis did consider the possibility of conferring halakhic validity on the courts. Among these were Shlomo Goren, Moshe Zvi Neriah, Shimon Federbusch, and to some extent also Shaul Yisraeli. For a discussion of their views, see Shapira, *Halakhic Status*, and sections on Israeli Law and Jewish law, later. These rabbis, however, had no followers.

Content of Jewish Law

The Jewish legal system is total in its scope. It seeks to regulate not only the personal life of individuals, but also the public domain. And yet, given that Jews in the Diaspora did not fully control the public domain, the potential for developing a Jewish public law was not fully realized. Although the communities spread throughout the world enjoyed legal autonomy and maintained judicial religious systems of their own, in the absence of territorial control the rabbinic courts dealt mainly with personal matters. In the establishment of Israel as a Jewish state is a potential for reviving a unique Jewish expression in the public domain. How have halakhists responded to this challenge? Their instinct is traditional and their nature conservative – they therefore reject revolutions. Consequently, halakhists find it difficult to grapple with the challenge of sovereignty and have not developed a stand on basic questions such as the halakhic validity and status of Knesset laws, state institutions (including the courts), and elected officials. But if Jewish law fails to answer these questions, a chasm opens up between halakhic life and public life in Israel. Instead of creating an experiential fusion of horizons between the religious world (including its legal facet) and the political-public domain, the horizons of Jewish law and of Israeli law exist in parallel universes, which do not meet.

This general background can help us understand the alienation from the courts. If Israel is not a reality that Jewish law knows how to digest, it is only natural that its judiciary has not been the subject of serious halakhic discussion. Barring such a discussion, the courts are placed in the classic category that Jewish law used during exile when dealing with alternative legal systems: Gentile courts.

Rabbinic Establishment

Beside the general difficulty characterizing Jewish law's encounter with sovereignty, a specific difficulty marks its encounter with the Israeli legal system: contemporary halakhists are more alienated from the judicial than from the legislative and executive powers. The latter two powers are not a priori perceived as illegitimate. Why this difference? It is even more puzzling given that all the substantive grounds mentioned in halakhic literature against recourse to the judiciary – opposition on national grounds, as well as professional and religious opposition – could be used even more effectively as a basis for rejecting cooperation with the other powers as well.

It seems that the difference is related to the institutional aspect of the rabbis' function. Jews in the Diaspora were minimally involved in legislation. They conducted their lives bound by external systems of legislation and government in the country where they lived, and they accepted this reality. Traditional Jewish law validated the external laws by determining that "the law of the kingdom is law" (*dina de-malkhuta dina*). This mental disposition was easily extended to the State of Israel, so that

Israeli law is perceived as if it were the law of a foreign kingdom. As the foreign law was valid, so is Israeli law. By contrast, in the context of judicial autonomy, judicial roles remained in Jewish hands during the Exile. The rabbinic judiciary system played a crucial role in the shaping of Jewish life in exile, especially given that other instruments of power were mostly denied to Jews. It is thus clear why halakhists in previous generations were on guard and eliminated competition by forbidding recourse to Gentile courts. The historical construct in use during the Exile has persisted in Israel: the Israeli legal system is perceived as a variation on the powers that threatened the rabbinic establishment for 2,000 years, and is therefore perceived as a rival.

The halakhic alienation from the courts conveys the enormous disappointment of rabbis and halakhists with the new circumstances: precisely at the time of the most astonishing transition in Jewish existence, from exile to independence, a central public role they had fulfilled so skillfully and so responsibly over all those years slipped from their hands. Religious historical memory ascribes to the rabbis "ownership" of the judicial function, and the Israeli judiciary subverts this. The reasons behind the united front of halakhists against the courts are thus clear: even Zionist or liberal or Sephardi rabbis share in the sense that their standing as judges of Jews has been challenged. The disappointment conveys deep currents, not always conscious, of hostility to the establishment that pretends to occupy the halakhists' historical role in contemporary Jewish leadership.

A Zero Sum Game

The general picture is that of a struggle between two legal systems, set up so that one's success is necessarily perceived as the other's failure. For the generation of the founders of Israeli law, Jewish law was an obstruction to the realization of the Zionist ideal, preventing the liberation of the "new Jew" from the fetters of exile. Halakha, which was religious and irrational, was a central expression of the people's abnormality and was therefore an obstacle in the path of the State of Israel that sought to return the Jewish people to history. For halakhists today, Israeli law is a Trojan horse that seeks to instill into the national life cycle of Jews a foreign system of values, originating in Western-liberal culture. In doing so, the Israeli judiciary also deprives rabbis of their historical role as the ultimate interpreters of the Jewish way of life.

And so it is that one's dream is the other's nightmare.

ISRAELI LAW AND JEWISH LAW: A POSITIVE SUM GAME

Can we think about Jewish law and Israeli law coexisting without mutual alienation? Can normative multiplicity be a basis for the accumulation of cultural capital rather than for spiteful competition between the Israeli and the religious establishments? Can the current zero sum game be turned into a positive sum game for the benefit of Israel's public domain? I will suggest initial thoughts for amending this situation, from the perspective of both Israeli and Jewish law.

Israeli Law

To this day, halakha is, in the consciousness of both its interpreters and its subjects, above all a religious legal system. Consequently, full responsibility for the preservation, development, and implementation of the religious norm lies with the religious authorities – the halakhists. The State of Israel, which rests on secular sources of authority, has neither the authority nor the responsibility for promoting a halakhic agenda. In other words, a clear and sharp separation is required between the Jewish legal system and the Israeli legal system.

Beside its religious-theological meaning, however, another crucial meaning is hidden in halakha – a cultural one: intellectually, the shelf of halakhic literature is the most prominent in the Jewish library; spiritually, it is the pungent spice that has enriched the Jewish soul throughout history; behaviorally, halakha has drawn the map guiding the Jews' ways of life in all circumstances and in all places. Halakha has decisively influenced Jewish identity, Jewish historical memory, Jewish collective consciousness, and the singularity of Jewish civilization. Hence, removing the cultural significance of Jewish law from the agenda of Israeli Judaism could leave it without depth, inarticulate, fragmented in its context, and detached from the rich horizons of its past.

Indeed, the alienation of Israeli law from Jewish law, as described previously, cleared the way for the entry of American law, which expresses liberal-Western preferences. The Americanization of law is part of a broad process of domination – Western culture eclipsing the unique aspects of small cultures; the processes overtaking media, art, taste, language, and leisure are taking place in law as well. Interestingly, most Israeli law professors were trained between the Charles and Hudson Rivers (rather than between the Jordan River and the Mediterranean). Their motto, then, is "I am in the East, and my (professional and cultural) heart is deep in the West." As a result, the curriculum in Israeli law faculties, the reading materials, the contents studied, the paradigmatic figures, the definition of standards, and even the language are imported from the United States. On the one hand, this is a worthy imitation of a splendid professional system worth joining, since it upgrades professional standards in Israel. Yet on the other hand, it is a process of association with contents, values, and outlooks from another culture and another society, with all that this implies.

Let me illustrate. Generally (and I apologize in advance for the gross generalizations and insensitivity to nuances), American culture sanctifies the individual, disregards the community, and views the state, in some contexts, as a danger. The American public domain is perceived in American society as a neutral space, devoid of the particularity of religion or national identity (in its European sense). The American individual is, above all, a rights-bearer, charged with duties mainly insofar as these are meant to implement the rights of the other toward him or her. Democracy in American society and culture assumes liberal garbs of a particular kind, pushing aside alternative interpretations of the democratic way of life. The guiding principle of American capitalism is to prefer the interests of the suppliers of capital to those of others, among them the workers. The American ethos hesitates to impose on the state responsibility for the welfare of the individual, and the United States is therefore not a welfare state. All these preferences are promoted by the American legal system. Hence, insofar as Israeli law is influenced by the contents of American law, be it directly or indirectly, Israelis voluntarily submit to the preferences of others and accept the meaning of a "good life" as formulated largely in American terms. The direct consequence of the alienation of Israeli law from its Jewish sources is that the normative system in Israel, which functions as a cultural mediator, serves as an amplifier for American values in the Israeli market of ideas.

I believe that Israeli law should be exposed to the influence of varied cultural voices, and the Jewish voice should be central among them. Halakha, which bears the fundamental genome of Jewish culture, offers alternatives for each one of the American preferences noted. Most Israeli Jews, not only religious ones, can relate to the halakhic preferences on the place of the community in Israeli society (extremely important); the duties of Israeli citizens (and not merely their rights); the unique nature of the public domain (which should reflect Jewish particularity, as befits a nation-state); the deep-rooted value of solidarity and mutual responsibility; and communal responsibility for the welfare of the underprivileged (leading to a welfare state) and for the minorities in our midst ("loving the stranger"). The Israeli public should examine the suitability of the fundamental values of Jewish law to Israeli national culture, not on a religious basis. According to this suggestion, Jewish law can contribute to Israeli law by serving as a critical model – a proposal for a good life and a good society, to the citizens of the Jewish and democratic state. It can enable Israeli law a space for reflection, a source of inspiration from an ideal system for a concrete-practical one. Moreover, it can emerge as a functioning system that also offers Israeli law concrete arrangements worthy of imitation. All of them will serve to temper the provincial tendency of Israeli jurists to wander in foreign fields. A serious, sincere search on the home turf of Jewish civilization may uncover rich lodes, potential sources of legal inspiration for twenty-first-century Israel.

Jewish Law

The Jewish law enacted in exile has yet to deal seriously with the normative meaning of a Jewish state. A halakhic lacuna has been revealed concerning central aspects of public law. In the absence of halakhic activism to fill the normative space, and in light of the institutional tension between rabbis and judges, halakhists have decided to categorize Israeli courts as Gentile courts. This choice has far-reaching implications, both ideologically and educationally.

Ideological-Conceptual Considerations

In exile, Gentile courts represented a genuine threat to the very possibility of preserving Jewish singularity, which is why Jewish law sharply censored any option of crossing the community borders by turning to foreign courts. The current situation is entirely different. The establishment of the State of Israel enables the shaping of a national domain where Jews are the dominant voice. In the State of Israel, a Jew feels at home. The Jewish state, the product of the Zionist political idea, upgrades the Jews' mode of existence and grants them – as owners – full authority for their lives (and the lives of the minorities living among them) and, consequently, also full responsibility. Jews, as the majority group, are responsible for developing public products and shaping the public arena wherein Jewish society exists according to its preferences.

The Israeli legal system is one of the crucial signs of renewed Jewish sovereignty, which involves symbolic aspects (such as the state flag and the state emblem placed in the court), as well as practical ones. The halakhic decision making Israeli courts a variety of Gentile courts thus reproduces in the state of the Jews the existential mode that prevailed in exile. In the consciousness of religious Jews who conduct their lives according to halakhic commandments, it establishes a distance between themselves and the Jewish democratic state; it detaches them from the feeling of normalcy that Zionism aspired to create in Jews and returns the exile mentality – existence in the shadow of a dominant "other" – to the Land of Israel. It involves a denial of the most important Jewish phenomenon of the last 2,000 years.

Educational-Cultural Considerations

As a matter of fact, despite the categorical halakhic rejection of the courts, the religious and haredi public in Israel fully participates in the entire range of actions involving Israeli courts. Observant Jews routinely turn to the courts to solve their legal disputes; thousands of Israeli lawyers are observant Jews; the number of religious judges in the current Supreme Court is higher than their proportion in the population; they hold key positions in the Ministry of Justice (Minister of Justice,

State Attorney, and Director of the Courts); and their presence in legal academia, where the Israeli legal system is studied and taught, is impressive.

An intense dissonance thus prevails between the view widely adopted by halakhists and the actual reality of their followers. On the one hand, prominent halakhists zealously disqualify the courts.[28] On the other hand, the masses of the religious public are an inherent part of Israel's legal system. The religious establishment must take into account that intensifying the struggle against the legal establishment leads to harsh educational-cultural consequences, regardless of whether the religious public will heed its call. Let us consider both possibilities.

Should the religious public continue to ignore halakhic ruling on Israeli law, the result could be a loss of the rabbis' prestige and even a systemic injury to the institution of the rabbinate as a whole. Not in vain does the halakhic principle state: "No decree should be imposed upon the community unless the majority are able to abide by it."[29] When the religious establishment makes an extreme decision against the courts, it sets the stakes very high, and it must be aware of it.

By contrast, should the religious public be persuaded by the rabbinic establishment to accept the religious prohibition and, contrary to its current practice, refrain as far as possible from turning to state courts, the educational-religious damage described earlier will be avoided, but a heavy religious-cultural price will be exacted from us all. In these circumstances, an alternative judicial rabbinic instance will be established, where disputes will be settled according to Jewish law. A regime that could be called "legal pluralism" will then prevail in the State of Israel. Two systems – one Israeli and one Jewish – will compete with one another for the citizens' hearts. Should one of the parties to a dispute choose it, the state system will consider the conflict; should all the parties be interested in turning to the religious system, the dispute will be decided there.

A plausible assumption is that each system will then aspire to expand its scope at the other's expense, leading to prolonged friction and severe conflicts between Jewish and Israeli law. The courts of the Jewish system will strengthen their resistance to the Israeli "other" and radicalize the rhetoric against liberal values. The fear of a *Kulturkampf* will grow, with judicial norms and institutions as its weapons. Furthermore, in response to the establishment of a separate Jewish legal system, pressure may well grow to eradicate any religious influence from Israeli law. Thus, for example, the persuasive power of the demand to regulate issues of identity in

[28] Thus, for example, R. Abraham Yosef, Chief Rabbi of Holon, who is also a member of the Council of the Chief Rabbinate in Israel, went so far as to state that religious judges are not qualified to be included in a ritual quorum or serve in a religious function as representatives of the public; Abraham Yosef, *Do Not Include Judges in a Ritual Quorum*, YNET (Aug. 23, 2010) (www.ynet.co.il/aricles/0,7340,L-3942286,00.html).

[29] Babylonian Talmud, *Avodah Zarah* 36a.

Israel according to religious law will lessen. I refer to such issues as personal status (marriage and divorce) or to modes of joining the Jewish people, which are currently regulated by religious norms as determined in state law. Should this be the case, the Jewish people will split into two groups, so that members of the religious group will be unable to marry members of the other group.

Generally, religious isolationism within the borders of a separate legal autonomy could result in the transformation of the State of Israel from a "Jewish state" into a "state of all its communities." Imprisoning religion within a communal framework will deprive it from influence on the general Israeli discourse and on the shaping of the public domain, thereby limiting and eroding the active elements of Israel's Jewish identity.

Halakhic Activism

To avoid these consequences, halakhists should endorse halakhic activism. They should develop Jewish law to cover the area of public law. This move is extremely important at several cumulative levels: it can enrich and deepen the Jewish character of Israel; it can contribute to the clarification of the conceptual attitude of religious Jews toward Israel; it can provide a response to the personal distress of religious individuals, given the duality that characterizes their life; and it can enable Jewish law to submit its position on the key issues on Israel's agenda.

Some hold that, given that the source of religious Jewish law – halakha – is a one-time divine revelation on Mount Sinai, its content is set and unchanging. Halakha is, as it were, a "black box," a system hermetically sealed that determines the behavior of Jews in all its details, without any consideration for the real context wherein they conduct their lives. According to this view, halakha neither is nor should be influenced by variables external to the individual – such as the passing of time or geographic location or a scientific discovery – or by variables dependent on the individual – such as conceptual and cultural changes, new social organizations, and so forth.

And yet, serious observation of the history and the philosophy of halakha reveals the mistake of cataloguing halakha as a closed system operating outside human history. Indeed, the relevance of halakha until the present days relies on and derives from its self-perception as a "Torah of life," which reacts to life as it is, including the ceaseless changes typical of human existence. When a gap emerges between life and the norm, the halakhic authorities of the time know how to renew the norm in a way responsive to the challenge posed by reality without changing the system's spirit or the commitment to its values.[30] The same should be done in our time.

30 Yedidia Z. Stern, *Public Leadership as Halakhic Authority*, in JUDAISM: A DIALOGUE BETWEEN CULTURES 235 (ed. Avi Sagi et al.; Hebrew, 1999).

A Positive Sum Game

Jewish law, then, at the cultural level, can contribute to the enrichment of Israeli law and to its adaptation to the character of the nation whose life it regulates, without demanding that Israeli law renounce its secular, rational, and "normal" character. The same is true vice versa: there are religious interests – conceptual and educational – that require new thinking on the standing of Israeli law from the perspective of traditional Jewish law. Lowering the wall of alienation is a shared interest of both the Israeli and the Jewish legal systems, for the benefit of the Israeli collective.

SUMMARY

The establishment of a Jewish state was supposed to clarify the question of Jewish national identity. Concentrating a scattered group in one place, imposing on it full political responsibility, and creating a cultural hegemony in the public sphere were supposed to serve as the raw materials of nation building. In reality, however, instead of deciding on the question of national identity, the Jewish state – which has been in existence for two-thirds of a century – has become the central arena of the controversy on the nature of Jewish identity. The success of political Zionism has raised, in all their intensity, questions requiring ideological and practical decisions on the nature of collective Jewish existence and its meaning. The real function of the Jewish state has instilled life into mutually competing visions of the interpretation, meaning, and orientation of Judaism itself.

This chapter has considered expressions of the Israeli identity struggle in the legal field. The mutual alienation between Israeli law and Jewish law is a sign of their disagreements. The high price of this struggle is exacted from Israeli society in general and from its religious segment in particular. Serious thought is needed to develop concrete alternatives to this mutual alienation. The challenge is indeed unique and serious: the State of Israel is one link in the chain of Jewish existence, tying it to its heritage, but it is also a link in the chain of democratic existence, tying it to its time. It does not resemble any of the other links in these chains: it is a unique manifestation of a dominant democratic culture and of democratic sovereignty in the history of the Jewish people, as well as a unique manifestation of dominant Jewish culture and of national Jewish sovereignty among democratic nations. This duality of belonging should be reflected in the contents of the state laws and in the contents of Jewish law, in each legal system according to its way.

5

Why "Live and Let Live" Is Not a Viable Solution to the Difficult Problems of Religious Accommodation in the Age of Sexual Civil Rights

Mary Anne Case

For about a decade, some well-intentioned scholars of religious liberty have insisted that, as Douglas Laycock put it, "conflicts ... between religious conservatives and the gay rights movement have live-and-let-live solutions in the tradition of American liberty."[1] More recently, they have tried to concretize this claim in proposals for accommodation of religious objectors in the context of state laws recognizing same-sex marriage.[2] Because of continuing religious conscientious objection to abortion, and newly vigorous religious objection to contraception[3] (including but not limited to demands for exemptions from the contraception mandate of the Patient Protection and Affordable Care Act [ACA] such as those recently considered by the US Supreme Court in cases like *Burwell v. Hobby Lobby*[4]), some have now expanded the reach of their proposals for religious accommodation from the narrow issue of same-sex marriage to more broad "disagreements over sexual morality,"[5] renewing their claims, first, that to arrive at a live-and-let-live solution is not only desirable but possible, and second, that to do otherwise than accommodate would be untrue to this nation's tradition of religious liberty.

1 Douglas Laycock, *McElroy Lecture: Sex, Atheism, and the Free Exercise of Religion*, 88 U. Det. Mercy L. Rev. 407, 429–30 (2011). See also Douglas Laycock, *Religious Liberty and the Culture Wars*, 2014 U. Ill. L. Rev. 839, 840.

2 See, e.g., Letter from Robin Fretwell Wilson et al. "Religious Liberty Implications of Legalizing Same-Sex Marriage" (May 1, 2013), in Thomas Berg, *Archive: Memos/Letters on Religious Liberty and Same-Sex Marriage*, Mirror Just (http://mirrorofjustice.blogs.com/mirrorofjustice/2009/08/memosletters-on-religious-liberty-and-samesex-marriage.html).

3 I describe these objections to the provision of contraception as newly vigorous because, until the contraception mandate in the ACA publicized and crystalized the issue for them, many religious employers who now demand exemptions had quietly been providing to their employees exactly the health benefits to which these employers now object.

4 Burwell v. Hobby Lobby 134 S. Ct. 2751 (2014).

5 Laycock, *Religious Liberty*, 846.

A longer version of this chapter was published in 88 U.S.C. L. Rev. 463 (2015).

This chapter will sharply contest both of these claims with respect not so much to their normative desirability as to their descriptive accuracy. Even when the claim for a live-and-let-live solution is limited to same-sex marriage or to gay rights generally, I have long been skeptical as a descriptive matter that such a solution could be concretely constructed, let alone successfully implemented In part, this is because proponents of accommodations they claimed were designed to live and let live initially tended to

> isolate issues of gay rights without ever even acknowledging that they are far from the only issues as to which there is strong religiously motivated objection, let alone discussing the extent to which [their] proposed framework should be or the reasons why it should not be applied to any of these other issues.[6]

One of my longstanding fears[7] has indeed come to pass – the insistent claim for religious accommodation now extends far beyond gay rights to other sexual rights, other reproductive and family recognition rights, and women's rights. I have a strong personal normative stake in fighting this expansion, committed as I am to what I have called feminist fundamentalism,[8] which is defined in my case as an uncompromising commitment to the equality of the sexes and to the abolition of fixed sex roles. But my principal focus here will remain on the practical and legal, not the ideological problems with this expansion. In particular, this expansion of claims for accommodation does not solve, but rather compounds the problem of selective attention to only a subset of the laws and regulations to which religiously motivated actors might have a conscientious objection. Among my central concerns are: first, there are serious problems under both the Establishment Clause and the Equal Protection Clause if only a certain subset of religious claims for exemption – those propounded largely by conservative Christians in conflict with laws guaranteeing liberty and equality in matters of sex, gender, and sexuality – are favorably received; and second, there would be even more serious problems with administrability, of the sort Justice Scalia warned of in his opinion for the Court in *Employment Division v. Smith*,[9] if an even broader set of religious accommodation claims is given traction.

This chapter thus rests on the normative view that *Smith* was correctly decided and that the Religious Freedom Restoration Act (RFRA)[10] was a mistake, even if

6 Memorandum from Mary Anne Case to Andrew Koppelman and George Dent, 1 (Dec. 4, 2009).

7 Memo to Koppelman and Dent 10: "Whether under the Equal Pay Act or Title VII, numerous employers have litigated and lost their claim that their religious views justified them in refusing to hire or promote women or to pay them equally with men. Would your proposal not only upset this settled law but expand the range of employers who could use religious exemptions to discriminate against women?"

8 See generally, Mary Anne Case, *Feminist Fundamentalism as an Individual and Constitutional Commitment*, 19 AM. U. J. GENDER SOC. POL'Y & L. 549, 550 (2011)

9 Employment Division v. Smith, 494 U.S. 872, 888–89 (1990).

10 Religious Freedom Restoration Act, 42 U.S.C. §§ 2000bb et seq. (2012).

for no other reason than because of the descriptive impracticability of an approach to religious exemptions from generally applicable law contrary to that of the US Supreme Court in *Smith*, as the Court explained when it first squarely confronted the issue in *Reynolds v. United States*:[11]

> Laws are made for the government of actions, and while they cannot interfere with mere religious belief and opinions, they may with practices … [To permit] a man [to] excuse his practices to the contrary because of his religious belief … would be to make the professed doctrines of religious belief superior to the law of the land, and in effect to permit every citizen to become a law unto himself.[12]

Not only in (in)famous cases like *Reynolds* and *Smith*, but also in somewhat less notorious ones, such as *Estate of Thornton v. Caldor*[13] and *United States v. Lee*,[14] and in regrettably nearly forgotten ones such as *Hamilton v. Regents of the University of California*,[15] the Supreme Court repeatedly set forth convincing arguments why the sorts of religious exemptions from generally applicable laws typically proposed by proponents of a live-and-let-live solution to the sexual culture wars are neither workable nor "in the tradition of American liberty."[16]

Not even with respect to the concrete proposals for religious exemption actually endorsed, let alone with respect to the host of comparable claims for accommodation foreseeably waiting in the wings, have the proponents of live and let live set forth in any detail how the proposed religious accommodations they urge legislatures and courts to adopt would actually work in practice. Moreover, while it is clearly correct to say, as Laycock does, that, "[i]f we are to preserve liberty for both sides in the culture wars, then we have to preserve some space where each side can live its own values and where its rules control,"[17] no proposal I have seen offers my side in the culture wars anything like the "space … [to] live its own values and where its rules control" that such proposals insist our conservative religious opponents are entitled to. As a strong supporter of rights to sexual liberty and equality, I instead observe that many religiously motivated opponents of such rights seem to want not only to have their cake and eat it too, but also to shove it down my throat; and that most, if not all, religious liberty scholars who claim their goal is a live-and-let-live

11 Reynolds v. United States, 98 U.S. 145 (1878).

12 Reynolds, 166–67.

13 Estate of Thornton v. Caldor, 472 U.S. 703, 709–11 (1985) (striking down under Establishment Clause statute giving employees an "absolute and unqualified right not to work on their Sabbath," because "the statute takes no account of the convenience or interests of the employer or those of other employees who do not observe a Sabbath").

14 United States v. Lee, 455 U.S. 252 (1982) (rejecting claim by Amish employer to exemption from Social Security tax).

15 Hamilton v. Regents of the Univ. of Cal., 293 U.S. 245 (1934).

16 Laycock, *McElroy Lecture*, 429–30.

17 Laycock, *Religious Liberty*, 876.

solution seem to support my religious opponents in their ongoing efforts to realize these desires at my expense.

Following are some of the descriptive claims I am seeking to encapsulate with this admittedly tendentiously formulated imagery.

First, as proponents of living-and-letting-live themselves have to admit, few conservative participants in the sexual culture wars showed any interest in settling for accommodation so long as there was any chance of complete victory for their side. Second, religious objectors in the United States have been increasingly successful in recent years at obtaining unprecedentedly robust constitutional and statutory protection for enclaves in which they can "live [their] own values and [have their] rules control," despite the contrary commands of secular laws specifically designed to protect the liberty and equality of their opponents in the culture wars. Among these enclaves are not only (a) churches themselves and institutions sponsored by or affiliated with them, but (b) for-profit corporations and perhaps also (c) units of local government.

The first Supreme Court case ever to hold that religious institutions were constitutionally entitled to an exemption from civil rights laws was *Hosanna-Tabor Evangelical Lutheran Church and School v. Equal Employment Opportunity Commission*.[18] Although the law at issue in this case was the Americans with Disabilities Act (ADA),[19] the sexual culture wars nevertheless played a central role at oral argument, with justices from both the left and the right of the Court taking it as a central and legitimate premise in support of the "ministerial exception" to the employment discrimination laws that "[t]he government's general interest in eradicating discrimination in the workplace is simply not sufficient to justify changing the way that the Catholic Church chooses its priests [or other authority figures], based on gender roles that are rooted in religious doctrine."[20] More broadly, Chief Justice Roberts's opinion for a unanimous court in *Hosanna-Tabor* has the potential to become what I have called "Citizens of the City of God United,"[21] eviscerating the holding in *Smith* and ceding to religious institutions a constitutionally protected sphere of liberty they have never before enjoyed under US law. While the Justices in *Hobby Lobby-Tabor* took discrimination in employment on grounds of sex as the paradigm case of what churches must be protected in doing if they so choose, the majority in *Hobby Lobby* and its progeny took government protection of women's

18 Hosanna-Tabor Evangelical Lutheran Church and School v. Equal Employment Opportunity Commission, 132 S. Ct. 694, 699 (2012).

19 42 U.S.C. §§ 12101 et seq. (2012).

20 Transcript of Oral Argument Hosanna-Tabor, 2011 WL 4593953, *32.

21 Cf. Citizens United v. FEC, 558 U.S. 310 (2010) (overruling previously upheld limitations on the speech and political expenditures of corporations). For further discussion, see Mary Anne Case, "Citizens of the City of God United? The Confused Premises and Radical Implications of Hosanna Tabor" (unpublished ms, on file with the author).

reproductive freedom and equality, another centerpiece of the sexual culture wars, as the paradigm case of what might be trumped by religious objectors claiming a right to accommodation under RFRA.[22] Finally, while there is little discussion today among supporters of a live-and-let-live solution to the sexual culture wars of having the spaces in which the respective sides can "live [their] own values and [have their] rules control" be truly public spaces (that is to say, units of government into which people would be encouraged to self-sort), the Supreme Court's recent decisions have not only declared church space to be newly inviolable and private corporate space to be newly protected for the religious, they have also vastly increased the ability of the religious to exert control over public governmental space[23] and resources.[24]

While conservative religious individuals and institutions insist on the freedom to exclude and discriminate against their opponents in the sexual culture wars, they, and the proponents of live-and-let-live solutions who support them in their demands to exclude, simultaneously insist that individuals and institutions committed to sexual equality and liberty should not be permitted to exclude or discriminate against, and indeed should be forced to accommodate and subsidize religious applicants who do not share and wish to be exempted from facilitating an institution's commitments to, for example, LGBT equality, the equality of the sexes, or reproductive rights. As the examples discussed later will demonstrate, the proposal to live and let live is radically asymmetrical, with religious opponents of sexual rights demanding both legal protection for their own space and the legal right to invade the space of their opponents.

This insistence on nondiscrimination against and non-exclusion of religious opponents of sexual rights extends to an insistence that their access to government recognition and government funding be unimpeded, even when the reason government gives for declining recognition and funding is the religious organization's or individual's discriminatory policies with respect to sex, gender, or sexuality. For example, a draft accommodation proposal sent to states considering legislative exemptions for those who claim a religious objection to providing goods and services for or recognition of a same-sex marriage not only would protect the objecting service providers from suit by individuals to whom they refuse service or recognition, but would also legally guarantee that the refusal will not

> result in any action by the State or any of its subdivisions to penalize or withhold benefits from any protected entity or individual, under any laws …, including but

[22] See, e.g., Hobby Lobby 2783: "[O]ur decision in these cases is concerned solely with the contraceptive mandate. Our decision should not be understood to hold that an insurance-coverage mandate must necessarily fall if it conflicts with an employer's religious beliefs. Other coverage requirements … may be supported by different interests."

[23] See Town of Greece v. Galloway, 134 S. Ct. 1811 (2014).

[24] See, e.g., Hein v. Freedom from Religion Found., Inc., 551 U.S. 587 (2008).

not limited to laws regarding employment discrimination, housing, public accommodations, educational institutions, licensing, government contracts or grants, or tax-exempt status.[25]

This not only seeks to make discrimination as costless as possible for the religious, but would also deny to those states and their subdivisions committed to guaranteeing liberty and equality with respect to sex, gender, and sexuality the ability to vindicate these commitments, even in their choice of contracting partners and subsidy recipients. What then remains of the promise of letting not only religious conservatives, but also those with liberal egalitarian commitments in matters of sexuality and gender "live their own values"? What remains of a space in which they, too, can have their "rules control"?

Most proponents of live and let live treat any refusal to recognize, include, or subsidize religious opponents of sexual liberty and equality as unjustifiable discrimination against these religious opponents, rather than as merely an attempt by proponents of sexual equality and liberty to maintain a space in which to live their own values. In the name of living-and-letting-live, for example, many express indignation rather than support for the result in *Christian Legal Society v. Martinez*,[26] even though all Hastings College of the Law sought to withhold in that case from a campus group that excluded some students on the basis of sexual orientation was official recognition and subsidies, not categorically the ability to meet or advertise on campus.[27] In the name of living-and-letting-live, many similarly complain of and would seek to reverse, through legislatively mandated accommodations and exemptions, the results in cases such as those involving Ocean Grove Camp Meeting in New Jersey,[28] Catholic Charities in Illinois,[29] and the Boy Scouts in Connecticut,[30] although in each of these cases the harm suffered by the religious organization in question was simply its inability to benefit

[25] See, e.g., Wilson, "Religious Liberty," 5.

[26] Christian Legal Soc'y Chapter of the Univ. of Cal., Hastings Coll. of the Law v. Martinez, 561 U.S. 661 (2010) (upholding policy of a state-sponsored law school of only giving official recognition to student groups that agreed to admit "all comers" and not exclude students based on forbidden grounds, including religion and sexual orientation).

[27] Christian Legal Society, 671–73. For an example of the hostile reaction of live and let live proponents to the result in Christian Legal Society, see, e.g., Laycock, *McElroy Lecture*, 428–29.

[28] See Jill P. Capuzzo, *Group Loses Tax Break Over Gay Union Issue*, N. Y. TIMES, Sept. 18, 2007, B2 (www.nytimes.com/2007/09/18/nyregion/18grove.html) (reporting that pavilion associated with the Methodist Church forfeited a tax exemption granted on condition that it be open to the public, when it declined to allow a same-sex couple to hold a commitment ceremony there).

[29] See Summary Judgment Order at 2, 3, Catholic Charities of the Diocese of Springfield v. State, 2011 WL 3655016: "The fact that [Catholic Charities] has contracted with the State to provide care and adoption services for over forty years does not vest [it] with a protected property interest."

[30] See Boy Scouts of Am. v. Wyman, 335 F.3d 80, 84 (2d Cir. 2003) (rejecting Boy Scouts' challenge to exclusion from Connecticut's employee charitable contributions campaign).

from certain government subsidies or government contracts so long as it refused to abide by the nondiscrimination conditions placed on the contracts and subsidies by the government entities paying for them, which were themselves committed to a policy of nondiscrimination.

Finally, the accommodations and exemptions now being sought by religious conservatives in the sexual culture wars are vastly more expansive than the paradigm cases of religious accommodation in US law to which proponents of granting such exemptions under the banner of live and let live seek to assimilate them, notably the exemption of pacifist Quakers from the draft and of Catholic hospitals from performing nontherapeutic abortions.

Perhaps the best way of illustrating just how far from "honor[ing] America's … long and rich tradition of religious freedom"[31] granting these expansive new claims for exemption would be is to examine them in light of Justice Benjamin Cardozo's concurring opinion in a case that should be far more prominent than it is in discussions of religious accommodation. In *Hamilton v. Regents of the University of California*,[32] the Supreme Court unanimously declined to grant a religious exemption from a required course in military science to pacifist Methodist students at a state-sponsored school. Cardozo began his analysis of why the case involves no "obstruction by the state to 'the free exercise' of religion as the phrase was understood by the founders of the nation, and by the generations that have followed," by observing:

> The petitioners have not been required to bear arms for any hostile purpose … They have not even been required in any absolute or peremptory way to join in courses of instruction that will fit them to bear arms. If they elect to resort to an institution for higher education maintained with the state's moneys, then and only then they are commanded to follow courses of instruction believed by the state to be vital to its welfare. This may be condemned by some as unwise or illiberal or unfair when there is violence to conscientious scruples, either religious or merely ethical. More must be shown to set the ordinance at naught.

Cardozo went on to note that, while "[f]rom the beginnings of our history, Quakers and other conscientious objectors have been exempted … from military service," this was not only a mere "act of grace," but also "the exemption, when

31 Wilson, "Religious Liberty," 1. Wilson et al. claim that it is part of the American tradition of religious liberty that accommodations should "serve the purpose of insulating conscientious objectors from penalties at the hands of the government." They then treat as the sort of penalty from which conscientious objectors ought to be insulated any refusal by government to exempt the objector from generally applicable conditions on government subsidies or contracts. (p. 13) Do they therefore see the result and the reasoning in Hamilton (see following note) as contrary to the American tradition of religious liberty?

32 Hamilton v. Regents of the Univ. of Cal., 293 U.S. 245 (1934); 265–68 (Cardozo, J., concurring).

granted, ha[d] been coupled with a condition, at least in many instances, that they supply the army with a substitute or with the money necessary to hire one."[33]

These specific points are illuminating enough when translated to the present situation. As Cardozo makes clear, the history of American free exercise demonstrates that a religious accommodation, even when granted, need not be costless to those who receive it, and that conditioning state subsidies on compliance with state policies does not violate the religious liberty of those who choose to avail themselves of the subsidy. He goes on to speak more generally:

> Never in our history has the notion been accepted, or even … advanced, that acts thus indirectly related to service in the camp or field are so tied to the practice of religion as to be exempt, in law or in morals, from regulation by the state … Manifestly a different doctrine would carry us to lengths that have never yet been dreamed of. The conscientious objector, if his liberties were to be thus extended, might refuse to contribute taxes in furtherance of a war … or in furtherance of any other end condemned by his conscience as irreligious or immoral. The right of private judgment has never yet been so exalted above the powers and the compulsion of the agencies of government. One who is a martyr to a principle – which may turn out in the end to be a delusion or an error – does not prove by his martyrdom that he has kept within the law.[34]

Every point Cardozo makes about the claims of the plaintiffs in *Hamilton* is true *a fortiori* of the new proposals for religious exemption now championed in the context of the sexual culture wars.

Having set forth in general terms my concerns about the viability of a live-and-let-live approach to religious accommodation in the sexual culture wars, I will now examine a few of the many serious problems in more detail. One overarching theme is that of an asymmetry I'm tempted to call "live and let die." The proponents of living-and-letting-live disregard (or in some instances actively embrace) extremely troubling asymmetries: (1) in the accommodation sought to be granted to religious opponents of sexual civil rights as compared with that offered to religious opponents of almost anything else that secular law requires or protects; (2) in the space sought to be granted to religious opponents of sexual civil rights and those they would offer to proponents of those rights; and (3) in the harms suffered by religious objectors seeking accommodation and the harms suffered by those whom they would be excused from serving, including, or treating equally.

As I have previously observed, what helped the Free Exercise and Establishment Clauses work so well together to maintain religious peace and freedom for so long was that, as concerns free exercise, "most of the deepest disagreements between

33 Hamilton, 265–68.
34 Hamilton, 267–68.

major religious groups in the United States in prior centuries happened to be about what to believe and how to worship rather than how to live in society."[35] One major exception, the Mormon practice of polygamy, was not in fact accommodated, but promptly and harshly quashed, as Scalia noted in his *Romer v. Evans* dissent.[36] As the outcomes in *Reynolds* and *Smith* demonstrate, accommodating religiously motivated differences in how to live has always been much more difficult and less readily attainable than accommodating differences about what to believe. The problems of accommodating religious differences about how to live in society, such as those at issue in the sexual culture wars, are compounded in present-day America, not only by the increasing diversity of religious views about how to live, but also by the increasingly interconnected way groups and individuals do in fact live. Moreover, in contradistinction to most of the exemption claims put forward in the context of sexual rights, earlier free exercise claims such as those in *Reynolds* and *Smith* involved efforts on the part of believers to engage in primary religiously mandated conduct, rather than efforts to avoid being complicit with, tainted by, or implicated in the religiously condemned conduct of others. In these and many other respects, claims for exemption made in the context of the current sexual culture wars extend well beyond what was even claimed by, let alone granted to, earlier religious conscientious objectors to secular law.

Proponents of live and let live have also yet to come to terms with the fact that issues of sexual rights are far from the only issues about how to live in society regarding which there is strong religiously motivated objection by some to the lives and

35 Case, *A Lot To Ask*, 108. Similarly, the vast majority of the disputes involving the scope of the Free Exercise Clause brought before the Supreme Court in the past 100 years have been directly or indirectly about how to worship. The two major successful exceptions are Thomas v. Review Board, 450 US 707 (1981) (extending unemployment benefits to an employee who lost his job because of a religiously motivated refusal to work on the production of armaments) and Wisconsin v. Yoder, 406 US 205 (1972) (providing an exemption from a compulsory school attendance law for Amish children), which were seen by many scholars as outliers. To make this descriptive observation is not at all to claim that religion should be or is confined to belief and worship. Of course, many devout believers incorporate their faith into every aspect of their lives, but let me repeat: in my view, the Reynolds Court had it right that this cannot make the religious laws unto themselves.

36 Romer v. Evans, 517 U.S. 620, 648–51 (1996) (Scalia, J., dissenting) (drawing analogies between condemnation of polygamy in the nineteenth century and condemnation of homosexuality in the twentieth and observing the numerous respects in which the Supreme Court had found it constitutional to make criminal and otherwise legally disadvantage the religiously motivated conduct of polygamists). A more minor exception, the use of controlled mind-altering drugs in religious ritual, was held by the Supreme Court not to require a religious exemption from a general law making use of such drugs illegal. See Smith, 494 U.S., 890. Because it involved the sacramental use of controlled substances, the Smith case is also a dispute about how to worship, but the particular form of worship also quite directly involves a contested way of living in society. This is a familiar issue in free speech cases – all speech is also noise; all press, at least before the computer age, is also litter. Just as government is not categorically barred from regulating noise because it takes the form of words, it is not categorically barred from regulating actions because believers invest them with religious significance.

actions of others. They need to clarify the extent to which their proposed framework should be, or the reasons why it should not be, applied to any of these other issues. As Justice Ruth Bader Ginsburg pointed out in her *Hobby Lobby* dissent, even if one limits the field of inquiry only to the very narrow question of religiously motivated objections to aspects of the provision of health care coverage, there are "religiously grounded objections to blood transfusions … antidepressants … medications derived from pigs … and vaccinations," each of which must either be accorded the same deference granted to religiously motivated objections to the contraceptive mandate or adequately distinguished.[37] Broadening the horizon, Ginsburg also enumerated just a few of the many "commercial enterprises [in addition to *Hobby Lobby*] seeking exemptions from generally applicable laws on the basis of their religious beliefs," citing already litigated cases in which enterprises objected to dealing with blacks, unmarried heterosexual cohabitants, "young, single wom[e]n working without [their] father's consent," "married wom[e]n working without [their] husband's consent," and any person "antagonistic to the Bible," including "fornicators and homosexuals."[38] She asked, "Would RFRA require exemptions in cases of this ilk? And if not, how does the Court divine which religious beliefs are worthy of accommodation, and which are not? Isn't the Court disarmed from making such a judgment?"[39]

Similarly, I warned in 2009 that even if, *arguendo*, the proponents of live and let live are correct going forward about the small number of likely exemption claims arising from gay rights issues, "[t]here is every reason to think that" a multiplicity of other analogous "religious exemptions will … often be sought. A glance at the docket of a single federal judge, my colleague Frank Easterbrook, gives some sense of the range of already litigated cases on such issues."[40] Religious opposition to gay people was involved in some of Easterbrook's public employment cases – for example, the case of a cosmetology instructor who persisted in proselytizing students in her clinic[41] – but he also was faced with the complaints of a Catholic FBI agent who refused on religious grounds to investigate peaceful antiwar protestors,[42] a Baptist police officer who refused on religious grounds to accept an assignment at a casino,[43] a black Muslim prisoner who refused on religious grounds to clean pork off food trays while on kitchen duty,[44] and a Christian

37 Hobby Lobby, 2805.
38 Hobby Lobby, 2804–05.
39 Hobby Lobby, 2805.
40 Case, Memo to Koppelman and Dent, 5.
41 Piggee v. Carl Sandburg Collection, 464 F.3d 667, 668–69 (7th Cir. 2006) (Wood, J., opinion).
42 Ryan v. DOJ, 950 F.2d 458 (7th Cir. 1991).
43 Endres v. Ind. State Police, 349 F.3d 922 (7th Cir. 2003).
44 Chapman v. Pickett, 801 F.2d 912 (7th Cir. 1986).

prisoner who objected on religious grounds to being exposed to observation by female guards.[45]

Holding that the Baptist policeman, just like the Catholic FBI agent, was not entitled to the requested religious accommodation and could be fired, Easterbrook observed:

> Many officers have religious scruples about particular activities … If [plaintiff] is right, all of these faiths, and more, must be accommodated by assigning believers to duties compatible with their principles. Does [religious accommodation] require the State Police to assign Unitarians to guard the abortion clinic, Catholics to prevent thefts from liquor stores, and Baptists to investigate claims that supermarkets mis-weigh bacon …? … Firefighters must extinguish all fires, even those in places of worship that the firefighter regards as heretical.[46]

Looking beyond one judge's cases, to the newspaper headlines, would multiply the potential claims for exemption. For example, when it was first reported that Muslim cab drivers at the Minneapolis-St. Paul Airport would not serve passengers carrying duty-free liquor, "officials … proposed color-coded lights on cab roofs to indicate whether the driver would accept a passenger carrying alcohol."[47] After more than 5,000 documented taxi refusals at the airport and countless more passengers involuntarily dropped off somewhere between the airport and their destination as soon it became clear to their driver that they were carrying alcohol, authorities dropped all talk of a religious exemption and instead upped the penalty for refusal from being sent to the end of the cab line to a thirty-day taxi license suspension for a first offense and a two-year revocation for a second offense.[48] The overwhelming majority of cabbies in the airport area are Somali Muslims, and there is every reason to think that offering a religious exemption to such drivers would serve to increase the number who insist on such an exemption, because failure to do so will mark the driver as a bad Muslim in the eyes of his community.[49] (Compare, here, the argument that civil rights laws mandating that blacks be served by businesses in the South solved the collective action problem faced by business owners pressured by their white racist customers to remain segregated.) Advocates of exemptions from

[45] Johnson v. Phelan, 69 F.3d 144 (7th Cir. 1995).

[46] Endres, 349 F.3d at 925, 927.

[47] Katherine Kersten, *A Two-Tiered Airport Taxi System Could Lead to 'Chapter Two'*, MINNEAPOLIS STAR TRIB. (Oct. 16, 2006) (www.startribune.com/local/11585696.html).

[48] See *Minnesota's Muslim Cab Drivers Face Crackdown*, REUTERS (Apr. 17, 2007) (www.reuters.com/article/2007/04/17/us-muslims-taxis-idUSN1633289220070417).

[49] See, e.g., Katherine Kersten, *Shariah in Minnesota?* WALL STREET J. (Mar. 24, 2007) (www.wsj.com/articles/SB117470053320547681): "Islam prohibits the consumption of alcohol but not its transportation, say Somalis who reject the taxi drivers' stance. Yet in June 2006, the Muslim American Society's … Minnesota chapter issued a 'fatwa' forbidding drivers here from carrying alcohol to avoid 'cooperating in sin.'"

public accommodation laws for service providers who refuse to provide service for same-sex wedding celebrations have yet to explain whether and why the claims of these Christian bakers and florists are more worthy of accommodation than those of Minneapolis's Muslim cab drivers, who also wish to avoid what they consider "cooperating in sin."[50]

Some proponents of religious exemptions in the context of the sexual culture wars have also suggested that the state should be foreclosed from telling students of social work that it is "simply not acceptable for social workers to view homosexual people as perverse."[51] This too, opens up the possibility of a host of analogous religious accommodation claims going far beyond gay rights. Would the same analysis apply to a school telling students it was training in clinical psychology that it was not acceptable for them to view mentally ill people as possessed by demons, especially considering that many traditional religions still practice exorcism? If not, why not?

Although the first inclination of those arguing for live-and-let-live solutions to the sexual culture wars may be to say that addressing any other religious exemption questions is beyond the scope of their project, a law reform proposal that cannot be generalized to other similar issues is at best of limited usefulness, at worst dangerous and unconstitutional. Ginsburg is clearly correct to warn, in her *Hobby Lobby* dissent, of the risk of "havoc"[52] and the absence of a "stopping point"[53] if exemptions are granted to all those with claims analogous to those put forth by religious opponents of sexual rights. On the other hand, granting exemptions only to religious objectors to sexual rights and not to other similarly situated conscientious objectors on other issues could itself raise constitutional problems under the federal Establishment and Equal Protection Clauses, as well as state constitutional provisions such as California's No Preference Clause.[54] As Ginsburg also warned in her *Hobby Lobby* dissent, "approving some religious claims while deeming others unworthy of accommodation could be 'perceived as favoring one religion over another,' the very 'risk the Establishment Clause was designed to preclude.'"[55]

It is important to look at the risk of potentially unconstitutional favoritism implicit in proposals for special religious accommodations in the sexual culture wars from

50 Kersten, *Shariah*.

51 See George W. Dent Jr., *Civil Rights for Whom? Gay Rights Versus Religious Freedom*, 95 KY. L. J. 553, 596 (2006–07).

52 Hobby Lobby, 2787.

53 Hobby Lobby, 2802.

54 The California Constitution guarantees the "[f]ree exercise and enjoyment of religion without discrimination or preference" and has been interpreted "as being broader than the Establishment Clause of the First Amendment." CAL. CONST. Art. I, § 4; Vernon v. City of L.A., 27 F.3d 1385, 1395 (9th Cir. 1994).

55 Hobby Lobby, 2805 (quoting United States v. Lee, 455 U.S., 252, 263 n.2 (1982) (Stevens, J., concurring in the judgment).

two distinct angles, considering the risk of problematic discrimination in both the questions of (a) which religious groups and viewpoints are deemed worthy of special accommodation and (b) which societal groups will be singled out for diminished protection and thus for harm by the proposed accommodation. Establishment Clause problems arise when a certain group of believers (notably the conservative Christians who would be the principal beneficiaries of religious accommodations in the context of the sexual culture wars) is extended accommodation not granted to others with analogous claims for accommodation, especially when those denied analogous accommodations come from faiths less numerically or culturally dominant. The constitutional concerns are compounded when one considers not only that the views of certain dominant religious groups are favored for accommodation by proponents of live and let live, creating Establishment Clause problems, but also that the brunt of the proposed exemptions will fall almost exclusively on individual members of historically disadvantaged groups, notably gay men and lesbians and other women, creating equal protection problems. The problem here is precisely what caused the Supreme Court to strike down the Defense of Marriage Act (DOMA) as unconstitutional.[56]

In addition to potentially opening up floodgates to a host of new potential claims for religious exemption by a host of different kinds of service providers who seek to avoid serving a host of different clients for a host of different religious reasons, proposals to live and let live, if taken seriously, risk upsetting settled law denying religious accommodation to those who claim a religious objection to associating with blacks or Jews or women on terms of equality. Though few today would seek an exemption from dealing with blacks, there is every reason to believe that had such an exemption been made available earlier, it not only would have been asserted, it might have become entrenched. As William Eskridge has documented, the interaction of traditional religions with the black civil rights movement in the United States has been dynamic – denied an accommodation for the exclusion of blacks, traditional religious groups gradually accommodated themselves to their inclusion.[57]

Unfortunately, traditional religions have not yet internalized US constitutional norms of sex equality to even a significant fraction of the same extent as they have internalized such norms on racial integration over the course of the last half-century. Nor, unfortunately, is it likely as a matter of fact that judges and legislators would view religious exemptions from constitutional and statutory sex equality norms to

[56] See United States v. Windsor, 133 S. Ct. 2675, 2693 (2013) (striking down DOMA as a "[d]iscrimination[s] of an unusual character," targeting for disadvantage and stigma a group the state had specifically chosen to protect but that was condemned by the "traditional [especially Judeo-Christian] morality" legislators wished to reinforce [first alteration in original]).

[57] See William N. Eskridge Jr., *Noah's Curse: How Religion Often Conflates Status, Belief, and Conduct to Resist Antidiscrimination Norms*, 45 Ga. L. Rev. 657, 665–85 (2011).

be quite as far out of bounds as exemptions from norms on race,[58] as the carefully phrased dicta in Justice Samuel Alito's *Hobby Lobby* majority opinion confirm.[59] Whether or not there have been or will continue to be few cases in which "a right is asserted to discriminate against gay people precisely as such,"[60] there have been an abundance of cases in which on religious grounds a right is asserted to discriminate against women precisely as such. Whether under the Equal Pay Act or Title VII, numerous employers have litigated and lost their claim that their religious views justified them in refusing to hire or promote women or to pay them equally with men.[61] I am even more afraid now than I was when I first squarely confronted the issue that live-and-let-live proposals risk not only upsetting this settled law, but also expanding the range of employers who could use religious exemptions to discriminate against women.[62] This worries me profoundly both as a feminist and as a constitutional lawyer.

Nor am I reassured by the insistence of proponents of live and let live that while religious liberty may be in great peril, women's rights are secure and there is of course no danger of retrogression on aspects of our current law crucial to women's legal and social equality. I am also a comparativist and a student of history. I look at the women of Afghanistan, who were in modern dress and in the labor force in the mid-twentieth century and in burkas and confined to the home as a matter of law by that century's end; and similarly at the women of Iran, Iraq, and Israel,[63] to

58 But see Case, *Feminist Fundamentalism* (arguing that, as a matter of law, an uncompromising commitment to the equality of the sexes is incumbent on state actors in the United States whenever they act or speak).

59 See Hobby Lobby, 2783: Very carefully mentioning only race and not, for example, sex, let alone sexual orientation, Alito insists: "The principal dissent raises the possibility that discrimination in hiring, for example on the basis of race, might be cloaked as religious practice to escape legal sanction. Our decision today provides no such shield. The Government has a compelling interest in providing an equal opportunity to participate in the workforce without regard to race, and prohibitions on racial discrimination are precisely tailored to achieve that critical goal" (citation omitted). Note how the words "for example," central to Ginsburg's challenge, drop out of Alito's reassurances, such that only race, but not other forbidden grounds for employment discrimination, are announced by the majority to be immune from interference through RFRA. This is just one of many ways in which Alito's opinion in Hobby Lobby is slippery.

60 Case, Memo to Koppelman and Dent, 5.

61 See, e.g., EEOC v. Fremont Christian School, 781 F.2d 1362, 1365 (9th Cir. 1986) (rejecting religious exemption from Title VII claimed by a Christian school that wished to use "doctrinal beliefs held by the Church" to give lesser pay and benefits to female teachers).

62 See, e.g., Nick Anderson, *Religious Colleges Get Exemptions to Anti-bias Law*, WASH. POST, Dec. 18, 2015 (listing more than thirty colleges who have successfully sought religious exemption from Title IX requirements of sex equality in the past two years).

63 See, e.g., Ricky Shapira-Rosenberg, *Excluded, For God's Sake: Gender Segregation in Public Space in Israel* (Israel Religious Action Center, 2010) (www.irac.org/userfiles/Excluded,%20For%20God's%20Sake%20-%20Report%20on%20Gender%20Segregation%20in%20the%20Public%20Sphere%20in%20Israel(1).pdf).

name just a few of the other countries in which increasing religious demands for sex segregation, for the exclusion of women from the public sphere, and even for outright female subordination have gained rather than lost traction in law as the result of religious demands in the course of my lifetime, and I am anything but reassured. I also note that, as members of the *Hobby Lobby* majority have very recently acknowledged, demands for religious accommodation are infinitely expandable: in many religions, as a matter of religious principle, a believer strives asymptotically to approach perfect observance, demanding ever more of himself or herself, and correspondingly of the state by way of accommodation or exemption from laws that stand in the way of more perfect observance. This is yet another sense in which there is, as Ginsburg says, no "stopping point." In her *Hobby Lobby* dissent, Ginsburg asked, about the majority's proposed less restrictive alternative of having the government pay directly for contraception, "where is the stopping point to the 'let the government pay' alternative?"[64] There is similarly no stopping point with analogous claims and no stopping point down the slippery slope to demands to be exempt from ever more remote connection with the religiously impermissible act. Consider the ever expanding reach of persons who seek accommodation or exemption due to their conscientious objection to participating in abortions: the range of individuals raising such claims has expanded from physicians actually performing abortions, to ambulance drivers and IV nurses, to pharmacists objecting to dispensing not only the morning-after pill, but also condoms.

This ever expanding circle of conscientious objectors to the provision of various aspects of women's reproductive health care has had among its powerful legal weapons the Church Amendment, which provides:

> No individual shall be required to perform or assist in the performance of any part of a health service program or research activity funded in whole or in part under a program administered by the Secretary of Health and Human Services if his performance or assistance in the performance of such part of such program or activity would be contrary to his religious beliefs or moral convictions.[65]

One way to probe the extent to which proponents of live and let live are serious about the symmetry of their assertion that "[i]f we are to preserve liberty for both sides in the culture wars, then we have to preserve some space where each side can live its own values and where its rules control"[66] is to consider what support they would offer to someone who sought to mobilize the Church Amendment as a conscientious objector *against* the values of traditional conservative religion in the sexual culture wars. The Church Amendment on

64 Hobby Lobby, 2802.
65 42 U.S.C. § 300a-7(d) (2012).
66 Laycock, *Religious Liberty*, 876.

its face protects persons motivated not only by "religious beliefs," but also by "moral convictions." I myself have a profound moral conviction that no child, but especially not a girl child, should be born into a family in which women are systematically subordinated to men and forced into traditional sex roles. I have previously called this moral conviction feminist fundamentalism, defined as an uncompromising commitment to the equality of the sexes and the abolition of fixed sex roles. If I were an obstetrician-gynecologist, would I be fully accommodated in a refusal to provide services that would facilitate the reproduction of a Christian fundamentalist Quiverfull family or an FLDS (Mormon) family or a woman who came to my office in a burka with a husband who did all the talking for her? Would the supporters of live and let live be as eager to defend me as they are to defend religiously motivated conscientious objectors to the provision of contraceptives?

I could ask similar questions with respect to any of the proposals for accommodation and exemption that proponents of live and let live urge be passed in connection with state recognition of same-sex marriages. First, let me observe that the legislation proposed by Wilson and colleagues speaks very generally, extending exemptions to those whose "sincerely held religious beliefs" would be "violate[d]" by their "provid[ing] services, accommodations, advantages, facilities, goods, or privileges for a purpose related to the solemnization or celebration of *any* marriage," or by "treat[ing] as valid *any* marriage," or by "provid[ing] counseling or other services that directly facilitate the perpetuation of *any* marriage."[67] This would on its face extend exemptions to those (and there are many) with a sincere religious objection to facilitating or recognizing interfaith marriages, the remarriage of the divorced, even interracial marriages. When one adds in the objections those with a faith in egalitarian marriage may have to marriages in which wives are subordinate to their husbands, very few couples could remain secure that their marriage would be recognized as necessary by all those from whom they may require services in the course of their married lives.

Far from promoting the social peace that proponents of live-and-let-live solutions to the sexual culture wars claim to offer, such a broad license to disrespect the validity of such a broad array of potentially disfavored marriages seems to encourage insecurity on the part of those in need of services and hostility on the part of providers. It moves us farther along the road to what I call the new feudalism,[68] rather than promoting the liberty and equality of all.

67 Wilson, "Religious Liberty," 3–4 (emphasis added).

68 See Mary Anne Case, "The New Feudalism," keynote address delivered at Tulane Law School's Forum on Law and Inequality, Nov. 7, 2014 (discussing the extent to which our rights are becoming more and more, rather than less and less, a function of our hierarchical attachments, whether to state, church, employer, or family).

6

Control by Accommodation: Religious Jurisdiction among the Palestinian-Arab Minority in Israel

Michael Karayanni

INTRODUCTION

The various religious communities of the Palestinian-Arab minority in Israel have adjudicative and prescriptive jurisdiction over their members in a variety of family law issues.[1] In matters of marriage and divorce, this jurisdictional authority is exclusive in nature: these members cannot opt for any other institution or judicial body but those of their respective religious communities when seeking to conduct or adjudicate their marriages and divorces.[2] In other matters of family relations, such as custody over children, maintenance allowances, alimony claims between the spouses, inheritance, and more, these religious courts possess a concurrent jurisdictional capacity.

What this means is that the members of the specific religious community can use the courts of their community on these matters instead of turning to the regular civil courts (usually the Court of Family Affairs) upon establishing a certain precondition.[3] A common condition is that of consent: the religious court will be competent to deal with one of the listed family law matters if all parties to the action have consented to such jurisdiction. What exactly is included in an action pertaining to

[1] See YÜKSEL SEZGIN, HUMAN RIGHTS UNDER STATE-ENFORCED RELIGIOUS FAMILY LAWS IN ISRAEL, EGYPT AND INDIA 84–93 (2013).

[2] See Adam S. Hofri-Winogradow, *Plurality of Discontent: Legal Pluralism, Religious Adjudication and the State*, 26 J. RELIGION & STATE 57, 62 (2011). It is true that marriages can be celebrated in a civil manner outside of Israel and then be recognized in one form or another through the rules of Israeli private international law. It is also true that parties can live together as partners and gain a status and a bundle of rights similar to that of married couples. However, these alternatives have their shortcomings and do not always prove to offer an adequate alternative. See Menashe Shava, *Civil Marriages Celebrated Abroad: Validity in Israel*, 9 TEL-AVIV STUDIES IN LAW 311 (1989).

[3] See Daphna Hacker, *Religious Tribunals in Democratic States: Lessons from the Israeli Rabbinical Courts*, 27 J. RELIGION & STATE 59, 63 (2012).

An expanded version of this chapter appeared as *Tainted Liberalism: Israel's Palestinian-Arab Millets*, 23 CONSTELLATIONS (2016).

marriage or divorce, what is the exact list of family law matters that are subject to concurrent jurisdiction, as well as what forms a consent for such jurisdiction, have drawn much litigation. Given the different options and prospects of litigation, parties naturally engage in "forum shopping" in order to maximize their interests, given that the religious courts and the civil courts do not necessarily see eye to eye on the different disputed matters, nor on the procedure of adjudication.

Notwithstanding these controversies, there is a general agreement in the literature dealing with law and religion in Israel that the jurisdictional authority granted to the Palestinian-Arab religious communities is a form of minority accommodation.[4] Consequently, scholars commonly refer to this jurisdictional authority as a "group-differentiated right,"[5] "group right,"[6] design of "self-government,"[7] or "autonomy."[8] In addition, scholars and public figures frequently make calls to enhance the recognition granted to Palestinian-Arab religious institutions (*millets*), in the name of such values as liberal multiculturalism and inclusive democracy toward an indigenous minority.[9]

This basic feature of the jurisdictional authority granted to the Palestinian-Arab religious communities as accommodational is what distinguishes it from the jurisdictional authority granted to the Jewish rabbinical courts. When evaluated in terms of liberalism, rabbinical jurisdiction comes out as intolerant and even coercive. As to why Israel has nonetheless maintained this jurisdictional authority, claims center on it being a matter of necessity, stemming from the quest to maintain governmental coalitions, preserve Jewish unity, or manage the deep conflict among Jewish Israelis as a form of consociational politics.

These basic distinctions pertaining to the perceived nature of the jurisdictional authority granted to each of the religious communities have been the subject of my research for more than a decade now. One major implication I have explored relates to the effects of this distinction on individual members who are especially

4 See Michael Karayanni, *Separate Nature of Religious Accommodations for the Palestinian-Arab Minority in Israel*, 5 NW. J. INT'L HUMAN RIGHTS 41 (2006).

5 Ilan Saban, *Minority Rights in Deeply Divided Societies: A Framework for Analysis and the Case of the Arab-Palestinian Minority in Israel*, 36 NYU J. INT'L. L. & POLITICS 942–48, 954–60 (2004).

6 See DAVID KRETZMER, LEGAL STATUS OF THE ARABS IN ISRAEL 163–68 (1990), discussing the religious organization of the Palestinian-Arab religious communities under the heading of "group rights"; Itzhak Zamir, *Equality of Rights for Arabs in Israel*, 9 LAW & GOVERNMENT 26, 30 (Hebrew, 2005).

7 Amnon Rubinstein and Barak Medina refer to the religious organization of the Palestinian-Arab religious communities as a limited form of self-government. See A. RUBINSTEIN & B. MEDINA, CONSTITUTIONAL LAW OF THE STATE OF ISRAEL 429–35 (Hebrew, 2005).

8 Jacob M. Landau, ARAB MINORITY IN ISRAEL, 1967–1991: POLITICAL ASPECTS (1993) 24; Ori Stendel, *Rights of the Arab Minority in Israel*, 1 ISRAEL YEARBOOK ON HUMAN RIGHTS 149 (1971).

9 See ILAN PELEG & DOV WAXMAN, ISRAEL'S PALESTINIANS: THE CONFLICT WITHIN 7, 149–51 (2011); Yousef T. Jabareen, *Constitution Building and Equality in Deeply-Divided Societies: Case of the Palestinian-Arab Minority in Israel*, 26 WISCONSIN INT'L. L. J. 346, 357–59, 397 (2008–09).

vulnerable to the encroachment of religious patriarchy, namely, women and children. I have argued that, given the supposed liberal character of the Palestinian-Arab religious jurisdiction, Palestinian-Arab women, for example, have a harder battle enforcing their individual autonomy against their religious community, since Israeli "liberalism" in matters of religion and state is equally attuned to the collective right of their respective religious community as such.[10] A second implication concerns the option of reforming the internal family law norms of the Palestinian-Arab religious communities. Should a reform movement crystalize within one of these communities, the same group-based liberal conception guarantees a free sail forward.[11]

A second part of my research compared this accommodating Israeli policy when it comes to the Palestinian-Arab community as separate religious communities and the far less (if not entirely) repressive policy when it comes to the Palestinian-Arab community as one national group.[12]

A third part of this project sought to question the basic characterization of the jurisdictional authority of the Palestinian-Arab religious communities as liberal and accommodational.[13] My argument in this respect rests on the proposition that what sounds liberal and accommodational might not actually be so – just as one might be speaking a language that others may understand as such, but actually not be speaking that language according to its grammar. The false liberal nature of this accommodation also has some important normative implications. For example, the mere characterization of a legal arrangement as liberal and accommodating creates the impression that it is inherently positive and desirable, when in fact it may be repressive and backward. The labeling works as a normative laundering machine, conveying the idea that the accommodation is supposedly serving the interests of the group, when in fact it is serving interests that are foreign to it.

From an analytical point of view, it is imperative, therefore, to identify what I called multicultural qualifications. Group-based arrangements need to meet certain standards in order to qualify as multicultural. One such standard requires that the group arrangement should have the best interests of the group and group members as its principal objective when prescribed and maintained by

[10] See Michael Karayanni, *Acute Multicultural Entrapment of the Palestinian-Arab Religious Minorities in Israel and the Feeble Measures Required to Relieve It*, in MAPPING THE LEGAL BOUNDARIES OF BELONGING: RELIGION AND MULTICULTURALISM FROM ISRAEL TO CANADA 225 (ed. Rene Provost, 2014).

[11] See Michael Karayanni, *Multicultural Nature of the Religious Accommodations for the Palestinian-Arab Minority in Israel: A Curse or a Blessing?* in ISRAELI NATION STATE: POLITICAL, CONSTITUTIONAL, AND CULTURAL CHALLENGES 265–89 (ed. F. Oz-Salzberger & Y. Stern, 2014).

[12] See Michael Karayanni, *Two Concepts of Group Rights for the Palestinian-Arab Minority under Israel's Constitutional Definition as a "Jewish and Democratic" State*, 10 INT'L. J. CONSTITUTIONAL L. I-CON 304 (2012).

[13] See Michael Karayanni, *Multiculture Me No More! On Multicultural Qualifications and the Palestinian-Arab Minority of Israel*, 54 DIOGENES 39 (2007).

the state. Similarly, when certain groups are not under the threat of assimilation, or happen to be overrepresented in government bodies, then it is questionable whether such a group is entitled to any special accommodations other than recognition of the members' right of association. If, notwithstanding these conditions, the group is accorded certain rights, especially with the power to instruct members to act by certain norms, then the group-based arrangement may not qualify as multicultural. This is certainly true in respect of the ultra-Orthodox community in Israel, whose internal norms happen to be patriarchal in nature, thereby discriminating against women, on the one hand, but enjoy substantial accommodations in terms of funding, educational autonomy, exemptions, and more, on the other hand.[14]

My intention in this chapter is to look into the historical motivations behind Israel's recognition of the jurisdictional authority granted to the Palestinian-Arab religious communities through the *millet* system. Though this jurisdictional authority existed from the times of the Ottoman Empire[15] and was maintained by the British when granted the Mandate over Palestine and then adopted by Israel, my claim is that each of these regimes had its own objectives when accepting this jurisdictional authority. Building on newly discovered archival materials, as well as on international legal instruments that predate the establishment of the State of Israel, I argue that the central motivation behind the recognition accorded to the Palestinian-Arab religious communities was primarily an institutional interest of control, rather than a concern for the well-being of the minority communities.

The study is limited mainly to Israeli policy in the first two decades after the establishment of the state (1948–67). An Israeli sociologist has claimed that until the Six Day War of June 1967, Israel could have developed a political culture that would have transcended religious, ethnic, and national boundaries by adopting a secular concept of Israeli citizenship with substance.[16] However, things did not develop in this direction. Tensions between the civil identity of the Israeli and the primordial definitions of the Jewish collective came to dominate Israeli society. These tensions were fueled also by the fact that from June 1967 onward, Palestinian identity took on a more crystalized form with the weakening of Pan-Arabism and the unification of the local Palestinian population – i.e., Palestinians who had been living inside Israel since 1948 and those in the territories occupied by Israel occupied in the West Bank

[14] See Ruth Halperin-Kaddari, *Women, Religion and Multiculturalism in Israel*, 5 UCLA J. INT'L L. & FOREIGN AFF. 339, 343 (2000).

[15] Kamel Abu Jaber, *Millet System in the Nineteenth-Century Ottoman Empire*, 57 MUSLIM WORLD 212–23 (1967).

[16] Baruch Kimmerling, *Boundaries and Frontiers of the Israeli Control System: Analytical Conclusions*, in ISRAELI STATE AND SOCIETY: BOUNDARIES AND FRONTIERS (ed. Baruch Kimmerling, 1989).

and the Gaza Strip from 1967.[17] Among the various options available to the Israeli polity in defining the relations between religion and state from 1948 to 1967, the decisions and actions that were actually taken are particularly telling.

INTERNATIONAL LEGITIMACY

The first major factor that influenced Israel's policy of maintaining the Palestinian-Arab *millets* was its quest to gain international legitimacy. In the years following the establishment of the state in 1948, a vital foreign policy interest was to acquire international recognition and secure economic support, especially from Western democracies. At the time, Israeli policy makers believed that without the material and normative backing of major foreign powers, Israel would face an existential threat.[18] In order to secure international support, Israel followed the provisions of the international documents on which its establishment was based, which linked the establishment of a Jewish state to the recognition of minority religions living there. This included the Palestinian-Arab *millets*, and Israel fashioned its policies accordingly. This may be called the *balancing formula*.

The roots of the balancing formula can be found in the historic Balfour Declaration of 1917, which asserted that the British government viewed "with favor the establishment in Palestine of a national home for the Jewish people," and balanced this with the proviso "that nothing shall be done which may prejudice the civil and religious rights of the existing non-Jewish communities in Palestine." Following the 1920 San Remo Resolution, the League of Nations granted Great Britain the mandate over Palestine, and the 1922 document in which the Mandate for Palestine was outlined incorporated the pledge of the Balfour Declaration and explicated the Mandate's commitment to respect "the personal status of the various peoples and communities," according to which "their religious interests shall be fully guaranteed."[19] These instruments are mentioned in Israel's Declaration of Independence of 1948[20] as documents that grant international legitimacy to the establishment of the State of Israel. Consequently, an essential relationship was established between Israel's character as a Jewish state and the recognition it needed to accord to its non-Jewish religious minorities. This relationship was conditional in nature: the Jewish nation-state structure was to be balanced against recognition accorded to non-Jewish religious institutions.

[17] See, e.g., PELEG & WAXMAN, ISRAEL'S PALESTINIANS, 54; JACOB M. LANDAU, ARAB MINORITY IN ISRAEL, 1967–1991: POLITICAL ASPECTS (1993) 2; Elie Rekhess, *Evolvement of an Arab-Palestinian National Minority in Israel*, 12 ISRAEL STUDIES 3–28 (2007).

[18] Uri Bialer, *Top Hat, Tuxedo and Cannons: Israeli Foreign Policy from 1948 to 1956 as a Field of Study*, 7 ISRAEL STUDIES 2–3, 14–15 (2002).

[19] League of Nations, Mandate for Palestine (1922), Art. 9 (www.mfa.gov.il/mfa/foreignpolicy/peace/guide/pages/the%20mandate%20for%20palestine.aspx).

[20] Declaration of Independence 1948, OG no. 1, May 14, 1948.

From the start, Israel's action towards the institutions and sites of its religious minorities came under close scrutiny.[21] During the 1948 war, David Ben-Gurion himself issued special orders instructing Israeli soldiers "not to loot or defile a Christian or Muslim Holy Place."[22] Possible negative repercussions on world public opinion made Ben-Gurion revoke an order already issued by an Israeli military commander to expel the inhabitants of Nazareth.[23] Following these measures, local Christian leaders were asked to send out cables reporting that all was well with the Christian communities and holy places.[24] This same attitude proved central to Israel's foreign policy after the establishment of the state. In other words, the recognition accorded to the local non-Jewish religious communities was considered vital in the context of Israel's relations with the international community, rather than being merely a local policy beneficial to local religious communities. Accordingly, Israel was willing to recognize the international community's interests in the holy places under its territorial control, notwithstanding its sovereignty.[25] This policy surfaced again as a counter-effort against the campaign to internationalize Jerusalem in the early 1950s – a proposal Israel resisted[26] and resists to this day.

The balancing formula also explains how the Shari'a and Christian courts ended up having a more enhanced capacity than the rabbinical courts, regarding matters of personal status that came under the exclusive jurisdiction of the religious courts. In fact, the widest jurisdictional capacity was that of the Shari'a courts.[27] Beyond issues of marriage, divorce, and alimony, these courts had exclusive jurisdictional capacity in matters of maintenance allowances for children, custody issues, paternity declarations, and more.[28] During the Ottoman Empire, the *millets* were the official state courts.[29] Although during the British Mandate the Shari'a courts no longer held this status, they continued to have the widest jurisdictional capacity. Given Israel's effort not to disrupt the existing jurisdictional capacity of Palestinian-Arab *millets*, in conformity with the balancing formula, the Shari'a courts retained their expanded authority in the Jewish state as well.

21 Alisa Rubin Peled, *Crystallization of an Israeli Policy towards Muslim and Christian Holy Places, 1948–1955*, 84 MUSLIM WORLD 95 (1994).

22 URI BIALER, CROSS ON THE STAR OF DAVID: THE CHRISTIAN WORLD IN ISRAEL'S FOREIGN POLICY, 1948–1967, 8 (2005).

23 BIALER, CROSS, 8.

24 BIALER, CROSS, 8.

25 WALTER EYTAN, FIRST TEN YEARS: A DIPLOMATIC HISTORY OF ISRAEL 74–75 (1958).

26 EYTAN, FIRST TEN YEARS, 74–75.

27 MARTIN EDELMAN, COURTS, POLITICS, AND CULTURE IN ISRAEL 77 (1994).

28 Moussa Abou Ramadan, *Judicial Activism of the Shari'a Appeals Court in Israel (1994–2001): Rise and Crises*, 27 FORDHAM INT'L. L. J. 264 n. 50 (2003).

29 Ido Shahar, *Forum Shopping between Civil and Shari'a Courts: Maintenance Suits in Contemporary Jerusalem*, in RELIGION IN DISPUTES: PERVASIVENESS OF RELIGIOUS NORMATIVITY IN DISPUTING PROCESSES 150 (ed. Franz von Benda-Beckman et al., 2013).

The balancing formula was also evident in the way Israel treated its Christian communities.[30] These communities retained their judicial hierarchy, which for some communities meant recognition of the authority of appellate courts sitting outside of Israel in countries such as Lebanon, a country Israel considers an enemy state.[31] These Christian courts retained their exclusive discretion to appoint whom they saw fit to their courts, a privilege that neither the Shari'a courts nor the rabbinical courts enjoyed. When Israel was established, Western nations such as France, Italy, and the Vatican showed special interest in the well-being of the local Christian communities. In an effort to resist the pressure of these countries and the influence they might have on the rest of the Christian West, Israeli authorities became especially sensitive to maintaining the interests of local Christian communities. Thus, local Christian property was retained by these communities.[32]

Intragovernmental correspondence during this period reveals the extent of Israeli sensitivity to Christian interests in particular. A letter from Yaacov Herzog, director of the Christian Department at the Ministry of Religion, to Gershon Avner, director of the West European Department at the Ministry of Foreign Affairs, urged that "we should reconsider our relations with the Christians and in the meanwhile deal with them with special care."[33] A year earlier, in 1950, Walter Eytan, the director general of the Ministry of Foreign Affairs, wrote to the director of the West European Department, "we shall be prepared to take into consideration Christianity's concern for the Christian faith in our country … therefore it is necessary to bring before the Christian world a detailed and defined plan that provides actual guarantees."[34] He went on to assert that Israel's sovereignty would not be undermined by guaranteeing the maintenance and functioning of religious institutions, and concluded, "this is a tax that we have to pay in return for the fact that our country exists in the Holy Land." It is no wonder, therefore, that in cases where there was disagreement between governmental departments on how the affairs of the Christian communities should be handled, it was the Ministry of Foreign Affairs that took the more accommodating policy, while other departments, in the Ministry of Religious Affairs and in the Ministry of the Interior, took a more reserved view.[35]

Sarah Ozacky-Lazar and Yoav Gelber have called attention to another component of this balancing formula. In a memorandum of May 1948 titled "The Arab Problem," the Ministry of Minorities expressed concern about lawlessness in the

30 LAURENCE LOUËR, TO BE AN ARAB IN ISRAEL 15–19 (2007).

31 Karayanni, *Two Concepts*, 328–29.

32 By contrast, Muslim property in Israel was massively diminished, on the pretext of it having become absentee property of formerly Ottoman landlords who lived outside Israel. See BIALER, CROSS, 144, 179, 180–81.

33 ISA/MFA/2550/5 (Feb. 8, 1951).

34 ISA/MFA/2550/5 (Jan. 30, 1950).

35 BIALER, CROSS, 104–05, 130–31, 189; Rubin Peled, *Crystallization*, 96, 103.

country and what was deemed disgraceful acts committed by "the best of us." The memo called on the Israeli government to apply its international commitments toward the Arabs who remained in the new state, and noted that living up to these commitments was justified since foreign states would presumably treat their Jewish minorities in the same manner as Israel treated its Arab minority.[36]

When Israel was established, this balancing formula had already guided the British Mandate authorities, at least during the years immediately following its institution. Committed as it was under the Balfour Declaration to the establishment of a national home for the Jewish people in Palestine, the British Mandate was well aware that Muslims had become the most disadvantaged group in Palestine. They had lost their majority status, as well as the prominence of the Shari'a courts as official state institutions. The Christians lost nothing by the advent of the British Mandate and even gained some advantage, given that the Mandate was in the hands of a Western Christian state. To balance things, the British Mandate established two official Muslim bodies: the office of the Grand Mufti of Palestine and the Supreme Muslim Council.[37]

This balancing formula suggests that maintaining the Palestinian-Arab *millets* was done in order to facilitate Israel's diplomatic efforts. This consideration took foreign affairs into account first, with domestic affairs coming second, if at all. Somewhat paradoxically, according to this formula, the constitutional nature of Israel as a Jewish nation-state served, and to a large extent still serves, as a guarantee for the maintenance of the jurisdiction of the Palestinian-Arab religious courts.

DIVIDE AND CONQUER

In his seminal book *Arabs in the Jewish State*,[38] Ian Lustick started his analysis by noting how in spite of Israel's deep divisions, especially among Arabs and Jews, at the time of his writing Israel had not witnessed ethnic disturbances, as had other countries. The reason for this, he argued, was the quiescence of the Israeli Arabs achieved through various means of control.[39] One important instrument of control was segmentation and fragmentation.[40] In this respect, the existing religious divisions among the Palestinian-Arab community as dictated by the *millet* system proved

36 Sarah Ozacky-Lazar, *Crystallization of Mutual Relations Between Jews and Arabs in the State of Israel: The First Decade*, 1948–1958, 57–58 (PhD diss., University of Haifa; Hebrew, 1996); Yoav Gelber, *Israel's Policy Towards Its Arab Minority*, 1947–1950, 19 ISRAEL AFFAIRS 55 (2013).

37 Daphne Tsimhoni, *Status of the Arab Christians under the British Mandate in Palestine*, 20 MIDDLE EASTERN STUDIES 169–70 (1984).

38 IAN LUSTICK, ARABS IN THE JEWISH STATE: ISRAEL'S CONTROL OF A NATIONAL MINORITY (1980).

39 LUSTICK, ARABS, 25–26.

40 LUSTICK, ARABS, 82–83.

to be an important resource, the exploitation of which could optimize segmentation and therefore control.[41] This policy of divide and conquer is the second factor behind Israel's policy of preserving the Palestinian-Arab religious courts.

The argument that the Israeli establishment has sought to enforce religious divides within the Palestinian-Arab community has occasionally surfaced in scholarly writings.[42] Sabri Jiryis, writing already in 1976, claimed that by "feeding and reinforcing confessional loyalties" based on religious divisions, the Israeli government "hoped to consolidate its own political position."[43] This supports the claim that Israel maintained the *millet* system in order to effectuate its policy of control.[44] The system itself not only maintains religious divides among the different Palestinian-Arab religious communities and by so doing nourishes the religious identity of each, it also mandates that members of different religious communities can marry and divorce only within their own communities, thereby discouraging the emergence of a nonsectarian national identity.

One powerful circumstantial piece of evidence in this respect is the split in the Israeli establishment's attitude toward the recognition and maintenance of non-Jewish religious communities, on the one hand, and the official policy regarding recognition of non-Orthodox Jewish religious streams and sects, on the other. Israel has been extremely accommodating when it comes to the non-Jewish religious communities. New communities have been recognized, such as the Druze[45] and the Anglican Evangelical Church, and very small Christian religious communities are still officially maintained despite the fact that they number only a few thousand members.[46] Yet the quest of the Jewish Reform and Conservative movements and the Karaites to gain official recognition has been firmly opposed by the Israeli establishment.[47] The oft-sounded argument against recognition of these groups is that it will endanger Jewish unity.[48] But of how much interest to the Israeli establishment is it to preserve and nourish Palestinian national unity?

This divide-and-conquer policy is corroborated by newly released documents from the Israeli State Archive: minutes and memos produced by senior Israeli government officials in the first two years following the state's establishment.

[41] LUSTICK, ARABS, 133.

[42] PELEG & WAXMAN, ISRAEL'S PALESTINIANS, 21–22; BARUCH KIMMERLING & JOEL S. MIGDAL, PALESTINIAN PEOPLE: A HISTORY 179–80 (2003); KAIS M. FIRRO, DRUZES IN THE JEWISH STATE (1999), 102–04.

[43] SABRI JIRYIS, ARABS IN ISRAEL 197(1976).

[44] Gad Barzilai, *Fantasies of Liberalism and Liberal Jurisprudence: State Law, Politics and Israeli Arab-Palestinian Community*, 34 ISRAEL L. REV. 436 (2000).

[45] Druze Religious Courts Law, 5723-1962, 17 LSI 27 (1962–63).

[46] Asher Maoz, *Religious Human Rights in the State of Israel*, in RELIGIOUS HUMAN RIGHTS IN GLOBAL PERSPECTIVE: LEGAL PERSPECTIVES 352–53 (ed. Johan D. Van der Vyvert & John Witte Jr., 1996).

[47] Michael Corinaldi, *Social, Educational and Cultural Aspects of Religious Pluralism in Israel: Discussion*, in STATUS OF RELIGIOUS PLURALISM IN ISRAEL, 17–18 (American Jewish Committee, 1982).

[48] Pinhas Shifman, WHO'S AFRAID OF CIVIL MARRIAGE? 10 (Hebrew, 1994); Charles Liebman, *Religious Pluralism in the United States*, in STATUS OF RELIGIOUS PLURALISM, 23–25.

In the immediate aftermath of the 1948 War, some Israeli government officials envisioned a better future for Jewish–Arab relations in the country. They called for a governmental policy that would promote a tolerant attitude toward the Arab minority, and total equality between the Jews and Arabs living in Israel.[49] The Israeli provisional government also established a separate ministry to oversee the status and conditions of the Arab minority, the Ministry of Minorities. The minister in charge was Bechor-Shalom Shitrit (who at the same time also served as the minister of police). Shitrit was seemingly keen in his efforts to promote this tolerant liberal attitude toward the Arab minority, and on August 26, 1948, he sent a draft of a bill titled "Public Council Assisting the Ministry of Minorities Ordinance" to Minister of Religious Affairs Yehuda Leib Hacohen Fishman.[50] In the accompanying letter, he asked for comments.

In substance, the bill was rather bold. It proposed the establishment of a public council composed of government officials and the general public in order to offer advice to the Ministry of Minorities on such issues as the rehabilitation of relations with minorities; how to seek the input of minorities on questions relating to the national economy; and even the advancement, empowerment, and recognition of minorities' problems.

The first to respond to this initiative was Haim Hirshberg, head of the Muslim Department at the Ministry of Religious Affairs,[51] apparently at Fishman's behest.[52] Hirshberg sounded a strong reservation, questioning the "necessity and effectiveness" of such a public council. He reasoned that issues of education and culture should be handled separately by each of the religious communities (*eidot*). Additionally, if the members of the proposed council were dominated by Jewish members, then the public council would appear to be one in which Jews told Arabs what to do. If, on the other hand, the intention was to have minority members appointed to the council, it would set "a dangerous precedent" of establishing a semi-parliamentary body, representing the minorities, which would be "totally undesirable for us." Fishman was evidently impressed by these arguments, and in a letter to the minister of minorities he suggested that this bill be dismissed, or more accurately, shelved. His first argument was explicit: "The bill will consolidate the different religious communities in the country into one national minority, which would be not only undesirable for us at all, but [also] … unnecessary and even damaging." … It is not our job to imprint upon this culture, and to empower, the stamp of Arab nationalism."[53]

49 Ozacky-Lazar, *Crystallization*, 57–58.

50 ISA/RG 98/G/4778/39 (Aug. 26, 1948).

51 Hirshberg's biography indicates that he was a trained academic in Jewish history, a rabbi, and familiar with Arabic language and culture; see ALISA RUBIN PELED, DEBATING ISLAM IN THE JEWISH STATE: DEVELOPMENT OF POLICY TOWARD ISLAMIC INSTITUTIONS IN ISRAEL 26 (2001).

52 ISA/RG 98/G/4778/39 (Aug. 31, 1948).

53 ISA/RG 98/G/4778/39 (Sep. 6, 1948).

The seeds of this vision were present in a meeting that took place some weeks before, when the minister of minorities met with representatives from the Ministry of Religious Affairs, among them Hirshberg and the head of the Christian Department at the time, Rabbi Yaacov Herzog. In the minutes documenting this meeting, Shitrit sought to address the issue of appointing *qadis* to the Shari'a courts, suggesting, among other things, that the minister of religious affairs himself make the appointment while the Muslim community had the right to elect *qadis* or even establish a high Muslim council in order to deal with the matter. Herzog had reservations about *qadis* being appointed by the minister of religious affairs, for this would detract from their autonomy, especially when compared to the rights granted to the Christians to appoint their own religious leaders. Herzog then added that caution was called for in these matters and that, in general, "we are not interested in forming national minorities, and should try to handle all matters on the basis of religious communities."[54]

This explicit divide-and-conquer policy soon spread to other departments. In a "secret" memo to the minister of education and culture written in 1949, Supervisor of Arab Education Y. L. Blum wrote that his own approach to the "Arab problem" was to eliminate or minimize all differences "between us and them," which would promote "stability and tranquility."[55] He then related a discussion he had had with Hirshberg, who held a completely different view. Hirshberg was of the opinion that they should retreat from the idea of an "Arab minority" and "look at them as Israeli citizens who are members of different religions and communities, such as Muslims, Christians of different sects, Druze, Circassians, Greeks, Armenian and just Arabs … In other words, we do not have one problem of the Arabs, but problems of different communities and nations, and we should tend to each problem separately and stress and develop the conflicts between the different sects and diminish their Arabness. Thus they will forget that they are Arabs and know that they are Israelis of different creeds." Blum noted that these ideas of Hirshberg's were revolutionary in the political sense, but "based on facts." He then added that "each one of us who is closely familiar with the Arabs … knows how great is the hatred between Muslims and Christians … and between all of these and the Druze." Blum ended this secret memo by speculating whether he should accept Hirshberg's position or stick to his own, suggesting that both positions should be considered.

In due course, the more accommodating outlook advocated by Shitrit was completely rejected.[56] The Ministry of Minorities was dismantled, and the Office of the Advisor to the Prime Minister on Arab Affairs became the principal government organ in charge of handling issues regarding the Arab minority.[57] Ben-Gurion

54 ISA/RG 98/G/4778/39 (Aug. 17, 1948).

55 ISA/G/1733/1 (Apr 19, 1949).

56 PELED, DEBATING ISLAM, 18.

57 PELED, DEBATING ISLAM, 18.

"vehemently objected" to the Public Council bill and vetoed the whole idea.[58] When it was clear that the Ministry of Minorities would no longer exist, a committee was appointed by the Israeli government, headed by Yehoshua Palmon. The committee recommended that broad autonomy in religious matters be accorded to the different religious communities that would henceforth come under the jurisdiction of the Ministry of Religious Affairs.[59] Palmon became the advisor to the prime minister on Arab affairs, acquiring the informal title "czar of Israel's Arabs."[60] The divide-and-conquer formula was then adopted by a committee that was established in 1957 by the ruling party, Mapai, to advise on policies toward the Arab minority. Archival documents recording the minutes of the committee's meetings show that the course advocated by Hirshberg and his ministry advocated became the course followed and advocated by this influential committee.[61]

NATION BUILDING

Identity is relational. This is a sociological fact.[62] A group defines itself not only by stressing its past, its culture, and its aspirations, but also by stressing the divides that separate it from other groups. These divides become clearer if other groups are also pushed into preserving their own identity. Preserving the system of religious courts for the Palestinian-Arab minority was also guided by the hegemonic Jewish majority in Israel's will to preserve its distinctiveness and identity.[63] Israel is a Jewish nation-state that prioritizes Jewish collective interests,[64] and its maintenance as such mandates the preservation of Jewish identity, which is ethnic and hereditary.[65] An essential mechanism for enforcing Jewish identity is promoting endogamy among the Jewish majority.[66] Granting religious communities exclusive jurisdiction as prescribed by the *millet* system is a very efficient design to circumvent intermarriage,

58 Gelber, *Israel's Policy*, 55.
59 Gelber, *Israel's Policy*, 67.
60 Gelber, *Israel's Policy*, 67.
61 Yair Bäuml, *Principles of the Discrimination Policy towards the Arabs in Israel, 1948–1968*, 16 STUDIES IN ISRAELI AND MODERN JEWISH SOCIETY 403–04 (Hebrew, 2006).
62 Aziza Khazzoom, *Great Chain of Orientalism: Jewish Identity, Stigma Management, and Ethnic Exclusion in Israel*, 68 AM. SOCIOLOGICAL REV. 481 (2003).
63 Sammy Smooha, *Model of Ethnic Democracy: Israel as a Jewish and Democratic State*, 8 NATIONS & NATIONALISM 478, 483 (2002).
64 Mark Tessler, *Identity of Religious Minorities in Non-secular States: Jews in Tunisia and Morocco and Arabs in Israel*, 20 COMPARATIVE STUDIES IN SOCIETY AND HISTORY 359–60 (1978).
65 Uzi Rebhun & Chaim I. Waxman, *Challenges for the Twenty-First Century*, in JEWS IN ISRAEL: CONTEMPORARY SOCIAL AND CULTURAL PATTERNS 469 (ed. Uzi Rebhun & Chaim I. Waxman, 2004).
66 See STEVEN V. MAZIE, ISRAEL'S HIGHER LAW: RELIGION AND LIBERAL DEMOCRACY IN THE JEWISH STATE 174 (2006); Simha Meron, *Freedom of Religion as Distinct from Freedom from Religion in Israel*, 4 ISRAEL YEARBOOK ON HUMAN RIGHTS 223 (1974).

which the Jewish majority has considered particularly threatening to its collective interests and to Israel's identity as a Jewish state. Sammy Smooha makes this argument when depicting the characteristics of Israel as an "ethnic democracy," observing, "So long as Israel remains a Jewish-Zionist state, Jews will continue to have a vested interest in sustaining Arabs as an ethnic minority in order to reduce the danger of assimilation and intermarriage."[67]

Interest in preserving Jewish identity was especially intense in the first two decades after the establishment of the state in 1948. When asked by a journalist which fundamental laws characterize Israel as a Jewish state, Zerah Warhaftig, a long-time member of the Knesset and minister of religious affairs from 1961 to 1974, answered that there are two-and-a-half such laws.[68] The first is the Law of Return that guarantees Jews all over the world the right to immigrate to Israel and regard it as their homeland.[69] The second is the law on marriage and divorce. This law, he said,

> guarantees the physical unity of the nation [and] the stability of the Jewish family. Only by this law is the state a Jewish state. Abrogating this law – the introduction of civil marriages and divorces with the possibility of mixed marriages – could bring about the abolition of the concept of Jewish state. This would be a democratic but not a Jewish state.[70]

Collective Jewish sentiments about preserving the exclusive jurisdiction of religious norms and courts over matters of marriage and divorce proved to be instrumental in the enactment of the Rabbinical Courts Jurisdiction (Marriage and Divorce) Law, 1953 (RCJ). This law mandates that marriages among Jews in Israel be conducted under the Jewish (Orthodox) law and that rabbinical courts have exclusive jurisdiction over divorce proceedings. The common perception that this law came about due to the Jewish religious parties' excessive political power is erroneous and misleading.[71] In addition, the historic status quo letter of 1947 did not include any explicit mention of exclusive jurisdiction for the rabbinical courts in matters of marriage and divorce. On the contrary, the text is vague in this respect, with some interpretations saying that the promise as made would also sustain the prospect of having a civil marriage regime alongside the religious option.[72] However, as

[67] Sammy Smooha, *Ethnic Democracy: Israel as an Archetype*, 2 ISRAEL STUDIES 222 (1997).

[68] Zerach Warhaftig, *State of Israel as a Jewish State*, in RELIGION AND THE STATE 72 (ed. Matityahu Rothenburg; Hebrew, 1964). (The "half law" Warhaftig mentioned was the one that recognizes the Sabbath as the official day of rest in the country.)

[69] Warhaftig, *State of Israel*, 74.

[70] Warhaftig, *State of Israel*, 75.

[71] Zvi Triger, *There Is a State for Love: Marriage and Divorce between Jews in the State of Israel* in TRIALS OF LOVE 173–225 (ed. Orna Ben-Naftali & Hanna Naveh; Hebrew, 2005).

[72] Triger, *There Is a State*, 193.

the Knesset discussion of RCJ reveals, a strong sentiment of Jewish-Zionist nation building was pivotal in adopting the exclusive jurisdiction of rabbinical courts over marriage and divorce, as well as the exclusive jurisdiction of other religious communities over these matters in their respective spheres.[73] These Jewish-Zionist sentiments centered on the Jewish unity that might be threatened by a civil marriage regime – given that such a regime would eventually lead to lesser restrictions on marriage between Jews in Israel[74] and on the threat of mixed marriages that might lead to assimilation and from there to the weakening of Jewish identity.[75] Warhaftig, who was the deputy minister for religious affairs at the time, asserted that: "Any prospect for mixed marriages will not be possible when religious marriage is obligatory," and applauded this exclusive jurisdictional authority as a way to prevent such "disastrous" marriages.[76] The intent was to safeguard the interests of the Jewish community,[77] as they were perceived at the time, not the interests of the non-Jewish minorities.

Historically, the process of nation building has been intertwined with regulation of the family, especially the institution of the family.[78] Perceiving the nation in terms of a certain culture, be it national, ethnic, secular, or religious, most often translates itself into legal institutions that define the formation of family relations.[79] So the Israeli experience of maintaining the exclusive jurisdiction of the rabbinical courts and other religious courts is by no means a peculiar one. Yet, if the regulation of marriage is a reflection of how the nation is perceived, then the divides maintained by the *millet* system maintains are a testament to another important feature of Israeli society: that it is a non-assimilative society when it comes to the Jewish and Palestinian-Arab communities. Thus far, Israel has resisted the creation of an inclusive Israeli identity. In terms of nationality, to date a citizen of the State of Israel cannot be registered as simply "Israeli" in public records.[80] One must register under

73 Triger, *There Is a State*, 198.
74 Triger, *There Is a State*, 198.
75 Triger, *There Is a State*, 204.
76 Triger, *There Is a State*, 204.
77 As a part of the process of building a nation based on the "ingathering of exiles," for a number of decades after its establishment, the State of Israel adopted policies that encouraged intermarriage among Jews of different cultural backgrounds as a legitimate and "even a desirable option." See Oren Yiftachel, *"Ethnocracy" and Its Discontents: Minorities, Protests, and the Israeli Polity*, 26 CRITICAL INQUIRY 742 (2000); Sammy Smooha, *Jewish Ethnicity in Israel: Symbolic or Real*, in REBHUN & WAXMAN, JEWS IN ISRAEL, 51; Yochanan Peres, *Ethnic Relations in Israel*, 76 AM. J. SOCIOLOGY 1026 (1971).
78 Philomila Tsoukala, *Marrying Family Law to the Nation*, 58 AM. J. COMP. L. 874 (2010).
79 Michael Karayanni, *In the Best Interests of the Group: Religious Matching under Israeli Adoption Law*, 3 BERKELEY J. MIDDLE EASTERN & ISLAMIC L. 33–36 (2010).
80 HCJ 8140/13 Ornan v. State of Israel 2013 (Dec. 9, 2013) (Nevo Electronic Database).

such definitions as Jew, Arab, Druze, or nothing. So nation building in Israel is also upheld by containing Israelis within their separate identities, and in this sense, the existing divides between the religious courts have proved instrumental as well.

All in all, in the Israeli context, marriage has been perceived as an instrument intended either to delineate or to blur the divides between different Israeli groups. When the divide was deemed inappropriate, barriers that prevented intergroup marriage were lifted; but when the divides were perceived as appropriate, the policy was to maintain the existing divides so as make intergroup marriage difficult to achieve. For this latter objective, the *millet* system was a resource that the State of Israel was set from the start to exploit.

INTERNAL FORCES

When Israel was established, the political and religious leadership of the Palestinian-Arab community displayed a position that favored the maintenance of their religious courts.[81] This formed the fourth factor that worked to maintain the Palestinian-Arab *millets*, but it was a rather weak one.

First of all, the Palestinian-Arab minority, like the Jewish majority, was against assimilation and antagonistic to the creation of an inclusive Israeli identity.[82] In fact, this minority was interested in maintaining its separate identity, an aspiration that might be jeopardized were the state to introduce a territorial-secular regime for marriage and divorce. So endogamy was a Palestinian-Arab interest as much as it was a Jewish one.[83]

Other internal forces favored the policy of opting for separateness. The non-Jewish religious leadership understandably supported the maintenance of the existing *millets*,[84] as the system formed the power structure that sustained their authority.[85] This became evident whenever a reform was proposed that encroached on the jurisdiction of the existing Palestinian-Arab *millets*. Each time, religious community leaders argued that the restriction would undermine the autonomy of the Palestinian community over their religious affairs

[81] Yet when pressed it was not always clear that the Palestinian-Arabs were positively for the system and in fact "tried not to emphasize their interreligious and interethnic differences"; KIMMERLING & MIGDAL, PALESTINIAN PEOPLE, 180.

[82] Sammy Smooha, *Arab-Jewish Relations in Israel: A Deeply Divided Society*, in ISRAELI IDENTITY IN TRANSITION 43 (ed. Anita Shapira, 2004).

[83] Karayanni, *In the Best Interests*, 33–36.

[84] NADIM N. ROUHANA, PALESTINIAN CITIZENS IN AN ETHNIC JEWISH STATE: IDENTITIES IN CONFLICT 183 (1997).

[85] See David M. Neuhaus, *Between Quiescence and Arousal: The Political Functions of Religion: A Case Study of the Arab Minority in Israel: 1948–1990*, 16 (PhD diss., Hebrew University of Jerusalem, 1991).

or even infringe on the freedom of religion of their group members.[86] In Haim H. Cohn's autobiography, he mentions a reform proposal advanced by the minister of justice immediately after the establishment of the State of Israel, according to which one secular-territorial law that applied to all Israeli citizens alike would replace religious jurisdiction over matters of personal status, including marriage and divorce.[87] When the proposal came up for discussion before the government, it was soon seen that it had no real prospects of succeeding. In large part, this was due to the opposition of the ministers and parties that wanted to preserve rabbinical jurisdiction, but Cohn also mentions an argument made by representatives of the Muslim Shari'a court, who protested the initiative as an act of ingratitude: when the Muslims were the majority in the country and the Jews were only a small minority, the Jews were accorded full autonomy and jurisdiction over their personal status, but now that things were the other way around, the Jewish majority wanted to abolish the jurisdiction of the Shari'a courts.[88] Elsewhere, Cohn noted that "the various Christian churches likewise insisted on retaining, in the full, the ecclesiastical jurisdiction they had enjoyed in this country for a century or more."[89]

The political leadership of the Palestinian-Arab community, too, sent a strong message that it was interested in maintaining the religious courts. Traditional political representatives, authorities based on clan leadership, preferred the jurisdiction of religious courts over matters of family law because this preserved the patriarchal order and therefore bolstered its own power base. Additionally, the seemingly secular leadership (led, incidentally, by the Communist Party) concentrated its efforts on the national struggle of the Palestinian-Arab minority, leaving aside issues of religion, especially in the domain of family law.[90] Given the fact that the Palestinian-Arab minority was still heavily dependent on patriarchy as a social order,[91] the secular leadership calculated that, should it raise the secular flag and push for a territorial regime of family law, it could lead to internal divisions that might weaken its national agenda.[92] Additionally, the

86 See ROBERT H. EISENMAN, ISLAMIC LAW IN PALESTINE AND ISRAEL: HISTORY OF THE SURVIVAL OF TANZIMAT AND SHARI'A IN THE BRITISH MANDATE AND THE JEWISH STATE 168–95 (1978).

87 HAIM H. COHN, PERSONAL INTRODUCTION: AUTOBIOGRAPHY 227 (Hebrew; 2005).

88 COHN, PERSONAL 227.

89 Haim H. Cohn, *Religious Freedom and Religious Coercion in the State of Israel,* in ISRAEL AMONG THE NATIONS 94 (ed. Alfred E. Kellerman et al., 1998).

90 See ELIE REKHESS, ARAB MINORITY IN ISRAEL: BETWEEN COMMUNISM AND ARAB NATIONALISM, 1965–1991 (Hebrew, 1993).

91 KIMMERLING & MIGDAL, PALESTINIAN PEOPLE, 188–90.

92 Manar Hassan, *Politics of Honor: The Patriarchy, the State and the Murder of Women in the Name of Family Honor* in SEX, GENDER, POLITICS 297–301 (ed. Daphna N. Yizre'eli et al.; Hebrew, 1999).

Communist Party, with which the Palestinian-Arab community identified, called for the establishment of institutions to teach Islam, given the lack of such institutions among Muslims in Israel, as well as working to promote the increase of salaries of Shari'a court judges and other funds for the administration of Muslim religious endowments.[93]

In comparison with the three factors that resulted in the retention of the religious court system, assessed earlier, this one seems weaker. The Palestinian-Arab minority that ended up inside the borders of the State of Israel as drawn by the 1949 Armistice Agreements was relatively small, comprising about 150,000 people. This community, which only a few years earlier had been part of the majority group, now lacked an elite, was politically unorganized, was traumatized by internal displacement and detachment from family and friends, and had no meaningful economy of its own to depend on.[94] Above all, Palestinian Arabs in Israel were now under the rule of a military government and remained so for eighteen years, until 1966. It is true that as the years went by, this minority became more politically mobilized. Yet when Israel was established it seems that they would have settled for a lesser jurisdictional authority than the one granted.

CONCLUSION

Looking at the jurisdictional authority of the Palestinian-Arab religious communities from a historical perspective reveals that what many regard as a form of accommodation is essentially a form of control. Defining the Palestinian-Arab community in religious terms instead of as a national minority has better served the Israeli policy of control than the interests of the Palestinian-Arab minority itself, at least in terms of its aspirations as one national unit. From a broader perspective, this chapter offers the view that one needs to be cautious when characterizing a group-based juridical arrangement as a form of a multicultural accommodation. Past critical writings on multiculturalism have sought to highlight the adverse effect of accommodating religious groups on vulnerable members within them, especially women.[95] Given the inherently patriarchal nature of religious norms, it will

[93] Danny Rubinstein, *Religious-Secular Rift Among Israeli Arabs* in STATE AND RELIGION YEARBOOK 5753–5754, 90 (ed. Avner Horwitz; Hebrew, 1994).

[94] See Mark Tessler & Audra Grant, *Israel's Arab Citizens: The Continuing Struggle*, 555 ANNALS OF AM. ACAD. POLIT. & SOC. SCI. 99 (1998); PELEG & WAXMAN, ISRAEL'S PALESTINIANS, 48–50; KIMMERLING & MIGDAL, PALESTINIAN PEOPLE, 170–71, 187; JIRYIS, ARABS IN ISRAEL, 162.

[95] See Susan Moller Okin, *Is Multiculturalism Bad for Women?* in IS MULTICULTURALISM BAD FOR WOMEN? (ed. J. Cohen et al., 1999).

thus be inevitable that the interests of women will be subordinate to those of men when a religious group is granted juridical authority over the family law affairs of its members. Apparently, this is not all. In addition to this predicament, one needs to be aware of the external circumstances associated with the accommodation of religious groups.

7

Decentralizing Religious and Secular Accommodations

Roderick M. Hills Jr.

It is common for laws to accommodate religious practices by exempting them from otherwise generally applicable rules. Although the term *accommodation* is not conventionally used to refer to protections for secular belief, the law sometimes also "accommodates" secular principles by excluding religious activities (say, studying theology) from otherwise generally available benefits provided by the state (for instance, state-funded college scholarships). The first sort of accommodation is associated with the Free Exercise Clause of the US Constitution,[1] while the second is associated with the First Amendment's Establishment Clause. Both, however, are just as frequently the result of either express statutory language[2] or constitutionally inflected statutory construction in which courts strain to construe apparently general laws to contain exemptions.[3]

Regardless of the form of the accommodation, such exemptions present the dilemma of defining what it means to coerce the faithful or nonreligious, because both the existence and the absence of the accommodation might be taken to be coercive. If the state enforces its laws without any religious accommodation, the constituents of religious bodies (shareholders, officers, employees, etc.) may be forced to violate their conscience. If the state makes an exception for religiously motivated organizations, then other constituents of such bodies (employees, customers, tenants, etc.) with different views will be stripped of otherwise applicable protections from those organizations' power. The same dilemma confronts secular accommodations. If the state provides a benefit such as subsidies for religious and secular schools alike, secular taxpayers may complain that they are being coerced into paying for religious education with which they disagree. If the state excludes

1 See, e.g., Hosanna-Tabor Evangelical Lutheran Church v. EEOC, 565, 132 S.Ct. 694 (2012).

2 See, e.g., 42 U.S.C. §2000e-1(a), exempting "religious corporations" from liability for discrimination based on religion; Burwell v. Hobby Lobby, 573, 134 S. Ct. 2751 (2014).

3 See, e.g., NLRB v. Catholic Bishop of Chicago, 440 U.S. 490 (1979).

religious schools alone from such otherwise generally available subsidies, then religious schools may complain about antireligious discrimination.

The problem of religious and secular accommodations can be understood as a species of a more general difficulty that I shall call "reasonable and deep disagreement" (or RADD, for the sake of convenience). A RADD arises whenever the enforcement of one person's reasonable conception of fundamental liberty deprives another person of an equally reasonable and equally fundamental conception of liberty. The depth of RADDs arises from disagreement over baselines of entitlement. When social and legal consensus provides no commonly acknowledged baseline against which the disputing parties can measure their rights, one side of the dispute can plausibly claim that any resolution of the RADDs constitutes an invasion of their fundamental rights. There is no neutral ground between coercing the organization into violating its religious scruples or allowing that organization to coerce its constituents (employees, customers, contractors, etc.) into obeying the organization's religious commitments. There is likewise no neutral ground between forcing a taxpayer to help pay for subsidies to religious organizations' activities and discriminatorily singling out those religious organizations by depriving them of subsidies that secular organizations receive. Losers in political fights over such religious or secular accommodations, therefore, are unlikely to acquiesce in political compromise. Because they are reasonable disagreements, RADDs also present no plain, crisp solutions: each side has plausible arguments to back its position, giving it all the more reason to dig in its heels.

This chapter suggests that decentralization of a federal regime can help reduce these RADD-induced maladies. Rather than assign the power to resolve RADDs exclusively to the national government, the law ought to allow subnational governments to modify or waive national rules on accommodation. The choices of such subnational bodies will inevitably leave the secular or religious side of a RADD dissatisfied in any particular case. The federal system as a whole, however, extends equal concern and respect to rival and reasonable conceptions of religious liberty by giving each conception a larger area in which it can be acknowledged as authoritative. Such federalism broadens what Jeremy Waldron calls the "right of rights"[4] – that is, the right of citizens to say what their rights mean, where disagreement about the rights' content is reasonably disputed. The final part of this chapter explores specific mechanisms with which some mix of constitutional law and statutory construction can safeguard subnational governments' power to define religious and secular accommodations.

[4] See JEREMY WALDRON, LAW AND DISAGREEMENT (1999).

HOBBY LOBBY AS *ILLUSTRATION OF THE IRREPRESSIBLE CONFLICT*

The firestorm of controversy ignited by *Burwell v. Hobby Lobby*[5] and government-mandated, employer-financed contraception for employees illustrates how disagreement over baselines leads to unresolvable RADDs about religious and secular accommodations. The Affordable Care Act[6] (ACA) mandates that employers provide their employees with health insurance covering the cost of "preventative care and screenings ... with respect to women."[7] After ACA was enacted, the Health Resources and Services Administration construed this phrase to include contraception.

Does this contraception mandate invade the religious liberty of employers with religious objections to some mandated contraceptives? Or would an exemption from such a mandate to protect employers' religious scruples invade the employees' right to be free from religious coercion or discrimination? Because the constitutional traditions and precedents support affirmative answers to both of these questions, the dispute over the contraception mandate is both reasonable and deep – a fight with no obvious winners but plenty of acrimony.

Consider, first, religious employers' arguments against the contraception mandate. Those arguments can be framed either as objections to coercion or discrimination. By forcing them to pay for medical services that they deem sinful, the mandate can be characterized as forcing employers to violate their consciences. Religious employers can find a home for such objections in the Religious Freedom Restoration Act's (RFRA's) codification of some version of *Sherbert v. Verner*'s "compelling state interest" limit on generally applicable laws[8], requiring religion-specific exemptions to mandates substantially burdening religious free exercise.[9] Against these arguments, however, opponents of a special religious exemption from the contraception mandate have precedents of their own. In particular, they can rely on precedents like *Estate of Thornton v. Caldor, Inc.*[10] that limit the power of the government to discriminate in favor of religion in ways that burden third parties' interests.[11]

Is there any way to resolve this conflict to the reasonable satisfaction of the contestants? The problem is that the definition of a permissible religious accommodation turns on concepts of harm and baselines of entitlement that are themselves

[5] Paul Horwitz, *Hobby Lobby Moment*, 128 HARV. L. REV. 154 (2014).
[6] Patient Protection and Affordable Care Act, Pub. L. No. 111–148, 124 Stat. 119 (2010).
[7] 42 U.S.C. §300gg-13(a) (4) (2011).
[8] 374 U.S. 398 (1963).
[9] 42 U.S.C. §§ 2000bb–2000bb-4 (2011).
[10] Estate of Thornton v. Caldor, Inc., 472 U.S. 703 (1985).
[11] For examples of this argument, see Frederick Mark Gedicks & Rebecca G. Van Tassell, *RFRA Exemptions from the Contraception Mandate: An Unconstitutional Accommodation of Religion*, 49 HARV. CIV. RTS-CIV. LIB. REV. 343 (2014).

reasonably disputed. Consider, for instance, Gedicks and Van Tassell's argument that *Hobby Lobby*'s broad construction of RFRA's exemptions violates the Establishment Clause.[12] Gedicks and Van Tassell argue that, by depriving employees of their statutory right to contraception, RFRA (as construed by *Hobby Lobby*) harms workers and therefore exceeds the scope of permissible religious accommodation. Gedicks and Van Tassell's argument, however, turns on their assumption that the baseline for defining third-party harms is the distribution of burdens and benefits immediately preceding the Court's decision in *Hobby Lobby*.[13] If one instead uses a predictive baseline by which to define harm, then the harmfulness of RFRA's religious exemption from ACA's contraception mandate becomes much more obscure. Predictive baselines maintain that a limit on an entitlement is not harmful if one predicts that the entitlement would never have been created by the legislature without the limit on the legislation. The intuition underlying predictive baselines is that no one is left worse off by a condition limiting a benefit, if the legislature would never have enacted the benefit in the first place absent the conditional limit.

Applying the theory of predictive baselines to ACA and RFRA, one would ask a question of statutory interpretation roughly akin to an inquiry into severability of an unconstitutional provision in a statute: If Congress had known that RFRA's protections for employers would be held unconstitutional under *Estate of Thornton*, would Congress have simply eliminated the contraception benefit entirely from the set of services that employers were obligated to finance? If Congress had eliminated the contraception mandate entirely rather than force religiously minded employers to fund it against their consciences, then workers would be no worse off as a result of RFRA's religion-based limit on the contraception mandate, for the mandate would not exist at all but for RFRA's relieving the burden on religious employers. RFRA's limits, therefore, would impose no harm on anyone. To the contrary, such limits actually benefit female employees by giving them at least some contraceptive benefit that, but for RFRA's protections for religious objectors, would not exist at all.

Unlike Gedicks and Van Tassel's confidently simple view of baselines, applying this sort of predictive baseline to ACA transforms the inquiry into harm into a tangled metaphysical knot resistant to any simple unraveling. One can make a plausible case that Congress would have eliminated the contraception mandate entirely, rather than force employers to fund it against their conscience. ACA, after all, expressly preserves all "federal laws regarding conscience protection,"[14] suggesting

[12] Gedicks & Van Tassell, *RFRA Exemptions* 343 (barring "permissive accommodations" of religion that "impose significant burdens on third parties who do not believe or participate in the accommodated practice").

[13] Gedicks & Van Tassell, *RFRA Exemptions*, 371–72; see also Gedicks & Van Tassell, *Of Burdens and Baselines: Hobby Lobby's Puzzling Footnote* 37, 13 (http://papers.ssrn.com/sol3/papers.cfm?abstract_id=2602028) and in RISE OF CORPORATE RELIGIOUS LIBERTY 336 (ed. Chad Flanders et al., 2015).

[14] 42 U.S.C. section 18023(c) (2) (a) (1).

a congressional preference for preserving RFRA. By contrast, ACA makes no specific mention of contraception, referring instead generally to "preventative care and screenings … with respect to women."[15] One could, therefore, surmise that, had Congress been forced to choose between providing employer-financed contraception to workers and providing conscience protection for religious employers, it would have chosen the latter by carving contraception benefits out of ACA's "preventative care and screenings … with respect to women." The US Supreme Court apparently invoked a similar sort of predictive baseline in *Amos v. Presiding Bishop*[16] in holding that employees were not harmed by Title VII's exemption for religious corporations, reasoning (plausibly) that Title VII's prohibition on religious discrimination might not have been enacted at all absent Title VII's exempting religious corporations from its scope.[17]

Such an inference of Congress's likely preferences, however, is merely an educated guess. It is also possible that Congress would have faced down religious objections to contraception and left the Mikulski Amendment untouched. In favor of this alternative view, one could note that ACA has detailed provisions limiting insurance benefits for abortions – a response to vociferous opposition to abortion funding from Democratic Representative Bart Stupak.[18] One might infer from the absence of similarly detailed provisions limiting contraception funding that protecting religious employers from contraception mandates was simply not a congressional priority.

The problem with predictive baselines, in sum, is that the complex counterfactuals they require give rise to the same sorts of RADDs that they are intended to resolve. This problem is not unique to predictive baselines, but to any effort to define coercion by reference to some controverted counterfactual state that would putatively exist absent the coercive condition.[19]

15 42 U.S.C. section 238(n); Pub. L. No. 111–8, section 508(d) (1), 123 Stat. 524, 803. Sen. Mikulski's press release accompanying this amendment was equally discrete, referring to preventative screenings for female-specific diseases like breast cancer, not to contraception or family planning. *Senate Approves Mikulski Amendment Making Women's Preventive Care Affordable and Accessible*, Thu, Dec. 3, 2009; www.mikulski.senate.gov/newsroom/press-releases/senate-approves-mikulski-amendment-making-women-and-39s-preventive-care-affordable-and-accessible.

16 483 U.S. 327 (1987).

17 *Amos*, 483 U.S. at 337 ("we find no persuasive evidence … that the Church's ability to propagate its religious doctrine through the Gymnasium is any greater now than it was prior to the passage of the Civil Rights Act in 1964").

18 David M. Herzenhorn & Jackie Calmeson, *Abortion Was at Heart of Wrangling*, N. Y. TIMES (Nov. 7, 2009).

19 Michael W. McConnell, *Religious Freedom at the Crossroads*, 59 U. CHI. L. REV. 115, 148–49 (1992); Ira C. Lupu, *Reconstructing the Establishment Clause: The Case Against Discretionary Accommodation of Religion*, 140 U. PA. L. REV. 555, 577 (1991) (noting that the definition of coercion is "a matter of serious debate and difficulty").

For instance, Douglas Laycock has proposed a theory of what he calls "substantive neutrality" under which the baseline distinguishing coercion from neutrality is defined by balancing the likely effect of a government's decision on religious choices.[20] Under Laycock's theory, if the enforcement of a generally applicable law against a religious practice would impede that practice, while granting an exemption for that practice from that law would not substantially increase the attractiveness of the religion to nonbelievers, then the absence of that exemption counts as constitutionally forbidden coercion. Laycock offers an intuitively easy case to illustrate his theory, arguing that a general prohibition on minors' consuming alcoholic beverages should contain an exception for the minors' consumption of wine for religious rituals like the Roman Catholic Eucharist. The absence of such an exemption, Laycock notes, will "powerfully discourage … an act of worship," while the inclusion of such an exemption "is unlikely to encourage any child to take communion, or any parent to take his child to a communion service, who is not already religiously motivated do so."[21]

Like predictive baselines, however, Laycock's baseline of substantive neutrality turns out to be tricky to apply. RFRA's exempting employers from a contraception mandate might, at first glance, seem to qualify as substantively neutral, because few businesses would appear to be tempted to adopt a religious rationale for resisting a mandate that has few material costs. On the other hand, appearances can be deceptive. One could imagine that any religion-specific exemption might create subtle incentives for secular libertarian opponents of all mandates to frame their general objections to governmental regulation in religious terms, launching their assault on the regulatory state with a Bible (or Quran or whatever) opportunistically in their hand, even when their real agenda is weakening state regulation more generally for purely secular ideological reasons.[22]

With either sort of baseline, in sum, one must assess a hypothetical counterfactual – with predictive baselines, what the legislature would do if the religious classification were forbidden; with substantive neutrality, what secular actors would do if the religious classification were allowed. Either counterfactual provides rich ground for further divisive RADDs.

The complexity of calculating baselines by which to measure coercion has led some commentators to embrace an equality-oriented antidiscrimination principle of religious liberty in place of anti-coercion theories. In their simplest form,

[20] Douglas Laycock, *Formal, Substantive, and Disaggregated Neutrality Toward Religion*, 39 DePaul L. Rev. 993, 1001 (1990).

[21] Douglas Laycock, *Substantive Neutrality Revisited*, 110 W. Va. L. Rev. 51, 55 (2007).

[22] For a discussion of the subtle ways in which the availability of religion-specific exemptions might shape incentives of those challenging facially neutral regulations, see Mark Tushnet, *Accommodation of Religion Thirty Years On*, 38 Harv. J. L. & Gender 1, 11 (2015).

antidiscrimination principles condemn religion-based classifications in much the same way as equal protection doctrine condemns race-based classifications – as justifiable only if necessary to advance some compelling interest of equal constitutional weight.[23] Such formal neutrality, however, has few fans today.[24] As Laycock has noted, the simple prohibition on all religion-based classifications ignores constitutional history and constitutional intuitions alike.[25] Few scholars or courts are willing to swallow the idea that, for instance, the prohibition of alcoholic beverages must be extended to the ceremonial use of wine in a religious ceremony.

As soon as one moves away from the more wooden versions of formal neutrality, all of the ambiguities and controversies associated with anti-coercion theories crop up again, albeit in a different form. Rather than struggle with the definition of baselines and harm, antidiscrimination theorists have to struggle with the definition of equality and analogous actions. Defining these ideas creates just as many RADDs as defining the baseline of neutrality by which coercion is measured.

Consider, for instance, Larry Sagers and Christopher Eisgruber's theory of "equal liberty."[26] On this theory, religion-based exemptions from regulatory burdens are permitted just so long as "persons [are] not … treated unequally on account of the spiritual foundations of their deep commitments."[27] To defend such religion-specific accommodations, therefore, one must show that the accommodation relieves religious believers of some burden from which "analogous" secular conduct is exempt. They offer the example of a federal court's striking down a landmark law enacted by the City of Cumberland, Maryland, that subjected historically significant buildings, religious and secular alike, to landmark restrictions.[28] According to Sagers and Eisgruber, the court properly held that Cumberland's landmark law illegally discriminated against a Roman Catholic church by barring the church from replacing an aging monastery building with a more modern structure, because the law allowed variances where landmarking imposed economic hardship. By not making religious hardship an equal basis for receiving a variance, the law covertly discriminated against religious reasons.

Applying Sager and Eisgruber's equal liberty theory to ACA, however, illustrates why their concept of analogous activities creates as many RADDs as it resolves. In place of arguing whether a facially neutral law improperly coerces religious or secular persons, the theory requires one to determine whether the burdens the

[23] This anti-classification idea is sometimes denoted "formal neutrality" and associated with Philip Kurland.

[24] Mark Tushnet is one. See *Accommodation of Religion*, 28 HARV. J. L. & GENDER 26–27.

[25] Laycock, *Formal, Substantive, and Disaggregated Neutrality*.

[26] LARRY SAGERS & CHRISTOPHER EISGRUBER, RELIGION AND THE CONSTITUTION (1996).

[27] SAGER & EISGRUBER, RELIGION AND THE CONSTITUTION, 241.

[28] Keeler v. Mayr & Council of Cumberland, 940 F.SUPP. 879 (D. Md. 1996).

law imposes on some secular or religious activity are analogous to each other. The critics of ACA's mandate, for instance, argue that ACA's various exemptions for secular employers require that employers with religious objections receive an exemption from the contraception mandate.[29] The defenders of the mandate argue that the existence of such secular exemptions is irrelevant.[30] Sager and Eisgruber would counsel these disputants to ask whether the employers' religious hardship of complying with ACA's contraception mandate is analogous to the small businesses' economic hardship having to provide insurance for their employees. The answer to this question of analogy is wholly indeterminate. If one casts a cold eye on religious scruples, then the law's drawing a distinction between religious and economic hardships may seem perfectly rational. If one is more deferential to religious persons' claims of substantial burdens, then the distinction will seem like a denial of equal liberty. Such searches for analogies between religious and secular objections do not resolve any RADD: they merely provide a new opportunity for reasonable and fierce disagreement. Sager and Eisgruber resolve such disagreement by straining for secular analogies to religious practices, in order to give the former all the benefits enjoyed by the latter, as a sort of most-favored-nation status for religion. As Michael McConnell has noted, such a version of equal liberty surreptitiously smuggles in special solicitude for religious objections under the guise of treating such objections equally to secular ones, by straining to find analogies between religious and secular conduct and giving the former the benefits of regulatory exemptions enjoyed by the latter.[31]

Judged by their aspiration to ensure merely equal treatment for religious reasons, Sager and Eisgruber's special solicitude for religion is a flaw. The flaw, however, is compelled by Sager and Eisgruber's ambition to accommodate all of our precedents and intuitions about religious liberty and secular equality. The truth is that we Americans disagree about what religious liberty means, and the theoretical efforts to reconcile the divergent strands of our legal traditions simply mask but do not really resolve such RADDs.

Here, then, is our predicament. That some sort of accommodation ought to be drawn for at least some sorts of generally applicable burdens on religion and secular beliefs has been a "nearly unanimous" opinion in the United States.[32] That such exemptions can constitute unconstitutional establishments of religion when they impose excessive

[29] Hobby Lobby, 723 n.3d at 1143 ("the interest here cannot be compelling because the contraceptive-coverage requirement presently does not apply to tens of millions of people").

[30] Frederick Mark Gedicks & Andrew Koppelman, *Why an Exemption for Hobby Lobby Would Violate the Establishment Clause*, 67 VAND. L. REV. 51, 63–64 (2014).

[31] Michael McConnell, *Problem of Singling Out Religion*, 50 DEPAUL L. REV. 1, 36–37 (2000).

[32] ANDREW KOPPELMAN, DEFENDING AMERICAN RELIGIOUS NEUTRALITY 5 (2013).

costs on third parties is equally uncontroversial.[33] Between these two propositions lies a mass of legal and factual disagreement impossible to hedge by any general nationwide rule. In the end, we are faced by unbridgeable, reasonable, and vociferous disagreement. Taking rights seriously means taking this disagreement about rights seriously.[34]

To take disagreement seriously, each side of that disagreement needs to surrender the pretension that it can persuade the other to yield on the question of how to define religious and secular accommodations. Rather than impose one side's view of an appropriate accommodation of secular and religious scruples, the law could offer a meta-accommodation, meaning an accommodation of each theory of accommodations. Such a meta-accommodation would need to be a principle of deciding disputes about accommodations that gives each side of a RADD the comfort of knowing that its view of its liberties was given a fair shake.

DECENTRALIZATION OF RADDS AS EQUAL CONCERN AND RESPECT

Suppose that a nation afflicted with RADDs about religious and secular accommodations already possesses a system of decentralized jurisdictions. Suppose, for instance, that, in the ordinary case, subnational jurisdictions normally have broad autonomy to govern education, a field in which disputes over religious accommodations frequently arise. In such a regime, national decision makers have an option available to them aside from deciding the RADD themselves: they could devolve the choice between the various and equally reasonable antidiscrimination and anticoercion theories to subnational governments.

Under what circumstances might such a decentralization of RADDs constitute a better meta-accommodation than a single, uniform national decision?

How Decentralization of RADDs Promotes Democratic Equality

To appreciate the egalitarian advantages of decentralization, it is helpful to recount how legislation more generally provides an egalitarian process for resolving disputes about rights. As Jeremy Waldron has persuasively argued, the legislative process provides a mechanism by which citizens can "resolve disagreements about what rights they have among themselves and on roughly equal terms."[35] He felicitously

[33] See, e.g., Texas Monthly v. Bullock, 489 U.S. 1 (1989) (striking down special sales tax exemption for religious periodicals alone).

[34] For other more general arguments about the persistence of disagreement about rights, see AMY GUTTMAN & DENNIS THOMPSON, DEMOCRACY AND DISAGREEMENT, 35–36 (1996); JEREMY WALDRON, LAW AND DISAGREEMENT, 243–49 (1999).

[35] WALDRON, LAW AND DISAGREEMENT, 264.

describes this right to a fair dispute-resolution process as the "right of rights," meaning the right to have an equal say over the definition of one's rights. If each citizen has an equally weighted vote for legislative representatives who, in turn, each have an equally weighted vote to cast for legislation, then the process by which decisions are reached by a majority vote of legislators respects the equality of citizens. Assuming that the disagreement settled by the vote is a reasonable disagreement and that everyone agrees that it must be resolved collectively, then the minority cannot invoke what it regards as the substantive wrongness of the result as a reason to overturn the decision, because the wrongness or rightness of the outcome is, by hypothesis, the very question subject to a reasonable disagreement.[36] Instead, any complaint needs to be directed at the egalitarian merits of the process by which the decision is made: does that process respect the contestants by treating their views with equal concern and respect, giving equal weight to their views on a topic that "is the subject of a good-faith disagreement"?[37]

An important aspect of that process is the definition of the constituency entitled to vote on the dispute about rights. Should the decision be made for the entire nation by a vote of the entire nation (or its elected representatives)? Such a question could itself be a subject of reasonable dispute, with some citizens arguing that the decision has nationwide effects requiring a nationwide constituency, while others argue that the scale of the effects will mostly be confined within each subnational jurisdiction's boundaries, allowing each subnational unit to decide the question for itself. Are there any general principles or presumptions that might suggest how such a disagreement ought to be resolved?

Consider two principles suggesting a weak presumption in favor of subnational decision making. First, the question of scale should be made on an outcome-neutral basis. By hypothesis, the underlying substantive dispute that the constituency, whatever its proper scale, is called on to decide is a reasonable disagreement. Disagreements about the process by which the disagreement is decided, including the scale of the constituency that should do the deciding, cannot therefore be determined by one side's view of the merits of that underlying substantive dispute, because those merit are precisely what is up for grabs. Decentralizing or centralizing the decision opportunistically to achieve one's preferred substantive outcome is like rigging the voting rules to ensure one's own team's maximal success. It is intuitively unacceptable for a legislative majority to change the voting rules in the legislature (say, from a pairwise Tournament method to a modified Borda Count) with each vote to ensure that the majority's preferred outcome always triumphs. Either method might be perfectly acceptable, but switching the rules for outcome-based reasons is not.

[36] WALDRON, LAW AND DISAGREEMENT, 294.

[37] WALDRON, LAW AND DISAGREEMENT, 303.

The same intuition applies to opportunistic decisions to switch the level of decision maker or size of constituency to ensure maximum victory for one's side.

Second, where deep disagreements are at stake, there should be a presumption in favor of decision making by subnational constituencies if there is unresolvable procedural doubt about the proper scale of constituency to decide a RADD. The justification for this presumption is rooted in the definition of deep disagreement. With such disagreements, each side reasonably believes that a decision for the other side constitutes an invasion of its own fundamental interests. Any resolution of the disagreement, therefore, will provoke maximum resentment that needs to be assuaged by assurances of fair play. Subnational decision making provides such assurance by producing a multiplicity of substantive outcomes under normal demographic circumstance, because the population of federal regimes (which tend to be large republics) is heterogeneously distributed across subnational jurisdictions. Some jurisdictions will tend to opt for the more secular accommodation, while others will lean toward the more religious outcome. By foreclosing winner-take-all outcomes especially favorable to one side, this multiplicity of outcomes reassures each side that its interests have been treated with respect. Just as proportional representation better ensures the representation of each interest than first-past-the-post plurality voting, federalism better assures representation for each reasonable point of view than national legislation.

One might object that a single uniform decision by the national legislature is just as likely to embody compromise as multiple spatially divided decisions by subnational governments – just a different sort of compromise. According to the prediction in James Madison's *Federalist #10*, legislative moderation increases with the size of a republic's territory, population, and resulting demographic heterogeneity, because such heterogeneity undermines the cohesiveness of any majority in the national legislature. On Madison's theory, each side of a RADD would have to bend a bit in the national legislature, offering a watered-down version of its ideal version of accommodations, in order to secure a stable majority from which the minority cannot pick off defectors with a different bill. This legislative moderation is itself a compromise that the majority could cite to placate losers.[38] One might reasonably ask why such a centralized form of moderation is not just as good as the decentralized version in which the two sides agree to divide up territory and go their separate ways.

Imagine, for instance, that Congress is debating colleges' and universities' eligibility for federal aid. The hard-core secularists might demand a secular accommodation barring any use of taxpayers' money to purchase any services from any religiously affiliated institution. The hard-core religious believers might demand

38 On Federalist #10 as a liberal theory for promoting pluralism, see Roderick Hills, *Federalism as Westphalian Liberalism*, 75 FORDHAM L. REV. 769 (2006).

absolute nondiscrimination. On this view, religious institutions ought to be eligible for federal funds precisely to the extent that they provide services similar to analogous secular organizations – and the analogies should be construed broadly to require religious institutions to get "most favored organization" status. Given the results of the last legislative election, however, neither faction can press through its ideal form of accommodation, because neither contains a solid majority of legislators, and its opponents are able to pick off allies by trading votes on unrelated legislation. Congress, therefore, settles for a middle ground unsatisfactory to each side – say, a special ban on religious colleges' and universities' receiving direct aid but allowing such schools to receive aid indirectly as a result of students' using their federal loans and grants at religious institutions.

The problem with such a centralized compromise is that it does not actually acknowledge the reasonability of each side's views of a RADD. The religious side believes, with some reason grounded in national precedents, that the special ban on direct aid to religious schools is unconstitutional antireligious discrimination. Also citing plausibly relevant precedents, the secular side regards the religious schools' eligibility to receive federal money through students' using their federal aid at religious schools as impermissible federal subsidies for theology studies. The moderate congressional solution brands both as too extreme, despite these extreme views' reasonable basis in American traditions of liberty and equality. While satisfying to the congressional moderates, the outcome is actually an insult to both the extremist factions in the legislature, whose views have thereby either been branded beyond the pale of polite legislation or traded away in a compromise based on voting power rather than constitutional principles.

If the extremists are, in fact, offering reasonable positions, then the enforced compromise can only be expected to make them smolder in resentment as what they believe to be the just resolution is drowned in an orgy of political horse-trading. By contrast, the decentralized solution acknowledges the legitimacy of both sides, by allowing both the sides' "pure" versions of accommodations to be enforced against some subset of citizens. The decentralized solution also gives the national legislature a reason to wash its hands of an unresolvable debate. In a decentralized system, the acrimony of interminable debate can thereby be reduced by a simple vote, but that simple vote does not suppress truly legitimate differences of opinion with a gratuitous compromise.

Reasonability as a Limit on the Decentralization of RADDs

The presumption of decentralization for RADDs set forth previously presupposes that subnational power is limited by a principle of reasonability. Subnational governments can only choose one of the versions of religious and secular accommodations that fit within the range of reasonable disagreement defined by national traditions of religious liberty. There is, for instance, reasonable disagreement about baselines (predictive or otherwise) defining coercion or harm to third parties. Under the proposal for decentralization defended here, subnational governments could choose among these equally reasonable conceptions of harm or coercion in deeming some accommodation for religious practices non-harmful or non-coercive. These governments, however, could not adopt some proposal for religious accommodation falling outside the range of reasonable disagreement.

One might reasonably ask: Why have such a reasonability limit at all? If some decentralization of RADDs is comforting to the losers in a national debate, then why should not total decentralization be totally comforting? The reasonability limit follows from the same principle as the presumption itself: On issues of deep disagreement where citizens' fundamental beliefs and values are at stake, citizens want some assurance that their own views are treated with equal concern and respect. Giving subnational governments unlimited power to impose any settlement of a RADD on that government's residents, however, invites the insult of disparaging discrimination in subnational jurisdictions. One would expect, therefore, that citizens would hedge the benefits of prevailing in subnational jurisdictions where they comprise a majority, with some assurance against being subject to the rules of their opponents in subnational jurisdictions where they are in a minority. Such a tradeoff suggests that decentralization would be constrained by some sort of norm of reasonability.

This interest in hedging the risks of decentralization can be illustrated with a simple federal regime containing only four subunits, A through D. Because the nation's population is heterogeneously distributed, imagine that the attitude of each subunit's population toward religious and secular accommodations can be arrayed on a single left-right dimension from most secular (A) to most religious (D). On Madison's theory, the national legislature, constrained by the heterogeneity of the constituencies that it represents, is predicted to adopt some sort of mushy compromise measure somewhere in roughly the center of the spectrum. As noted earlier, that compromise will still leave many citizens dissatisfied: The extremists in Subunits A and D would each feel that their preferences were given short shrift by moderates in subunits B and C, because the national legislature's decision would be closer to the views of the moderates than the extremists.

Decentralization of all accommodations without any constraints of reasonability, however, would also aggrieve these same extremist national minorities, because they would resent the treatment of their views and fellow citizens in the subunits that adopted policies furthest from their own ideal point. For instance, the residents of A (the most secular regimes, analogous to, say, Massachusetts) would not regard the national legislature's choice of accommodations as ideal – but that choice, although a defeat for their ideal position (leftward of the likely outcome in the national legislature), would still be much closer to the more secular citizens' choice than the likely much more pro-religious policies in Subunits C and D. Citizens in A, therefore, might logically be willing to sacrifice their own right to subnational self-rule for the sake of saving their fellow citizens from C's and D's extremism. National legislation is in effect an insurance policy against local extremism, purchased at the price of sacrificing the right to obtain one's most preferred outcome in those subunits of the nation where one's views are dominant.

If all subnational jurisdictions are constrained by a norm of reasonability, then the value of such "moderation insurance" from the national legislature diminishes, because the distance between what the national legislature might enact and the laws of the most extreme subnational jurisdiction disappear. Subnational jurisdictions in such a constrained system of decentralization would be limited to choosing among accommodation policies falling within the broad but nonetheless constrained traditions on national liberty. This constrained set of policies can still be arrayed on a single dimension from most secular to most religious, but the range of permissible subnational outcomes is narrower, clustered in the middle and – critically – largely overlapping with outcomes that the national legislature (constrained by its heterogeneity) might plausibly approve.

In effect, the subunits, constrained by law, would simply gain a local option to choose one of the accommodations policies that the national legislature, constrained by demographic heterogeneity, could also choose if the electoral stars were properly aligned. That set of options is still capacious: Just because the national legislature is more moderate than any given subunit does not mean that it would not lean right or left at any given moment after any given set of elections. Decentralization that is constrained by a norm of moderation simply allows the losers at the national level to opt out of one among several possible moderate accommodation policies in favor of another moderate policy closer to their ideal point. No one would gain much by allowing the national legislature to trump subnational accommodations that are so constrained by a norm of reasonability, because the national legislature's choices would not necessarily be any more moderate than any of the (properly constrained) subunits.

Scale Economies as Rebuttal of the Decentralization Presumption

This presumption in favor of decentralization of RADDs is only a presumption. By its own terms, it ought to be rebuttable. How?

The rebuttal of the presumption, like the limits of reasonability, follows from the presumption's justification. The point of the presumption is to show special solicitude for losers at the national level on matters of deep disagreement – that is to say, matters each side regards as issues of fundamental principle, where a victory for one side is an invasion of the other side's fundamental rights. On other matters of mere disagreement, reasonable or otherwise, there is no special reason to show such special sensitivity. Democracies must govern themselves by majority votes of one sort or another, and mature citizens understand that they will lose some and win some. If the national legislature enacts a national accommodations rule for reasons having nothing to do with the majority's views about a RADD, then such reasons ought to be sufficient to assuage hurt feelings of the losers. (For convenience, such reasons can be denoted RADD-neutral reasons). The question of whether a centralized solution is needed, after all, is just one more question about which citizens can reasonably disagree, and such disagreements are normally resolved by a majority vote. If there are RADD-neutral reasons to believe that, with respect to some RADD, the citizens of a nation "should act [as] one community" (to quote Locke), then the defeated minority cannot complain about its defeat, because such a unified community "should move that way whither the greater force carries it, which is the consent of the majority."[39]

One such set of RADD-neutral reasons are scale economies in lawmaking. There might be reasons to believe that the national government can produce some national benefit at a much lower price than subnational governments. This scare-quoted price includes all considerations, economic and noneconomic, about which citizens might care. These encompass not only collective action problems confronted by subnational jurisdictions in apportioning the costs of national public goods (e.g., national defense), but also disruption of market harmonization produced by the "interfering and unneighborly regulations of some States" (in the phrase of *Federalist* #22).[40] Such bads might theoretically be suppressed by subnational jurisdictions' voluntarily cooperating through intergovernmental compacts, but the cost of negotiating such deals in the face of strategic behavior might be insurmountably high.[41] Consider, for instance, the provision of chaplains for the US Army. Soldiers fight for the nation as a whole and are stationed disproportionately in territory dictated by defense needs. To subject soldiers' religious liberties to the accommodations rules of those states where the soldiers happen to be stationed would give disproportionate influence to those few states that happen to be the physical location of bases, inspiring resentment from the others. In theory, they could work out a complex pact to decide how much to subsidize the religious needs of the armed services through grants from religious to secular states (or vice versa). But the desire to avoid the hassle of such dickering constitutes a RADD-neutral reason to let the question be

39 John Locke, *Second Treatise on Government* §96 (1689).

40 *Federalist* #22 (http://avalon.law.yale.edu/18th_century/fed22.asp).

41 The point is as old as the *Federalist Papers*, but has usefully been restated in Robert Cooter & Neil Siegel, *Collective Action Federalism: A General Theory of Article I, Section 8*, 63 STAN. L. REV. 110 (2010).

worked out in Congress. The losers can take comfort in the savings produced by such efficiency, secure in the knowledge that these efficiencies, and not hostility to their view of the RADD, are the reason for the centralized decision about chaplains.

One might object that the existence of such scale economies might itself be the subject of reasonable disagreement. It is plausible, however, to believe that questions of assigning powers in a federal system are not RADDs, but merely RDs (with a single D), as such disputes are often reasonable but rarely very deep. In particular, they lack religious fervor. Religions typically deal in the scale of personal responsibility, not the scale of governmental responsibility. A firm's owner, for instance, might have a sincerely religious belief that filling out a form makes that owner complicit in a sinful decision of another person to use a particular form of contraception. By contrast, whether personal mobility of insureds requires that markets in health insurance be regulated at the national level is not generally a question about which religious doctrines have much to say. In theory, therefore, the conversion of disputes about religious accommodation into disputes about scale economies in government should reduce the depth of disagreement inspired by RADDs. Where a plausible argument for centralization of a RADD is offered that sounds in scale economies rather than in the rightness of one side of the RADD, then such an argument should suffice to rebut the presumption of decentralization.

INSTITUTIONALIZING DECENTRALIZATION OF ACCOMMODATIONS: CONSTITUTIONAL LAW AND STATUTORY CONSTRUCTION

Suppose that one is persuaded to adopt a presumption against preemption for RADDs. What legal form should such a presumption take? *City of Boerne v. Flores*[42] provides an example of one constitutional antidote to over-centralization of constitutional RADDs.

In *Boerne*, the US Supreme Court trimmed back on Congress's power to impose on state governments a duty to accommodate religious practices by carving out exemptions in religiously neutral state laws. The subnational law at issue in *Boerne* was a land-marking ordinance enacted by the City of Boerne that prevented Archbishop Flores from expanding a church to accommodate a growing congregation. RFRA arguably required the City of Boerne to justify this imposition on a church with some compelling governmental purpose, but *Boerne* struck down the RFRA as applied to subnational governments, reasoning that Section 5 of the Fourteenth Amendment authorized Congress to enact only those laws that were "congruen[t] and proportional" to the likelihood of a constitutional violation as

[42] 521 U.S. 507 (1997).

defined by the Court. RFRA lacked such "proportionality or congruence between the means adopted and the legitimate end to be achieved," because it preempted a broad swathe of facially neutral state laws that were not intended to target any person's or group's religious free exercise. Congress could not impose any presumption that religious groups were entitled to accommodation from the burdens of such laws, because the Court itself did not require such accommodations.

Boerne thus chained Congress to the Court's narrower definition of religious accommodations, thereby earning criticism from scholars arguing that Congress should have the power to expand federally protected rights beyond the judicially defined minimum.[43] The claim that *Boerne* imposed judicial supremacy over popular constitutionalism, however, overlooked the decentralizing effect of the limit on Congress that, in combination with lenient Establishment Clause decisions, opened the way for subnational popular constitutionalism. Nineteen state legislatures have taken advantage of this option by enacting mini-RFRAs imposing a broad obligation of religious accommodation on themselves and their subdivisions, thereby engaging in a variety of popular constitutionalism. By curbing Congress's power to impose a single regime of accommodations on the nation, *Boerne* also enabled a form of popular constitutionalism compatible with equal concern and respect for rival conceptions of accommodations that are more secular than those selected by Congress.

Hobby Lobby illustrates how *Boerne* converts judicial enforcement of one side of a RADD into a default rule that states with a different view can set aside, thereby preserving a space for both views of religious accommodation. *Hobby Lobby* involved a federal statute (ACA) with an ambiguous accommodation of religion (RFRA). In construing the latter broadly to exempt religious employers from the duty to finance their employees' contraception, *Hobby Lobby* adopted the least secular resolution of a hotly contested RADD, protecting employers' religious liberty at the expense of employees' access to contraception. By relying on statute, however, *Hobby Lobby* left unaffected the power of state legislatures under *Boerne* to impose precisely the same employer mandate to provide contraceptives that federal law precludes, without any obligation (insofar as federal law is concerned) to justify such measures as necessary for a compelling purpose.

If one regards the system of voice and exit in private government to be flawed, then one might regard *Boerne*'s federalism-based limit on Congress's powers as providing a rival and different system of voice and exit. Congress's RFRA-based limits on its own federal laws create private governments with the power to discriminate against constituents on religious grounds. States' regulation in the gaps opened by those

[43] See, e.g., Robert Post & Reva B. Siegel, *Popular Constitutionalism, Departmentalism, and Judicial Supremacy*, 92 CALIF. L. REV. 127 (2004)

limits allows subnational governments to curb those private governments' religious regimes. Underlying both the federally protected private government and the state regulation hedging those protections are those minimum accommodations that the federal courts enforce against both levels, such as the ministerial exception to anti-discrimination law.[44] So long as those judicial protections do not resolve RADDs, the system of decentralized accommodations can give each side of the culture wars a voice and a chance to resolve a RADD in their favor in a small part of the nation.

[44] Hosanna-Tabor.

8

In Search of the Secular

Yishai Blank

INTRODUCTION

This chapter is an attempt to locate and defend "the secular" in present-day Israeli legal doctrines, institutions, and discourse of religious liberty. While some degree of state non-religiosity has been a fairly consensual political and legal value, secularism has never been recognized as more than a personal attribute of individuals or a coincidental trait of Israeli society as a whole. In addition to the partial guarantee of separation between the state and its official (Jewish) religion, secular persons have been protected by a set of individual rights and freedoms. Secular sentiments, secular communities, and secular ways of living, however, have never been legally recognized or protected. In addition, the management of various aspects of religious freedom and of religious affairs has been, to a significant extent, delegated to local authorities.

This legal structure has arguably served as sufficient barrier against religious oppression and coercion – or at least it did when seculars formed the majority of the population, or while they still enjoyed hegemonic political and legal status. However, as the balance of power in the legislature, administration, and judiciary shifts from seculars to religious Jews, and as Orthodox Jewish religion gains prominence in the public sphere and state policies, this legal structure needs to be reevaluated and possibly reconsidered. Freedom of conscience and other individual rights may no longer adequately protect seculars and members of minority religions and non-Orthodox Jewish denominations. Seculars can be considered a national majority only if we include among them people who identify as "traditionalists" (*masorti*), and in certain localities seculars are already a minority.[1] Unlike members

[1] The two most recent comprehensive studies of religiosity among Jews in Israel were conducted in 2009, one by the Israeli Bureau of Statistics (IBS) and one by the Israeli Institute of Democracy together

I wish to thank the participants of the "Religions, Rights and Institutions" workshop at Princeton University's Program in Law and Public Affairs for wonderful and enriching discussions. I am grateful to Hanoch Dagan, Allan Patten, and Dori Spivak for helpful comments and suggestions.

of institutionalized religions, seculars in Israel do not form a coherent group with a more-or-less clear set of beliefs, practices, and ways of life. Nevertheless, inasmuch as secularist communities signify the aspiration to create a plurality of experimental public spaces where liberal and counter-hegemonic values are protected (albeit in different ways), they themselves deserve to be protected against the growing enmeshing of state, dominant religions, and nationality. Thus, I argue that secularism in Israel should be understood as an effort by various nonreligious minorities to confront and oppose the dominant and empowered state religion. As such, these communities should be given protection.

RELIGIOUS FREEDOM IN ISRAEL: ASYMMETRY BETWEEN RELIGION AND SECULARISM AND DECENTRALIZATION

Israel is often thought to be an exceptional case as regards religious liberty, given its formal characterization as a "Jewish and democratic state."[2] Despite the characterization of the state as Jewish, the position of the Supreme Court and of most jurists is that the Israeli legal system ensures both freedom from religion and freedom of religion.[3] Indeed, these two complementary and often also conflicting freedoms have been part of Israel's unwritten constitution almost since the establishment of the state,[4] and with the legislation of Basic Law: Human Dignity and Liberty in 1992, the Court read them into the constitutionally protected value of human dignity.[5]

What enables jurists and political actors to argue that, although the state is defined as Jewish, it is still committed to a separation of religion from state, is that the Jewishness of the state can be – and indeed has been – interpreted nationally rather than religiously. The dual meaning of Jewish – both a religion and a nation – is a source of much debate among scholars, judges, and policy makers, and this is

with the Avi Chay Israel Foundation. Both have found a growth in the religiosity of Israelis; both confirm that full seculars are a nationwide minority. According to the IBS, 8 percent of Jewish-Israelis defined themselves as ultra-Orthodox, 12 percent as religious, 13 percent as religious-traditionalist, 12 percent as traditionalists, and 42 percent as secular. According to the Avi Chay survey, seculars count for only 46 percent of Jews. See PORTRAIT OF ISRAELI JEWS: BELIEFS, OBSERVANCE, AND VALUES OF ISRAELI JEWS, 2009 (Hebrew, 2011).

2 Basic Law: Human Dignity and Liberty, 1992, SH 1391, 150, s. 1A; Basic Law: Freedom of Occupation, 1994, SH 1454, 90, s. 2.

3 See, e.g., Haim Cohen, *Religious Coercion in Israel*, in 2 BERENSON BOOK 297 (ed. A. Barak & H. Berenson, 2000); DANIEL STATMAN & GIDEON SAPIR, STATE AND RELIGION IN ISRAEL: A PHILOSOPHICAL-LEGAL INQUIRY 266–82 (Hebrew, 2014); AVIHAY DORFMAN, FREEDOM OF RELIGION AND FREEDOM FROM RELIGION: A DEMOCRATIC PERSPECTIVE 14–16 (Hebrew, 2015).

4 Zvi Berenson, *Religious Freedom and Freedom of Conscience in Israel* (Hebrew), 3 TEL-AVIV U. L. REV. 405 (1974).

5 See, e.g., HCJ 953/01 Solodkin v. City of Beit Shemesh, 58(5) PD 595 [2005] (Isr.); CA 6024/97 Shavit v. Hevra Kadisha GHSHA Rishon Le-Zion, 53(3) PD 600 [1999] (Isr.); HCJ 5016/96 Horev v. Minister of Transportation, 51(4) PD 1, 34 [1997] (Isr.).

one of the main reasons it is almost impossible to convincingly argue that Israel has a formal system of disestablishment.[6] This duality also leaves the door open for religiously motivated legislatures, policy makers, and judges to infuse their various actions with religious content.[7] More and more, the religious interpretation of the Jewishness of the state is becoming entangled with, not to say indistinguishable from, its national one.

Numerous legal factors entangle the Israeli state with religion. Most known and talked about are the religious monopoly over marriage,[8] extensive funding of religious services and institutions, ongoing exemption from military service for religious women and ultra-Orthodox men and women, and the prohibition on public transportation during the Sabbath. I will not discuss these, since they have been aptly documented. Instead, I would like to describe three other factors, which are more systemic and have not received sufficient attention until now: a systematic asymmetry between the categories of religion and secularism; decentralization of the management of aspects of religious freedom and religious affairs; and the unique compromise that has created in some instances two parallel public systems, one religious and the other "general" but not secular.

Asymmetrical Treatment of Religion and Secularism

Israel has developed fairly wide accommodation doctrines for religious practices by creating special protection for religious feelings and religious communal ways of life. These protections run parallel to the formal freedom of religion (or "free exercise," in American terminology), and in fact they often bypass the prohibition on legislating religious norms. Secular feelings and ways of life, however, have not received the same recognition.

What lies at the heart of this asymmetry is that the secular is theoretically and sociologically nonexistent in Israeli legal doctrine and discourse. Religions in Israel are based in and on recognizable communities, traditions, holy texts, sets of beliefs, practices, ways of living, sentiments, and feelings.[9] The secular, on the other hand,

6 See STATMAN & SAPIR, STATE AND RELIGION 4, 199–202.

7 See JEWISHNESS OF ISRAEL (ed. A. Ravitzky & Y. Z. Stern, 2007). See also Yishai Blank, *Localizing Religion in a Jewish State*, 45 ISRAEL L. REV. 291 (2012).

8 See, for example, Gila Stopler, *Free Exercise of Discrimination: Religious Liberty, Civic Community and Women's Equality*, 10 WILLIAM & MARY J. WOMEN & THE LAW 459, 485–92 (2004); Gideon Sapir & Daniel Statman, *Religious Marriage in a Liberal State*, in CONSTITUTIONAL SECULARISM IN AN AGE OF RELIGIOUS REVIVAL 269–82 (ed. S. Mancini & M. Rosenfeld, 2014).

9 One of the inheritances Israel received from the British Mandate is a list of "recognized religious communities" that had authority and autonomy over their members in personal matters. These recognized religious communities still have monopoly over religious matters of their members, as well as over certain aspects of personal law such as marriage and divorce.

has remained a normative void, a legal absence[10] and a sociological enigma.[11] It is seen either as the simple lack of all the things that religions possess and signify, or is understood to be an idiosyncratic personal trait: each secular person is thought to have different preferences, behave differently, have a distinct conscience, and so on. Secularism as a positive value or worldview – rather than an opposition to religious coercion or signification of a societal sector – has never been systematically pursued or adopted.[12]

The lack of secularism as a theoretical or political project has also meant that there was no "secular" around which a definable community with a protection-worthy way of life, sentiments, or preferences could be formed.[13] This negativity and vacuity of the secular has had particularly grave results in the Israeli legal system, which has veered in recent years in the direction of acknowledging collective and cultural group rights.

Recognizing Religious (But Not Secular) Feelings

Despite traditional liberal reluctance to protect individuals from harms to their feelings,[14] Israeli law protects religious sentiments in several ways. The most traditional is criminal prohibition of "offenses against religious sentiments," which dates back to the British Mandate.[15] More important, however, is the doctrine, developed by the Supreme Court, concerning "religious feelings" (*rigshct dat*). According to this doctrine, which is extremely rare in Western democracies, state action aimed at

10 A petition by a secularist group to be recognized as an official religious community entitled to the same status as others was rejected by the Supreme Court. See HCJ 6168/92 Israeli Secularist-Humanist Society v. Israel, 51(4) PD 289 (1997).

11 Scholarship dealing with secularism (as well as "traditionalism") in Israel has started to appear. See the very recent collection Y. FISHER, ED., SECULARIZATION AND SECULARISM: INTERDISCIPLINARY PERSPECTIVE (Hebrew; 2015).

12 Parts of the kibbutz movement included secularism into their comprehensive ideology. It was not, however, an independent component, nor did it reach beyond the radical communist parts of this movement. In the urban sector, the Canaanite movement advocated radical secularism, but it remained extremely small and marginal.

13 Secularism has remained by and large a civil project, that is, led mostly by organizations of civil society, rather than by political parties or prominent and salient ideologies. Such organizations still exist; among them one could mention Israel Hofshit. Another leading organization that deals with issues of state and religion is the Israeli Organization for Reform and Progressive Judaism (but, as its name suggests, this is not a secularist organization, but rather a Reform Jewish one).

14 Dating back to John Stuart Mill, liberal scholars have repeatedly argued that liberalism denies curbing people's speech or acts simply because they hurt the feelings of others. For a summary, see Daniel Statman, *Offence Against Religious Sentiments* (Hebrew), in MULTICULTURALISM IN A JEWISH AND DEMOCRATIC STATE 133–88 (ed. M. Mautner et al., 1998); MORDECHAI KREMNITZER ET AL., RELIGIOUS FEELINGS, FREEDOM OF EXPRESSION AND CRIMINAL LAW (Hebrew; 2002).

15 Penal Code, s. 170–74. For a detailed analysis of these prohibitions, see Statman, *Offence Against Religious Sentiments*; KREMNITZER ET AL., RELIGIOUS FEELINGS.

preventing offense to religious feelings can be justified under certain conditions.[16] At its heart lies a distinction between religious motivation or purpose and religious feelings. While administrative actions specifically intended to enforce a religious norm are not permitted, the same actions can be sanctioned if they are aimed instead at protecting the feelings of religious individuals and communities.[17] The Supreme Court has even ruled that in certain instances, it is the duty of the state to provide such protection.

The need to balance general public considerations and individual rights against offended feelings became a dominant path through which religious consideration de facto entered into Israeli law. In some cases – such as blocking roads during the Sabbath[18] and regulating areas where sex shops could operate – the Court ruled that no specific authorization was required, and the relevant authority could factor the feelings of religious communities into its decisions even if the law did not mention religion at all.[19] In other cases, however, such as when local governments tried to prohibit the selling of pork or to shut down cinemas on the Sabbath, the Court ruled that they could not use their regular zoning and business licensing powers, since they were primarily motivated by religious considerations rather than by protecting religious feelings. This caused the Knesset to legislate "special enabling laws" whereby it authorized local governments to regulate where pork could be sold[20] and places of entertainment could be open during the Sabbath.[21]

16 This doctrine is not limited to the domain of religious feelings, but has been extended to other, non-religious feelings. Such was the case in artistic or political speech that offended soldiers, in the case of the film *Jenin-Jenin*. For an analysis and critique of this doctrine, see Meital Pinto, *Offense to Feelings or Offense to Cultural Identity?* 15(2) HAMISHPAT 647 (2011).

17 This distinction appeared soon after the establishment of Israel and has been repeated in numerous cases. See CA 217/68 Izramex Ltd. v. Israel, 22(2) PD 343 (1968) (Isr.).

18 HCJ 531/77 Baruch v. Tel Aviv District Traffic Controller, 32(2) PD 160 (1978) (Isr.); HCJ 174/62 League for the Prevention of Religious Coercion v. Council of Jerusalem, 16 PD 2665 (1966) (Isr.). The Court ruled that it was legal for a locality to use its ordinary traffic and road control powers in order to close down streets and roads during the Sabbath in order to prevent "direct infringement" on the lives and feelings of the religious community living nearby.

19 In the Horev decision, however, where the closure of a large and central road (Bar Ilan) near a religious neighborhood in Jerusalem was considered, the Court ruled that although the transit authority was allowed to take into consideration religious feelings, it had to pass a three-pronged test: first, factoring in the feelings had to fit with the specific purpose of the authorizing legislation; second, it could not coerce religion, in the sense of forcing a secular person to perform a religious duty; and third, the offense to religious feelings had to be insufferable. See HCJ 5016/96 Horev v. Minister of Transportation, 51(4) PD 1, 55 (1997) (Isr.).

20 The issue of selling pork is complicated and has attracted much attention. See DAPHNE BARAK-EREZ, OUTLAWED PIGS: LAW, RELIGION, AND CULTURE IN ISRAEL (2007); Issachar Rosen-Zvi, *Pigs in Space: Geographic Separatism in Multicultural Societies*, in LAW AND SOCIOLOGY: CURRENT LEGAL ISSUES 225 (ed. M. Freeman, 2006) 225; Blank, *Localizing Religion*.

21 The Sabbath has spurred debates and legal battles since the establishment of Israel. For lengthier discussion, see, e.g., Cohen, *Religious Coercion*; Blank, *Localizing Religion*.

No equivalent doctrine was developed as regards secular feelings, which might be offended by seculars being exposed, for example, to certain religious services, practices, rituals, or symbols. On the contrary, in the rare cases where such an argument was raised, courts have tended to reject it.[22] While taking seriously claims that individual rights might be infringed upon by religious practices or legislation, the courts have not been willing to entertain the idea that these might cause any offense to the feelings of seculars, as long as no direct religious "coercion" was involved. Thus, seculars have only individual rights, whereas religious people have legal recognition of their feelings in addition to their general rights and freedom of religion.[23]

Recognizing Religious (But Not Secular) Unique Ways of Living

Side by side with the emergence of the doctrine of offense to religious feelings, the Supreme Court developed the idea that ultra-Orthodox Jews are a religious minority with a unique way of life worthy of special protection. While this idea dates back to the 1960s and 1970s and issues related to the Sabbath, in 2000, the Supreme Court went much further and ruled that the uniqueness of this lifestyle could even justify such measures as creating segregated towns on government-allocated lands.[24] Affirming the policy of establishing a "separate but equal" ultra-Orthodox town, the Court stressed that recognizing the right of the religious community to sustain its lifestyle "represents a well-accepted contemporary notion among jurists, philosophers, social scientists and educators, according to which the individual is entitled – among his many other rights – to fulfill his belonging to a community and its unique culture, as part of his right for personal autonomy."[25]

This ruling opened the floodgates for the establishment of more and more towns solely for ultra-Orthodox Jews.[26] Furthermore, groups of religious-Zionist

[22] For example, in the conflict among seculars and religious communities in the city of Rehovot, the Court refused to consider that there was any offense to secular feelings posed by the construction of a municipal religious service center. HCJ 10907/04 Solodoch v. Municipality of Rehoboth (unpublished, 2010). For further discussion, see Yishai Blank, *Islands of Pluralism: Segregation and Integration among Religious and Secular Jews in Israel* (Hebrew), 6 *Haifa U. L. Rev.* 85, 115–16 (2011).

[23] Admittedly, offense to feelings often proved a weak weapon (such as in the Horev case), especially when the conflicting rights were constitutionally protected basic rights, such as freedom of speech and demonstration, freedom of movement and more. Yet in other cases and in the daily routine of the administration, offense to religious feelings became crucial in mediating secular/religious conflicts and tensions.

[24] HCJ 4906/98 Am Hofshi v. Ministry of Building and Housing, 54(2) PD 503 (2000) (Isr.) (While affirming the general policy, the Court disqualified the specific instance since no "equivalent" secular settlement was established). For detailed analysis, see Blank, *Island of Pluralism*, 95–99, and Blank, *Localizing Religion*, 312–13.

[25] Am Hofshi, 508–09. Although this segregation is often presented as self-segregation, the fact that it is mandated by the government makes it hard to assess whether it is voluntary. See Blank, *Localizing Religion*.

[26] Such new towns include El'ad, Beitar Illit, Modi'in Illit, Kiryat Sefer, and Immanuel. Two additional ultra-Orthodox cities (Kasif and Harish) are currently being planned by the government. See N.

Orthodox Jews started claiming that they were entitled to the same, since they too were a religious minority with a unique lifestyle. While as a matter of legal doctrine, this religious-Zionist claim is still contentious, in practice there are a growing number of religious-Zionist localities, neighborhoods, and developments that are strictly homogeneous and formally exclude secular Jews, non-Jews, and even ultra-Orthodox Jews.[27]

Here, too, the doctrine was crafted in an asymmetrical manner. When secular Jews tried to demand a "separate but equal" land allocation from the government, or when local governments were suspected of creating development schemes for seculars only, the courts vehemently opposed them.[28] Seculars were described as a "majority," belonging to the "general stream" rather than being members of a distinct minority, and therefore creating segregated neighborhoods for them was "an administrative intervention in natural, spontaneous and legitimate social processes."[29] (The "natural process" alluded to was what popular debates sometimes refer to as "ultra-Orthodox takeover," which turns neighborhoods into enclaves where seculars can no longer lead their secular lifestyle.)

Long before the evolution of the (multi-)culturalist license for ultra-Orthodox-only segregation, small settlements such as *kibbutzim*, *moshavim*, and other communal settlements restricted membership with screening committees.[30] Although mostly intended to exclude Arabs, this practice nonetheless created high levels of segregation between secular Jews, Zionist-religious Jews, and the ultra-Orthodox in rural areas of Israel. Though parts of this system were declared illegal by the

GUROVICH & E. COHEN-KASTRO, ULTRA-ORTHODOX JEWS: GEOGRAPHIC DISTRIBUTION AND DEMOGRAPHIC, SOCIAL AND ECONOMIC CHARACTERISTICS OF THE ULTRA-ORTHODOX JEWISH POPULATION IN ISRAEL, 1996–2001 (Hebrew; July 2004) (www.cbs.gov.il/www/publications/int_ulor.pdf).

27 In the Saba'a case, the district court ruled that although the land auctioned was state land, the winners – a private company called Be'emuna – could still maintain an exclusive criterion and sell apartments to religious-Zionist Jews only. The court ruled that there was "nothing wrong in a group of people organizing in order to live next to each other to be able to lead their life according to their ways of life." AdminC 2002/09 Saba'a v. Israel Land Administration (unpublished, 2010). An appeal to the Supreme Court was rejected, since the project was already under construction, and the Court ruled that it was a "done deal." However, the Court made remarks that cast doubt on the ruling of the district court, as well as on the legality of the practice. AdminA 1789/10 Saba'a v. Israel Land Administration (unpublished, 2011).

28 AdminC 209/01 Fintz v. Minister of Housing and Planning (unpublished, 2002) (the Jerusalem District Court ruled that the decision of the locality to cancel the development plan was likely to have been the result of too many ultra-Orthodox that won the public tender; it thus ruled that the withdrawal of the locality was illegal); AdminC 1888/09 Edri v. Minister of Housing and Planning (unpublished, 2010) (rejecting the petition of Zionist-religious Jews to be allocated a land from which ultra-Orthodox Jews would be formally excluded).

29 Edri, para. 18.

30 Neta Ziv & Chen Tirosh, *Legal Battle Against the Screening of Candidates to Communal Settlements: A Trap in a Pierced and Muddy Web*, in GATED COMMUNITIES 311 (ed. Amnon Lehavi, 2010).

Supreme Court, screening committees were legislated into law by the Knesset and are still responsible for much residential segregation in rural Israel.[31]

Nevertheless, there is something new and far-reaching about the principle of "a minority with a unique lifestyle worthy of protection." First, it imports the exclusionary logic of the relatively small rural sector into the urban environment and serves as a legal vehicle for the creation of all-religious neighborhoods or developments within cities, where the large majority of the population lives.[32] Second, it expands the license to exclude and opens up the potential of recognizing more religions and communities as being worthy of "pure" segregated settlements. Third, it adopts the view that religion is a culture – rather than a set of beliefs, rituals, practices, etc. – whose members have a common wish to exclude others and whose fixed identity requires protection from "external" threats.

This asymmetry also exists in other areas, where the Court has been extremely hesitant to identify and recognize a collective secular way of life. Instead, as mentioned previously, courts translate claims about a secular way of life into claims about individual rights that are supposedly infringed: freedom of movement (in cases of road closures), freedom of speech (in cases of religiously offensive speech), freedom of occupation (in the pork and Shabbat cases), and more. Even if these individual rights win over religious ways of life in judicial and administrative balancing, it is important to note the conceptual difference and its possible ramifications.

I do not mean to claim that seculars should be acknowledged and protected as a social minority, or that secularism should be treated merely as a set of cultural beliefs and practices. Such an approach would be anathema to what secularism should stand for: a principled and general position against political religion (rather than a sectorial one), a commitment to the pursuit of a public good (rather than a private one), and an insistence on the plurality of worthy ways of life, individual and collective. But this particular asymmetry between secularism and religiosity in Israel must end, given that religion is turning into a dominant – if not the dominant – political force, and considering that religious communities are becoming a social majority. While religious Jews have culture, community, and the "national" on their side, seculars have abstract individual rights that do not adequately capture

[31] The law is highly ambiguous and seems to be self-contradictory. While it allows the screening committee of settlements with up to 400 families to exclude applicants on the basis of "lack of fit to the social-cultural fabric" of the settlement, it is prohibited to discriminate on the basis of race, religion, nationality, country of origin, political views, and more. Clearly, however, the sociocultural fabric of the settlement is mostly based on these attributes. It is therefore very unclear what courts will do once cases of excluded individuals begin to get to courts. A petition to strike down this legislation was submitted by ACRI but was rejected by the Supreme Court as too hypothetical and too early, for lack of evidence as to the application of the law. See HCJ 2311/11 Sabbach v. Knesset (17.9.2014) (Isr.); also www.acri.org.il/he/97.

[32] Israel's rural settlements comprise less than 10 percent of the population.

the indispensability of communities with shared public spaces for the formation of a positive secularism.

Religious and Secular "Federalism" in Israel: The Localization of Religiosity/Secularism

Local governments are uniquely positioned vis-à-vis tensions that arise from daily interactions between individuals and groups, over the character of their shared spaces. Local governments have authority over zoning, land use, business licensing, road and traffic control, sanitation, water, housing, safety, taxing and spending, and more. These traditional powers are applied in many issues that touch on religious freedom.

Given the residential patterns in Israel, which are marked by a high degree of voluntary segregation along lines of religious creed and ethnicity, localities are often fairly homogeneous polities, and the application of local authority frequently reflects the religious or secular composition of the population.[33] For instance, localities may use their transit powers to close down roads on the Sabbath, their business licensing authority to prohibit selling of pork, their zoning bodies to prohibit or permit religious kindergartens, their tax policies to give deductions to religious institutions, or their zoning boards to allocate lands for religious activities.

The initial response of the Supreme Court to this situation was contradictory: on one hand, it tried to prevent localities from applying their regular authorities for religious purposes by declaring that such actions were beyond the scope (*ultra vires*) of local authority and ruling that religion should thus rest solely in the hands of the central government.[34] Yet in other cases, where the religious purpose was not too overt, the religious coercion minimal, and the allocation of budgets "transparent" and equal,[35] the Court allowed the local action. In addition, the special enabling laws enacted by the Knesset specifically authorized local governments to take religious considerations into account when applying their business licensing powers.[36]

As courts took their cue from the legislature and affirmed such local action, and local officials catered to their local constituencies, the distinction between predominately ultra-Orthodox localities, majority religious-Zionist localities, all-Muslim localities, predominately traditionalist localities, and majority-secular localities

[33] See Blank, *Localizing Religion.*

[34] HCJ 72/55 Freidi v. Municipality of Tel Aviv, 10 PD 734 (1955) (Isr.).

[35] See HCJ 262/62 Peretz v. Chairman, Council Members and Residents of Kfar Shemaryahu, 16 PD 2101 (1962) (Isr.). This legal principle enables localities to express their religiosity by giving money to synagogues, churches, and other religious enterprises, but is a source of much contention and many legal battles. See AdminA 343/09 Jerusalem Open House v. City of Jerusalem (unpublished, 2010).

[36] Local Authorities Act (Special Enablement), 1956, S 249(21); Municipalities Act (religious holidays and days of rest); Prohibition of Opening of Amusement Places (Special Enablement), 1997.

became more and more accentuated. For instance, the Supreme Court allowed a predominately Druze local government to prohibit "Western music" in its coffee shops,[37] and a Jewish town to draw maps of where pork could be sold, based on the residential distribution of religious people and "pork-eaters."[38]

These Court rulings, combined with the special enabling laws and the background of existing residential segregation, have promoted further segregation and self-sorting and further entrenched the territorialization of religiosity and secularism. Although the Court seems to protect minorities by these rulings, it also incentivizes localities and neighborhood residents to exert pressure to obtain an overwhelming majority so that they will not be required to accommodate others. It has put a premium on homogeneous, "pure" spaces, and promoted (perhaps unwittingly) what Rosen-Zvi calls "geographic separatism."

A Unique Compromise: Parallel Public-General and Public-Religious Systems, but None Fully Secular

Another unique characterization of the Israeli state is that in various important realms, the state has chosen to establish two parallel systems: one "general" and the other "religious." This was seen as a compromise between the two aspects of religious freedom: in order to uphold freedom *from* religion, the general system remained supposedly secular, but in order to protect freedom *to* religion for religious people, a parallel public-religious system was established. Leading examples of this are public schools, the military, and state religious courts. The establishment of parallel systems should have made the general system an overtly secular one, entirely separate from religion, so that any involvement with religion could be a matter of individual personal choice. However, this did not happen. Instead, the general system maintained a constant compromise between secularism and religiosity.

Public Schools: Religious and General (but not Secular)

The most salient debates about the schooling system in Israel revolve around the fact that ultra-Orthodox private schools, which are generously funded by the state, fail to teach the basic modern core studies (such as mathematics, English, and civics) required for public funding.[39] This highly visible public debate stands in stark contrast to the complete acceptance of another fundamental aspect of the public schooling system: in addition to funding fully private religious schools, the state

37 HCJ 166/71 Halon v. Ussfiyeh, 25(2) PD 591 [1971] (Isr.).

38 Solodkin v. City of Beit Shemesh.

39 This issue is routinely used as a battle cry for secularist parties such as Shinuy, Meretz, and Yesh Atid. It has become a symbol of the political power of ultra-Orthodox political parties and the inability of the state to enforce its own decisions.

also funds and runs both a general (*klali* or *mamlachti*) public school system and another public-religious one (*mamlachti-dati*, for religious-Zionists).[40] But the general one is far from being truly secular: religious texts (the Bible, Mishnah, and often the Talmud) are taught in general public schools; religious attire is permitted for students and teachers alike; Jewish religious holidays are celebrated; and the curriculum is set by the Pedagogical Council of the Ministry of Education, which is currently – but also historically – committed to strengthening the identity of Israel as a Jewish state.

While these characteristics of a general public education may seem natural and consensual in the Israeli context, they would be controversial in many other liberal democracies, as they seem to entangle the state with religion. In such places as France, Italy, and the United States,[41] courts and administrators are constantly grappling with demands to maintain public schools wholly devoid of any religious signs, including personal religious attire, religious symbols, and the like. Although the concrete outcomes of these legal and political battles change from time to time and from place to place, they are seen as lying at the heart of the perennial dilemma of church and state relations, which is often most intense in the context of public schools.

In Israel, however, such bitter conflicts concerning the secular nature of the general public system have never taken place, and there has never been a legal or political campaign aimed at radically secularizing the general public schools. By radical secularization I do not mean a sectorial, atheist education, but rather the opposite: a truly inclusive public education system that would not prefer Orthodox Judaism over other religions and would be truly open to all religions and all strands of Judaism, as well as atheism. I do not claim here that extreme secularist measures (such as the prohibition of religious attire) should be adopted. Rather, I want to emphasize, once more, the asymmetry of the religious and the secular in Israeli law: while religious communities (at least the Zionist-religious ones) receive a separate public educational system, seculars do not, as the general public schools still incorporate both secularist and religious demands.

Moreover, in recent years, the balance has shifted in the opposite direction from secularism: with the growth of the political power of the National-Religious Party and its overt mission to strengthen the Jewish aspect of the state, the general public schools have become a main target. There is an intensified campaign to infuse the general schooling system with Jewish (national and religious) contents, and to tilt

[40] Public Education Act s. 1. For a comprehensive description of Israel's public school system, see Yishai Blank, *Brown in Jerusalem: A Comparative Look on Race and Ethnicity in the Public Education System*, 38 URBAN LAWYER 367 (2006).

[41] For comparative analysis, see, e.g., STEPHEN MACEDO, DIVERSITY AND DISTRUST: CIVIC EDUCATION IN A MULTICULTURAL DEMOCRACY (2000).

the balance between the Jewish pole and the democratic one in the direction of the former.[42]

The Military

There are other places where a religious system and a general public one exist in parallel, and yet the public system does not really attempt to be secular. The same situation exists in the Israel Defense Force (IDF). Although ultra-Orthodox citizens are exempted from mandatory service,[43] in recent years, units have been created for religious soldiers only. Yet the general units, where nonreligious soldiers serve, have not become more secular, nor have they even maintained the same level of non-religiosity. There are "religious officers" in every unit, and only kosher food is served in the whole military, including the nonreligious units. While the common justification for these accommodations is the desire to keep all units welcoming to all soldiers, the establishment of special units for religious soldiers proves that the general state service can never be accommodating enough, that there will still be a demand for a parallel religious service, and that this demand will have good chances of being met. There is evidence that, with the appearance of religious units, the influence of religion on the general military units has become more intense, often coercing secular soldiers into religious norms and activities (mostly related to the status of women and to the military rabbinate). Pressure to accommodate, transform, and "theocratize" (as Yagil Levi calls it) the military as a whole, including its general units, has grown and hardened.[44]

What becomes apparent from these principles is that Israel has, in fact, no legal notion of secularism. Israel is defined as Jewish, and even if this is meant in the national, cultural, or moral sense, the state is still closely tied to Jewish religion – and mostly to its ultra-religious definition – and very far from a secular state. In addition, the Supreme Court has created exemptions and accommodations for religious individuals and communities by recognizing their feelings and their unique ways of life. It has not recognized equivalent secular feelings, communities, and ways of life. Overall, this decentralized and asymmetric system of religious liberty has allowed the state to be understood as religious by some and

[42] A recent example of this has been the battle over the teaching of civics in public high schools. After much debate, a new edition of the obligatory textbook came out, showing signs of the growing influence of the new religious leadership of the Ministry of Education. For example, citations from the Declaration of Israeli Independence were replaced by a Jewish prayer.

[43] This is one of the most controversial aspects of the status quo between the ultra-Orthodox community and the state and is seen by many as one of the areas where the greatest injustice is done to the secular majority.

[44] Yagil Levi, *Theocratization of the Israeli Military*, 4 ARMED FORCES & SOCIETY 269 (2004); YAGIL LEVI, DIVINE COMMANDER: THEOCRATIZATION OF THE ISRAELI MILITARY (2015).

secular by others; it has enabled the expression of religious feelings and norms by public bodies, funded and established by the state; it has mitigated some "religion wars" at the national level, while inciting and encouraging them at the local level; and it has exacerbated existing residential segregation between persons of different creeds.

IN SEARCH OF THE SECULAR

Should we worry about the lack of the category of the secular in Israel? Is it a problem that seculars are seen only as individuals who bear rights, while religious people belong to communities who deserve special protection and whose feelings and ways of life are valued? And should the legal rules change in order to amend the situation?

What Is Secularism?

Secularism is often construed as the idea that the state should be separate from religion, or at least that religion should be depoliticized,[45] and seculars defined as individuals who do not believe in God, practice any religion, or belong to any institutionalized religious group. Yet recent studies show that secularism is a dynamic, complex, and often contradictory set of ideas that cannot be limited to the relationship between religion and the state, and secular people are an extremely diverse group of people, not necessarily identifiable merely by their approach to God, faith, institutionalized religions, or religious practices.[46]

A large body of literature has unmasked secularism as a European construct that was developed against the backdrop of colonial expansion and has continually failed to stand up to its own promise of being value-neutral. Critics of secularism have convincingly claimed that, instead of being universal and liberal, secularism has often been sectarian and oppressive, both internally and externally.[47] It has also been used for political purposes that have little to do with real liberal values and a lot to do with other ambitions – imperialistic, nationalistic, racist, and classist.[48]

45 See Susanna Mancini & Michel Rosenfeld, *Introduction* xv, in CONSTITUTIONAL SECULARISM IN AN AGE OF RELIGIOUS REVIVAL (ed. S. Mancini & M. Rosenfeld, 2014).

46 Although religion is diverse, too, it is much easier to define, since there is a clearer set of texts, traditions, and institutions that helps in determining what religious people "are."

47 See TALAL ASAD, FORMATIONS OF THE SECULAR: CHRISTIANITY, ISLAM, MODERNITY (2003); Saba Mahmood, *Secularism, Hermeneutics, and Empire: The Politics of Islamic Reformation*, 18(2) PUBLIC CULTURE 323 (2006); CHARLES TAYLOR, A SECULAR AGE 3 (2007).

48 Gil Anidjar, *Secularism*, 33 CRITICAL INQUIRY 52 (2006); SABA MAHMOOD, RELIGIOUS DIFFERENCE IN A SECULAR AGE: A MINORITY REPORT (2015).

Against the Sectarian-Sociological Interpretation of Secularism

In Israel, seculars have traditionally been identified with the Ashkenazi, a group of middle- and upper-middle-class Jews of European descent who maintained hegemony in Israel during the formative years of the state.[49] For them, secularism was part of the "new Israeli" – as opposed to the ultra-Orthodox Jew of the Exile, the traditionalist Mizrahi Jew from Muslim countries, and the Arabs (Muslim and Christian). Thus, for decades, secularism in Israel did much more than neutrally describe an attitude to God or religion; it also represented values that oppressed, delegitimized, and marginalized certain groups of people, marking them as primitive and inferior, and created a cultural and social hierarchy within the new state.

It is therefore crucial that this interpretation not just be set aside, but that it serve as a warning against a sectarian, provincial, and racist understanding – and practice – of secularism. In some of the battles between seculars and religious groups in Israel, it is precisely this indefensible conception of secularism that motivates action against religion. It can be difficult to distinguish the legitimate from the sectarian. Moreover, not all sectarian secularist claims should necessarily be dismissed, especially when religious sectarian claims are accepted by the state and the courts. In this sense, I argue that at least the asymmetries that have been created with respect to religious feelings[50] and segregated religious residential areas need to be abolished.

Additionally, although I reject the idea that secularism in its sectarian, sociological sense deserves legal protection in general, there is an important reservation to be made: in light of the multicultural turn in Israeli jurisprudence, there could be a moment when such cultural protection might be appropriate for seculars – unless we reject the expansive multicultural protection given to other communities.[51] Ruling out communal protection for secularists comes from the asymmetry between majority and minority groups, which is fundamental to the legitimation given to collective cultural rights in the multicultural discourse and doctrine. Hence, if the political and demographical context changes even further and secular groups become more marginalized and minoritized, a good argument might be made for recognizing them as a minority group with a way of life worthy of protection.

Last, another reason to adopt and protect a semi-sociological understanding of secularism might exist in the (rare) case where it is possible to identify a secular social group as the bearer of values that are worthy of protection in themselves. In this sense, "seculars" can sometimes be shorthand or a proxy for the values that they represent, adopt, or are committed to. In such a case, the protection given to

49 Baruch Kimmerling mentions secularism as a characteristic trait of this group, together with Ashkenazi ethnicity, socialist ideology, and Zionist nationalism. See BARUCH KIMMERLING, END OF THE ASHKENAZI HEGEMONY (Hebrew; 2001).

50 See also DORFMAN, FREEDOM OF RELIGION, 84–85.

51 See also Blank, *Islands of Pluralism*, 85.

a certain group would stem not from the value-neutral protection of its culture, but from the worthiness of the values it represents. Although this cannot be said in general of all, or even the majority, of secular individuals and communities in Israel, there might be cases where protecting a particular secularist community would in fact be valid on the basis of its values.

Against Secularism as Just (Narrow Negative) Liberalism

Perhaps the most complicated, yet crucial reservation to make regarding secularism is to reject the full identification of secularism with liberalism (and modernity). Seen as merely another aspect of liberal moral and political theory, secularism has receded into the background and became synonymous with it.[52]

As Charles Taylor demonstrates, there is no justification for identifying liberalism with secularism: various secularisms have existed in non-liberal settings.[53] Understanding secularism as a negative and narrow type of liberalism would mean that the only stance secularism has vis-à-vis religion is distance and detachment, embodied in the principle of freedom from religion (or freedom of conscience). But secularism can include positive and active responses and engagements with religion. Even more important, in Israel, thin, narrow, and individual liberal rights are at risk of losing out to the public interest, since public interest has been thoroughly captured by the religious, as a result of the duality of the idiom "Jewish and democratic."

These conditions – the pervasive presence of Judaism in the public sphere, and the inherent entanglement between state and Judaism – require that oppositional communities be able to constitute themselves in secularized public spaces. Hence, although it would be hard to articulate such protection in narrow liberal terms, a more expansive reading of liberalism might enable its creation.

Against the Anti-faith Interpretation of Secularism

Another understanding of secularism to which I take exception is that secularism is by necessity purely rationalistic, reason-based, anti-faith, and anti-spiritual. Although political liberalism requires a commitment to public reason and the exclusion of God-centered explanations for public action, I do not believe that secularism necessitates a complete expulsion of faith. Once secularism is unlinked from liberalism, there is more leeway for understanding and formulating its relationship to reason and spirituality. While it would be impossible to label a position as secular if it endorses God as its ultimate political authority or if it publicly adopts the viewpoint of one particular religion, it is not unthinkable that secularists themselves have faith

52 See ASAD, FORMATIONS OF THE SECULAR.

53 See TAYLOR, SECULAR AGE.

or spirituality. Nor is it impossible that a secular polity would eschew a strict separationist approach, and instead choose an ecumenical approach toward religions and other faiths and spiritual pursuits.

Secularism as Concrete, Local, and Pluralist Public Spaces of Resistance to Political Religion

Having articulated my objections to the more common notions of secularism, I will describe my interpretation of the secular in general, what it might mean in the Israeli context, and why it is worth defending and protecting. Following Taylor, I argue that secularism needs to be understood as something more than the principle of the separation of church from state and as something additional to the secularization of public spaces. Rather, it must be understood in a third sense, as the emergence of conditions in which belief in God shifts from being "unchallenged, and indeed, unproblematic, to one in which it is understood to be one option among others, and frequently not the easiest to embrace."[54] I view this as one of the greatest moral values of secularism, and why it deserves to be protected and even promoted by the state: it frees individuals from an oppressive, monolithic acceptance of the existence and supremacy of God.

Creating the conditions in which acceptance of God becomes one option among others requires much more proactive and positive measures than simple freedom from religion, especially in Israel.[55] Taking secularism seriously requires taking into account its context, the way it operates and the content of the religion against which it is positioned. Hence, one needs to understand secularism as being necessarily embedded in concrete places, and positioned vis-à-vis specific appearances of religion and concrete religious practices and beliefs. In this sense, secularism is also, by necessity, plural and experimental. We should enable individuals and communities to explore what it means to be secular for them, in different settings, different contexts, and different historical moments.

Secularism as a personal choice should be protected, but as long as it is merely a desire not to be coerced into a religious practice, assurance of common individual rights, including freedom from religion, will suffice. But in contexts such as the Israeli one, freedom from religion may not be enough, and more effective protection may be required. Where the environment is suffused with religious relics, symbols, and meanings, and official bodies of the state strengthen its Jewish character

54 See TAYLOR, SECULAR AGE, 3.

55 See Martha Nussbaum's interpretation of freedom of conscience, which should protect every individual's "capacity to search for the ethical basis for her life and after their ultimate meaning." MARTHA NUSSBAUM, FREEDOM OF CONSCIENCE 19 (2008).

by various means, secularism becomes a value that deserves more stringent defense. Put differently, secularism means different things in different contexts, and accordingly, it merits different means of protection.[56]

What is Israeli secularism, then, and where can it be found? Given the entanglement of religion and state at the central level, and in light of the decentralized nature of religious liberty in Israel, both religiosity and secularism in their more extreme and pure forms have been found mostly at the local level. While the central state has constantly compromised between secular and religious groups and been stuck in gridlock over many issues, local governments have not only been able but even forced to define and maintain secular as well as religious locales. In these smaller-scale settings, religious and secular communities were mutually constituted and were able to try out their concrete visions of what it might mean to be secular, as well as religious.

I do not want this chapter to be read as one of the "urgent calls for the reinstatement of secularism" propelled by the fear of Islam[57] or, in the context of Israel, by a desire to reinstate old elites for fear of the growing power of previously excluded societal groups and minorities, including religious ones. It is one thing to call for secularization in the United States or France in certain political contexts, but another to defend it in Israel, where religion is currently associated not with oppressed and disempowered minorities, but with an increasingly powerful right-wing national political movement.

Israel as a state never fully adopted a doctrine of separation of religion from state. Religious laws, public services, national symbols, and public spaces are the norm rather than the exception. Although not a theocracy, the state has maintained a constant compromise between religiosity and non-religiosity. Yet at local levels, experimentations in more radical religiosity and secularism have taken place. In this sense, the localization of religious liberty presents both the dangers and the promises associated with decentralization of such an issue. On one hand, it has enabled greater religious pluralism,[58] allowed for more democratic involvement in public matters for excluded and marginalized religious minorities, and mitigated conflicts at the national level between competing religious groups and seculars; on the other hand, it may have exacerbated residential segregation on the basis

56 This approach parallels, in a way, the disaggregation approach that Cécile Laborde advocates as regards religion. According to her, the concrete protection we should grant religion depends on the value or the meaning that religion has in a particular context. Likewise, secularism would mean different things in different contexts, and the protection that we should give it would vary accordingly. See Cécile Laborde, Chapter 1, this volume.

57 See Mahmood, *Secularism*.

58 This is the main argument Richard Schragger makes in favor of the decentralization of religious liberty, since it destabilizes the monopoly of dominant religions; see Richard Schragger, *Role of the Local in the Doctrine and Discourse of Religious Liberty*, 117 HARVARD L. REV. 1810 (2004).

of religion, contributed to growing religious and secular extremism, and oppressed local minorities.[59]

Here I emphasize the impact that this structure has had on secularism in Israel, and I argue that localities have been the only place – materially and socially – where individuals and communities have been able to materialize a fuller idea of secularism, secularizing public spaces, disentangling their locality from religion, and making belief in God one choice among others. Recently, the dual meaning of Judaism as religion and nationality has become more and more inseparable as religious-Zionists and secular-nationalists advance a program of strengthening the Jewish identity of the state. With this process, some secularism begins to also operate against this duality, becoming more identified with non- or even anti-nationalism.

Given this context, enabling secularism in its different meanings seems to depend on the continuous existence of local, smaller-scale polities that are sufficiently authorized to allow for individuals and groups to pursue their vision and their life meanings, especially when they are in opposition to the increasingly religious central state apparatus. Searching for secularism in Israel means attempting to create a mode of secularity that has never really been tried as a nationwide Israeli project: a public secularity – an ensemble of secular public spaces and secular public reason – which is not enmeshed with religion in general or Judaism in particular. Such secular locales would enable the emergence of public spaces of secularity that would go beyond individualized secular choices and hopefully serve as public forums where communities could experiment with non-political religion, and the interpretation of Judaism might be altogether detached from religious authorities, texts, and institutions.[60] Such places might become beacons and models for others to imitate and learn from.

I am not advocating the creation of pure secular spaces, nor am I suggesting that seculars are currently discriminated against. To the contrary, the model I am advocating is "islands of pluralism" where individuals from different communities will be exposed to each other, learning from daily experiences the art of living together in spite of radical differences.[61] But this pluralism should not be unidirectional, and it should not mean that nonreligious people are the only ones who submit to religious-Zionist ideologies (in schools, in the military, in public holidays, and more), while religious groups opt out of the general system into their public or private religious systems. I am calling for greater symmetry, not in exclusion but in inclusion.[62]

59 For discussion of these consequences in detail, see Blank, *Islands of Pluralism*.

60 For an elaboration of this point in the American context, see Richard Schragger & Micah Schwartzman, *Against Religious Institutionalism*, 99 VIRGINIA L. REV. (2013).

61 See Blank, *Islands of Pluralism*.

62 Thus, current demands by secularist groups to obtain a separate, non-general, secular strand within the public education system should be opposed, as this gives up on the basic commitment to every individual, regardless of his or her group belonging. Yet, while tolerance toward various communities

Although the process and structure I have described is particularly Israeli, it is not detached from the world: there is a remaking of the relations between religions and states, between religious communities and secular ones, and more generally, as Michael McConnell puts it, "a new whiff of intolerance is in the air."[63] Yet while McConnell thinks this intolerance is directed by secularists toward religious beliefs and practices, the religious revival, especially in its more virulent and radical forms of fundamentalist Christianity, Judaism, and Islam, is just as crucial to understanding the new construction of religion and state relations. Searching for secularism in small polities might be a beginning to combat this new intolerance.

in the educational system is a reasonable liberal accommodation, these separate systems should not be as autonomic as they are, or the general system be as religiously inspired as it currently is.

[63] Michael W. McConnell, *Why Protect Religious Freedom?* 123 YALE L. J. 770, 773 (2013).

PART II

The Challenges of Religious Institutions for the Secular State

9

The "How Many?" Question: An Institutionalist's Guide to Pluralism

Ori Aronson

INTRODUCTION

A policy decision to involve the state in either the accommodation or the provision of institutional pluralism entails a crucial design question that is often undertreated in the political morality literature on pluralism. The fact that a pluralist agenda has won the policy debate – that political agency has been mobilized in support of public institutions that would tolerate or express multiple alternatives and respect individual and community choice – does not in itself tell us a lot about the quantity and character of the alternatives that ought to be included in the pluralist regime. Most of the normative inquiry in this area has focused on the external boundaries of the field of options to be devised – that is, whom it might be justified to exclude from the sphere of public respect and accommodation. The typical discussion in this context concerns the variety of illiberal practices exercised by communities that present an otherwise morally sustainable demand for pluralist recognition, and positions vary familiarly.

But assume that the external boundaries of the field have been relatively settled: that we have a reasonably articulated theory of what qualifies as a non-legitimate cultural practice, such that we know what is not going to be part of the recognized field of alternatives in our pluralist regime. We are still left with the issue of how to design the field itself, and here the discussion is lacking. Specifically, two interrelated questions arise: (1) What is the pluralistically optimal amount of alternatives a state is required to (strive to) sustain in order to fulfill its political ideal (the N question); and (2) what is the optimal degree of variance the state should (seek to) maintain among the given alternatives (the Δ question)? How large or distinct should a cultural group be in order to warrant political recognition and differentiation? What kinds of courts should a judicial system include, and what variety of schooling

Thanks to Joshua Cohen, Marie-Therese Hoelscher, Turkuler Isiksel, Chris Kutz, and Sarah Song for helpful comments and to Dana Zamir for valuable research assistance.

should an education system uphold? Should legally recognized familial structures, contractual associations, or property relationships be limited in kind or open-ended?

Obviously there is no available method to answer these questions in the abstract, as different pluralistic contexts lead to different institutional demands, and even in particular cases we are not likely to reach something like an exact figure –a “42” à la Douglas Adams. But we should be able to make an effort to theorize the institutional implications of normative pluralism and to identify workable, useful benchmarks, considerations, or heuristics for pluralist institutional design. This work is essential for constructive as well as critical engagement with current practices from a pluralist perspective.

In this chapter, I suggest an analytical framework for working through these questions. The framework identifies two fundamental paradigms of pluralist institutionalism: *mimetic pluralism*, in which the pluralist field is meant to accommodate an existing diversity of practices within the state apparatus; and *poietic pluralism*, in which the state engages in the design or fosters the development of new institutional alternatives. Each presents an ideal type of institutional design, deriving from a different moral conception of pluralism as a political imperative, and therefore also suggesting a different approach to the “how many?” question. Through the elucidation and juxtaposition of these ideals, I hope to open up useful avenues for treating questions of pluralist institutional design in context, and not only in the abstract.

To keep the discussion grounded, I draw on the near history of Israel’s politics of law, religion, and identity and some of the institutional variations they have brought about, as examples and illustrations. This chapter begins therefore with the tale of two Israeli stories of institutional innovation, each representing a different model of pluralist design. From the context-specific stories, I turn in the second section to present and discuss the two paradigms of pluralist institutional design, which are to anchor the discussion throughout. The third and fourth sections are dedicated to analyses of two central complications or challenges faced by pluralist institutional designers of either paradigm, but shows how they play out differently in each of the two approaches. One challenge is the ever-changing nature of the social spheres that are subject to pluralist treatment (dynamism of the pluralist field); the other has to do with the effects of a constituency failing to avail itself of a pluralist structure (problem of convergence). Finally, in the fifth and final section, I return briefly to the question in the title and draw initial practical implications of the discussion for pluralist institutional design.

DESIGNING PLURALIST INSTITUTIONS: TWO ISRAELI STORIES

Marriage Registration

In October 2013, Israel’s parliament enacted an amendment to the law on marriage and divorce registration, which had until then provided that Jewish couples were to register for marriage with the local rabbinate of their places of residence or wedding. The 2013 legislation provided instead that couples may register for marriage with any rabbi authorized to register marriages in Israel, "regardless of [the couple's] place of residence or the location of their wedding."[1] The formal justification for the legislation, presented in the explanatory notes to the bill, focused on the fact of young persons' geographic mobility in contemporary Israel, which renders the requirement of local registration needlessly burdensome.

A highly visible subtext, however, had to do with the matter of variety: not so much a measure of administrative streamlining, the legislation was above all another act in a decades-old culture war around the system of marriage and divorce in Israel, still dominated by the Jewish Orthodox. Unable to muster the political force to enact a comprehensive civil marriage reform, representatives of secular constituents instead recurrently opt for second-best solutions that seek to circumvent or to mitigate the costs the Orthodox monopoly incurs on couples and individuals who have no other option but to marry the religious way. In this case, the legislation was meant to enable couples to register for marriage with a local rabbinate that is not as strict as the one they might have been bound to under the previous place-of-residence regime.

Because it is part of a religious system, marriage registration in Israel is not a mere clerical function: the registrar – a male Orthodox rabbi appointed by the Chief Rabbinate – is expected to employ his knowledge of Jewish law to ascertain that both parties are Jewish and that there are no other obstacles to consummating the marriage according to Jewish religious law (*halakha*). The degrees of diligence in insisting on these issues can vary, however: a modern-Orthodox registrar might treat couples differently than his ultra-Orthodox counterpart, and a rabbi in an urban setting might diverge from a rabbi in a small-town or rural setting. And due to the diffuse and nonhierarchical nature of rabbinical authority, there is no practical way to ensure the application of uniform halakhic standards throughout the local rabbinates. This meant that by the virtue of chance – where you or your future spouse happened to live – one's marriage registration experience could vary significantly, albeit only within the boundaries of the Orthodox spectrum vetted by the Chief Rabbinate. The new law therefore allows couples to "shop" for a more hospitable rabbi-registrar from among those available in the existing distribution of local rabbinates throughout Israel.

Civil Adjudication

Devising a choice mechanism among several providers of public service along the secular-religious fault line has been suggested in Israel not only in the context

[1] Marriage and Divorce Ordinance (Registration) § 2A (Isr.).

of marriage registration. As in many other countries over the past few decades, adjudication of civil disputes in Israel has undergone a process of institutional diffusion and pluralization, with diverse adjudicatory units and forums springing up both within the state apparatus (specialized courts, administrative tribunals) and in the so-called private sphere (the Alternative Dispute Resolution variety). One of these developments has taken the form of a burgeoning industry of Jewish religious tribunals, *battei din*, which, pursuant to parties' authorization, hold court in diverse civil disputes according to halakhic principles and procedures, and at the same time can enjoy the backing of state enforcement under Israel's arbitration laws.

The development of a competitive, client-oriented market for Jewish-religious arbitration, out of what was once an intra-community service premised mostly on cultural commitments and charismatic leaderships, is a multifaceted story. It involves multiple agents and points of institutional innovation, including a 2006 landmark Supreme Court opinion that turned out to reinforce the privately run forums' claim of religious attractiveness.[2] In that decision, the Court clarified that state-run *battei din* – rabbinical courts with exclusive jurisdiction in marriage and divorce – lack jurisdiction over civil or commercial disputes. This decision in turn led to still-ongoing political efforts to draft and enact a novel jurisdiction-conferring statute, one that would formally establish state-sponsored Jewish-religious jurisdiction in civil matters, alongside the secular courts that normally adjudicate such disputes.

These attempts to formally introduce a "public option" in the market for religious adjudication of civil disputes are yet to bear legislative fruit. However, as a matter of institutional vision they represent a clear intention to add into the institutional mix of civil adjudication in Israel a novel forum that would be different than existing form of civil dispute resolution, in significant ways.

Commonalities

Both episodes, I suggest, can be appropriately understood as political exercises of a pluralist normative agenda: they employ state institutions in order to enlarge and diversify the set of alternatives available for individuals acting socially, and they do so in a social context that is deeply sensitive to demands for difference and distinction – that is, religious attachment and belief.

But the two episodes are also distinguishable from each other in their approaches to institutional design. The marriage registration reform was conducted through a minor tinkering with the mechanism of choice: it took the field of existing alternatives (the already-established local rabbinates) as given, and merely reworked the

[2] HCJ 8638/03 Amir v. Grand Rabbinical Court, 61(1) P.D. 259 (2006).

process through which couples are paired with registrars. The proposed religious adjudication reform, on the other hand, would change – enlarge – the field of available choices, by introducing a new alternative for parties to choose from. So, while the two episodes tell comparable stories of pluralist normative agendas in the design of state-backed religious institutions, they also present two competing strategies of how to do pluralism. It is the aim of this chapter to conceptualize these two strategies as paradigmatic versions of pluralist institutional design and to unpack some of their moral, political, and practical foundations and implications.

In what follows, I term the two paradigms *mimetic pluralism* and *poietic pluralism*. Each presents an ideal type of pluralist institutional design, involving distinguishable modes of institutional imagination and formation and deriving from different liberal conceptions of pluralism as a political imperative. I define these two concepts with an aim to distinguish between them, but note already that in reality both necessarily overlap and feed into each other, such that they are more accurately conceived as instances on a continuum of pluralist strategies, rather than as separate, let alone mutually exclusive, possibilities. Still, through their elucidation and juxtaposition we may come up with some generalizable insights about the pluralist method of institutional design.

PLURALIST INSTITUTIONALISM: MIMESIS AND POIESIS

Mimetic Pluralism

A pluralist agenda is mimetic when it calls for designing public institutions that respect and reflect existing variations in belief systems, in social norms and understandings, and in demands from the public sphere. In such cases, the public intervention is characterized by imitation – mimesis – of already-existing practices, through their representation in state institutions. Mimetic pluralists rely on the multiplicity of alternatives developed by members of the constituency as the principal determinants of both N (amount) and Δ (variance). They ask the state to take the field of alternatives as given and ensure that it retains its pluralistic character, either by creating institutions that recognize these practices and sustain their multiplicity or by taking over a sphere of social action and making it public. The "how many?" question for mimetic pluralists is concerned primarily with determining which groups, practices, or institutions qualify as viable for recognition as distinct alternatives under the pluralist regime: What are the foundational elements of a religion, how many members constitute a tribe, what procedures are required to establish an association?

The marriage registration reform in Israel is an example of mimetic pluralism. As we saw, what the reform involved was a mere tweak in the assignment mechanism of couples to registrars – in place of a bounded geographical criterion, it opted for a national choice-based market structure. It used the known diversity in registrars' halakhic rigidity as the basis for institutional reform that would inject pluralism into a system often perceived as arbitrary, coercive, and discriminatory. The state overlaid the existing map of alternatives with its system of marriage registration and adopted the existent pluralistic field as its solution to local religious disparities.

Mimetic pluralism can thus be thought of as a bottom-up project of institutional design. In its ideal type, it is a passive-responsive political strategy, which identifies diversity in morally consequential social spheres and then makes room for that diversity in the design of public institutions. It does so ostensibly without engaging in a critical evaluation of the nature or content of the existing alternatives (except for the purpose of defining the external limits of the regulated field and excluding illegitimate options).

Of course, these spheres of plurality, to which the state attaches its public superstructure when it "goes pluralist," do not develop organically out of some stateless zone of pre-political communal life. The state (through law) has a background role in the processes of creation or evolution of most social arrangements, and so it is hardly ever a purely mimetic agent. The marriage registration case shows this: the Jewish-religious alternatives endorsed by the state in that case were themselves state institutions – local rabbinates, funded, managed, and regulated by law as part of the government apparatus. Other instances of mimetic pluralism, however, apply to institutions that evolve with lesser statist involvement. Consider the *millet* system, in which the Ottoman Empire recognized acts of tribunals of certain religious minorities that came under its control – an arrangement whose central features are still in force in Israel today. Still, as theories of representation have long recognized, any mimetic act by definition alters that which is being represented, and in that sense as well there is no such thing as pure mimesis.[3] Existing religious courts that are granted state imprimatur are no longer the same tribunals they were without their position within a political context.

When theorized as the realization of a liberal political ideal, mimetic pluralism is best understood as a mechanism for coping with the (sociological) fact of reasonable pluralism and the demands and constraints this fact imposes on the state.[4] Framed in terms of autonomy, dignity, or equality,[5] as an expression of respect or of recognition,[6] or indeed as a signification of the diversity of human experience as an

3 "Mimesis is poiesis, and poiesis is mimesis"; see PAUL RICOEUR, THE RULE OF METAPHOR 39 (trans. Robert Czerny et al., 1977). For an analysis, see, e.g., Jenna Sunkenberg, *Between Reality and Fiction: Paul Ricoeur's* La Metaphore Vive, 29 SCRIPTA MEDITERRANEA 21, 23–24 (2008).

4 JOHN RAWLS, JUSTICE AS FAIRNESS: A RESTATEMENT 32 (2003).

5 E.g., WILL KYMLICKA, MULTICULTURAL CITIZENSHIP: A LIBERAL THEORY OF MINORITY RIGHTS (1995).

6 E.g., Charles Taylor, *Politics of Recognition*, in MULTICULTURALISM: EXAMINING THE POLITICS OF RECOGNITION 25–73 (ed. Amy Gutmann, 1992).

intrinsic social good,[7] mimetic pluralism seeks to express, accommodate, and facilitate through public institutions the multiple visions of social welfare that exist in a community or in a certain social structure at a given time.

Poietic Pluralism

A pluralist agenda is poietic when it engages the state in the creation – *poiesis* – of multiple institutional alternatives that would sustain, overall, a sufficiently pluralistic field. Poiesis may vary in degrees of activism: the state could itself put in place new institutions, or it could incentivize creation by non-state actors. Poietic pluralists face the "how many?" question in a more direct sense than mimetic pluralists, because they are required to introduce new institutions into an existing field or indeed to produce a whole new institutional scheme where the state was not formerly involved at all. The determinants of N and Δ under poietic pluralism are not necessarily existing practices or expectations, rather a conception of what ought to be the set of alternatives that constitute the pluralist institutional structure. And because the limits of reason preclude the possibility of an accurate *ex ante* prediction as to the optimal set of alternatives, poietic pluralism would likely take the form of an experimentalist institutional agenda, leaving open ends for the introduction of new institutional possibilities down the road.

The proposal in Israel to establish state rabbinical courts with jurisdiction over civil disputes is an example of poietic pluralism. Although a field of diverse forums for civil dispute resolution already exists (in religious ADR tribunals and in secular state courts), the proposal of a new forum expresses a view that this field is not diverse enough to fulfill a sufficiently pluralist vision of adjudication; namely, it lacks the option of a state-backed religious process. The state therefore actively enters the field and produces the missing alternative. In this process, it engages the "how many?" question: while it does not provide a finite number, it does take the position that in civil adjudication, two is not enough – the choice between private-religious and public-secular is a pluralist state of affairs, but it is not sufficiently so. At the same time, the state reflects on the degree of variance question: the normative gap between the private-religious and public-secular alternatives is too wide, compelling parties to litigate in forums that are either too private or too secular.

Notably, there are other ways of construing the poietic project expressed in the proposed legislation. Applying a more nuanced lens, the story can also be told not as a binary setting (private-religious/public-secular) into which a third option

7 E.g., Albert W. Musschenga, *Intrinsic Value as a Reason for the Preservation of Minority Cultures*, 1 Ethical Theory & Moral Practice 201 (1998).

(public-religious) would be introduced, but rather as a broad field in which multiple judicial forums would operate, located on various points along a private-public/religious-secular spectrum. Thus, not all ADR-based *battei din* are the same, and not all secular state courts are the same. Religious tribunals vary from extreme ultra-Orthodox forums to modern-Orthodox systems that willingly endorse the legitimating shadow of secular arbitration law and seek to serve diverse litigants. The civilian judicial system is also made of diverse units, with varying degrees of procedural rigidity and distance from statist control. In this portrayal, the addition of a state rabbinical court with jurisdiction over civil disputes seems a more nuanced institutional move, and one that can therefore raise more particular questions along the N and Δ lines: Why only one kind of state religious court? Why Orthodox and not Conservative or Reform?[8] The degrees of poietic design therefore vary according to context and perspective.

Compared with mimetic pluralism, poietic pluralism is thus conceived as a top-down creative exercise in political agency: having decided to go pluralist, designers of public institutions are asked to employ their prescriptive imagination to come up with what could be, rather than their descriptive skills of tracking and identifying what already is. In doing so, poietic pluralists cannot avoid issues of content and quality, which at least some mimetic projects can treat as given. In that sense, poietic pluralism can prove a more demanding effort in institutional design, although it comes with the uniquely redeeming potential of introducing people to novel and unfamiliar paths.

Poietic pluralism as a liberal project would most sensibly be grounded in a moral understanding of autonomy as self-authorship, requiring meaningful choice in important life junctures as the core of autonomous fulfillment.[9] In terms of political obligation, this version of autonomy requires the liberal state to ensure that in significant spheres of human development, multiple and diverse institutions be made available to choose from and thus made one's own.[10] Capabilities-based approaches to distributive justice,[11] as well as pluralist accounts of legal constructs in property[12] or

[8] I do not attend here to the bigger question of the non-Jewish communities in Israel and their needs and expectations with regard to state-based religious adjudication. A full account of the Israeli pluralist agenda in this respect would necessarily include those communities as well, but is excluded from the present chapter for the purpose of theoretical focus and clarity. For an enlightening treatment, see Michael Karayanni, *The Acute Multicultural Entrapment of the Palestinian-Arab Religious Minorities in Israel and the Feeble Measures Required to Relieve It*, in MAPPING THE LEGAL BOUNDARIES OF BELONGING: RELIGION AND MULTICULTURALISM FROM ISRAEL TO CANADA 225 (ed. Rene Provost, 2014).

[9] E.g., Joseph Raz, *Autonomy and Pluralism*, in MORALITY OF FREEDOM 369–99 (1986); ELIZABETH ANDERSON, VALUE IN ETHICS AND ECONOMICS 1–16 (1993).

[10] See Hanoch Dagan, *Pluralism and Perfectionism in Private Law*, 112 COLUM. L. REV. 1409 (2012).

[11] E.g., AMARTYA SEN, COMMODITIES AND CAPABILITIES (1999); Martha C. Nussbaum, *Foreword: Constitutions and Capabilities: "Perception" Against Lofty Formalism*, 121 HARV. L. REV. 4, 10–56 (2007).

[12] See HANOCH DAGAN, PROPERTY: VALUES AND INSTITUTIONS 3–75 (2011).

marriage,[13] fit this category. Such pluralists must face the quantitative nature of the poietic challenge, because even where multiple institutions already exist, the available alternatives may fail to provide genuine or meaningful choice, and therefore state intervention is required.

Of course, in the mirror image of the constitutive element that inheres in all mimesis, poietic pluralism as well cannot really escape the boundaries of that which is already in existence, and so, at least to us humans, there is no pure poiesis – what we can imagine is bound by what we already know. The histories of administrative states (and of judicial systems therein) are stories of experimentation in institutional novelties like regulatory agencies, specialized courts, and privatized endeavors; however, few of those come from nowhere. Consider, for example, community courts and other innovations in therapeutic and restorative justice, which have been gaining traction in rule-of-law democracies over the past two decades:[14] while these variations certainly chart new pluralist courses alongside the liberal orthodoxies of criminal justice, they often draw on communal, indigenous, and traditional social practices for inspiration and legitimation.

Institutional design in both the mimetic and poietic strands emanates from a liberal commitment – framed in one way or another – to pluralist accommodation or provision of difference in the public sphere. The two modes are not mutually exclusive, indeed, as we saw and as will be further elaborated, they sometimes converge or overlap. Still, they are distinguishable in the kinds of inquiry and expertise that institution makers employ in the pluralist project. Mimesis requires a keen grasp of what exists in the social world that demands public recognition or protection. Poiesis requires a sensitivity to that which is missing from social practice and thus demanding of public provision or fostering.

Dynamism of the Pluralist Field

Both mimetic and poietic pluralists must face the dynamic nature of the fields they regulate. In both models, sufficient (optimal) degrees of plurality are contingent on the practices, beliefs, expectations, and choices of individuals and groups, and all these can change as societal and cultural connections and commitments develop or alter. We can already sense that the "how many?" question presents a moving target, which can at best produce a workable algorithm rather than a finite number. Here I unpack the different sorts of dynamism each pluralist model has to tackle.

[13] See Shahar Lifshitz, *Pluralistic Vision of Marriage*, in MARRIAGE AT THE CROSSROADS 260 (ed. Marsha Garrison & Elizabeth Scott, 2012).

[14] See, e.g., Bruce J. Winick, *Therapeutic Jurisprudence and Problem Solving Courts*, 30 FORDHAM URB. L. J. 1055 (2003).

In some contexts, mimetic pluralism can be a static exercise, requiring a one-time choice and relying on a given institutional background as the determinant of the field of alternatives. In the Israeli marriage registration example, the choice-based pluralist framework was superimposed on an existing institutional structure – the system of local rabbinates, which is not expected to fluctuate without further deliberate design choices. Thus even if some of the local rabbinates turn out to share similar levels of *halakhic* rigidity, or if an existing rabbinate would shift in one direction or another, the attachment of the pluralist scheme to the existing jurisdictional structure is not likely to change; people's choices might shift, but not the institutional design. A similarly static pluralist account can be seen in familiar functional explanations of the jurisdictional redundancy characterizing the US judicial structure – fifty-one systems with often overlapping jurisdiction over identical or similar cases. Classic accounts of this arrangement as a "judicial laboratory"[15] or as a mechanism for bringing out "interest, ideology, and innovation"[16] rely on the fact of the American federal structure, with its given number of states that is not likely to change, regardless of the actual pluralist pay-off it produces.

But other mimetic projects are dynamic, requiring an ongoing engagement with fluctuating social and political fields. This occurs when the pluralist project involves the creation of public institutions that are to accommodate existing social practices (hence their mimetic quality). Here the state needs to continually track the fluctuations in the field that is subject to pluralist accommodation, in order to ascertain whether new groups, communities, or practices have emerged (or withered), so as to require a remodeling of the mimetic structure. The continued evolution of the *millet* system even after the establishment of the State of Israel is a case in point: since 1948, three "new" religious groups were formally recognized by the Israeli government and entrusted with various degrees of autonomous control over internal affairs and/or jurisdiction over their members' personal status. Thus in 1957, the Israeli Druze community was recognized as a separate religious group, leading to the establishment of Druze religious courts in 1962; in 1970, the Evangelical Episcopal Church in Israel became the tenth Christian denomination to be officially recognized (the other nine having been recognized already by the British Mandate in 1939); and in 1971, the Baha'i faith was added to the list.

An institutional project of mimetic pluralism, if it is to serve more than the political moment that led to its adoption, must therefore involve a mechanism for tracking and evaluating the development of new practices that would require institutional accommodation: Have new possibilities evolved, and do they qualify under

15 See, e.g., Barry Friedman, *Valuing Federalism*, 82 MINN. L. REV. 317, 397–400 (1997).

16 Robert Cover, *Uses of Jurisdictional Redundancy: Interest, Ideology, and Innovation*, 22 WM. & MARY L. REV. 640 (1981).

the pluralist criterion to enjoy institutional accommodation? This mechanism can take different forms – it can rely on private party petitioning (such as the US federal process for acknowledging Indian tribes)[17] or on public outreach through surveys and censuses (such as demography-contingent multilingual ballots).[18] The dynamism of the mimetic process lies in the dynamism of the reality it seeks to respect and imitate, and so a genuine mimetic pluralism has to answer the "how many?" question by accepting the potential of a constantly shifting number of institutional variations.

At the same time, such episodes of mimetic dynamism of course do not merely reflect a passive process of tracking and observation, in which the state would grant institutional accommodation to any qualifying group under some predetermined objective threshold (e.g., membership size). Rather, these processes are likely to involve identity politics, which in Israel include the special complexities of a state whose constitutional ethos is defined along exclusionary ethno-religious lines. Thus, for example, while the Druze, who have shown a strong allegiance – as minority outsiders – to the Jewish national project (notably by encouraging young men to serve in the Israel Defense Forces), won jurisdictional recognition, requests for recognition by Jehovah's Witnesses, who challenge the deeply rooted anti-proselytizing sentiment in Israel, are recurrently declined.

Indeed, in some contexts, a practice that may seem a straightforward exercise in mimetic distinction can turn into a hot-button pluralist challenge when confronted with identity politics and intergroup anxieties. Consider the registry of nationalities administered by the Israeli Interior Ministry: once a security-profiling tool distinguishing primarily between two categories – Jewish and Arab – the registry has taken on the additional role of serving as an active turf for the Israeli culture wars of group definition, recognition, and belonging. In this context, the dynamics of mimetic pluralism have been evident, in the inclusion over time of such nationalities as Druze, Circassian, and, lately, Aramaic in public expressions of these groups' differentiation from the (Muslim) Arab collective, as well as in the denial of a petition to enter "Israeli" in the list, in what was a failed attempt to symbolically entrench a republican version of citizenship in Israel.[19] By employing the nationalities registry to imagine new communities and block the access of others, Israel has in a sense switched from a mostly symbolic exercise in mimetic pluralism into a poietic project of redesigning the very field of alternatives.

Like mimetic pluralism, poietic pluralism can also sometimes seem a relatively static act of institutional design. This is the case when the institutional

[17] See 25 CFR Part 83 (2015).

[18] Endorsed in the United States in the Voting Rights Act for "language minorities" that comprise more than 5 percent of the relevant constituency's citizens of voting age. 52 USCS § 10303(f) (3).

[19] CivA 8573/08 Ornan v. Ministry of Interior (ISC, Oct. 2, 2013).

imagination employed to create the field of new alternatives is bound either by an attachment to familiar and existing institutions that serve as inspiration or source of borrowing for the new field, or by an ideological or political capture that, while supporting pluralism, limits the effectively available resources of innovation and diversity. The proposal to entrust existing state rabbinical courts with jurisdiction over civil matters arguably suffers from both pathologies of poiesis. The existing tribunals are all Jewish Orthodox, presided over by only-male judges, most of whom were educated in ultra-Orthodox institutions of rabbinical learning. Thus, while the new forum would add a novel judicial alternative to the existing field (making it a pluralist move), it would be one that represents only a segment of Jewish legality – one that already enjoys accommodation in state institutions, as well as a strong base in Israeli interest group politics. None of the current bills proposed, for example, adding judicial forums that would apply non-Orthodox halakhic innovations.

The choice to limit the proposed pluralist legislation to an Orthodox option could be explained in terms of variance – there simply aren't enough potential "customers" in Israel for a non-Orthodox Jewish religious court to justify the creation of two systems of state rabbinical adjudication. In other words, the primary demand for religious adjudication can be satisfied by an Orthodox court; another tribunal would simply not be distinct enough to justify the investment. But note that this explanation reflects a mimetic reasoning, rather than a poietic one: it derives an institutional agenda from existing practices and preferences, and in that way entrenches the status quo rather than challenges it.

The dynamic nature of poietic pluralism lies therefore in its goal of stimulating the capacity of individuals to keep engaging in the lifelong project of self-authorship. This is a challenge, since we suffer from an inherent epistemic deficit when we try to design an *ex ante* optimal array of institutions for individuals through which to achieve this ideal of autonomy. Because the needs and beliefs of people vary and change, and because social conditions keep evolving, the poietic project necessarily entails some measure of uncertainty. This does not mean that poietic exercises in pluralist institutional design are futile. It does mean, however, that we can only measure the success of poietic acts of institutional pluralism in retrospect: Did we manage to develop a field of valuable alternatives?

The open-ended nature of autonomy-enhancing poiesis leads to institutional experimentalism as a central feature of the pluralist enterprise.[20] This poses a special challenge for designers, who have to construct systems that are robust enough

20 I use "experimentalism" here following Unger, in the sense of institutional design that leaves room for reflection, critique, and reform within the very structure of the social arrangement. See ROBERTO MANGABEIRA UNGER, DEMOCRACY REALIZED: THE PROGRESSIVE ALTERNATIVE 16–27 (2000); compare Michael C. Dorf & Charles F. Sabel, A *Constitution of Democratic Experimentalism*, 98 COLUM.

to serve institutions' purpose of providing order, structure, and direction to social life, but at the same time are also flexible and malleable enough to be able to incorporate new information and new interests (and to forgo defunct elements) in their own design.[21]

This can be attempted in different ways. One is to institutionalize "poietic moments" – predetermined points along the projected life of an institution, in which its pluralist ideal comes under examination and its resistance to reform is relaxed (e.g., by a temporary change in amendment procedures or a reversal of a default norm). Another is to create modes of learning and of critical reflection in the ongoing functions of the institution, in order to mitigate the risks of entrenchment and ossification. Thus a pluralist design can institutionalize meaningful interaction between agents of different units, such that the discourse of each is infused by the knowledge and experience of the other.

While always dynamic, the universe of pluralist institutions – mimetic or poietic – does not always expand. In different contexts, institutional designers can face the predicament of a contracting field of choices or alternatives. This is a special challenge of pluralist dynamism.

THE PROBLEM OF CONVERGENCE

What happens if the field subject to pluralist regulation does not play along? That is, what if pluralist theory prescribed institutional reform in a given context, but the people intended to benefit from the pluralist design fail to do so? This is not merely a problem of poor design, of giving the incorrect answer to the "how many?" question; it can also arise due to the very nature of choice-based systems.

Mimetic pluralism can reach a dead end when the amount or the variety of the social practices that were the basis for the pluralist project dwindles – when people abandon certain associations or practices and converge around fewer options, or even a single one. Language usage sometimes raises these kinds of concerns; this is a familiar issue in indigenous communities overrun by colonial forces of cultural assimilation, but other paths can also lead to the death of a language, as in the decline of Yiddish and Ladino, which was the combined result of Jewish secularization, the Holocaust, and a resurgence of (modern) Hebrew.[22] When state institutions are mimetically designed to accommodate lingual pluralism – in formal

L. Rev. 267 (1998) (conceiving of experimentalism in the context of policy development and application, rather than in institutional design).

[21] See, e.g., Robert E. Goodin, *Institutions and Their Design*, in THEORY OF INSTITUTIONAL DESIGN 1, 39–43 (ed. Robert E. Goodin, 1996).

[22] See Sarah Abrevaya Stein, *Asymmetric Fates: Secular Yiddish and Ladino Culture in Comparison*, 96 Jewish Q. Rev. 498 (2006).

correspondence, in the modes of petitioning the government, in public education – what is the pluralist to do when a language is dying? The simple answer would seem to be that if the pluralist project is about dignifying the actual preferences of people, recognizing existing practices, and accommodating them in public institutions, then the state should simply eliminate alternatives that have gone out of favor with the relevant constituency.

But this result can be problematic to the mimetic pluralist in several respects. First, the more likely scenario is not a complete abandonment of a certain practice, but rather its gradual decline until it is shared by only a small group of people. Then the question implicates the allocation of public resources and raises the question of a pluralist threshold: Which groups or practices are sufficiently substantial to justify their accommodation in the state apparatus? Second, mimetic pluralism need not necessarily be conceived of as a synchronic overlay of present conditions. It can also justify taking account of past practices worth preserving or reviving. This could be done in order to respect a cultural memory shared by members of living communities – for example, if it is constitutive to their ongoing association. It can also be required as a measure of corrective justice, when the state had a causal role in the decline of the cultural practice.

The underlying question here has to do with the kind of obligation a state is subject to when it opts for mimetic pluralism: Should it merely provide the opportunity for the different groups to make use of pluralized public institutions, and then it is up to individuals and communities to determine whether the pluralist design will endure or wither? Or is the state also expected to ensure that the different alternatives in fact thrive and are expressed in the products of its institutions?[23] Take, for example, the case of public support for non-Orthodox Jewish rabbinates in Israel. In 2012, following Supreme Court brokering, the state took on an obligation to fund a fixed number of posts for non-Orthodox rabbis in local councils across Israel.[24] Membership in non-Orthodox communities in Israel is low;[25] assume it drops to meager and the consumption of non-Orthodox rabbinical services becomes rare. Should the state continue funding these positions? Should it make a positive effort to get people to know and appreciate them, and keep its mimetic vision alive?

It is at these junctures that mimetic pluralism and poietic pluralism seem closest to each other, and their character as positions on a continuum (rather than

[23] This question echoes a long-standing debate among individualist and communitarian liberals regarding the role of cultural attachments in one's identity – a constitutive element, or a result of unencumbered choice – and the ensuing implications in terms of political morality. See, e.g., KYMLICKA, MULTICULTURAL CITIZENSHIP, 89–93.

[24] HCJ 8944/05 Brachat Shalom Congregation v. Prime Minister's Office – National Authority for Religious Services (ISC, May 29, 2012).

[25] www.idi.org.il/ ספרים-ומאמרים/מאמרים/הרפורמים-והקונסרבטיבים-בישראל-—פרופיל-ועמדות

discrete alternatives) becomes evident. A decision to use state institutions not only to accommodate and enable existing practices, but also to create a space for ones that once did, or ones that sometime could, necessarily involves a position on how the field of alternatives ought to look – that is, an essentially poietic perspective.

Poietic pluralism faces the problem of convergence in a similar but distinct way. Recall that the plausible liberal foundation for poietic pluralism lies in the value of autonomy and the need to ensure meaningful choice. Suppose that a poietic project takes place and multiple institutions are created by the state in order to provide the needed choice. But it turns out that people do not choose the options presented to them through the pluralized institutional scheme; rather, they coalesce around only a few of the alternatives, if not a single one. This can be the result of one of three failures: (1) Designers' failure in identifying the field warranting pluralist treatment. Autonomous people do not exercise self-authorship through all of their social interactions, and sometimes make choices according to one-dimensional metrics like price or time. (2) Designers' failure in creating the appropriate institutions, for instance in terms of N and Δ. Incorporating an open-ended experimentalist element to the pluralist structure ought to help in correcting this kind of failure over time. (3) Constituents' failure in utilizing the full array of the pluralist structure, due to communal pressures, prejudice, lack of information, or behavioral biases. Here the problem of convergence lies with the "client," rather than with the "product," and so institutional designers may consider means of overcoming the forces that work against the pluralist ideal. In other words, should people be "nudged"[26] toward a pluralist life of choice and meaningful self-authorship, in hope of making them more autonomous? And if so, how does one do this?

Take the civil adjudication case discussed earlier under Designing Pluralist Institutions. Assume that institutional designers properly perceive the new state religious tribunal as the missing link in the field of available judicial forums, such that its provision would allow individuals sufficient choice (between sufficiently diverse alternatives) to fulfill the autonomy-based pluralist ideal. But once constituted, people don't use it. This could be because they are not aware of its existence or nature, because they are wary of approaching religious institutions regardless of merits, or because they share an ideological bias against state institutions. Can the state nonetheless lead some litigants into that forum, to ensure that it thrives and furthers the autonomy-enhancing function it was designed to serve? From a normative perspective, this question involves familiar concerns with the ironies of paternalism, in which coercion is used to promote autonomy.[27] Different coercive

[26] See RICHARD H. THALER & CASS R. SUNSTEIN, NUDGE: IMPROVING DECISIONS ABOUT HEALTH, WEALTH, AND HAPPINESS (2009).

[27] See, e.g., Luc Bovens, *Ethics of Nudge*, in PREFERENCE CHANGE 207–19 (ed. Till Grüne-Yanoff & Sven Ove Hansson, 2009).

measures obviously invoke different levels of objection – subsidizing court fees in the new forum is not the same as compelling randomly selected parties to litigate their cases in that forum; although even the latter method can be defended in certain contexts.[28]

THE "HOW MANY?" QUESTION

Having drawn an analytical map for pluralist institutional design, described its moral underpinnings, and identified some of its central practical challenges, I return to the question in the title of this chapter. By now, it should be clear that we are not likely to reach a conclusive answer. But could we perhaps identify conditions in which the alternatives provided are too few or too many to accomplish the pluralist ideal? This sounds like a question mostly for poietic pluralists, since they are engaged in the creation and alteration of the institutional field and therefore have to decide on the contours of their design. Mimetic pluralists, on the other hand, are supposed to track existing conditions, and so should ostensibly be indifferent to numbers, once the sphere of pluralist accommodation has been chosen. But this is, of course, not the case in reality. While poietic projects confront the "how many?" question as a matter of logical necessity, mimetic projects do so as a matter of pragmatic means-end calculation, given limited resources of governmental accommodation.

In *poietic* projects centered on choice and diversity, institutional designers will have to take account of our knowledge of how people choose and how choice mechanisms can be tweaked and biased through strategic design of the supply side. Thus, for example, we know that in some contexts, the availability of many alternatives may numb the skills of deliberate choice:[29] the resources required to understand and evaluate the multiple alternatives may become prohibitive, leading to a reinforcement of the status quo and in fact inhibiting exit, experimentation, and effective choice. At the same time, allowing choice between just two options can lead to a flattening of the choice experience, framing it as a binary juxtaposition with stakes seeming higher than what they actually are. Inserting additional alternatives, especially ones framed as in between, can significantly shift individuals' choices.[30] An illuminating analogy can be drawn from party-system politics, with the extensively

[28] I survey justifications for randomized case allocation in Ori Aronson, *Forum by Coin Flip: A Random Allocation Model for Jurisdictional Overlap*, 45 Seton Hall L. Rev. 63, 90–100 (2015).

[29] See, e.g., Barry Schwartz, Paradox of Choice: Why More Is Less (2005); Sheena Iyengar, Art of Choosing (2011).

[30] See, e.g., Amos Tversky & Itamar Simonson, *Context-Dependent Preferences*, 39 Management Science 1179 (1993).

studied tradeoffs between two- and multiparty systems, including their effects on voter choice.[31]

In mimetic projects centered on recognition and accommodation, institutional designers will have to engage in setting thresholds and determining variables. How large, old, or prevalent should a group or a practice be, in order to qualify for pluralist accommodation in state institutions? Subjective claims of distinctness will not do: although such a criterion simplifies the screening process, it could lead to an overflow of claims for inclusion in the institutional scheme. So an objective, non-discriminatory method has to be devised, and it has to be one that does not end up entrenching an existing distribution of cultural or political capital. Such a system could, for example, begin from accommodating a set number of prominent groups, but include a guaranteed mechanism for adding or rotating more members down the road, in a process not controlled by the original inductees.[32]

Under either paradigm, a mechanism for tracking pluralist effectiveness has to be devised: Are the challenges of dynamism and convergence met? Here modes of experimentalism, destabilization,[33] and revision[34] are to be instituted in order to allow for defunct institutions to be abandoned, newly needed ones to be introduced, and variations to be reworked. In addition, designing institutions that are optimally disparate, and so as to allow difference and choice to coexist peacefully, can also raise concerns as to the effects on notions of political community, civic engagement, and democratic deliberation – all concepts that assume some degree of shared public space. Clearly these are not anti-pluralist concepts, as they all rely on difference to enrich and inform the social dynamics they support. But they do require exposing this project to additional levels of normative inquiry. The process of pluralist institutional design thus entails a host of problems that are beyond the scope of the current chapter, but I hope that they become more readily accessible thanks to the analytical framework it has laid out.

[31] E.g., AREND LIJPHART, ELECTORAL SYSTEMS AND PARTY SYSTEMS: A STUDY OF TWENTY-SEVEN DEMOCRACIES, 1945–1990, 57–77 (1995).

[32] Compare, for example, with the process of ascension into the EU or with membership in the UN Security Council.

[33] See Charles F. Sabel & William H. Simon, *Destabilization Rights: How Public Law Litigation Succeeds*, 117 HARV. L. REV. 1015 (2004).

[34] See Thomas Jefferson, *Reform of the Virginia Constitution: Letter to Samuel Kercheval* (Jul. 12, 1816), www.constitution.org/tj/ltr/1816/ltr_18160712_kercheval.html.

10

Equality in Religious Schools: The *JFS* Case Reconsidered

Haim Shapira

INTRODUCTION

Education has become a battlefield on which different religious and nonreligious worldviews are fighting each other. One may discern two contexts in which these conflicts occur: that of public schools, which are intended to serve the general heterogeneous community, and that of parochial faith schools, which are meant to serve specific religious communities. In the former case, the challenge of the schools is to serve the general community and at the same time respect religious diversity in it. It is common wisdom that the key principle in addressing this challenge is neutrality. Public schools intended for the general community must remain neutral with respect to religion, enabling teachers and students from different religious backgrounds, as well as nonreligious ones, to study together freely and equally. Conflicts in this context arise when individuals feel that neutrality has been violated and their religious freedom infringed upon.[1]

In the latter context, the challenge of faith schools is to serve a specific religious community and at the same time respect general state norms. Faith schools are not committed to neutrality, but identified with a specific religion.[2] State recognition

[1] The question of what is exactly neutrality in this context and when it is violated is not a simple one, and different jurisdictions relate to it in different ways. For a review of the American approach, see KENT GREENAWALT, RELIGION AND THE CONSTITUTION VOL. 2 (2008) 103–56. The European approach is diverse, and different countries have their own approaches. One can find an illustration of this pluralism in the decision of the European Court of Human Rights allowing Italy to put crucifixes in school classrooms; see Lautsi and Others v. Italy, no. 30814/06 (Mar. 18, 2011). See in this regard, Lorenzo Zucca, *Lautsi: A Commentary on a Decision by the ECtHR Grand Chamber*, 11 INT'L. J. CONSTIT. L. 218–29 (2013). For a review of some European models, see MYRIAM HUNTER-HENIN, LAW, RELIGIOUS FREEDOMS AND EDUCATION IN EUROPE (2011).

[2] The level of religiosity of faith schools varies. The religious identity of some faith schools is mainly nominal or symbolic, and their curriculum and educational program are neutral. The religious identity of other faith schools is more significant, and their curriculum and educational program are designed accordingly. These schools are designated to serve a given religious community and prefer

of such schools is based on the right of individuals to religious freedom and on the right to education, which includes the right of parents to determine the kind of education they would like to grant their children. For religious communities, education is an essential vehicle to pass their heritage to future generations, cultivate their unique way of life, and maintain their identity. In this context, religious freedom is manifested in the right to be associated with religion. Imposing neutrality on faith schools would violate their right to religious freedom. Nevertheless, schools of this type must also comply with state norms, including equality and antidiscrimination laws. Conflicts in the context of faith schools arise when individuals, students, or teachers feel that they have been discriminated against on various grounds by school policy. In most cases, the school argues that the divergent treatment is the result of the religious policy of the school. When such conflicts reach the courts, a clash ensues between equality and the right to religious freedom. Judicial intervention protecting these individuals may undermine the religious freedom of the school, but abstaining from intervention may ignore individuals' right to equality.[3]

In this chapter, I address the problem of equality in religious schools, with special reference to judicial intervention in related conflicts. To this end, I investigate the Jews' Free School (*JFS*) case decided by the Supreme Court of the United Kingdom in 2009,[4] involving a Jewish school that refused to admit a child on grounds that he was not Jewish. The child's father sued the school for racial discrimination. The Supreme Court decided in favor of the child and declared that the school admission policy, based on Jewish law criteria of Jewishness, was discriminatory on racial grounds and therefore unlawful. This dramatic decision was tantamount to accusing the JFS, an old and important Jewish school in London, the Chief Rabbi of the United Kingdom, who guided the school, and by implication the Jewish religion as a whole, of racism. The case exceeds the Jewish context because it marks a new judicial policy of intervention in religious life.

The case has been discussed in detail by Christopher McCrudden, with a focus on the history of the British legal system.[5] He situated the case within two broader debates. The first concerns the treatment of minority groups and multiculturalism.

admitting students from a specific religious background. The discussion in this chapter focuses on faith schools of the latter type.

3 There is no necessary correspondence between the neutral-religious and the public-private distinctions. Such a correspondence exists in the United States, where as a result of the Establishment Clause every public school must be neutral, and every religious school must therefore be private. This is not the situation in other countries, including the United Kingdom, where there are both faith and non-faith state schools.

4 R (on the application of E) v. Governing Body of JFS and the Admissions Appeal Panel of JFS and others (2009) UKSC 15.

5 See Christopher McCrudden, *Multiculturalism, Freedom of Religion, Equality, and the British Constitution: The JFS Case Considered*, 9 INT'L J. CONSTIT. LAW 200–29 (2011). See also the discussion in this volume by Peter G. Danchin.

According to him, the *JFS* case represents a new phase of "post-multiculturalism," starting at the beginning of the twenty-first century, characterized by intervention of the courts in ethno-religious practices, which they scrutinize in light of liberal values. The second debate pertains to the shifting approaches to "constitutionalism." With the arrival of the European Convention on Human Rights and EU law, the United Kingdom has seen a shift away from a pragmatic approach to constitutional thinking toward one that allows the judiciary to expand greatly its role in protecting individual rights. In the current critical analysis of the *JFS* decision, I pursue two objectives: to refute the court determination that the JFS admission policy, based on Jewish law, was discriminatory on racial grounds, and to draw some conclusions regarding the general question of judicial intervention in cases of conflict between equality and religious freedom in religious schools.

THE PROBLEM IN ITS LEGAL CONTEXT

JFS, formerly known as the Jews' Free School, is a Jewish school in London, maintained by local authorities and supported by public funds (formally: a voluntary aided school). The school was recognized as a faith school, and it declares itself to be a follower of Orthodox Judaism, accepting its worldview and practices. The school also declares that it admits students from all other branches of Judaism, such as the Masorti (traditional), Reform, and Liberal. The school has a long and distinguished history that can be traced back to 1732. It is reputed to be highly successful and is in great demand, so that the number of applicants exceeds the number of available places. The school admission policy gave preference to students who were defined as Jewish according to Jewish law (*halakha*), as determined by the Office of the Chief Rabbi (OCR). Because the school was in a constant state of oversubscription, in practice it accepted only students who met this definition.[6]

M was a child born of a Jewish father and a mother of Italian Roman Catholic descent who converted to Judaism under the auspice of the Masorti synagogue. The OCR did not recognize M's mother's conversion, JFS did not recognize the child as Jewish, and the school refused to admit him. M's father sued the school, claiming that the school rejected his child on ethnic grounds, and thus it discriminated against him unlawfully. Conversely, the school argued that the boy had been rejected on religious grounds, which is permitted by law.

To understand the judicial decisions, we must first introduce the legal framework. The Equality Act of 2006 prohibits discrimination against students on religious grounds, but it includes an exception by which the prohibition does not apply

[6] According to British law, a faith school may prefer religious students only if it is oversubscribed. In case of under-registration, it must accept every student, regardless of religion.

to faith schools, which are allowed to discriminate on religious grounds in their admission policy. Regulations issued under the Equality Act state that for this purpose the school is at liberty to determine the student's religious identity. The Race Relations Act of 1976 (RRA) prohibits discrimination on the basis of race and does not exempt faith schools, which are therefore not permitted to discriminate against students on racial grounds in their admission policy. The RRA defines "racial" as one of the following grounds: color, race, nationality, and ethnic or national origin. The conclusion from these two statutes is that JFS, being a faith school, is allowed to discriminate on religious but not on ethnic grounds.

How does British law define discrimination? The RRA distinguishes between direct and indirect discrimination. A person directly discriminates against another when he treats the other less favorably on racial grounds.[7] By contrast, a person discriminates against another indirectly if he discriminates on the basis of other criteria, which are applied equally to persons of different racial groups but result in racial discrimination.[8] This distinction corresponds to the American distinction between disparate treatment and disparate impact. But in contrast with American law (and laws of other countries as well), where a person complaining of disparate treatment (or direct discrimination) must show that the defendant intended to discriminate on racial grounds, according to the British approach direct discrimination does not depend on discriminatory intent, but on the objective criteria that were applied. Furthermore, direct discrimination cannot be justified under any circumstances. Indirect discrimination is different in these two aspects: it does not depend on the criteria that were applied (including intent), and it can be justified. Indirect discrimination is determined through a two-step decision. First, does the contested policy have an adverse effect on a certain racial or ethnic group? Second, can it be justified in light of legitimate aims (applying proportionality tests)? An affirmative answer to the former question and a negative one to the latter constitute indirect discrimination.

The claimant, M's father, argued that the school did not admit his son because his mother was of Italian ethnic origin. Had she been Jewish, he would have been admitted. Although if she had converted to Judaism under the supervision of the OCR, she would have been considered Jewish and M would have been admitted, this requirement also resulted from the fact she was not of Jewish origin. Had she been Jewish, she would not have been required to convert. JFS treated M less favorably on grounds of ethnic origin and therefore engaged in direct discrimination on racial grounds. Alternatively, according to the claimant, the policy was indirectly discriminatory against the group of students whose mothers were not of Jewish origin.

7 RRA, Para. 1(1) (a). Racial grounds include all the grounds mentioned previously, and in particular for this case, ethnic origin.

8 RRA, Para. 1 (1) (b) and (1A).

In response, JFS argued that it applied criteria that determine Jewish religious identity according to halakha. It is in accordance with law for JFS, as a faith school, to prefer Jewish applicants, and it is the prerogative of the school to determine who is Jewish. M was not admitted to the school because he was not religiously Jewish. Had M's mother undergone a valid conversion, recognized by the OCR, she would have been considered Jewish, and so would her child, despite her Italian ethnic origin. It is therefore a not a matter of ethnic but of religious identity. JFS did not engage in discrimination on grounds of ethnic origin, directly or indirectly.

The heart of the problem was in the fact, acknowledged by all parties, that Jewish identity is at the same time ethnic and religious. All parties accepted that in its admission policy JFS engaged in discrimination on religious grounds, which was within the exemption granted to faith schools, and therefore lawful. The case was fought around the question of whether the school also discriminated on ethnic grounds.

The High Court rejected both claims of the father and accepted the arguments of JFS. The father went to the Court of Appeals, which unanimously reversed the High Court decision, holding that JFS discriminated directly against M on grounds of ethnic origin. JFS appealed to the Supreme Court, and the case was decided on December 2009 by a panel of nine justices, which dismissed the appeal of JFS. The decision on the issue of direct discrimination was by a majority of five[9] to four.[10] The majority decided that JFS engaged in direct discrimination against M on grounds of ethnic origin. Two justices of the minority, while exonerating JFS from direct discrimination, held that it was engaged in indirect discrimination against M.[11] Only two justices[12] held that the JFS admission policy was lawful.

The decision of the court did not depend on the fact that JFS was funded by the state. Had it been a private school, fully funded by parents, the result would have been the same. The court based its decision on the prohibition against racial discrimination in the RRA, which applies to individuals and organizations regardless of their ties to the state. The following discussion focuses on the decision of the Supreme Court.

THE SUPREME COURT DECISION: A CASE OF RACIAL DISCRIMINATION

The court first established the legal framework and held that direct discrimination is decided by the objective criteria that were applied in practice, and not by the subjective intent of the discriminator. The court cited a series of previous decisions that

9 Lord Phillips, Lady Hale, Lords Mance, Kerr, and Clarke.

10 Lords Hope, Rodger, Walker, and Brown.

11 Hope and Walker.

12 Rodger and Brown.

established this doctrine and reaffirmed it,[13] and based on this legal tradition, it drew yet another conclusion, namely that British law does not recognize any justification for direct discrimination. A policy that is directly discriminatory by its criteria is unlawful, regardless of any legitimate purpose or need to redress a social or historic situation. Lady Hale described it as "a model of formal equality."[14] After establishing this doctrine, the court turned to the main question of the case: the ground on which M was refused admission, or in more general terms, the objective criteria on which the JFS admission policy was based. It was clear and agreed that the school applied the criteria of Jewish law that define Jewishness. According to Jewish law, a person is a Jew if he or she was born of a Jewish mother or has converted to Judaism. The mother's Jewishness is determined in the same way. The court called this the "matrilineal test." M's father argued that the matrilineal test is clearly of ethnic origin, whereas JFS argued that it determines Jewish religious membership.

To explain this argument, JFS argued that one must distinguish between two different categories: "ethnically Jewish" and "religiously Jewish." Although there is some overlap between them, the two are not identical. Most Jews belong to both categories, but some belong to one but not to the other. The criteria by which one determines each category are different. For the criteria by which one determines Jewish ethnic identity, JFS was relying on a previous decision of the House of Lords, in the case of *Mandla v. Dowel-Lee*,[15] where the House of Lords held that Sikhs are an ethnic group. The House of Lords emphasized that ethnicity should not be determined by a biological approach, but by a sociological and anthropological one (in other words, a cultural one). Lord Frazer mentioned seven criteria by which one can identify an ethnic group, such as shared history, common culture, common language, and so on.[16] JFS asserted that these criteria define who is ethnically Jewish.

[13] The leading case on direct discrimination is R v. Birmingham City Council, ex p Equal Opportunities Commission (1989)1 AC 1155. The city council of Birmingham did not intend to discriminate between boys and girls, but in practice there were more grammar school places for boys than for girls. The result was that girls had to perform better than boys on the entrance examination to secure a place. The House of Lords found the city guilty of direct discrimination on grounds of sex. A second case that followed this doctrine was James v. Eastleigh Borough Council (1990) 2 AC 751, where the council exempted women over the age of sixty from entrance fees to city facilities, whereas men were exempted only from age sixty-five. The purpose for the policy was to exempt people of pensionable age, but the House of Lords decided by majority that the policy was directly discriminatory on grounds of sex. The court in the *JFS* case reaffirmed this controversial decision.

[14] Paras. 59, 67.

[15] Mandla v. Dowell Lee (1983) 2 AC 548.

[16] Frazer (p. 562) mentioned seven characteristics: (a) a long shared history; (b) a cultural tradition of its own; (c) a common geographic origin or descent; (d) a common language; (e) a common literature, peculiar to the group; (f) a common religion, different from that of neighboring groups or from the general community surrounding it; and (g) being a minority or an oppressed or dominant group within a larger community. A group that shares some of these characteristics is considered an ethnic group.

Conversely, the criteria established by halakha define who is religiously Jewish. Some people are ethnically Jewish, but not religiously. M is an example of such a person. He meets most of the characteristics of the Jewish ethnic group, if not all, but he does not meet the halakhic criteria, and therefore he is not religiously Jewish. Some Jews do not share any cultural or religious characteristics with other Jews, and therefore are not part of the Jewish ethnic group, but they meet the halakhic standards, and therefore they are religiously Jewish. In applying the criteria required by Jewish law, JFS identified those applicants who were religiously Jewish. M was refused admission because he was not religiously Jewish.

The justices of the majority rejected JFS's argument on the grounds that the distinction suggested by the school was based on the purpose of discrimination and not on the factual criterion being applied. The court accepted that the purpose of the discrimination was indeed religious. There was unanimous agreement that JFS and the Chief Rabbi did not intend to discriminate on racial or ethnic grounds. But the court held that purpose and intent are irrelevant for determining direct discrimination. The criterion that was applied in this case was the matrilineal test, which the court held was by nature a test of ethnic origin and therefore constitutes direct discrimination on ethnic grounds. The fact that if M's mother had converted to Judaism in a procedure recognized by the OCR she would have been deemed Jewish did not change the outcome, because the court held that it was also related to M's mother and therefore part of the criteria of determining M's ethnic origin. The court concluded that M received less favorable treatment only because of his ethnic origin, which constituted direct discrimination on racial grounds.

The minority of four justices accepted the school's argument and determined that JFS should not be held responsible for direct discrimination on ethnic grounds. Lord Hope expressed the view that although direct discrimination should be decided based on objective criteria, in some cases intent may be relevant, as, for example, where the factual criteria are unknown and in order to identify them, the court must explore the mental process and intent of the discriminator. The majority agreed with this argument. But according to Hope, intent is also relevant when the question is how to categorize the criteria. In the case at hand, the criteria are known, but the question is how to categorize them. Are they ethnic or religious? For Hope, it was not clear that the criteria applied by JFS were of ethnic origin. The purpose of the school and of the Chief Rabbi, who guided it, was religious; therefore, the criteria should be categorized as such.

Two of the minority justices, Lords Hope and Walker, ruled that JFS engaged in indirect discrimination.[17] Applying the two-step decision, the judges found, first, that the JFS admission policy placed children of M's ethnic group (those whose

[17] Paras 205–15 (Hope), 235–37 (Walker).

mother is not Jewish) at a disadvantage; second, that the question of whether such a policy could be justified by legitimate aims was answered in the affirmative. The educational and religious objectives of JFS, as a Jewish faith school, are legitimate aims that may justify discrimination of effect against some racial groups. But the school failed to asses this effect and consider alternative ways to reduce or eliminate adverse effects on this racial group. Hope suggested that the school should accept also students who are recognized as Jewish by other branches of Judaism, such as the Masorti and the Reform, who go to JFS.[18] Because the school failed the proportionality test, it was guilty of indirect discrimination on racial grounds.

Only two justices, Lords Rodger and Brown, held that the admission policy of the school was lawful. Rodger stated that the purpose of faith schools was their religious character. Such schools are allowed by law to grant preference to applicants from their religion, and they are at liberty to decide which applicants belong to their religion. The JFS admission policy followed this legal framework. The decision of the majority to interfere with Jewish religious criteria, he said, "leads to extraordinary results and produces such manifest discrimination against Jewish faith schools in comparison to other faith schools, that one can't help feeling that something has gone wrong."[19] Brown asked simply: "Can a Jewish faith school ever give preference to those who are members of Jewish religion under Jewish law?" and answered in the affirmative,[20] leading to the conclusion that JFS did not engage in indirect discrimination. It was completely legitimate to prefer applicants who were Jewish under Jewish law according to the OCR interpretation. The suggestion that the school should endorse the criteria of other branches of Judaism would undermine its character as an Orthodox Jewish faith school. These strong views remained in the minority, however. The discussion next focuses on the court decision and the majority opinions.

EVALUATING THE COURT DECISION: RELIGIOUS FREEDOM PERSPECTIVE

Although the case was addressed by the court as a discrimination case, its implications are beyond this realm. In order to assess these, we explore the court decision from the perspective of freedom of religion. Let us begin with what may be called the expressive dimension. The decision that the JFS admission policy, which was based on Jewish law, was discriminatory on racial grounds implies that the school administration and the Chief Rabbi, who guided it, committed an act of racism. It

[18] Para. 212.
[19] Para. 226.
[20] Para. 249.

implies also that Judaism uses racist criteria for determining religious membership. This is not the type of decision that courts reach every day. The court was troubled by this outcome, and several justices tried to explain why reaching such conclusions would be a mistake. Lord Phillips, the court president, opened his judgment as follows: "Nothing that I say in this judgment should be read as giving rise to criticism on moral grounds of the admissions policy of JFS in particular or the policies of Jewish faith schools in general, let alone as suggesting that these policies are 'racist' as that word is generally understood."[21]

Phillips distinguished here between legal and moral responsibility. The judgment determined the legal responsibility of JFS, but it should not be read as "criticism on moral grounds." The basis for this distinction was articulated by Lord Kerr: "One can have sympathy with the school authorities in their wish to pursue what must have seemed to them an entirely legitimate religious objective. It is plain that the Chief Rabbi and the governors of JFS are entirely free from any moral blame."[22] This is because the school authorities did not intend to discriminate on racial grounds, but rather on religious ones. Under this interpretation, it appears that the point on which the majority insisted, namely that direct discrimination should be decided based on objective criteria and not on intent, is restricted to the legal aspect, whereas from the moral perspective the decisive element is intent. In other words, the JFS policy is condemned as discriminatory only legally, but morally it can be justified.

This conclusion seems far removed from the text of the majority opinions, however. The justices do not express any serious reservation with regard to the antidiscrimination law, and the impression is that they endorse it as the correct doctrine. Their statements, therefore, should not be understood as a justification of the school or of the Chief Rabbi. They only show "sympathy" for them, meaning that the justices understood that they did not intend to discriminate on racial grounds and were not aware of the meaning of their actions. But the verdict that the JFS policy was discriminatory is valid both legally and morally. At the same time, the need of the justices to clarify their decision and limit its moral and social implications illustrates the problematic nature of the judgment, even from their own point of view.

The *JFS* case raises important questions regarding freedom of religion. Does a child, as part of his religious freedom, have a right to be admitted to the faith school he chooses? Does a faith school have a right to determine who is a member of its religion and give him or her preference in admission policy? Which of these conflicting rights takes precedence? The court did not consider the issue from this perspective and did not try to balance equality with religious freedom, because of the legal framework within which the court addressed the case. Had the court dealt with

[21] Para. 9. See also Paras. 54 (Hale), 124 (Kerr), and 156 (Clarke).
[22] Para. 124.

the case at the constitutional level, by referring to the Human Rights Act of 1998 and to the European Convention of Human Rights, equality would have been balanced (or at least considered) with religious freedom, because discrimination under ECHR Article 14 may be justified if it is necessary to protect the rights and freedoms of others. The court, however, scrutinized the case in light of antidiscrimination legislation, and the RRA does not require such balancing. To the contrary, the court held that direct discrimination cannot be justified, and therefore did not consider and did not balance equality with religious freedom or other rights and interests. From a constitutional perspective, balancing is possible and maybe even required, whereas from a statuary perspective, balancing is not permitted.[23] But when speculating on the case and evaluating the court decision, it is appropriate to consider its effect on freedom of religion.

It is possible to discern different sub-rights and aspects of religious freedom. One is the individual right to freedom of religion, at the core of which is the right to hold a certain belief and to be identified with a certain religion. This core meaning refers to the internal world and identity of a person. Another aspect of the individual right is the right to manifest one's religion in various ways. This aspect refers to acts in the external world. Both aspects are included in ECHR Art. 9 (1).[24] According to Art. 9 (2), the right to hold a belief and identify with a religion is absolute and cannot be infringed or limited in any circumstances, but the right to manifest religion may be subject to limitations under specific terms.[25] Another sub-right is the associational right to freedom of religion. Religious activities are usually conducted in community with others and within the framework of religious organizations. The associational right to freedom of religion is the right of individuals to associate with others for religious purposes and to become members of religious organizations. This sub-right is also mentioned in ECHR Art. 9 (1).[26]

But the associational right includes more than this. Religious organizations, such as churches, mosques, synagogues, religious schools, charity organizations, and so on, have their own rules of operation. These rules, or some of them, are conceived by believers as being sacred, even divine. The operation of religious organizations according to their rules is thus part of the religious activity and deserves protection

[23] See McCrudden, *Multiculturalism*, 215.

[24] "Everyone has the right to freedom of thought, conscience and religion; this right includes freedom to change his religion or belief and freedom, either alone or in community with others and in public or private, to manifest his religion or belief, in worship, teaching, practice and observance." A similar formulation is found in the Universal Declaration of Human Rights 1948, Art. 18.

[25] "Freedom to manifest one's religion or beliefs shall be subject only to such limitations as are prescribed by law and are necessary in a democratic society in the interests of public safety, for the protection of public order, health or morals, or for the protection of the rights and freedoms of others." This subsection has no parallel in the UDHR.

[26] "Either alone or in community with others and in public or private."

under religious freedom. Courts worldwide have recognized the right of religious organizations to independence or autonomy and consider this part of the right to religious freedom. The individual right and the associational right to religious freedom are part of what Americans call "free exercise." There is yet another sub-right that may be called "freedom from religion," which can also be seen as part of the individual's right to religious freedom. If a person has a right to be identified with a certain religion, he *ipso facto* has a right not to be coerced to partake in other religious activities than those with which he identifies. This right is also applicable when it comes to religion being forced on nonreligious people. Atheists and nonreligious people have, as part of their religious freedom, a right not to be coerced to partake in any religious activity. In the American context, this aspect is addressed under the Establishment Clause,[27] which naturally is broader than this aspect and reflects the principle of state neutrality toward religion. But for the purposes of this discussion, there is no need to explore the meaning and scope of this neutrality. As is well known, views with regard to this principle differ, and different countries endorse different approaches.

To examine the *JFS* decision in light of religious freedom, we must bear in mind that the decision was aimed at the JFS admission policy, which was based on halakhic membership criteria, as interpreted by the Chief Rabbi of the United Kingdom. The court was aware of the fact that this halakhic criterion is central to the Jewish religion instructed by official authority. Phillips opened his judgment with a citation from the book of Deuteronomy, which he presented as the source for the matrilineal principle and described as "a fundamental tenet of Jewish religion."[28] The determination that the JFS admission policy is discriminatory on racial grounds implies that this is also true of this fundamental Jewish tenet. Already at this point, one may wonder if we are witnessing an attack on the Jewish faith, this time in the name of human rights and equality. Naturally, this was not the intention of the court, but the decisions of the court are not to be judged by their intent, but by their implications and consequences.

The court declared that it did not contest the privilege of the school, as a faith school, to give preference to Jewish over non-Jewish applicants, but it disqualified the Orthodox criteria that are based on the matrilineal test. The court noted that the decision should be of a concern to all Jewish faith schools,[29] but in practice,

[27] See, for example, GREENAWALT, RELIGION, 1–16.

[28] Para. 2. Phillips's presentation follows the Jewish tradition and describes correctly the halakhic criteria of Jewishness in the past two millennia. Some historians believe that this doctrine was not valid in the biblical period and formulated only after the destruction of the Second Temple (70 CE), before which descent was patrilineal rather than matrilineal; see S. J. D. COHEN, BEGINNINGS OF JEWISHNESS (1999) 263–307.

[29] Para. 7.

it reaches far beyond that. All streams and movements of Judaism in Britain and elsewhere, including Orthodox, Masorti, Reform, and Liberal, share the fundamental principle that Jewish identity is defined by two (alternative) elements, descent, and conversion.[30] The differences between the various streams concern the details of these principles. For example, according to Orthodox halakha, descent is determined by the mother, whereas, according to Reform practice, it can be determined by either parent. Similarly, with regard to conversion, every stream sets its own terms for conversion. The Supreme Court was aware of these facts. Its ruling implies that any test of religious membership that is based on descent is by definition a test of ethnic origin and therefore discriminatory on racial grounds. That does not leave any Jewish organization free to manifest its own self-perception and self-definition of Jewishness.

The court ruling is not confined to schools, but includes other educational institutions, charity organizations, and perhaps even synagogues. Its ramifications can reach the absurd. Under the court's reasoning, it is difficult to see how synagogues could limit membership to Jews. If the definition of a Jew according to every Jewish synagogue depends on descent and conversion, and this can be deemed as a test of ethnic origin, given that purpose is irrelevant for the matter, a synagogue that applied this test would be engaging in direct discrimination on racial grounds.

From the perspective of religious freedom, the court decision interferes first and foremost with the associational right to religious freedom. It interferes with the autonomy of the school to create the proper educational and religious environment based on its religious beliefs, specifically, to accept students who are Jewish according to the religious rules that the school endorses. But the decision also interferes with the individual right to manifest religion. According to ECHR Art. 9 (1), this includes the right "to manifest [one's] religion or belief, in worship, teaching, practice and observance." An important part of the curriculum of every Jewish school is the teaching of Torah and Jewish studies in general. This act of learning is a religious commandment known as *talmud Torah* (Torah study). Some Jews wish to teach and learn Torah as a religious activity, in a community of Jews only.[31] This is no doubt their right as part of the individual right to manifest religion. For this purpose, the

30 See, for example, the words of Rabbi Tony Bayfield, the head of the movement for Reform Judaism: "all Jewish institutions worldwide – as far as I know – would say that Jewish identity is determined by either descent or conversion" (cited by Phillips, Para. 40; other justices also mention these common grounds of Judaism).

31 There are different views in the Jewish tradition on whether the act of Torah study is permitted to a non-Jew and whether a Jewish teacher is allowed to teach Torah to non-Jews. Some authoritative sources provide a formal prohibition against such teaching, whereas others permit and even praise it. See Babylonian Talmud, Hagiga 13a, Sanhedrin 59a; Maimonides, *Laws of Kings* 10, 9.

relevant definition of Jewishness is the one that is consistent with halakha. The court decision interferes with this right.

In addition to freedom of religion, we must consider also the right to education, which includes the right of parents to choose the kind of education their children will receive. Article 2 of the First Protocol to the ECHR emphasizes the right of parents to ensure that the education their children receive conforms with their religious conviction.[32] The decision in *JFS* interferes with this right. As noted previously, the court did not consider the issue from the perspective of religious freedom or the right to education, and did not balance equality with these rights, because under the antidiscrimination law it was not required to do so. But there is yet another aspect of religious freedom that is germane here, from the perspective of antidiscrimination laws alone. The role of antidiscrimination laws was originally to safeguard minorities and their religious freedom. In the *JFS* case, however, antidiscrimination laws were used against the religious freedom of a minority and undermined its way of life. In his dissent opinion, Rodger pointed out that the court decision produces a manifest discrimination against Jewish faith schools in comparison to other faith schools, which can determine who belongs to their religion, whereas Jewish faith schools cannot.[33] Perhaps this was the reason why Hale raised the possibility of allowing discrimination in cases in which it is justified to redress the historic or social situation of a minority. She insisted, however, that such allowances must be made by Parliament.[34]

Although the court did not have to consider religious freedom, when we assess the decision of the court, we must take into consideration its outcome and implications. The implications of this decision for religious freedom are quite dramatic. The decision interferes with several aspects of the right to religious freedom, and not with respect to a marginal issue, but a "fundamental tenet" of Judaism. It interferes with the individual right of parents to manifest their religion, and it interferes with the associational right to religious freedom by not respecting the autonomy of faith schools and the authority of the Chief Rabbi in internal religious matters. It also interferes with the right to education, and, above and beyond, it taints the school, the Chief Rabbi, and Judaism in general with racism. We must assume that the court saw itself compelled to adjudicate in this way in light of the statutory framework and of British legal tradition in the area of discrimination law. We must also assume that the court understood the case to indeed reflect discrimination on ethnic grounds. The question is whether it was truly a case of discrimination on ethnic grounds and whether it was necessary to rule this way. If there was at least a

[32] Universal Declaration of Human Rights, Art. 26 (3). ECHR first protocol, Art. 2.

[33] Para. 226.

[34] Paras. 69–70.

possibility of conceptualizing the case in a different way, then the question is why the court preferred this way, which led to such difficult and severe implications.

ON THE NATURE OF RELIGIOUS MEMBERSHIP

The court decision was based on two main propositions. The first is that direct discrimination should be determined by the objective criterion being applied, and therefore intent is irrelevant. The second is that the objective criterion applied by JFS was the matrilineal test, which is by nature a test of ethnic origin. The conclusion derived from these two propositions is inescapable: the JFS admission policy was directly discriminatory on ethnic grounds and therefore unlawful. The minority argued that the court should take a less rigid approach to the first proposition, that in some cases – and the *JFS* case was one of them – the court should consider the purpose of the discrimination. This approach leads to a different assessment of the JFS admission policy (one aimed to achieve a religious purpose) and ultimately to a different result.

I believe that there are good reasons for preferring the minority opinion in this regard, and I will return to it later. At this point, I want to focus on the second proposition and argue that the majority was wrong in determining that the factual test applied in this case was the matrilineal one. The matrilineal test was only part of the factual test that was applied. Attention to all the criteria applied by JFS would change the conclusion that this was a test of ethnic origin.

JFS applied the membership criteria of Jewishness according to halakha. Two main criteria are tested: whether the person was born to a Jewish mother, and (alternatively) whether the person converted to Judaism following a valid procedure. Each of these criteria is sufficient to determine one's Jewishness. To appreciate the nature of these criteria, one must take into consideration both elements. The criterion relating to descent fits well with the determination of the court that it reflects ethnic origin, but conversion does not. First, it is clear that by any classification conversion is a religious procedure. It is conducted in a religious context, and it expresses the convert's identification with Jewish belief and practices. Second, conversion, unlike descent, is a matter of choice. The fact that conversion is a sufficient condition for determining Jewish religious identity means that descent is not a necessary condition for this purpose. At this point already, it is possible to state that Jewish membership does not depend on ethnic origin. Indeed, the problem with M was not his or his mother's ethnic origin, but her invalid conversion. In his dissenting opinion, Rodger pointed out this crucial fact:

> Faced with a boy whose mother had converted under Orthodox auspices, the governors would have considered him for admission without pausing for a single second to enquire whether he or his mother came from Rome, Brooklyn, Siberia or Buenos

> Aires, whether she had once been a Roman Catholic or a Muslim, or whether he or she came from a close-knit Jewish community or had chosen to assimilate and disappear into secular society.[35]

The majority justices did not overlook conversion, but argued that conversion is ultimately part of the matrilineal test. Hale said, "The fact that the Office of the Chief Rabbi would have overlooked his mother's Italian origins, had she converted to Judaism in a procedure which they would recognize, makes no difference because M was rejected, not because of who he is, but because of who his mother is."[36] Phillips added that, based on a statement of the Chief Rabbi, he came to the conclusion that conversion is not only becoming part of the Jewish faith, it is also becoming part of the Jewish people. In order to be considered Jewish, M must be the child of a Jewish mother. Her Jewishness is determined by birth or by conversion. In both ways she would be considered part of the Jewish ethnic group. Phillips argued that ultimately it was a test of ethnic origin.

But there is something missing in the argument of the two justices. Conversion is relevant not only for M's mother, but also for M himself. If he converted with the approval of the OCR, he would be considered Jewish. Contrary to Hale's opinion, M was rejected not (only) because of who his mother was, but because of who he was. M was not considered Jewish because he himself did not meet either of the two alternative terms of Jewishness, according to halakha. The fact that conversion is a sufficient condition for determining Jewishness is also sufficient to determine that Jewishness does not depend on ethnic origin. Ascribing the proper weight to conversion would have led the court to the conclusion that the objective criteria applied by JFS were not of ethnic, but of religious nature.

But the court regarded descent as the central criterion that overshadows conversion, and this is what troubled it. For the court, religious membership should be based on the individual's conscious identification with faith or, in other words, in his belief. Phillips stated, "Membership of a religion or faith normally indicates some degree of conscious affiliation with the religion or faith on the part of the member."[37] From this point of view, M, who was affiliated with Jewish faith, attended synagogue with his father and practiced many Jewish rituals, should be deemed Jewish. So how should the court explain his rejection by JFS? The only reason was that his mother was not Jewish according to Orthodox law. The court conceptualized the problem as a conflict between the child's religious identity (Jewish) and his ethnic origin (non-Jewish). Under this conceptualization, the halakhic criterion of Jewishness is one of ethnic nature. Descent fits well with this conceptualization, but not

35 Para. 230.
36 Para. 66.
37 Para. 44.

conversion; therefore, the court portrayed conversion as a secondary test and as part of the ethnic origin criterion.

The main problem with this, however, has to do with the premise that religious identity is an expression of the individual's identification with the beliefs and practices of a certain faith. This widespread understanding of religious membership is not at all universal. Jewish religious membership is based on being part of the Jewish people. According to Jewish tradition, God made a covenant with the Jewish people.[38] To be part of this covenant or to be a member of Jewish religion, a person must also be part of the Jewish people. Although one does not have to be born Jewish, one can become Jewish by conversion, which is a double process that makes the convert part of both the Jewish people and the Jewish religion. This concept of religious membership that is dependent on peoplehood was challenged by the Christian idea of the New Covenant. In contrast with the old covenant made with the Jewish people, the New Covenant does not depend on peoplehood, but is open for every individual who believes in the ministry of Jesus Christ: "There is neither Jew nor Greek, there is neither bond nor free, there is neither male nor female: for ye are all one in Christ Jesus."[39] The idea of the New Covenant shaped the Western conception of religion and religious membership. Assuming that religious membership must indicate a "conscious affiliation with the religion or faith on the part of the member," the court endorsed the Christian and even the Protestant conception of religion. This assumption was so strong that the court was not prepared to consider an alternative view of religious membership that depends on being part of a people, which is the Jewish conception of religious membership.

An illustration for this religious diversity regarding ethnicity can be found in a comment made by Hale made when she considered the possibility of allowing Jewish schools to adopt criteria required by religious law even if these are ethnically based: "As far as we know, no other faith schools in this country adopt descent-based criteria for admission … The Christian Church will admit children regardless of who their parents are."[40] This comment was made to demonstrate the unusual approach of Jewish faith schools and implicitly to question the need to take their demand into consideration. Hale then explained that maybe the Jews should not be blamed for this approach, because it is what enabled them to survive through centuries of persecutions and discrimination. The court could have been expected to look more deeply to this phenomenon and try to understand this unique approach of Judaism, which was not only and not mainly a means of survival and a shield against persecution, but reflects the fundamental perception of

[38] Phillips indicates this principle in Para. 2. See Exod. 19:5–6, Deut. 29:13–14 (and 28:69).

[39] Gal. 3:28.

[40] Para. 69.

Jewish identity as combination of peoplehood and religion. This approach is taken not only in Jewish schools' admission policies, but in every Jewish community and organization.

One could argue that, according to the British doctrine of direct discrimination, if religious membership depends on ethnic origin, it is disqualified as a criterion of discrimination. A faith school may discriminate in its admission policy only if it applies purely religious criteria, which means Christian criteria of faith. But if it applies Jewish criteria, which include ethnic origin, it is guilty of racial discrimination. This argument may be countered on two dimensions. On the dimension of equality and fairness, it is clear that this approach generates discrimination against Jews for their belief. We used to think that citizenship and legal rights do not depend on religious identity, but now, following the court decision, it turns out that Jews who do not share the same concept of religion do not enjoy the same religious freedom that others do.[41]

The other dimension is the rationale behind the distinction between religious and ethnic grounds. Why does the law allow faith schools to discriminate on religious grounds but not on racial or ethnic ones? The reason is that having faith schools entails allowing them to select suitable students and forge a community of students who are interested in the religious and educational goals of the school. The law does not allow discrimination on racial and ethnic grounds, first and foremost because race and ethnicity are considered irrelevant for religious identity. If they are irrelevant, there is no justification for discriminating on these grounds. Furthermore, race and ethnicity are a matter of fate, not a matter of choice. A student or family may choose their faith, but they cannot choose their race. From a liberal point of view, it is right to allow schools to select students by their religious identity, which is subject to individual choice, but not by racial or ethnic identity, which is not. In the context of Jewish identity, however, this rationale is not valid. The element of ethnicity or peoplehood is a part of religious membership, and therefore it is a relevant criterion exactly as is "pure" religious membership. Furthermore, being part of the Jewish people is not entirely a matter of fate, but also a matter of choice. It is a matter of fate in the sense that if a person was born Jewish, he is religiously Jewish. But it is also a matter of choice, because he can become Jewish – both ethnically and religiously – by his own choice. Conversion is a procedure in which a person becomes at the same time a member of the Jewish people and of the Jewish faith. A fair judgment that would respect Jewish self-perception of Jewishness should classify the halakhic criteria of Jewishness as religious and therefore as lawful.

41 See again Rodger's observation that the court decision produces "manifest discrimination against Jewish faith schools" (Para. 226).

CONCLUSION

The decision of the court in *JFS* is based on two foundations: the legal framework of antidiscrimination law in the United Kingdom, and the evaluation of the case at hand. Conclusions can be drawn at each of these levels. The relevant legal framework for our purpose is the doctrines of direct and indirect discrimination on racial grounds, and especially the former. This doctrine was established in the RRA 1976 and further developed by courts. It is characterized by two main features: first, direct discrimination is determined by the objective criteria that were applied in practice; and second, it is construed as demanding formal equality, which means that there is no defense or justification for discriminatory policy.

The first feature is unique to the United Kingdom. Contrary to the parallel doctrines in other countries, where direct discrimination depends on discriminatory intent, according to the British doctrine, intent is irrelevant; only the factual test that was applied is relevant. *JFS* and other cases mentioned in the judgment illustrate the problem inherent in this doctrine. The objective criteria do not say much about the purpose of the contested policy or about its results, and therefore whether it is right or wrong. In some cases, discriminatory criteria are applied without discriminatory intent and even with benevolent intent, producing beneficial results. The *James* case cited by the court[42] is an excellent example. A municipality sought to grant benefits to pensioners by exempting them from entrance fees to municipal facilities and established a rule that pensioners would enjoy this benefit at their pension age, women at sixty and men at sixty-five. The rule reflects a benevolent intent and was supposed to reach a just outcome. Those who reached pension age and deserved the benefit would enjoy it, while those who did not reach that age and therefore did not deserve it, would not. But according to the objective doctrine of direct discrimination, this rule was deemed discriminatory on the grounds of gender and therefore was declared unlawful by a majority ruling of the House of Lords. The outcome of this ruling is patently absurd. If there was discrimination in this case, it was already in the legislation that set different pension ages for men and women. If this discrepancy between the genders is justified and valid, it makes no sense to disqualify the municipal rule that merely follows in its steps and brings about just results under these circumstances.

The same is true in the *JFS* case. The law allows faith schools to discriminate in their admission policy on religious grounds, so they can prefer students who are interested in and are suitable for the school's religious and educational goals. Since the exception of faith schools is justified because of a legitimate purpose, it seems logical to scrutinize contested policy according to its purpose. All parties agreed

[42] James v. Eastleigh Borough Council.

that JFS did not intend to discriminate on ethnic grounds and that the purpose of the JFS policy was religious. If the *JFS* case was decided by its purpose, the court would justify the JFS admission policy. But, according to the "objective doctrine," purpose is irrelevant; what is relevant is the factual criteria that were applied. The objective doctrine was developed by the House of Lords and has been followed by other courts. Hypothetically, the Supreme Court could reverse it, but the justices appear to treat it with reverence and are unlikely to consider a change. The minority suggested a less rigid approach, taking into consideration intent in some cases, but the majority opposed it for reasons of consistency and loyalty to the legal tradition. Perhaps future courts will reconsider it, or it will remain a matter for Parliament to address. In any event, the doctrine of objective criteria appears flawed.

The second feature of the doctrine of direct discrimination is that it is a model of formal equality, which means it cannot be justified under any circumstances. The *JFS* case was decided under this premise. Hale said clearly: "If Parliament had adopted a different model of protection we would not be here today. Parliament might have adopted a model of substantive equality, allowing distinctions which brought historically disadvantaged groups up to the level of historically advantaged groups."[43] The debate on formal versus substantive equality is an old one, but still going on. Many studies in various areas of equality – race, gender, religion, and others – have showed the limitations of the formal equality approach.[44] The *JFS* case is a good example. Antidiscrimination laws were designated to protect religious and ethnic minorities from discrimination. But in the case of JFS, the application of antidiscrimination law has led to depriving the minority of its religious freedom. Formal equality has led to the discrimination of Jewish schools relative to other faith schools. Non-Jewish faith schools may apply religious criteria in their admission policy, but Jewish faith schools are not allowed to do so. The justices of the majority were aware of this kind of argument, but saw themselves compelled by the law to the model of formal equality. At the beginning of his judgment, Phillips wrote, "there may well be a defect in our law of discrimination. In contrast to the law of many countries, when English law forbids direct discrimination it provides no defense of justification."[45] The implication of "defect" is clear: it must be fixed. Hale was attentive to the requirements that "discrimination law should modify its rigid adherence to formal symmetry and recognize a greater range of justified departures than it does

[43] Para. 66.

[44] I won't mention here the immense literature, only a couple of relevant references. For religion, see Douglas Laycock, *Formal, Substantive, and Disaggregated Neutrality Toward Religion*, 39 DEPAUL L. REV. 993 (1990). For general discussion of formal versus substantive equality in different areas in the European Community and the United Kingdom, see Catherine Barnard & Bob Hepple, *Substantive Equality*, 59 CAMBRIDGE L. J. 562–85 (2000).

[45] Para. 9.

at present."[46] Both justices, however, assumed that it is for Parliament to change the doctrine, to craft some exemption, or recognize certain justifications.

We can also draw some conclusions about the decision in the specific case of *JFS*. I argued earlier that even under the British doctrine of direct discrimination, the court could reach a different result and determine that the JFS criteria were not ethnic, but religious. I also argued that the reason the court did not reach a different result was because of its conception of religious membership, which was influenced by Christian and especially Protestant ideas of religion. Beyond the circumstances of the case at hand, this outcome highlights the limitations of courts in understanding the motivations of parties that are culturally and religiously different. *JFS* was a relatively easy case. The parties involved were both part and parcel of British society, and they all identified with liberal values and the democratic regime. Chief Rabbi Lord Jonathan Sacks is regarded as a spiritual leader of great stature, who stands for the highest moral and human values. He is respected not only within his community, but in British society at large. And yet the policy he and JFS endorsed was accused of being racist. One can only speculate what the outcome would be if the practices being reviewed by the court were those of foreign religions, represented in the country by less prominent figures. The *JFS* decision reflects a lack of willingness on the part of the court to reflect on different ideas of religion and religious membership. It evinces a rigid legalism and lack of the flexible thinking necessary to adapt liberal principles to variable situations.

I believe that the *JFS* case can teach a valuable lesson in judicial intervention in religious schools and other religious organizations. It is clear that religious organizations are not immune from judicial review. It is also clear that religious freedom is not an absolute right and may be subject to other rights or to balancing against such rights. But the fact that courts have difficulty in understanding religious minorities and fail to accommodate them properly raises a red flag. In recent years, the pendulum has swung toward the pole of intensive judicial intervention, imposing liberal values on religious minorities on the account of their rights. It may be time to change this course and reinforce religious freedom and other minority rights.

[46] Para. 69.

11

Religious Freedom as a Technology of Modern Secular Governance

Peter G. Danchin

Two marks of a mature field of inquiry are that its central problems are well-formulated and that its conventional wisdom is sound. Even in the most mature fields, however, the conventional wisdom can sometimes be misleading, and the central problems poorly cast … Progress can be made only if much of the conventional wisdom is displaced, and its central questions are reframed.[1]

INTRODUCTION

The conventional wisdom in religious freedom discourse rests on two core tenets: first, that sovereign authority must be secular in order to ensure neutrality toward religion and thus the separation of religion and state that is foundational to liberal democracy (the *neutrality thesis*); and second, that in order to ensure neutrality toward both religion and non-religion, political and legal authority must guarantee the universal (human) right to freedom of religion, conscience, and belief, so that individuals and communities may practice their faith freely without coercion or interference (the *universality thesis*).

The thesis of this chapter is that these two tenets of the conventional wisdom must be discarded if we are to gain a better grasp of the salience and structure of the contemporary politics of religious freedom. Recent scholarship on secularism has made clear that the neutrality thesis is no longer tenable. Rather than withdraw from the religious domain, the modern secular state has been shown constantly to intervene and seek to reconfigure substantive features of religious life by distinguishing what is properly religious, in order to render certain practices indifferent to religious doctrine and thus bring them legitimately under the domain of civil law. The result has been the constant intertwining of religion and governance as modern secular power operates incessantly to determine the scope of religion in the political order.

[1] Jules L. Coleman, *Architecture of Jurisprudence*, 121 YALE L. J. 2, 5 (2011).

The universality thesis has been shown to be similarly untenable. In fields as disparate as legal anthropology and intellectual history, the idea that a universal right to religious freedom exists that is neutral toward religion or protects all religions equally is today broadly criticized. Rather, it is more accurate to say that the human right to religious freedom purports to treat all rights-holders equally. In this move, however, a seismic shift occurs in the relationship between notions of normativity and authority.

It is now the rational, autonomous human being, as opposed to heteronomous "religion," that is the proper subject of normativity. The individual, now as a matter of right, decides questions of religion, conscience, and belief. Religion is hereby reformulated in accordance with a distinctive normative model of religiosity: as privatized belief in a set of creedal propositions to which an autonomous individual gives assent. This generates the distinctive and unstable co-imbrication of conscience and autonomy as the buffered self simultaneously chooses autonomously and believes freely.[2]

The genius and enduring appeal of modern discourse rests on the fact that each thesis is defined in terms of the other. On the one hand, the neutrality of the political order is said to be secured by the guarantee to protect the universal right to religious liberty. In this move, the disciplinary structure and secular practices of the public sphere combine to produce the believing subject and concomitant post-Protestant conceptions of religion (especially in relation to Scripture and rituals) and religious subjectivity (especially as regards moral and ethical sensibilities). On the other hand, the universality of the right is said to be secured by the neutrality of the public sphere toward religion. This requires the state constantly either to recognize or limit claims regarding the manifestation of religious belief and practice, generating the distinctive entanglement of religion and law in different domains of the public and private spheres.

This double structure necessarily generates two interrelated paradoxes. First, by defining the secular neutrality of the public sphere in terms of the universal right to religious freedom, the authority of religion is privatized relative to state authority and its normativity interiorized relative to individual subjectivity. Second and as a result, religious freedom is secured through subordination of religion to the secular power and public reason of the sovereign state. By defining the meaning and scope of freedom protected by the right in terms of secular neutrality, the claims of individuals and communities to religious liberty are in fact limited through a continuing praxis of legal recognition and regulation.

2 See Peter Danchin, *Islam in the Secular Nomos of the European Court of Human Rights*, 32 MICH. J. INT'L L. 663, 708 ff. (2011).

The oscillating dialectic between secular neutrality and individual right defines how the right to religious freedom functions as a technology of secular governance and is integral to the power of the modern nation-state. This can be seen in three key areas: first, in the foundational distinction common to all contemporary formulations of the right between a *forum internum* on the one hand, defined as the locus of religious belief and conscience ostensibly protected absolutely by law, and a *forum externum* on the other, where the outward expression or manifestation of this belief is subject to state regulation; second, in debates concerning the proper subject of the right and whether this can include collective subjects and actually existing systems of religious law adhered to by both majority and minority religions; and third, in cases where conflicts of value arise between two or more claims internal to the right to religious liberty itself, i.e., where both sides to a dispute frame their arguments as a claim to religious freedom.

The argument in this chapter proceeds in two parts. The first part, Rival Genealogies, outlines the two dominant genealogies that underlie the modern structure of the right to religious liberty and its twin theses of neutrality and universality. The *Jews' Free School* Case[3] then illustrates the three themes discussed previously by considering the recent decision of the Supreme Court of the United Kingdom in *R (on the application of E) v. Governing Body of JFS* (the *JFS* or *Jews' Free School* case).[4] Finally, the Conclusion notes how, counterintuitively, the three issues concerning the conceptual structure, subject, and authority of the right cut across the Western and non-Western divide. It thus becomes clear that the right to religious freedom is not a single, stable principle existing outside culture, spatial geographies, or power, but instead is a contested, polyvalent concept existing and unfolding within historical political orders.

RIVAL GENEALOGIES OF RELIGIOUS FREEDOM

There is a common origin story told about religious liberty in European history, namely, that "it helped establish the basis of political secularism by separating religion from politics and making the state indifferent [or in today's language 'neutral'] to claims of religious truth."[5] On this view, "since its initial formulation in seventeenth-century political thought, religious liberty has continued progressively to expand its tolerant ambit to all religions far beyond its initial mandate to institute peace across Christian denominations."[6]

3 This section draws on the discussion in Peter G. Danchin & Louis Blond, Unlawful Religion? Modern Secular Power and the Legal Reasoning in the JFS Case, 29 *Md. J. Int'l L.* 414 (2014).

4 UKSC 15 (2009), 2 A.C. 728 (S.C.) (2010) (appeal taken from Eng.).

5 Saba Mahmood & Peter Danchin, *Politics of Religious Freedom: Contested Genealogies*, 113 South Atl. Q. 1, 2 (2014).

6 Mahmood & Danchin, *Politics of Religious Freedom.*

In recent scholarship, however, this narrative has been critically revisited to show how religious liberty in its earliest formulation in European history was in reality "an unsteady and unstable concept, the result of a 'circumstantial casuistry' of historically embedded political concepts," rather than a principled commitment to the separation of church and state."[7] Ian Hunter has argued that the "rival and incompatible conceptions of religious freedom that emerged in early modern Germany – both among the Christian confessions and then among them and the institutions of public law and politics – have proved inscrutable to both normative philosophical ordering and to sociohistorical reconciliation."[8] On the basis of their regional and contingent nature,

> the various philosophical attempts to ground religious liberty in transcendent principles – whether in Catholic and Protestant scholasticisms, Lockean and Kantian rationalisms, or Taylorean philosophical hermeneutics – have been unable to supersede the incompatibilities at the heart of these conceptions since their early history.[9]

The result is that the rights forms we see today embedded in constitutional and international human rights instruments derive from heterogeneous traditions and specific political projects. Accordingly, divergent genealogies coexist within the capacious language of religious freedom, always submerging or reemerging in new ways to refract the political conflicts of the day.

Following Hunter's work on civil and metaphysical philosophy in early modern Germany,[10] we can identify two main rival traditions internal to liberal thought, which remain deeply entangled in the normative structure and jurisprudence of the right to religious liberty as formulated in provisions such as Article 9 of the European Convention on Human Rights (ECHR).

Civil Philosophy and Secular Neutrality

In the first, older liberal tradition, the public sphere was understood in terms of social peace and religious liberty conceived in jurisdictional terms.[11] This early conception derived from a civil philosophy that sought to desacralize the state

[7] Mahmood & Danchin, *Politics of Religious Freedom.*

[8] Ian Hunter, *Religious Freedom in Early Modern Germany: Theology, Philosophy, and Legal Casuistry*, 113 SOUTH ATL. Q. 37, 39 (2014).

[9] Mahmood & Danchin, *Politics of Religious Freedom*, 2 n. 4.

[10] IAN HUNTER, RIVAL ENLIGHTENMENTS: CIVIL AND METAPHYSICAL PHILOSOPHY IN EARLY MODERN GERMANY (2001).

[11] Although this civil jurisdictional conception differed markedly from the older "Two Realms" or "Two Kingdoms" tradition of church–state separation under which all authority was viewed as ultimately

and led over time both to the churches losing their civil and political authority and to the gradual spiritualization of religion.[12] The goal of this double strategy was not to protect religious freedom as a natural right against the state, but to end religious civil war by establishing a "neutral" juristic mode of governance over a multi-confessional society as the means of maintaining a legally enforced toleration between rival religious communities. Central to this strategy was the notion of *adiaphora*: the old Stoic idea of actions that morality neither mandates nor forbids, which within Christianity was understood to refer to matters regarded as inessential to faith but nevertheless permissible for Christians or allowed in the Church.

On this basis, civil philosopher Christian Thomasius declared "virtually the entirety of the visible church – all of its liturgies, sacraments and theological doctrines – to be morally indifferent with regards to salvation," while at the same time holding that "forms of worship were a matter of 'Christian freedom' to be left to the disposition of individuals or groups to the extent they posed no threat to social peace."[13] The result was that "should any form of worship pose a threat to public peace then, as something morally indifferent, it was legitimately subject to the civil sovereign, who had absolute authority over all matters capable of threatening public order."[14] In this late seventeenth-century civil philosophy, we already see the core features of modern secular power: the statist drawing of a line between the religious and the secular through simultaneous demarcation of the essentially religious (held to be absolutely free from sovereign interference) from the religiously permissible (external manifestations of religiosity held to be publicly recognized, but subject to limitation by the state on grounds of public peace and order).[15]

How this occurred in practice, however, was infinitely varied, contested, and ultimately settled by local and contingent forms of negotiation and resolved, if at all, by legal casuistry and the coercive imposition of judgments within regional jurisdictions and national state-religion settlements. For this reason, the intellectual origins

derived from God and the only question was to demarcate what was properly God's and what was Caesar's.

12 Danchin, *Islam in the Secular Nomos*, 731, n. 2.

13 See Ian Hunter, *Religious Offences and Liberal Politics: From the Religious Settlements to Multicultural Society* (2005) 9 (https://espace.library.uq.edu.au/view/UQ:9933).

14 Hunter, *Religious Offences*, 9. This employed a "juridical-ecclesial category to narrow the array of doctrine and liturgy where salvation was at stake and to expand the array that could be regarded as soteriologically indifferent and hence to be seen not from a sacramental-religious standpoint but from a juridical-political one." Hunter, *Religious Freedom*, 56.

15 Again, it is important to observe that this strategy was *not* rights-based. Modern accounts of neutrality as an objective principle in modern constitutionalism thus refer to it as creating a kind of "subjectless right." Christoph Möllers, *Limits of Differentiation: On the Role of Religion in Democratic Constitutionalism*, presented at LAPA workshop, Oct. 2014.

and meaning of the idea of political neutrality in religious freedom discourse are to be found not in philosophical foundations, but in the horizon of "the religious, political and juridical casuistries spawned by the national religious settlements themselves."[16] As we shall see later, this remains an important insight for understanding the contemporary politics of religious freedom.

A better-known argument for religious toleration was advanced by John Locke, also in the late seventeenth century. For Locke, toleration was a right of individuals against an intolerant state, whereas for Thomasius and the civil philosophers, it was a right of the state against intolerant religious communities.[17] The juridical construction of religious freedom in German public law thus sought to establish political neutrality toward ultimate theological principles as "the condition of establishing parity of legal treatment for rival religions as equally valid legal associations."[18] This marked a shift in the understanding of religious authority as Erastian control of churches by the state was effected to deny the coercive authority of religious institutions in enforcing the demands of conscience. This was the condition of freedom in the private sphere – a sphere defined, protected, delimited, and increasingly regulated by the state itself.

Similarly, Locke's empiricist epistemology led to a conception of civil power as directed to the regulation of things that can be objectively known, whereas religious belief was relegated to the status of subjective conviction.[19] On this view, the neutrality of civil law with respect to religion and the truth of particular religious practices was guaranteed epistemologically by relegating religious belief to the "realm of speculation."[20]

[16] Hunter, *Religious Freedom*, 40. The notion of negotiated and contingent relations between the state and actually existing religious communities, groups, and traditions is quite distinct from the notion of "a right," which implies a legal/moral relation between the state and an individual subject as rights-holder as well as a background justification not only of the right itself, but its distinctive function of holding others to correlative duties.

[17] Hunter, *Religious Freedom*, 52. Thus "Pufendorf's and Thomasius's conceptions were the instruments and effect of German imperial public law and the Brandenburg-Prussian settlement, whereas Locke's was an instrument of political-theological dissent from the Anglican settlement."

[18] Hunter, *Religious Freedom*, 55.

[19] Locke's theory of toleration thus equally relies on a particular conception of *adiaphora*: religious matters, properly understood, have no civil bearing as properly religious practices concern only a care for salvation and cannot harm the life, liberty, or estate of civil subjects. Conversely, there can be no coercion in religious matters, as one cannot correct belief, which is a matter of private concern. Kirstie McClure, *Difference, Diversity, and the Limits of Toleration*, 18 POLITICAL THEORY 361, 377 (1990).

[20] It is the discursive separation from other-worldly concerns that therefore underpins the capacity of civil discourse to convert incommensurable expressions of religious difference into a politically indifferent diversity of religious practices. McClure, *Difference, Diversity*, 385, n. 17. On this account, religion as a matter of facticity loses its epistemological privilege joining other mundane objects subject to civil regulation.

Moral Philosophy and Universal Right

The idea of religion as a subjective belief, which cannot be coerced because it is located in a private mental space, marks the beginning of a new religious psychology, and a corresponding shift from the privatization of religious authority in the early modern period to its normative interiorization in modernity. As Talal Asad has suggested, it is the idea that the mind is the impregnable bastion of true religious experience that provides the modern view with its plausibility, i.e., that coercion of religious belief is irrational because impossible.

Given that force can only secure an insincere profession of faith and outward conformity, true authenticity rests on the modern subject's ability to choose beliefs and act on them. This conception of belief as singular and inaccessible to other locations reinforces the idea of an autonomous buffered subject able to separate itself from objects by contemplation, reasoning, and interpretation, and choose from available beliefs.

This intellectual disposition and sensibility prefigures the second, later liberal tradition whereby the public sphere is reconceived in terms of a moral theory of justice and religious liberty, grounded in a complex (and unstable) notion of a right to freedom of conscience and belief. This conception derived from a metaphysical (or more accurately, transcendental) philosophical tradition that simultaneously sacralized reason and rationalized religion in a morally grounded state.

This Kantian scheme generated a new secular morality and theory of liberal political order premised on broadly Protestant conceptions of the individual, freedom, and religion. Unlike the civil philosophy of the early modern period, the subject of this moral philosophy was not religion per se, but the individual as both the subject and bearer of rights. The category of religion was rationalized and naturalized into a generically Protestant notion of conscience or belief, understood as internal to human subjectivity, while the notion of autonomy was asserted as the universal basis for political authority.[21]

While Kant himself maintained the distinction between public and private spheres,[22] over the past two centuries, these distinctions have substantially been reversed in the modern secular imaginary.[23] This has had a profound effect on conceptualization of the public and private spheres. If, for the civil philosophers and

[21] Danchin, *Islam in the Secular Nomos*, 733–34, n. 2.

[22] Immanuel Kant, *An Answer to the Question: What Is Enlightenment?* in WHAT IS ENLIGHTENMENT? EIGHTEENTH-CENTURY ANSWERS AND TWENTIETH-CENTURY QUESTIONS 58, 59–60 (ed. James Schmidt, 1996).

[23] As Foucault observed, Kant's conception of public and private is "term for term, the opposite of what is ordinarily called freedom of conscience." Michel Foucault, *What Is Enlightenment?* in FOUCAULT READER 32, 36 (ed. Paul Rabinow, 1984).

Kant alike, a spiritualized notion of religion as faith or conscience characterized the private sphere, today the duty to follow conscience has been reimagined as freedom of conscience, now understood in terms of autonomy as an individual right to do what one believes is right.[24] The private sphere remains a space of freedom from state interference, but the basis for this restraint is not respect for religion or conscience per se, but rather for the individual's right to choose not only the dictates of her religion or conscience, but any belief at all. This is reflected in the contemporary formulation of the *forum internum* as freedom of thought, conscience, and religion and comprises the modern category of the essentially religious, i.e., not subject to limitation by the state.

In this way, Kant's Copernican philosophical revolution had two main features: first, contrary to older traditions of Catholic natural law theory, it was non-naturalist: the ground of moral obligation was to be sought not in nature, human nature, external (clerical or traditional) authority, or any contingent circumstances of the moral agent; and second, contrary to Protestant theologies of God as the moral law-giver, it posited a new authoritative source of moral obligation now to be found a priori in transcendental concepts internal to pure reason alone. Moral judgment was thus to be given autonomously by the agent to herself – imposed upon the world – under the rational discipline of the categorical imperative. The first move defined enlightenment in terms of a particular conception of rationality – the right to think for oneself and be free of heteronomous (especially religious) sources of moral obligation – while the second defined freedom as acceptance of what reason dictates as duty (one should always act in accordance with what one can simultaneously will as universal law).

The difficulty is that each of these moves involves fraught and contested claims, not only about the phenomenal world, but about an imagined noumenal or transcendental realm internal to a particular (Protestant) conception of rationality.[25] This new moral economy marked the reversal in ethical thought in modernity, as what was previously external and objective (the authority of God) now became internal and subjective (the unstable co-imbrication of autonomy and conscience

[24] Thus, in *Religion Within the Boundaries of Mere Reason*, Kant develops the notion of a purely rational religion, which is premised on the exclusion of theology from theoretical reason and the grounding of faith in solely practical (moral) reason. In this way, religion is to be controlled by and be subject to the demands of (secular) morality. Immanuel Kant, *Religion Within the Boundaries of Mere Reason*, in RELIGION WITHIN THE BOUNDARIES OF MERE REASON AND OTHER WRITINGS 31 (ed. and trans. Allen Wood & George di Giovanni, 1998).

[25] As Foucault observed regarding Kant's 1784 essay *An Answer to the Question: What Is Enlightenment?*, the enlightenment as posited by Kant was the discovery of an exit, a "way out," a "process that releases us from the status of 'immaturity'" (a state where religious authority takes the place of our conscience) by a "modification of the preexisting relation linking will, authority, and the use of reason"; FOUCAULT READER, 35.

in the double bind of freely chosen conscience or belief), while what was previously internal and subject to God's natural order (human reason) now itself became external and objective (universal reason in the form of the categorical imperative). These reversals had the remarkable effect of simultaneously rationalizing religion and sacralizing reason – or what Kant himself in 1793 termed "religion within the boundaries of mere reason."

In this sequence of moves, the concept of religion and its authority in political order was fundamentally altered. We can see this along three broad dimensions. First, it was now irrational (as defined by rationality itself) for religion to be a source of moral authority, as the only non-contingent, objective source of such authority is secular rationality, which holds that no value other than freedom understood as autonomy (the right of each person to decide for themselves questions of moral value) is true. Second, religion as a category now became understood not as an external aspect of reality, but as an internal subjective value located in the inner mind or consciousness of the individual as subject. Religion was thus a set of beliefs, true if at all in only a non-naturalist conception of moral value. Such belief was not a genuine insight into the character of reality, but only the subjective attitude of the thinker who proposed and adhered to it. And third, the understanding of religion as belief or conscience became secondary to the master universal value of autonomy, such that any genuine religious beliefs must be autonomously chosen and affirmatively assented to by the individual as a set of propositions (subject to the overarching discipline of rationality itself). This is what scholars such as Talal Asad and Saba Mahmood refer to as the modern conception of religion and religious subjectivity.

THE JEWS' FREE SCHOOL *CASE*

These early histories and antinomies are consequential for our understanding of the formulation of religious liberty in provisions such as Article 9 of the ECHR, which, as Nehal Bhuta notes, represents a "bricolage of rights-forms derived from heterogeneous traditions and specific political projects."[26] This normative structure not only authorizes the state to intervene in what appear to be mere expressions of religious belief, but in fact involves the state in making substantive judgments about religion – a domain toward which it claims to be neutral. This has two paradoxical effects: first, by authorizing the state's intervention into the *forum internum* that it declares to be autonomous and sacrosanct; and second, by privileging the values

[26] Nehal Bhuta, *Two Concepts of Religious Freedom in the European Court of Human Rights*, 113 STH. ATL. Q. 9, 10 (2014).

and commitments of the religious majority as the norm against which the religious practices of minorities are judged and sanctioned in the *forum externum*.[27]

In order to see how these two paradoxes are generated, let us turn to consider the reasoning in the *JFS* case. The Jews' Free School (JFS) was founded in 1732 and is today one of the best, state-funded schools in London. JFS gives preference to Jews in its admissions decisions and recognizes the authority of the Office of the Chief Rabbi (OCR), as head of the United Synagogue, to determine who is Jewish for these purposes. This is permitted under English law, but only on the basis that the determination is made on grounds of religious belief, membership, or practice. Under the Race Relations Act 1976 (RRA 1976), there is no exemption for discrimination on grounds of race, which is defined to include "ethnic or national origins."

A twelve-year-old boy, M, applied for admission to the school. M's mother, who was Italian Catholic by birth, had converted to Judaism under the supervision of a non-Orthodox (Masorti) rabbinate. M was living with his father at the time, and they were both members of a Masorti synagogue. M was denied admission because he was not recognized as being Jewish according to Orthodox interpretation of Jewish religious law (*halakha*), according to which M would be considered Jewish only if his mother was Jewish (the matrilineal test) or if he underwent conversion under the supervision of an Orthodox rabbi. Given that the OCR did not recognize the conversion of M's mother, on the basis that it did not recognize the halakhic authority of the Masorti courts, and given that M himself did not wish to undergo an Orthodox conversion, M was denied admission to JFS.

M's father, E, sued JFS, arguing that the school's use of the matrilineal test in its admission policy violated the RRA 1976. A court at first instance upheld the school's right to deny M admission. This was reversed on appeal, and the case then came before the new UK Supreme Court. All nine judges wrote separate opinions, reflecting striking differences in judicial reasoning and the complexity of the issues under consideration. Despite their differences, most expressed "sympathy" with the governors of the school and anxiety about the court's decision, stating that they thought "something has gone wrong."[28]

A majority of five judges (Lords Phillips, Mance, Kerr, and Clarke, and Lady Hale) held that the admissions policy of JFS constituted direct racial discrimination under the RRA 1976, on the grounds that the criteria used by JFS to select pupils treated applicants differently on account of their ethnic origins. Two judges (Lords Hope and Walker) concurred in this result, but found instead that the admissions

[27] For detailed elaboration of this argument in a different context, see Saba Mahmood & Peter Danchin, *Immunity or Regulation? Antinomies of Religious Freedom*, 113 SOUTH ATL. Q. 129 (2014).

[28] See Heather Miller Rubens, *"Something Has Gone Wrong": The JFS Case and Defining Jewish Identity in the Courtroom*, 29 MD. J. INT'L L. 366 (2014).

policy of JFS constituted permissible religious discrimination that had the unlawful effect of indirect racial or ethnic discrimination. The remaining two judges (Lords Rodger and Brown) dissented, finding that JFS's admissions policy was neither directly nor indirectly discriminatory under the RRA 1976.

As a matter of history, there have been several ways to view neutrality and equality of treatment in religious matters. As Christopher McCrudden has observed, British legal policy toward majority and minority religious groups has moved through at least three phases: first, an early nineteenth-century phase of political compromises accommodating conflicting interests; second, a mid-1960s "multicultural" phase that relied primarily on antidiscrimination law and accommodation of "new" ethnic groups; and third, a contemporary phase of "constitutional idealism," which focuses more on principle and the notion of fundamental rights as enacted in legislation such as the Human Rights Act 1998, which incorporated the ECHR into British domestic law.[29] This shift toward quasi-constitutional liberal principles has supplanted both the legislative contingency toward religious traditions and groups of the pre-multicultural phase, and the integrationism and antidiscrimination focus of the multicultural phase. Consequently, it has been left to the judiciary to determine how to apply rights to conflicts involving religion, culture, and ethnicity. Practices previously regarded as ethnic and raising correlative duties of nondiscrimination are today often viewed as religious, to be adjudicated as a matter of individual rights.[30] It was in context of this normative shift toward liberal rights discourse in British constitutionalism that the *JFS* case was both argued and ultimately decided by the UK Supreme Court.

Given this background, what does it mean for a nation-state to be neutral toward Judaism as a religion? If neutrality previously meant affirmative engagement by the state with existing Jewish communities on matters pertaining to Jewish belief and practice, and later protection of such minority communities from acts of unlawful racial or ethnic discrimination, then today neutrality is understood as the protection of the right to freedom of religion and belief. In this sequence of moves, neutrality toward religion, understood as an institution, way of life, or tradition, has shifted almost imperceptibly to the question of the right to religious freedom – which suggests that the state adjudicates between competing rights and not neutrality toward competing religions. This is a shift fraught with consequences, as evident in the three domains of the conceptual structure, subject, and authority of the right. Let us consider each of these in turn.

29 Christopher McCrudden, *Multiculturalism, Freedom of Religion, Equality, and the British Constitution: The JFS Case Considered*, 9 INT'L J. CONST. L. (I-CON) 200 (2011).

30 Cf. Mandla v. Dowell Lee, [1983] 2 AC 548 (wearing of the turban held to be an ethnic practice) with R (Watkins-Singh) v. The Governing Body of Aberdare Girls' High School [2008] EWHC 1865 (Admin) (wearing of the Kara held to be both a religious and ethnic practice).

Forum Internum *versus* Forum Externum

The right to religious liberty is premised on the foundational distinction between the right to "freedom of thought, conscience and religion" in Art. 9(1) of the ECHR and the right to "manifest one's religion or beliefs" in Art. 9(2). The former, referred to as the *forum internum*, is held to be absolute, while the latter, the *forum externum*, is said to be subject to limitations where necessary to protect public order, morals, or the rights of others.

The European Court of Human Rights has long struggled with the issue of how to define the content and scope of Art. 9(1), and its religious liberty jurisprudence provides no clear guidance on the proper object of the protected sphere of the *forum internum*. What is of interest here is how the different conceptions advanced in *JFS* by the majority, concurring, and dissenting judgments closely track the three approaches adopted by the European Court of (1) autonomy, (2) conscience/belief, and (3) collective/institutional autonomy, respectively.

While *JFS* is framed and adjudicated as a race discrimination case involving unfair treatment by a school admissions board toward an applicant, the majority opinion begins neither by setting out the relevant criteria of antidiscrimination law nor by explaining the relations and duties of justice owed by one party to the other. Rather, it begins by citing Deuteronomy, the fifth book of the Hebrew Bible and the Jewish Torah, locating the source of the matrilineal test in the "clear commandment against intermarriage" (Deut. 7:3–4), which Phillips reads to yield the self-evident conclusion that it is a "fundamental tenet of the Jewish religion … that the child of a Jewish mother is automatically and inalienably Jewish."[31]

A genuine ambiguity is thus presented at the outset regarding who or what exactly is on trial before the court: Is it JFS for its treatment of M; or the ancient Israelite religion and its offspring, Judaism? This in turn generates deeper and deeply opposing anxieties. If the court is to permit discrimination on the basis of race, ethnicity, or descent solely because authorized by a religious tradition or justified on religious grounds, does this not pose a threat to the very foundations and conditions of our contemporary secularity and freedom? Conversely, if the court is to prohibit such a long-standing practice internal to a religious tradition, which entangles religious and descent-based criteria, does this not threaten the very idea of religious freedom, which has long been understood to encompass the right of religious persons, groups, and institutions to determine their own rules of belief, identity, and membership, free of state interference and regulation?

As the reasoning in the majority, concurring, and dissenting judgments unfolds, we see that the antinomies and contradictions characteristic of religious freedom

[31] UKSC 15 (2009), 2 A.C. 728 (S.C.) (2010), Para. 2.

discourse as the fundamental liberal premises of state neutrality toward religion and universality of the right to religious liberty are continually entangled with and defined in terms of their opposites. This is seen also in the arguments adduced by the parties. Having first claimed to be bound by immutable religious law, JFS and the OCR paradoxically invoke the right to decide for themselves matters of religious doctrine and orthodoxy, as a matter of religious freedom. Conversely, having claimed the right to be free from racial and ethnic discrimination and to practice their religion freely, M and his parents paradoxically rely on a distinctly modern conception of religion, understood in terms of individual belief regarded as freely chosen to apply to an Orthodox Jewish school.

But it is the divergences in reasoning in and across the nine separate judgments that best illustrate the modern politics of religious freedom. In contrast to his opening reference to Deuteronomy, Phillips thereafter steadfastly claims no interest in any religious rationale for JFS's actions: he says the court will rule on the facts alone, not on the basis of any religious motivation or reason. The implicit assumption is that the *forum internum* protects only the right to choose one's beliefs, not the immunity of the beliefs themselves. For Phillips, religious criteria are thus subjective, non-natural values or beliefs to which a person may choose to assent.[32] Religion is a matter of choice, while race and ethnicity are immutable, unchosen characteristics. Whether the matrilineal test is assented to as a matter of religious motive or belief is thus irrelevant to the objective fact that M and his mother's ethnic origins were the factual ground that determined the admissions decision made by JFS.

This reasoning reverses the normative understanding of the relationship between immutability and autonomy advanced by JFS and OCR in their argument before the court. The OCR acknowledged that "M was 'ethnically' Jewish, in the sense that he self-identified as Jewish, he was significantly involved with the Jewish community in various ways, and he was accepted as Jewish by at least parts of the community."[33] Ethnicity for the OCR was thus not biological, but sociological, involving deep historical practices of social choice and collective autonomy. On the other hand, the OCR did not acknowledge that M was "religiously" Jewish, because this was not a matter of individual or social choice, but rather was to be determined by an Orthodox interpretation of *halakha*, which, as revealed religious law, was in some vital sense immutable and unchosen. This telescopic reduction by the majority of an entire discursive tradition and its centuries-old traditions of reasoning and

[32] Phillips further states that "[m]embership of a religion or faith indicates some degree of conscious affiliation with the religion or faith on the part of the member" (Para. 44).

[33] McCrudden, *Multiculturalism*, 13. On the reasoning of the House of Lords in *Mandla v. Dowell-Lee*, if M was refused admission to a non-faith-based state school because he was Jewish, this would be racial discrimination because "he was being discriminated against on the grounds of his Jewish ethnicity"; UKSC (2009) 15, Para. 44.

interpretation into a mere subjective motive (then held to be entirely irrelevant), in contradistinction to a discriminatory fact or ground, calls for serious reflection.

The critical point, however, is that in arriving at this judgment, the majority draws a strong distinction between racial and religious grounds for exclusion, implicitly thus embracing a specific conception of religion as a nonracial and nonethnic category that itself is authorized by a prior understanding of the essential nature of religion in terms of interiorized belief. The distinctive bifurcation of the modern right to religious liberty between a *forum internum* of sovereign individual belief and a *forum externum* of manifestation of that belief open to limitation and regulation is in this way mapped onto the logic of antidiscrimination law: to discriminate for any reason (religious or not) on the ground of an immutable characteristic such as race, ethnicity, or descent is axiomatically unjust, because it irrationally denies the personal autonomy and valuable choices of others. In this moral economy, religion properly understood is reduced to a state of mind – belief in a set of creedal propositions to which a legal subject voluntarily assents – which is individual and otherworldly, rather than constituting any form of activity in the world.

Judaism does not fit into these categories and contests this conception of immutable characteristics and valuable choices. As noted earlier, for JFS and the OCR, the relevant immutable characteristic is religious, as constituted by halakha, while it is ethnicity that is a matter of social choice. Indeed, it was central to OCR's submissions before the court that one could be Jewish according to religious law while explicitly rejecting any conscious affiliation with the Jewish religion or faith. The veracity and rationality of these positions are reflected in the reasoning of the concurring and dissenting judgments taken together. These judgments reject the majority's interpretation of the distinction between racial and religious grounds, finding not only that the religious motivations and reasons for the exclusionary actions of JFS are relevant to the determination of this question, but that the exclusion of M was made on religious grounds as required by Orthodox Jewish law.

Unlike Phillips, Hope argues that both motive and reasons for action "may be highly relevant to the determination of the crucial question: was this discrimination on racial grounds?"[34] For Hope, there is a distinction between the reasoning that follows from an obligation to comply with Orthodox religious law on the one hand and from a personal decision or motive to apply that law on the other.[35] This yields the

[34] Para. 195. However, "once that conclusion has been reached, the fact that there may have been a benign reason for the discrimination is beside the point" (Para. 44).

[35] Rodger makes a similar point in dissent: "[M's] mother could have been as Italian in origins as Sophia Loren and as Roman Catholic as the Pope for all that the governors cared: the only thing that mattered was that she had not converted to Judaism under Orthodox auspices. It was her resulting non-Jewish religious status in the Chief Rabbi's eyes, not the fact that her ethnic origins were Italian and Roman Catholic, which meant that M was not considered for admission" (Para. 227).

first major divergence in reasoning in the case. In contrast to the majority's external, volitional, and subjective stance toward Judaism and the obligation to comply with halakha, the concurring judgments adopt an internal, cognitive, and objective point of view in adjudicating the first-level question of the distinction between racial and religious grounds. This opens the conceptual space for a different form of contestation, as the exclusion of M is now adjudicated at the secondary level of indirect racial discrimination, permitting JFS and the OCR to seek to justify the reasonableness of their actions toward M in the *forum externum*.

This, in turn, yields the second major divergence in reasoning in the case. In contrast to the cognitivist conception of religion adopted by the concurrence (albeit with its recognition of the objectivity of reasons and obligations deriving from a different source), the dissenting judgments respond to and are more sensitive to a conception of Judaism as a living discursive tradition that encompasses a way of life with its own established and internally contested sources, justifications, and hermeneutics, and thus its own conceptions of religious identity, authority, membership, and practice. It is this recognition that underlies the dissent's reliance on more classical liberal ideas of negative liberty and judicial abstention, which at the same time fail to take seriously or engage with the individual harm suffered by M as a result of the exclusionary actions of JFS and the OCR.

For the dissenting judges, it is implicit that JFS and the OCR as collective subjects have the right to profess and maintain a discursive religious tradition free of sovereign interference, even if this fails to address harms caused to members internal to the tradition itself. Only the concurring judgments of Hope and Walker squarely address this issue, seeking to balance the conflicting claims of right of both JFS and M, using concepts of "legitimate aim and proportionate means, common to both antidiscrimination and human rights law." Implicit in this analysis is an assessment of the harms imposed by JFS's admissions policy on the valuable life choices and autonomy of M and his parents. Importantly, this is held to include their right to choose among Orthodox, Masorti, Reform, and Liberal branches of Judaism, which the concurrence implicitly weighs more heavily than the (collective) right of JFS to devise its own admissions policy and follow the advice of the OCR in basing criteria for membership on halakha. In doing so, the reasoning in the concurring judgments implicitly makes an assessment of the reasonableness not of the matrilineal test, but of the application by JFS to M of Orthodox conversion criteria, which is found to be insufficiently inclusive and pluralistic. Thus the question of indirect racial discrimination based on immutable characteristics is subtly transformed into a reason-based jurisprudence premised on liberal criteria and fundamental values of individual freedom and autonomy.

When this reasoning is considered alongside that of the majority, we see how Judaism is in fact indicted twice: first categorically by the majority in the *forum internum* for irrationally prescribing an immutable characteristic as part of the matrilineal descent test, and second by the concurrence in the *forum externum* for unreasonably denying the valuable choices of M and his parents regarding religion, a judgment that also implicitly scrutinizes and is suspicious of beliefs and doctrines internal to the *forum internum* of the Jewish religion.[36]

In response to the court's ruling that Orthodox Judaism's membership and conversion criteria were unlawful for use in its admissions policy, JFS amended the policy to accept students on the basis of a Certificate of Religious Practice, which gauges synagogue attendance, formal Jewish education, and community participation. This change in policy has removed JFS's ability to accept children on the basis of the OCR's definition of Jewish membership criteria and substituted it with a state-supervised policy of religious practice that is nondiscriminatory, cross-denominational, and free of reference to ethnic or descent-based criteria. The school remains a faith-based school, but if it employs Orthodox halakha as its grounds for admission, it transgresses the boundaries of state law.

In this respect, the *JFS* case powerfully illustrates the distinctive modalities of the exercise of modern secular power. In defining the meaning, scope, and dialectical relationship between the public sphere and individual rights, the court regulates and delimits what constitutes religion and a proper religious subjectivity as a matter of English law. This raises considerable anxieties amongst the judges themselves, as the extent of intrusion of state law into the *forum internum* of the Jewish religion becomes visible, whether axiomatically as a matter of direct discrimination, or pursuant to the balancing of rights and interpretation of proportionality as a matter of indirect discrimination. In this complex set of moves, we see how the concept of neutrality toward Judaism is defined in terms of the right to religious liberty, which in turn is defined in terms of competing conceptions of neutrality as the majority, concurring, and dissenting judgments each grapple with the implications of state authority vis-à-vis a competing normative system. The right to religious liberty is in this sense best viewed as a sophisticated technology of modern secular power, which operates to discipline actually existing religious traditions so they conform to those secular spaces and sensibilities that religion properly should inhabit and express.

[36] The separation between private inner belief and public outer act or expression is in fact "reunited through a suspicion of motives of material interest or worldly power. In the context of the freedom of religious belief, it becomes imperative to determine whether acts or expressions of belief are genuinely religiously motivated. This presumes the power to pronounce upon, and if necessary probe into, the character of one's private convictions." Hussein Ali Agrama, *Religious Freedom and the Bind of Suspicion in Contemporary Secularity*, in POLITICS OF RELIGIOUS FREEDOM (ed. Winnifred Fallers Sullivan et al., 2015). There is a sense in the concurring judgments that JFS and OCR are exercising their institutional authority on the issue of conversion in a way that is not entirely or genuinely or necessarily religiously motivated.

In each of the three sets of judgments, no matter how the content and scope of the *forum internum* is demarcated, the court must make substantive judgments on what constitutes or falls within the protected category. The paradoxical result is that the courts must make determinations that are inescapably entangled with and premised on religious criteria and precepts, in order to define a sphere free from state authority – a private space of exception – which ostensibly limits legislative and other forms of governmental authority. This ever shifting and contested process of construction and demarcation of the *forum internum* is an integral part of the public order of the state itself.

As Hussein Ali Agrama has observed, the ability to control these distinctions involves the fashioning of religion as an "object of continual management and intervention," and this constitutes a mode of discipline not always articulated in the practice of liberal governance.[37] The reasoning in *JFS*, however, allows us to see how such modes of discipline function using the technology of modern rights discourse. What becomes clear is that both the subject of the right and the scope of freedom it encompasses are indeterminate categories. Further, the reasoning in the majority, concurring, and dissenting judgments alike inescapably entangles conceptions of the religious and the secular as part of the state's power and authority "to decide what shall count as essentially religious and what scope it can have in social life."[38]

This involves two critical determinations. First is the need to identify what about doctrine is essentially a religious matter. The court's five-to-four split on whether reliance by JFS and the OCR on the matrilineal test is a racial or religious ground of decision illustrates this first dilemma. Second is the need to distinguish between "the 'civil' and 'religious' dimensions of an act, and on that basis decide whether the act is enforceable, punishable, or otherwise deserving of protection or exemption under the law."[39] The divergence between the concurring and dissenting judges on whether the exclusion of M constituted indirect racial discrimination and the ensuing lines of argument concerning the legitimacy of JFS's aim and the proportionality of its means illustrate this second dilemma.

In both cases, the court must make an assessment of the religious beliefs at issue. This necessarily generates a modality of suspicion as the court considers whether acts or expressions of belief are genuinely religiously motivated and the nature of the belief itself.[40] What is critical to this liberal algebra is that religion be understood

37 Hussein Ali Agrama, *Secularism, Sovereignty, Indeterminacy: Is Egypt a Secular or Religious State?* 52 COMP. STUD. SOC'Y & HIST. 495, 499 (2010).

38 Agrama, *Secularism*, 503; for this reason, "secularism's power may lie more in the underlying question it continually provokes and obliges us to answer, than in the normativity of the categories it proposes."

39 Agrama, *Secularism*, 503.

40 Agrama, *Religious Freedom*, 304. A similar phenomenon can be traced in US religious freedom jurisprudence where courts routinely determine whether "religious acts or expressions are sincerely held to be essential to one's religion" and whether "these acts and expressions are authorized and mandated

essentially as a type of subjective belief, as opposed to any type of objective knowledge,[41] and that it not be allowed to express material interests or drives toward worldly power, which are seen as potentially dangerous or threatening, especially to those values foundational to the public order of the state. It is precisely the external, heteronomous, non-faith-based imperative of matrilineal descent in the Jewish religion that violates these secular imperatives. An unchosen imperative is, on one hand, deeply irrational for contradicting the foundational value of individual autonomy and, on the other, potentially threatening for suggesting a source of ultimate authority other than secular reason itself.

Individual versus Group or Associational Rights

The second dilemma for the court in *JFS*, as in all religious freedom cases, is the proper subject of the right. While the majority and concurrence differ on the nature of the *forum internum*, they agree that the essence of religion is to be found in a cognitive or rationalistic framework internal to the consciousness of the individual, whether autonomously to choose one's beliefs (for the majority) or to have and maintain a certain category of belief (for the concurrence). This conceivably includes the fiction of a corporate entity such as JFS viewed as a legal subject acting as an individual decision maker. For the dissenting judges, however, the proper subject of the right appears to encompass Judaism and Jewish religious practices more broadly construed.[42]

Over the last few decades, a rich (albeit poorly theorized) body of jurisprudence has been developed under Art. 9 of the ECHR, in which claims to collective religious autonomy have been adjudicated. The European Court has held in a series of cases that it has limited jurisdiction to review the processes, reasoning, or substantive

by orthodox religious texts"; Agrama, *Religious Freedom*, 304, citing WINNIFRED FALLERS SULLIVAN, IMPOSSIBILITY OF RELIGIOUS FREEDOM (2005).

[41] The "circumscribed sphere of religion already articulates the principle that it ought to be separated from material power." It is this understanding of religion and religious subjectivity that underlies the idea of state neutrality between religious and nonreligious but deeply held beliefs. If this were not the case, "it would be difficult to argue that the state should remain neutral between belief and what it sees as knowledge, especially in matters concerning public order and the governance of populations, when that knowledge is considered crucial to such governance." Agrama, *Religious Freedom*, 307.

[42] While neither Brown nor Rodger squarely address the question, their judgments appear to follow Asad's conception of religion as a "lived" or "discursive" tradition that encompasses a practical mode of living and "techniques for teaching body and mind to cultivate specific virtues that have been authorized, passed on, and reformulated down the generations." Talal Asad, *Re-reading a Modern Classic: W. C. Smith's "The Meaning and End of Religion,"* in RELIGION AND THE MEDIA 216 (ed. Hent de Vries & Samuel Weber, 2001). The danger of adopting a "pietistic conception of religion as faith that is essentially individual and otherworldly" is to situate religion ineluctably within a secular image of the world (p. 220).

decisions made by religious bodies within an area covered by religious autonomy.[43] In similar terms, the US Supreme Court has recently recognized a "ministerial exception" to generally applicable employment discrimination laws in the case of *EEOC v. Hosanna-Tabor*.[44]

The premise of such jurisdictional approaches to issues of religious autonomy is the notion that it is not for secular courts to make determinations on matters strictly ecclesiastical or involving religious teachings or orthodoxy. This proposition, however, leaves open a number of puzzles and dilemmas for the courts. The first relates to how the relevant autonomous sphere is to be drawn. If the RRA 1976 was intended to apply to religious schools and domains such as employment, why should it not apply to the internal activities of religious organizations in the case of acts of racial or ethnic discrimination? Conversely, if the right to religious freedom is interpreted to provide a form of collective immunity to religious organizations from legislative intervention in their internal affairs, on what basis does the RRA 1976 seek to regulate a religious school such as JFS, which has the express purpose of effectuating the obligation imposed by Jewish religious law to educate those students regarded by the OCR as Jewish? Some argument is needed to justify this particular demarcation of spheres, an argument that itself must be neutral toward religion and respect the right to religious liberty.

A second dilemma concerns how the state and state law are to relate to and recognize existing systems of religious law. There are a tremendous variety of constitutional arrangements in the world today prescribing different forms of relation between the state and religions,[45] and this includes a variety of forms of recognition of and formal relation to both majority and minority religions. In South Africa, for example, section 15(3)(a)(ii) of the post-apartheid 1996 constitution expressly contemplates legislation recognizing "systems of personal and family law under any tradition, or adhered to by persons professing a particular religion." Various contingent forms of legal relation between the state and South Africa's different religious communities, including groups living under customary law and religious minorities with their own family and personal status laws, have thus been developed through law reform efforts in the country over the last two decades.[46]

We have seen how British legal policy toward majority and minority religious groups has moved through at least two early phases of legislative accommodation

43 Obst v. Germany, no. 425/03 (Eur. Ct. H.R. Sept. 23, 2010); Lombardi-Valluari v. Italy, no. 39128/05 (Eur. Ct. H.R. Oct. 20, 2009); Scüth v. Germany, no. 1620/03 (Eur Ct. H.R. Sept. 23 2010).

44 Hosanna-Tabor Evangelical Lutheran Church & School v. EEOC, 132 S. Ct. 694 (2012).

45 Peter G. Danchin, *Of Prophets and Proselytes: Freedom of Religion and the Conflict of Rights in International Law*, 49 HARV. INT'L L.J. 249, 297–307 (2008).

46 Peter Danchin, *Politics of Religious Establishment: Recognition of Muslim Marriages in South Africa*, in VARIETIES OF RELIGIOUS ESTABLISHMENT 165 (ed. Lori G. Beaman & Winnifred Fallers Sullivan, 2013).

and multicultural recognition. But what is striking in *JFS* is how the courts today are employing constitutional liberal principles and alternatively classical ideas of negative liberty and judicial abstention evident in the dissenting judgments to adjudicate these forms of legal relation.

Conflicts of Rights

The final and arguably most intractable dilemma in religious liberty discourse arises when two or more claims of right come into conflict with each other. The issue here is not the conflict per se between M's right to be free from racial discrimination and JFS's right to discriminate in its admissions policy on the basis of religion and belief. We saw how the majority decided this issue by defining the *forum internum* of the right to religious liberty narrowly as individual belief and interpreting the RRA 1976 as a valid limitation on the right to manifest religion in the *forum externum* in order to protect the rights of others.

Rather, it is the disagreement between the concurring and dissenting judgments on the question of indirect racial discrimination that exposes a genuine conflict of rights internal to the right to religious liberty itself. The need to justify issues of legitimate aim and proportionate means of achieving that aim opened the deliberative space for claims to religious liberty to be advanced, albeit indirectly, by both M's father and JFS as reasons either to permit or prohibit the adverse impact of the school's admissions policy on M (and other children not of Jewish ethnic origin in the maternal line).

What is striking is the disagreement between the concurring and dissenting judgments in interpreting the concept of proportionality as to whether to privilege either the individual autonomy of M in matters of religion (i.e., the right to choose conversion under the authority of a non-Orthodox rabbinate) or the collective autonomy of JFS and the OCR to determine their own rules of religious membership.

For the concurrence, JFS was found to have failed to consider whether admitting children recognized as Jewish by any of the branches of Judaism would undermine the religious ethos of the school. Having found at the first stage of analysis that the OCR was bound by and had the right to apply Orthodox Jewish religious law, the implicit suggestion at the second stage is that Orthodox rules on conversion are insufficiently pluralistic and inclusive and that JFS should interpret and apply these rules more sensitively to the values of individual freedom and choice. This argument does not address issues of racial or ethnic discrimination (JFS accepted that M was ethnically Jewish), but rather substitutes the concurring judges' conception of what constitutes religion and a proper religious subjectivity for that of JFS and the OCR. This in fact reverses the logic of their claims, which were premised on the notion that halakha is immutable, while ethnicity is a social choice. It is precisely this danger of non-neutrality and interference in matters of religious doctrine and practice that drives the dissenting judgments toward judicial abstention and deference to the normative authority of JFS and the OCR that, in effect, privileges the right of JFS to collective freedom over the individual autonomy-based claims of M.

As a matter of justice, neither position seems entirely satisfactory. Regardless of the merits of the competing positions, the interesting question from the perspective of any theory of religious freedom is why such debates within religious communities create different normative claims from those between religious communities and the state. The idea of value pluralism allows us to see that there is in fact more than one substantive rights claim at issue. Because the right to freedom of religion is a complicated bundle of entitlements, each made up of a diversity of claims, it protects a range of human interests that are often at odds.[47] If this is correct, the critical question is why a majority of the UK Supreme Court so easily and at times without argument privileges one of the substantive rights claims at issue over the other. Further, if both claims are to be given their due, how should courts resolve such conflicts?

However approached, it is clear that the historical relationships between groups within particular societies and their complex interrelationship within the legal framework of the state are pivotal to any understanding of how and why conflicts raise concerns for the right to religious freedom. Such conflicts give rise to both moral and ethical questions that bear a complex relationship to different types of relations between individuals and groups. The conflicts that arose in *JFS* involving competing claims of religious freedom cannot meaningfully be addressed or properly understood without taking into account these collective dimensions of the question and the broader historical and intergroup context in which these forces and actors are operating. Paradoxically, this requires judges to turn to substantive (historical, cultural, religious) values and normative positions that transcend or lie beyond the competing rights claims themselves. This, of course, results in a constantly contested and thus oscillating series of antinomies in contradiction to the opening premises of neutrality toward religion and universality of the right.

CONCLUSION

This chapter has argued that the dialectical architecture of the right to religious liberty is a far more ambiguous instrument than conventionally assumed, which in practice often legitimates rather than alleviates discriminatory practices of the state against religious communities. This paradox haunts the jurisprudence of all

[47] Peter Danchin, *Suspect Symbols: Value Pluralism as a Theory of Religious Freedom in International Law*, 33 YALE J. INT'L L. 1 (2008).

contemporary legal systems, which face irreconcilable conflicts in maintaining that religious belief is immune from state intervention on one hand, while sanctioning its outward expression on the other.

What is striking in a wide variety of contexts is how courts have tended to privilege the values and sensibilities of the majority religion (on the basis of the universality thesis) and discriminate against minority religions through recourse to the secular concept of public order (on the basis of the neutrality thesis). These two features are not a result of the misapplication of the right to religious liberty or the particular religious personality of certain states; they are instead a product of the contradictions and antinomies internal to the conceptual architecture of the right itself, and emanate from the fraught and contested distinction between the *forum internum* and *forum externum*. It is for this reason that there are striking similarities in the conundrums entailed in regulating religious minorities across the Western and non-Western divide.

What is most deeply at issue in such cases is not primarily the belief-action distinction as between the *forum internum* and *forum externum*, but the distinction between individual belief as an inner dimension of human consciousness and religion as a discursive tradition and collective identity of distinct communities. This is a question that goes beyond public order limitations imposed on religious rites and rituals, and entails instead how the very category demarcated as religious in the *forum internum* is defined in the first place. Such a definition in cases such as *JFS* can be seen implicitly to challenge the equation of the *forum internum* with the neutral normativity of belief and the universal authority of the individual as subject alone.

12

Civil Regulation of Religious Marriage from the Perspectives of Pluralism, Human Rights, and Political Compromise

Shahar Lifshitz

INTRODUCTION

In many areas, Israeli law is modern, liberal, and Western. An exception to this is marriage and divorce law, which is subject to the authority of religious courts and religious law; civil marriage and civil divorce do not exist. Israeli secular law has developed certain civil alternatives to marriage that grant the couple some rights similar to those vested in married couples, but these solutions are not comprehensive, and many problems remain. This state of affairs has given rise to sharp liberal criticism focusing on human rights[1] and on the liberal values of equality and freedom,[2] and to proposals for the establishment of civil marriage.[3]

The present chapter addresses the debate in Israeli legal literature and the public discourse on the nature of civil marriage to be established. Currently, the discussion is divided between two polar views. According to one approach (the *exclusively civil track*), once instituted, the civil option would be the only one for marriage and divorce, and the civil marriage and divorce law would apply equally to all Israelis.[4] According to a second approach (*parallel tracks*), two separate tracks would be

[1] See SHAHAR LIFSHITZ, COHABITATION LAW IN ISRAEL IN LIGHT OF A CIVIL LAW THEORY OF THE FAMILY (Hebrew; 2005); also Amnon Rubinshtein, *Rights to Marriage*, 3 TEL-AVIV U. L. REV. 433 (Hebrew; 1973); Yuval Merin, *Right to Family Life and Civil Marriage under International Law and Its Implementation in the State of Israel*, 28 B. C. INT'L & COMP. L. REV. 79 (2005).

[2] RUTH HALPERIN KADDARI, WOMEN IN ISRAEL: A STATE OF THEIR OWN 235–36 (2004); Shahar Lifshitz, *Spousal Registry* (Israel Democracy Institute; Hebrew, 2006); Shahar Lifshitz, *Pluralistic Vision of Marriage*, in MARRIAGE AT THE CROSSROADS: LAW, POLICY AND THE BRAVE NEW WORLD OF 21ST CENTURY FAMILIES 260 (ed. Elizabeth Scott & Marsha Garrison, 2012); PINHAS SHIFMAN, CIVIL MARRIAGE IN ISRAEL: THE CASE FOR REFORM (Hebrew; 2000), but see Gidi Sapir & Daniel Statman, *Religious Marriage in a Liberal State*, 30 CARDOZO L. REV. 2855 (2009).

[3] See SHIFMAN, CIVIL MARRIAGE IN ISRAEL; Avishalom Westreich & Pinchas Shiffman, *A Civil Framework for Marriage and Divorce in Israel* (ed. Ruth Gavizon, Hebrew; 2012); Lifshitz, *Spousal Registry*; and Part II.

[4] See SHIFMAN, CIVIL MARRIAGE.

established, a civil one and a religious one, both recognized as state systems. Couples who married in the civil track would fall under the jurisdiction of the civil courts, whereas couples who married under religious law would be subject to the jurisdiction of the rabbinic courts and religious law in matters of marriage and divorce.[5]

I consider this debate from three liberal perspectives:

1. a liberal-pluralist perspective that (under certain conditions) regards an increase in the number of frameworks for establishing spousal relationships as a liberal value;
2. an outlook that seeks to protect the right to religious marriage and divorce for those who consider religious marriage and divorce their only legitimate option; and
3. a perspective that recognizes the non-liberal, national-religious arguments of those who support a track for religious marriage, and explores the ability of liberals to reach political compromises with those who do not share their liberal values.

Following the evaluation of these three perspectives, I present a complex model of civil marriage that is appropriate for Israel.

This chapter focuses on the regulation of Jewish marriages in Israel, and as such on the unique difficulties that arise owing to the divorce laws in Jewish religious law. Many of these difficulties are also relevant to religious laws of other religions that are practiced in Israel, but some characteristics of marriage and divorce in these religions are different from those of Jewish religious law, and the fact that most members of the non-Jewish religious communities are a national minority in Israel makes the regulation of marriage more complicated. Elsewhere I hope to complete the picture in a chapter that addresses the regulation of religious marriage of non-Jewish communities.

THE CURRENT SITUATION

Violations of Human Rights and Liberal Values

Following are, from a civil-secular-liberal viewpoint, the main grievances arising from the application of religious law in matters of marriage and divorce.[6]

Restrictions on eligibility to marry. The most severe problem is faced by those who are considered unfit to marry, according to Jewish religious law. In most Western countries, the right to marry is recognized as a basic human right, and

[5] See Ariel Rosen-Zvi, *Rabbinical Courts, Halacha and the Public: A Very Narrow Bridge*, 3 LAW AND GOVERNMENT IN ISRAEL (MISHPAT UMIMSHAL) 173 (Hebrew; 1995).

[6] For a survey, see Lifshitz, *Spousal Registry*.

therefore traditional limits to marriage have been reduced or eliminated.[7] Against this background, denial of the right to marry is particularly problematic, especially when the denial is related to personal and family circumstances perceived as irrelevant by the majority of the population (such as, for example, the personal status of *cohen* or *mamzer*).[8]

Mandatory religious marriage ceremony. Jewish law requires a religious ceremony, and state law supports this. Therefore, persons who desire to marry or divorce are obliged to do so in a religious ceremony even if they hold no religious beliefs.[9]

Orthodox hegemony. Only Orthodox rabbis are allowed to conduct marriage ceremonies. Clearly, this is a serious violation of religious pluralism and offends Jew of other denominations, such as Conservative and Reform.

Gender inequality. The religious Jewish wedding ceremony reveals a clear gender hierarchy that places the man in the active role of giver and buyer and the woman in the passive role of receiver and the one being bought.[10]

Inequities in divorce law. Laws of divorce in Jewish religious present unique problems, particularly in the way rabbinical courts in Israel apply them.[11] Under Jewish law, divorce is a personal act, in which the husband must give a document of divorce (*get*) to the woman. Therefore, a couple cannot be divorced if the husband refuses or is unable to do this, and a woman cannot remarry but remains "chained" (*agunah*), except when it can be proven that the husband is dead. In addition, religious divorce is based on fault in a traditional sense, contrary to modern liberal trends that have moved toward divorce as a matter of choice. Consequently, divorce disputes delve into the most intimate aspects of a couple's relationship, such as illness, defects, and sexual conduct,[12] as well as personal aspects of behavior, such as modesty and religiosity.

7 MARY ANN GLENDON, TRANSFORMATION OF FAMILY LAW: STATE, LAW AND FAMILY IN THE UNITED STATES AND WESTERN EUROPE 75–82 (1989); D. Coester-Waltjen & M. Coester, *Formation of Marriage*, in INTERNATIONAL ENCYCLOPEDIA OF COMPARATIVE LAW: PERSONS AND FAMILY 13–15 (ed. M. A. Glendon, 1997); L. D. Wardle, *Loving v. Virginia and the Constitutional Right to Marry*, 1790–1990, 41 HOWARD *L. J.* 289 (1998); J. Rubellin-Devichi, *Family Law: The Continuity of National Characteristics*, in EUROPEAN FAMILY 45–60 (ed. J. Commaile & F. de Singly, 1997).

8 A *cohen*, or member of the traditional priestly caste, is not permitted to marry a divorcee; a *mamzer*, one born of a forbidden union, is not permitted to marry anyone but another *mamzer*; a Jew is not permitted to marry a non-Jew. See Rubinshtein, *Rights to Marriage*; Aharon Barak, *On the Constitutional Right of Marriage and Divorce*, in HUMAN DIGNITY: THE CONSTITUTIONAL RIGHT AND HER DAUGHTERS (ed. A. Barak, Hebrew; 2014).

9 But see Sapir & Statman, *Religious Marriage* (arguing that the mere duty to participate in a religious ceremony does not abrogate freedom of religion).

10 See HALPERIN KADDARI, WOMEN IN ISRAEL.

11 This section is based on ARIEL ROZEN-TZVI, FAMILY LAW IN ISRAEL: BETWEEN HOLY AND SECULAR 255–69 1990)); MICHAEL J. BROYDE, MARRIAGE, DIVORCE AND THE ABANDONED WIFE IN JEWISH LAW: A CONCEPTUAL UNDERSTANDING OF THE AGUNAH PROBLEMS IN AMERICA (2001); B. JEXSON, AGUNAH: THE MANCHESTER ANALYSIS (2011).

12 Elimelech Westreich, *Husband's Claims in Matters of Infertility in the Rabbinical Court of Israel* (Hebrew), 25 *HEBREW U. STUDENT L. J.*, 241 (1995).

Modern Western law accepts the need for a person to disconnect himself from social frameworks in which he no longer wants to participate, including marriage. Contrary to this line of thinking, most rabbinical courts refuse to accept liberal grounds for divorce, such as separation, breakdown of the relationship, or unilateral no-fault divorce,[13] even when there is a basis for these grounds in religious law.[14] Consequently, a person in a religious marriage must either prove fault or obtain consent of the spouse for divorce. The fact that divorce depends on consent has created the ugly practice of extortion during divorce negotiations, whereby consent becomes contingent on payment of a fee, a generous property settlement, reducing or increasing the alimony, or even waiving child custody and visitation rights.

Special harm to women in religious divorce laws. Although neither a man nor a woman may initiate divorce unilaterally, without proof of fault or the consent of the other party, in other ways, religious divorce laws severely discriminate against women. A woman's infidelity is absolute grounds for divorce; by contrast, a man's infidelity, especially a one-time occurrence, is not generally considered grounds for divorce. A man whose wife has refused him a divorce may receive permission to marry another woman, even though he is not yet divorced from his previous wife; a woman, however, can never receive permission to marry again unless she has received a *get*. Rabbinical courts often refuse to insist on divorce even in cases of a man's extreme physical abuse of his wife.[15]

In cases of lengthy divorce proceedings, some people cohabit with new partners, and this practice has much more adverse consequences for women than for men in Israel. Under religious law, when a married woman has sexual relations with a man other than her husband, she loses financial support and rights to her property, and any child born of the new union is considered a *mamzer*. By contrast, halakhic sanctions against men are much more moderate: taking a new wife has almost no effect on property rights, and children born to a man who is still married to his previous wife are not considered *mamzerim*. Thus, women are much more vulnerable to the practice of extortion in divorce negotiations,

[13] Barak, *On the Constitutional Right*; Shahar Lifshitz, *I Want to Get Divorced Now! On the Civil Regulation of Divorce* (Hebrew), 28 TEL AVIV U. L. REV. 671 (2005); Carolyn J. Frantz & Hanoch Dagan, *Properties of Marriage*, 104 COLUM. L. REV. 75 (2004). See also Avishalom Westreich, *Right to Divorce in Jewish Law: Between Politics and Ideology*, 1 INT'L J. JURISPRUDENCE FAM. 177 (2010).

[14] See Avishalom Westreich, *Divorce on Demand: The History, Dogmatics, and Hermeneutics of the Wife's Right to Divorce in Jewish Law*, 62 J. JEWISH STUD. 340 (2011); Avishalom Westreich, *'Umdena as a Ground for Marriage Annulment: Between Mistaken Transaction (Kiddushei Ta'ut) and Terminative Condition*, 20 JEWISH L. ASS'N STUD., 330 (2010); AVISHALOM WESTREICH, NO-FAULT DIVORCE IN THE JEWISH TRADITION (2014).

[15] Mordechai Frishtik, *Physical Abuse by a Husband as Grounds for Divorce in Jewish Law* (Hebrew), 17 DINÉ ISRAEL 93 (1993–94).

mentioned earlier. The husband may already be living with another woman, but in court he may refuse to grant his wife a divorce unless she consents to a draconian settlement.

Alternatives to Religious Marriage and Divorce

Although there is no civil marriage in Israel, the secular public has found various means to cope with the religious system and the difficulties it poses. The most prominent of these are living together without marriage (cohabitation, or common law marriage) and marrying in a civil ceremony abroad.

Civil courts and, in some cases, legislators have joined in support of these secular alternatives. Cohabitation has been instituted as a general term in Israeli (civil) law for couples who maintain a marriage-like relationship even though they are not legally married.[16] As part of a trend to narrow the legal gap between cohabitation and religious marriages, a recent court ruling established that cohabiting couples are entitled to the same rights as legally married ones, even if the law does not state so explicitly. Moreover, couples may be recognized as cohabitating partners even if some of the accepted characteristics of a marital relationship do not exist – for example, sexual relations, mutual trust, and at times even permanent residence under one roof.[17]

Case law has also led to the legal recognition of civil marriage abroad.[18] Previously, Israeli case law made a distinction between the validity of such a marriage and its entry in the Population Registry.[19] But persons married in a civil ceremony abroad must be entered in the Israeli Population Registry as married, based on the marriage certificate presented, even if it is a marriage between persons who cannot marry in Israel. The practical result of this registration is quite close to what would have been achieved had there been a formal recognition of these marriages.

Although case law has not yet reached a final decision in the matter, for specific legal purposes, a person married in a civil ceremony is be treated as essentially married. And although divorce of Jews married in a civil ceremony is litigated in rabbinical courts, these courts allow civil marriages to be dissolved in the spirit of divorce laws enacted worldwide.[20]

[16] See at length, LIFSHITZ, COHABITATION.

[17] See Shahar Lifshitz, *Changes in Family Regulation: An Analytical and Prospective Look on the Effects of the Civil Revolution in Israeli Law* (Hebrew), 10 *L. & Bus.* 447 (2010) and Plonit v. Ploni 58(2) 213.

[18] For survey, see Lifshitz, *Changes*.

[19] HCJ 143/62 Funk Shlezinger v. Minister of Interior 17 PD 225 [1963] (Isr.)

[20] See File No. Rabbinical Court (High) 4276/03 H. S. v. H. Y. (11.11.2003) (Isr.)

Flaws in the Current Alternatives

Some believe that, from a liberal perspective, given the institution of common law marriage and the option of civil marriage abroad, the religious monopoly over marriage in Israel is legitimate.[21] My opinion is very different.

Need for a Civil Alternative to Cohabitation Law

Despite the widespread recognition of cohabitation rights in Israel, these rights do not provide a comprehensive solution to the civil distress caused by the monopoly of religious law.

First, civil legislation is not applied consistently, and there are cases in which cohabiting partners do not enjoy the rights of married couples. Although recent case law extends the rights of cohabitants, there is still not absolute equality with the rights of married couples. Second, because of the informal nature of cohabitation, its definition is based on factual circumstances surrounding the relationship between the spouses. Consequently, couples must prove in detail that their way of life suits the requirements of the law, including intimate details. Furthermore, the recognition of cohabitation rights is made at a given point, in accordance with a specific law and for specific agencies. Therefore, achieving these rights may involve an exhausting series of hearings before public and private entities. Third, because the dissolution of a cohabitation relationship does not require an official process, the legal defense enjoyed by such a relationship is weak. Fourth, even if cohabitation were granted all the practical rights of marriage, there would still be people who wish to marry because of the importance of marriage as a social symbol and an institution, but are unable to do so because of religious prohibitions.

In addition, for some couples, cohabitation reflects a rejection of the commitments of marriage. In these cases, imposing the duties of marriage does not respect the choice of the partners. There is a need for a mechanism that would separate cohabiting couples who wish to be married but cannot marry under Jewish law, from cohabiting couples who wish to participate in a relationship that is neither legal nor binding.[22]

Limitations of Civil Marriage Abroad

From the private perspective of the partners, there may be some advantages to the recognition of civil marriage abroad, compared to the granting of cohabitation rights.

[21] See Sapir & Statman, *Religious Marriage*.

[22] See LIFSHITZ, COHABITATION; see also Shahar Lifshitz, *Married Against Their Will? Toward a Pluralist Regulation of Spousal Relationships*, 66 WASH. & LEE L. REV. 1565 (2009).

Nevertheless, in my opinion, the civil recognition of such marriages cannot be considered a suitable solution for the difficulties that characterize marriage laws in Israel.

First, Israeli law has not given final and official recognition to the validity of civil marriage outside of Israel, despite its registration in the Population Registry. Second, in the present legal situation, it is the rabbinical courts, which do not recognize the validity of civil marriage, that have the authority to litigate the divorce of a couple married in a civil ceremony abroad.[23] Furthermore, the recognition of civil marriage has been largely a manipulation by the civil courts, not an overall civil solution that reflects a broad social consensus.

Finally, even if state law fully recognized the validity of civil marriages contracted abroad, it would still not be appropriate in the current circumstances. The court has already stated: "What kind of solution is it for the Israeli courts and legislators that requires sending residents of the state beyond its borders in order to correct the problem?"[24]

PROPOSALS FOR CIVIL MARRIAGE

For many years, the situation described previously has caused resentment among large sectors of Israeli society. As a result, proposals have been raised by the Israeli public,[25] in academia,[26] and in the Knesset[27] concerning the regulation of civil marriage.

These proposals differ one from each other in essential details. For example, it has been proposed to allow civil marriage only to those who are prohibited from marrying under present law. In this spirit, the Knesset passed the Civil Union for Persons of No Religion Act (2010), which enabled couples who do not belong to any recognized religion to establish a marital relationship and receive civil rights similar to those who are religiously married.[28] But restricting the law to persons of no religion does not solve the problem of others who are prohibited from marrying under Jewish law. Furthermore, limiting the possibility of civil marriage to those who are prohibited from marrying under Jewish law creates a serious problem for those who

[23] See the debate on this issue between Amichai Radzyner and Avishalom Westreich; see Amichai Radzyner *Problematic Halakhic "Creativity" in Israeli Rabbinical Courts Rulings*, 20 JEWISH LAW ANNUAL (2013) 103–17; *On Civil Marriage in Israel after HC 2232/03: A Response to Avishalom Westreich* (Hebrew) and *Yes, Only Rhetoric* (Hebrew), both in 6–7 FAMILY IN LAW (Academic Center of Law and Science, 2014); and Avishalom Westreich, *Rhetoric and Substance "Came Down Wrapped Together"? On Civil Marriage in Israel Following the Noahide Decision* (Hebrew), 6–7 FAMILY IN LAW (2014).

[24] See HCJ 51/69 Rodnitzky v. Rabbinical Court 24(1) PD 704, 713 (1970).

[25] YOAV ARTSIELI, GAVISON-MEDAN COVENANT: MAIN POINTS AND PRINCIPLES (Hebrew; 2004).

[26] Westreich & Shiffman, *Civil Framework*; SHIFMAN, CIVIL MARRIAGE.

[27] See, e.g., Draft Bill Civil Union, 2014, P/19/2604 (Isr.); Draft Bill Civil Marriage, 2014, P/19/2521 (Isr.); Draft Bill Civil Union, 2013, P/19/473 (Isr.); Draft Bill Civil Union, 2011, P/18/3034 (Isr.).

[28] See Sylvie Fogiel-Bijaoui, *Spousal Covenant (Brit Hazugiut), or the Covenant with the Status Quo*, 28 ISR. STUD. REV. 210 (2013).

object to religious marriage on principle. From a liberal perspective, we should seek a solution that makes civil marriage possible for all who wish to marry.

Another proposal offered in the past, the Gavizon-Medan proposal, distinguishes between marriage and divorce.[29] According to this plan, the procedures of marriage would be civil and uniform for the entire population (rabbis would receive a license to perform civil marriages), but all marriages would be subject to divorce in a religious court. The proposal, therefore, does not address in any way the problems associated with divorce under the existing system.

The late Ariel Rosen-Zvi believed that civil marriage should be established as a parallel track to religious marriage.[30] In this spirit, the Israel Institute for Democracy proposed a civil union bill according to which religious marriage would remain the official marriage, and those who choose it would be subject to the religious laws of divorce. But there would also an option for civil marriage, which, contrary to the current legal situation, would be open to anyone who cannot or does not want to enter into a religious marriage. All who choose this track would be entitled to all civil rights and able to divorce following a civil procedure.[31]

Alternatively, Pinhas Shifman supports an arrangement in which civil marriage is the only marriage recognized by the state.[32] In his opinion, there should be a separation between religious and civil marriage, and the civil validity of a religious marriage would be contingent upon its civil registration by the state. Furthermore, marriage could be dissolved in a civil procedure, according to civil rules, regardless of the manner in which the marriage was conducted.

There are nuances and variations in the application of each of the models, but the fundamental disagreement in the current discourse is between those who support the establishment of parallel tracks, civil and religious, and those who support the exclusively civil track.

A LIBERAL-PLURALIST ROADMAP FOR SELECTING THE PROPER MODEL

Intellectual Background: A Pluralist Model for the Role of the State in Regulating Spousal Relationships

The pluralist approach is based on perfectionist liberal philosophy, which emphasizes the inherent value of pluralism and its role in enhancing individual autonomy.[33] It underscores the idea that individual autonomy means not only the absence of

[29] ARTSIELI, GAVISON-MEDAN.

[30] Rosen-Zvi, *Rabbinical Courts.*

[31] See Lifshitz, *Spousal Registry.*

[32] See SHIFMAN, CIVIL MARRIAGE.

[33] See Lifshitz, *Spousal Registry.*

formal limitations imposed on individuals' choices, but also the existence of a range of plausible options. In light of the values of autonomy and pluralism, modern liberal approaches emphasize the obligation of the liberal state to create a diversity of social institutions that enable the individual to make genuine and meaningful choices among various alternatives.[34]

The liberal values of pluralism, autonomy, and human dignity, which lie at the core of the pluralist approach, not only justify state involvement in designing a variety of social institutions, but also lay down the substantive cornerstone for designing spousal institutions in at least three ways. First, the value of autonomy plays a central role; hence, the pluralist approach prefers egalitarian institutions that assist couples in developing their life plans, over spousal institutions that are potentially repressive and exploitative. Second, both partners must enjoy substantive freedom of choice within the spousal institutions. Third, the right of exit must be preserved for spouses who no longer wish to continue their relationships.

Civil Regulation of Religious Marriage in Light of the Pluralist Approach

Legal recognition of religious marriage tracks alongside the civil track appears consistent with a pluralist approach.[35] But a more thorough examination reveals great difficulties in justifying a method of parallel tracks in the Israeli reality.

First, the pluralist approach demands substantive freedom of choice. However, in closed communities that insist on a strict religious way of life and demand loyalty from their members, the marital track may be chosen as a result of community pressure rather than by free choice. Second, the double standard of sexual morality in Jewish religious family law does not conform to the commitment of the pluralist approach to prevent exploitation and inferiority within the spousal institution. Finally, the severe restrictions on the dissolution of the marital relationship that are characteristic of Jewish divorce law are inconsistent with the commitment of the pluralistic approach to the right of exit. Therefore, I believe that in the existing halakhic situation, from the point of view of the liberal-pluralist perspective, it is not possible to justify a proposal for an official (state) marriage track based on religious laws operating in parallel with the proposed civil track.[36]

[34] See J. RAZ, MORALITY OF FREEDOM (1986); J. RAZ, ETHICS IN THE PUBLIC DOMAIN: ESSAYS IN THE MORALITY OF LAW AND POLITICS (1994); Hanoch Dagan, *Pluralism and Perfectionism in Private Law*, 112 COLUM. L. REV. 1409 (2012).

[35] See J. A. Nichols, *Multi-tiered Marriage: Ideas and Influences from New York and Louisiana to the International Community*, 40 VAND. J. TRANSN'L L. 135 (2007).

[36] This theoretical position is based on the existing cultural reality and the specific content of the religious laws. Recently, a trend has been taking shape in rabbinic court rulings that are willing to adopt, in certain circumstances, Jewish traditions in divorce law that contain values of freedom, equality, and the right to exit. If such a trend becomes dominant, the pluralist perspective might be able to support a

Pluralism, Human Rights, and the Distress of Religious Persons in a Monopolistic Civil System

Marriage is a complex concept, laden with historical, religious, and cultural meanings that go far beyond legal issues, and many citizens perceive religious marriage as more significant to their identity than secular marriage. Therefore, a liberal pluralistic state must respect the religious significance of marriage.

At times, exclusive focus on secular and civil aspects can interfere with the values of individual autonomy and the prevention of exploitation that the pluralistic approach seeks to defend. Consider the case of Orthodox Jewish divorce. Although an exclusively civil divorce track would dramatically relieve the distress of divorce for those who are satisfied with a state divorce, such a track is liable to exacerbate the distress of religious women who require a *get* in order to be divorced and allowed to remarry according to religious law.[37] In the current situation, the rabbinical courts have the authority to achieve a religious *get*, but making divorce an exclusively civil institution would deny them such authority.

A comprehensive conception of human rights requires that the state not be satisfied with technically making it possible to realize various rights, but must act in a systematic and comprehensive manner to ensure that people can achieve their deserving interests and exercise their autonomy, by removing obstacles that might prevent this. In the context of marriage and divorce, an approach to human rights that is committed to the value of autonomy must examine whether additional circumstances are present, beyond state law, that significantly interfere.

How can the liberal state help those whose spouses refuse religious divorce? Some countries where civil marriage is the custom have developed approaches to remedy the situation. Certain jurisdictions support extensive use of contractual doctrines, such as duress and unconscionability, to invalidate divorce settlements achieved through extortion.[38] In other countries, civil remedies have been developed within the framework of torts. In New York, the *get* laws[39] impose civil sanctions on Jewish spouses who refuse to cooperate with the religious dissolution of their marriage, and also makes civil divorce contingent upon cooperation.

religious marriage track alongside the civil one. But regrettably, this is still a nascent trend, and there are many complexities to be resolved.

37 See BROYDE, MARRIAGE, DIVORCE AND THE ABANDONED WIFE; see also S. L. Stone, *Intervention of American Law in Jewish Divorce: A Pluralist Analysis*, 34 ISR. L. REV. 170 (2000).

38 See Golding v. Golding, 176 A.D. 2d 20 (N.Y. App. Div. 1992). See in a different context, Amichai Radzyner, *Annulment of Divorce in Israeli Rabbinical Courts*, 23 JEWISH LAW ASSOCIATION STUDIES (2013) 193.

39 There are two *get* laws. For the 1983 *Get* Law (as amended substantially in 1984), see N. Y. Dom. Rel. Law §253 (McKinney 1999 & Supp. 2010). For the 1992 *Get* Act, see N. Y. Dom. Rel. Law §236B(5)(h), (6)(d) (McKinney 1999 & Supp. 2010).

Although these methods can provide solutions for individual cases, they do not provide a comprehensive solution for the distress of women who are refused a *get*. Contractual and tort solutions can help only against refusers who are motivated primarily by financial reasons. Making the civil divorce contingent upon a religious *get* does not help those whose spouses are willing to forego the civil divorce. In Israel, where a majority of citizens would opt for religious marriage even if civil marriage were available, the topic should be addressed more radically. I propose that all those seeking a divorce undergo a divorce process in civil court. If the civil judge finds that the parties had a consensual religious marriage, he can transfer the divorce litigation to a religious court that has the constitutional authority it enjoys under the current legal situation to coerce cooperation in achieving the *get*, including imprisonment of the refuser.[40]

In sum, in my opinion, the civil track must be backed by a religious system operating under state sponsorship that has the authority to impose the obligation to grant a religious *get* and also to coerce it, at the request of the refused spouse and with the recommendation of the civil court. I refer to this track as an exclusively civil track backed by religious authority.

Although this model deviates significantly from the approach that advocates exclusive civil marriage, it is also quite different from the parallel-tracks model, in which all cases of religious marriage require a religious *get* in order for the spouses to remarry, even if they are personally satisfied with civil divorce. According my proposal, spouses may, by agreement, divorce in civil court and afterward remarry without the need for a religious divorce.

RELIGIOUS OPPOSITION TO AN EXCLUSIVELY CIVIL MARRIAGE TRACK

Liberals are not the only or even the main referees of the public discourse on this topic in Israel. Most of the prevailing views against civil marriage are formulated not in liberal terms, but in religious and national language. We now examine the extent to which the opposition to all the proposed models of civil marriage is valid from the internal point of view of these arguments, and then we examine the degree to which the liberal point of view should contain the religious-national one and compromise with it.

[40] According to some, being coerced to take part in a religious divorce ceremony represents illegal religious coercion toward the *get* refuser. To address this concern, religious coercion should be limited to cases where the spouses conducted a marriage ceremony that was clearly intended to grant their marriage halakhic validity. Participation in such a ceremony imposes an obligation on both parties to cooperate in the dissolution of the halakhic bond. If one of the parties refuses to cooperate in the divorce process, the rabbinical court should have the powers it enjoys at present to achieve the *get*.

Common religious-nationalist arguments against civil marriage[41] are that allowing the state to regulate marriage and divorce will

- increase cases of adultery and *mamzerut* by allowing halakhically married people to remarry without the dissolution of the halakhic marriage;
- legitimize mixed marriages between Jews and non-Jews;
- contribute to national conflict through the creation of private ancestry lists by religious organizations to determine marriage eligibility;
- undermine the Jewish nature of the state by secularizing an essential aspect of Jewish law and tradition.

I believe that, from the internal religious point of view, these fears are justified with regard to the exclusively civil marriage model. This model would result in genuine halakhic difficulties related to the status of improperly divorced women and *mamzerim*. It does not address halakhic and national concerns about mixed marriages and damage to the national unity or the symbolic significance of traditional Jewish marriage.

The relevance of these objections to the parallel-tracks model is less evident. For people married halakhically, the current situation would remain. Civil marriage would not increase the number of adulteries or the number of *mamzerim*, because civil marriage is not halakhically recognized as marriage, and a woman must be married in order for her behavior to constitute adultery or her child to have the status of a *mamzer*.[42] Thus, even if spouses who were married in a civil procedure do not obtain a religious divorce, there would be no halakhic issue involving the prohibition of a relationship with a married woman, and certainly no issue of *mamzerut*.

The weakening of the *mamzerut* argument blunts also the edge of the claim that civil marriage would contribute to a schism in the nation.

The argument that civil marriage would enable marriage between Jews and non-Jews is more persuasive halakhically, and some attribute to it general national importance beyond the narrow religious interest. But Israeli law already recognizes such marriages, both through common law marriage statutes and through indirect acceptance of civil marriage contracted abroad. Therefore, opposition to civil marriage, in the current situation, is only opposition to the official state recognition of such unions as proper marriage.[43]

[41] For a survey, see SHIFMAN, CIVIL MARRIAGE; Lifshitz, *Spousal Registry*; Westreich & Shiffman, *Civil Framework*.

[42] A few halakhic decisions have decreed that a union consummated by sexual relations constitutes a marriage, but the majority reject this view, denying that civil or common law marriage is valid. And while having a child out of wedlock may be immoral, such a child is not a *mamzer*. For the debate within Jewish law, see Rav S. Dichovsky, *Civil Marriage*, 2 TECHUMIN 252 (5741; Hebrew; 1980); Rav S. Y. Cohen, *Civil Marriage*, 3 TECHUMIN 154 (5742; Hebrew; 1981).

[43] See more broadly, Pinchas Shifman, *State Recognition of Religious Marriage: Symbols and Content*, 21 ISR. L. REV. 508 (1986).

Despite the fact that, as shown earlier, the parallel-track approach dispels a significant portion of the religious fears of civil marriage, it does not address the issue of religious divorce in cases of civil marriage. Nor does it address the opposition to state recognition of mixed marriages and the desire to preserve religious marriage as the national track.

These issues were the reason for the civil union proposal put forth originally by the Israel Democracy Institute as part of its constitutional project (described previously). Today this proposal serves as the basis for several legislative proposals before the Knesset, and many believe that politically it has the greatest chance of being enacted.

CIVIL UNION

The approach followed by the civil union proposal is to preserve the existing situation, in which state law recognizes only Orthodox religious marriage. At the same time, in order to meet the needs of those who cannot or do not wish to marry religiously, it establishes a new legal institution, referred to as civil union. Spouses who wish to have a common life that is legally meaningful, without marrying each other religiously, can contract a civil union and register with the registrar of civil unions as a couple, provided they sign a declaration stating that they do not wish to marry according to Jewish religious law (*halakha*).

The limitations on the qualifications for registering as a couple will only be civil in character (age, family proximity, etc.), not religious, and the civil union will be open to all who wish to use it. It will grant couples all the legal rights and obligations that civil laws in Israel grant to married couples, including inheritance, property, and alimony rights, the possibility of adopting children, and more. Religious divorce laws will not apply to civil union registrants, but a civil procedure will be established for the dissolution of the union, under court supervision.

The civil union proposal is designed to allay religious fears associated with the parallel-track approach.[44] Although it allows the union of partners of different (or no) religions and grants official state recognition to such unions, it preserves Orthodox religious marriage as the recognized marriage in Israel. This makes Israel unique among other Western nations and stresses the commitment of the state to its Jewish character. And the fact that this union would not be recognized as "marriage" is important from the religious and national points of view.

The civil union proposal does present certain problems from the Orthodox-halakhic point of view. The most substantial fear takes the form of the slippery slope argument. According to this claim, renouncing the traditional religious veto and granting

44 See Lifshitz, *Spousal Registry*.

recognition to secular couplehood may lead to far-reaching religious concessions, which would undermine the status quo and could harm the Jewish character of the state in other areas, such as Shabbat observance and *kashrut*

The civil advantages of civil union also raise fears that some of those who now opt for religious marriage might prefer a civil union. In addition, unions between Jews and non-Jews would receive greater acceptance because of the symbolic meaning of a civil union, which is relatively higher than that of common law marriage or marriage abroad. Furthermore, there are minority opinions of an extreme nature that would argue sexual relations can result in halakhically valid marriage that requires a *get* for dissolution, even if such a union is not recognized as marriage by the state (and therefore civil unions will increase the number of adulterous women and *mamzerim*).

In fact, the civil union proposal does change the status quo and erodes the religious monopoly over marriage and divorce in Israel. Nevertheless, it also takes into consideration religious-national concerns and provides a partial solution to them.

DIALOG BETWEEN GROUPS AND COMPROMISE IN DEMOCRATIC SOCIETY

Scholars of political theory believe that it is necessary to formulate fundamental arrangements in controversial matters in an area referred to as overlapping consensus.[45] But at this time, it is difficult to find an overlapping consensus in Israel on the matter of marriage and divorce between arrangements based on liberal considerations and those based on religious-national ones.

From the liberal-pluralist point of view, the requirements of essential freedom of choice, guarantee of equality, absence of exploitation, and the right of exit are not met by Jewish religious marriage. Therefore, the liberal-pluralist position rejects the two-track approach and adheres to the exclusively civil track (backed by state assistance in achieving a *get* when such assistance is required). The liberal approach does not support the civil union approach, which reserves the marriage track exclusively for religious marriage.

By contrast, the religious approach opposes vigorously the exclusively civil marriage track, even when it is attended by civil assistance in obtaining a religious *get*. Furthermore, halakhic considerations, and even more, national and meta-halakhic ones, make it difficult for many religious citizens to accept even a parallel model of civil marriage (unless softened by a distinction between marriage and civil union).

How is it possible, therefore, to make progress, when none of the areas of the available options overlaps those of the others? In recent decades, a vast liberal

[45] John Rawls, *Idea of an Overlapping Consensus*, 7 OXFORD J. LEGAL STUD. 1 (1987).

literature has developed dealing with the boundaries of autonomy that the liberal state should grant to non-liberal minority groups operating within its realm.[46] But this literature does not assist in resolving the question at hand. The literature usually deals with a society that is liberal at its governmental and social core, and it is therefore concerned with the legitimacy of non-liberal minority groups. By contrast, the controversy in Israel between the liberal point of view and the religious-national one in the matter of marriage and divorce reflects a basic tension with regard to the core identity of the state and the possibility of basing this identity on liberal values. Religious opposition to the civil-liberal approach is based on the desire of the religious to shape the laws of the state so as to reflect their own views of what is right. This opposition has to do with the identity of the state, not with the ability of religious-national groups to manage their lives autonomously.[47]

How it is possible to reconcile the liberal and non-liberal ways of thinking, which differ on the matter of the regulation of marriage and divorce, and more deeply, on the identity of the State of Israel? I propose a fundamental approach for conducting constitutional negotiations on these matters. My approach is based on several principles.

First, any arrangement should be the result of discussions between group representatives. Such discussions should include not only political negotiations in the conventional sense, but also dialog in which each group seeks to understand sincerely the position of the other side and its real needs. The intention is that following such a dialog, each side agrees to renounce the implementation of some of its principles in some areas, based on a genuine desire to establish cooperation and a willingness to compromise in area that are vital to the other side. Such concessions are not merely part of give-and-take based on a political understanding of limits of the power, but at times are made from a position of power.

Second, it is necessary to distinguish between the ideal positions of each group and the do-or-die boundaries of what is impossible for them to accept. Even when it is not possible to identify an overlapping consensus, in an open and sincere debate, it will be possible to combine and define the boundaries that would permit most groups in Israel to live within the state and participate in it.

Following these principles, two types of areas are defined: 1) An area of rules dealing with the do-or-die issues of the groups who participate in the dialog. These areas must be protected constitutionally, and are not open to the usual political decision

[46] See WILL KYMLICKA, LIBERALISM, COMMUNITY AND CULTURE (1989); WILL KYMLICKA, MULTICULTURAL CITIZENSHIP (1995); AYELET SHACHAR, MULTICULTURAL JURISDICTIONS (2001); MENACHEM MAUTNER, LAW AND THE CULTURE OF ISRAEL (2011).

[47] See Shahar Lifshitz, *Liberal Political Multiculturalism as a Remedy for Religion and State Relations* (Hebrew), 40 *HEBREW U. L. REV.* 887 (2011) (arguing this claim in the broader context of Israeli law and religious policy).

making. Therefore, even groups who have the political power to enforce their views will renounce their ability to do so out of recognition of the positions of the other groups. 2) An area of rules in which the contending groups have value-based positions that, even if very strong, do not represent do-or-die issues. Standard political decision making is applied with respect to these areas.

A distinction is derived from these principles, between the constitutionally protected portions and the public portions that are determined based on procedural democracy and majority rule. The narrow areas that are defined as the boundaries of the various groups will be marked as constitutional areas to which the standard procedural democratic majoritarian rules do not apply. Therefore, it will not be possible to change these rules with an ordinary majority, and laws that violate them will be subject to judicial review. By contrast, the other areas will be subject to the usual political arrangements, and it will not be possible to act against the decisions of the majority by anti-majoritarian means.

The proposed method involves two nontrivial processes: First, a process of essential internal clarification by each group, in which the groups define for themselves their values and distinguish between the two categories. This process is not trivial either for the religious or for the liberals.[48] The religious tend to describe the totality of their positions and values as sacrosanct. Liberals also have difficulty in compromising their values.[49] Second, the external relations between the groups must be characterized by sincerity. Each group must honestly expose which of its positions it can renounce, even at the cost of personal or moral discomfort, and which are do-or-die.

How can these principles be applied in the matter of civil marriage? As we have seen, the liberal position supports an exclusively civil regime. As long as current marriage and divorce laws contain elements of inequality and limitations on the right of exit, the liberal-pluralist position will not support a proposal for a state-sponsored religious marriage track. But what is the hard core of the liberal stance? In my view, it is the principle that it is the duty of the state to offer its citizens a way to marry and a means of divorce, irrespective of their religious faith.

48 See Larry Alexander, *Liberalism, Religion, and the Unity of Epistemology*, 30 SAN DIEGO L. REV. 763, 764 (1993).

49 The distinction between the political and the general liberal positions, and the argument that Israeli liberals must compromise on their general positions and settle for political liberalism, is at the heart of MAUTNER, LAW AND THE CULTURE. Ruth Gavizon also supports this distinction. See the introduction to the Gavizon-Medan Covenant; ARTSIELI, GAVISON-MEDAN. Nevertheless, there is a significant difference between an arrangement that is likely to be accepted on the basis of the constitutional method described in this section and the proposals of Gavizon and Mautner. In my proposal, the Israeli liberals renounce constitutional protection of general liberal values, but retain the ability to fight for these values in the political and democratic arena. By contrast, according to proposals by Gavizon-Medan and by Mautner, secular liberals renounce entirely the possibility that aspects of the regime would be based on general liberal principles.

Thus, proposals that limit civil marriage to those who are religiously ineligible to marry and make divorce subject to religious law are unacceptable to hard-core liberal thinking. By contrast, a tracked arrangement that makes civil marriage and divorce available to those who desire it, and makes only those who chose to marry halakhically subject to religious divorce, is not ideal, but neither is it a do-or-die matter – as long as opting for the religious track is conditional upon the agreement of the parties, and civil matters other than divorce (such as property relations) continue to remain subject to civil law (and provided that religious courts, operating under conditions of competition, increase their flexibility and blunt the harms to the exit right and gender equality).

What about the religious side? As we have seen, at the core of the religious opposition to civil marriage is the fear of state recognition of the remarriage of a married woman, fear of *mamzerut*, and the harm that follows from these to national unity. Therefore, the religious approach cannot accept exclusively civil arrangements that do not ensure that those who were married halakhically have to obtain a religious divorce before remarriage. Nevertheless, despite the halakhic concerns about the parallel-track approach, I believe that the religious must show flexibility in this matter, as they cannot expect the secular population to renounce any possibility of a form of civil marriage.

And what about civil union? From the liberal point of view, to settle for civil union involves painful concessions. First, the marriage label has great social and cultural value, particularly for those who would like to marry religiously, but are not permitted to do so. Second, acknowledgment that civil union does not represent marriage according to halakha strengthens the monopoly of Orthodoxy, which harms non-Orthodox streams that regard themselves as committed to Jewish law.

At the same time, accepting civil union also presents significant difficulties for the religious, especially with regard to the issues of remarriage and to unions between Jews and non-Jews.

I believe that, to the extent that civil union ensures the essential rights of the couples and the distinction between it and marriage is merely in the label, the issue is one of legitimate public-political decision by the state, and less of a constitutional matter in which majority rule is irrelevant. Therefore, weighing all the aforementioned factors, I propose the following roadmap:

1. Guarantee constitutionally the right to an independent civil track of couplehood that is open to all those who want it (or at least limit it to secular criteria).[50] Civil divorce rules will apply to those who choose this track, without a need for a religious *get*.

50 See also Barak, *On the Constitutional Right*.

2. Constitutionally guarantee a religious marriage track. Those who choose it will have to obtain a halakhic divorce in order to remarry.
3. Establish constitutional mechanisms to protect these two areas, so that even if parties achieve momentary political power, they cannot use it to subvert the do-or-die issue of the other group.
4. Decide whether the civil track is to be called marriage or civil union in the political arena, according to the regular procedures of majority decision and through coalition negotiations.[51]

SUMMARY

I have described the difficult current situation in Israel, where marriage and divorce take place only according to religious law, and examined several options for the establishment of civil marriage.

My discussion has focused on the liberal perspective on the matter, and I distinguished between several tiers in the liberal approach. First, I addressed the matter from a liberal-pluralistic point of view, which regards autonomy as a central value. Despite the fundamental sympathy of liberal-pluralist thinking for multiple marriage tracks, in the Israeli reality, a liberal approach will prefer an exclusively civil track as long as the religious courts refuse to adopt norms of gender equality and equitable divorce laws. However, a liberal approach committed to the value of autonomy must also take into consideration the experience and values of religious people; thus, an exclusively civil track must be backed up by civil tools and by authority granted to religious courts to ensure that religious divorce is justly obtainable for those who were married religiously.

Liberals must also take into consideration not only the private experiences of non-liberal individuals and groups, but also their approach to the role and identity of the state. In the area of marriage and divorce, liberals should agree to the parallel-tracks model even if they have the political strength to block it.

At the same time, it is the right and duty of liberals to carry on the political struggle for a civil marriage track that is legitimately considered marriage and not labeled something else. If a political compromise in the form of a civil union law is enacted, it would not be correct to abolish it by non-majoritarian means. Nevertheless, in constitutional negotiations, liberals must continue to insist that the state offer its citizens a civil marriage or a parallel track called marriage, and a means of divorce, irrespective of their religious faith, and this right should benefit from constitutional protection.

[51] Barak, *On the Constitutional Right.*

13

The Impact of Supreme Court Rulings on the Halakhic Status of the Official Rabbinical Courts in Israel

Amihai Radzyner

The privilege of exclusive State recognition, grants of legal powers ... seem to exact a rather heavy price on the Rabbinate, paid in loss of independence and religious freedom (Izhak Englard, 1987).[1]

INTRODUCTION

The fascinating and arguably tragic combination of religion and state in Israel is most visible in issues surrounding the official rabbinical courts.[2] Usually when we think about this matter, we think about substantive law: "marriage and divorce of Jews in Israel is conducted according to Torah law"[3] – that is, *halakha*. However, the combination of halakha and law has another interesting and perhaps less-known aspect: the halakhic significance, for better or worse, of the fact that the official rabbinical court operates by virtue of Israeli law. From the point of view of halakha, does a rabbinical court that operates by virtue of Israeli law have an advantage over private rabbinical courts that do not?[4]

Over the years, such a claim has been established, but because of events of recent years in the area of jurisdiction of the rabbinical courts, this claim has become

[1] Izhak Englard, *Law and Religion in Israel*, 35 Am. J. of Comp. Law 185, 197 (1987).

[2] The system of official rabbinical courts was established in the Land of Israel at the beginning of the British Mandate period (1921). Since then, the system has been recognized in Israeli law as an official judicial system of the state, and it has special authority to litigate matters of marriage and divorce for all Jewish residents of Israel, which must be carried out only according to Orthodox halakha. See Moshe Chigier, Husband and Wife in Israeli Law 12–22, 66 (1985); Talia Einhorn, Private International Law in Israel 168–70, 212–13 (2009).

[3] Rabbinical Courts Jurisdiction Act (Marriage and Divorce) 1953, S.H. 165, s. 2.

[4] In Israel, there are many private rabbinical courts, i.e., unofficial courts. Most of them deal only in monetary cases, as arbitrators, but some of the ultra-Orthodox courts deal also with marriage and divorce. See Adam S. Hofri-Winogradow, *Plurality of Discontent: Legal Pluralism, Religious Adjudication and the State*, 26 J. L. & Relig. 57, 63–74 (2010).

problematic. I refer in particular to the ruling of the Israeli Supreme Court, sitting as the High Court of Justice (HCJ) in the Amir case, that the rabbinical court must not litigate in areas that do not concern marriage and divorce, even if the parties have appointed it as an agreed-upon arbitrator to litigate their civil suit.[5]

Jewish Law and/or Israeli Law: The Debate on the Grundnorm *of the Official Rabbinical Courts*

One month after the verdict in the *Amir* case, the Great Rabbinical Court ruled in a technical matter resulting from an arbitration agreement.[6] During the debate, the court could not refrain from discussing the HCJ ruling in the *Amir* case. In addition to threatening to retroactively cancel bills of divorce (*gittin*) that had already been granted (a threat that was indeed carried out[7]), the rabbinical judges responded by saying the following:

> We must note, in parentheses, that the ruling of the HCJ is a severe blow to the *status quo* and to the relations of the rabbinical court with the civil courts. The rabbinical courts were not born with the establishment of the state. These courts have existed since the revelation on Mt. Sinai … There have been rabbinical courts in the Land of Israel for thousands of years … The State of Israel received the rabbinical courts as a living institution, but granted them formal authority in a narrow segment of family law. The courts, however, have continued to exist with their status intact in all other areas, with the consent of the parties. The formal procedure for carrying out any ruling was by means of a bill of arbitration, which was intended to allow the winner to enforce the judgment through the Execution Office. The HCJ and other judicial authorities have honored and enforced these judgments since the establishment of the state, without challenge. Every time the subject was raised in a legal debate, the authority and status of the rabbinical court in these issues was unquestioned. Note that citizens observant of the Jewish law are commanded by the halakha to litigate in rabbinical court, and they do so by agreement of both parties. The alternative offered to them is to turn to private courts; in many of these, the situation is unsatisfactory, and impairs the ability of religious citizens to observe the religious commandments properly … See the minority opinion of Justice Zvi Tal in the HCJ ruling in the Katz case.

I want to focus on the model presented by the Great Court. It is for good reason that it relies on the Tal's statement in the *Katz* case.[8] The Great Court does not specify what exactly is meant by this reference, but I believe the intention is clear. The *Katz* ruling dealt with the question of the authority of the rabbinical court

5 HCJ 8638/03 Amir v. Rabbinical Court of Appeals, Jerusalem (2006) (http://elyon2.court.gov.il/files/03/380/086/R08/03086380.R08.htm).

6 Appeal 5305-24-1 (14.5.06) (http://tinyurl.com/nq8ez8g).

7 Amihai Radzyner, *Annulment of Divorce in Israeli Rabbinical Courts*, 23 JEWISH L. ASSOC. STUD. 193 (2013).

8 HCJ 3629/95 Katz v. Jerusalem Dist. Rabbinical Court, PD 50 (4) 490 (1996).

to issue a writ of refusal and ban those who refuse to litigate civil suits before it. The majority opinion of Justices Zamir and Dorner rejected this practice, whereas Tal's minority opinion allowed the rabbinical court to impose this sanction. In his remarks, Tal wrote things that are reminiscent of the statements of the court quoted previously:

> Courts that litigate according to Torah law have existed in Israel since time immemorial. Our sages mention Moses' court, and from then onward, the chain of transmission of Torah law continues uninterruptedly to the present day ... The rabbinical court of our generation is also a link in this chain. Contrary to what might be inferred from the words of my colleague, Justice Zamir, and from his ruling, it was not the State of Israel that established the rabbinical courts. The rabbinical courts preceded the establishment of the State of Israel.[9]

I summarize the debate between the judges as follows: according to Zamir, the official rabbinical court is an institution that originated in the law of the British Mandate and subsequently entered into Israeli law. It has no other source of authority, and the historical question concerning the way in which rabbinical courts operated before they were authorized by law is of no importance. In any case, the rabbinical court is a single-tier institution, like any other judicial authority in the country, and it is the law that established this instance and defined its boundaries. There is no additional instance. By contrast, Tal represents the approach we have seen in the statement of the rabbinical court: the rabbinical court is a two-tier institution. The first tier, which has precedence both in time and importance, is the one created by halakha, which ordained the courts for generations and determined their mode of operation. The official rabbinical court in Israel received a second tier, created by law, by virtue of which "the rabbinical court operates as a government institution and an official organ of the state." Thus, the official rabbinical court in Israel is different from other courts that operated in the past and are operating today in Israel and abroad. In any case, this authority cannot harm the authority conferred by halakha. The second tier is merely supplemental, and the rabbinical court can operate based on its existing authority based on the first, halakhic tier.

As noted, Tal's was a minority opinion in the *Katz* ruling, but I would like to examine the halakhic significance of the two-tier structure he proposed, which the official rabbinical court has adopted.

In the context of the statements by Tal and the rabbinical court, the two-tier model is offered in an apologetic discourse directed outward, i.e., facing the Israeli judicial system, which is attempting to erode the powers of the rabbinical court. As part of this discussion, the rabbinical court, following Tal, answers as follows: the law

9 Katz v. Jerusalem Dist. Rabbinical Court, 615–6.

can take away our second tier, which it erected, but the law cannot take away what the halakha gave us, which is the first tier, on which we stand.

USING THE ISRAELI LAW AS A HALAKHIC ARGUMENT: RISE

I will focus on a similar discussion held in rabbinical court, an internal halakhic debate, aimed at the halakhic world and at private rabbinical courts that do not operate under the auspices of the state. This discussion uses the two-tier structure differently, not as part of a defensive argument intended to preserve the prerogatives of the rabbinical court from encroachment by the HCJ, but a discussion that lays claim to an added halakhic value of the official rabbinical courts. To use our analogy, the official court is indeed a two-tier structure, whose second tier is the authority that the law granted it, and it is this tier that makes it higher, in the halakhic sense as well, than the private courts – whose single tier parallels the first tier of the official rabbinical court.

Not all the judges of the official court accepted this position, but in the past thirty-five to forty years, it has been raised several times. Naturally, these discussions took place in circumstances of conflict between the official and the private rabbinical courts, which happened usually (but not exclusively) in cases relating to private law: various civil disputes where it was necessary to determine which court was preferable. Usually, the conflict has arisen when one of the litigants wishes to use the official court and the other is interested in using the private court. To which one are they to turn? Moreover, when a claim is filed with the official court, and the defendant wishes to litigate in a private court, is it possible to issue a writ of refusal[10] against him?

As noted, most of the forum disputes between official and private courts have surrounded claims relating to civil law, not matters of family law. Nevertheless, it seems that the best-known conflict between the courts – both because it was mentioned in an important, influential, and popular book of responsa, *Igrot Moshe*,[11] and because of the fact that it has become the cornerstone in the establishment of the preferred authority of the official courts – was a family case.[12]

In 1978–80, an alimony claim was litigated in the Tel Aviv (official) Rabbinical Court on behalf of a woman against her husband. The litigants were ultra-Orthodox

[10] A writ of refusal (Heb. *shetar seruv*) is a form of *herem* (which combines characteristics of shunning or excommunication) for a party who refuses to appear before a rabbinical court. See GINNINE FRIED, *Collision of Church and State: A Primer to Beth Din Arbitration and the New York Secular Courts*, 31 FORDHAM URB. L. J. 31 633, 651–52 (2004).

[11] Moshe Feinstein *Igrot Moshe* (9 vols., New York: c. 1959–).

[12] For the details of this case, see Asher Maoz, *Rabbinate and the Religious Courts: Between the Hammer of the Law and the Anvil of the Halakha* (Hebrew), 16–17 SHENATON HAMISHPAT HAIVRI [ANNUAL OF THE INSTITUTE FOR RESEARCH IN JEWISH LAW] 289, 345–48 (1991).

residents of Bnei Brak, and the husband served in an important religious position. The woman filed her claim in Tel Aviv, but the husband informed the court that because, according to halakha, "the plaintiff follows the defendant"[13] (i.e., the defendant determines the place of the litigation), the litigation must be held in the court of his choice, a private court in Bnei Brak headed by the head of the *yeshiva* in which the husband was teaching. The Tel Aviv court rejected the husband's request, among others, because it was the woman's right to demand that the litigation not take place in a court in which the judges are on good terms with her husband. However, more important,

> "The plaintiff follows the defendant" refers to two courts of equal standing, not to two different courts. The judgments of the state rabbinical court are legally valid and can be enforced, whereas the judgments of the private court have only moral force, and there is no possibility of enforcing them.[14]

But the ruling of the Tel Aviv court was not perceived as binding in Bnei Brak, and therefore the case was referred to an external arbitrator, Rabbi Moshe Feinstein from New York City, who adopted the position of the Tel Aviv court. According to him, the woman was right because

> Whatever comes out of the [private] court that the husband owes her and her daughters will not be possible to collect from him, because the government will not enforce the judgment, and whatever comes out of the district court they will force him to pay, and even if he does not have money and they are not able to collect from him – they will pay for her and for the girls from the money of the state, what they imposed in alimony … The imposition of alimony for his daughters is a very large amount, and there is no other authority that could collect from him except if she goes to the district court of the Chief Rabbinate.[15]

Feinstein also accepted the argument concerning the woman's fear of a miscarriage of justice in favor of her husband. Nevertheless, a close reading shows that Feinstein's response did not grant preferred status to the official court because of its being official. First, his arguments apply only to the facts of the case at hand: he talks about a woman's ability to resort to the Execution Office and to the National Insurance Institute if her husband does not pay the alimony. More important, he stresses explicitly:

> But perhaps the state will help collect what came out of another rabbinical court, and also if he does not pay the state will pay – it is possible to call her a refuser of Torah Law [so that the rabbinical court may place a ban on her].

13 R. Moshe Iserlish in *Shulhan Arukh*, Hoshen Mishpat 14:1.
14 Maoz, *Rabbinate* 346.
15 *Igrot Moshe*, Hoshen Mishpat, vol. 2, sec. 9.

In other words, if the powers of the official and the private courts are equal, the regular halakhic rules for choosing a forum apply, and the official court has no priority. Thus, it is clear that in civil law there is no difference from his point of view, because even the private courts make litigants sign an arbitration agreement so that it will be possible to enforce the verdict.

An interesting spin was applied to this answer. In 1981, an article was published by Rabbi Simha Miron, who was then director of the rabbinical courts.[16] This is perhaps the main article written on the topic of our discussion: the preferred halakhic status of the official courts in Israel over the other courts. Miron quotes Feinstein's words extensively, takes them out of context, and generalizes them. In his opinion, the enforcement and execution authority that the official court has in family law grants it preferred halakhic status even in areas in which it has authority only to arbitrate – that is, civil law. (Clearly, Feinstein did not intend any such thing; on the contrary, in cases in which the authority is equal, as in civil matters, it seems clear that he would say that the official court has no preference).

The substance of the article, however, is the independent creation of Miron, in which he argues that the official court has the status of a "permanent court" for the general population, a status that no other rabbinical courts in Israel have. I will not discuss the concept at length. It is sufficient to say that such a court should be the court of most of the Jewish population in a city. In *Shulhan Arukh Hoshen Mishpat* 3:1, there is an important definition by Rabbi Moshe Iserlish, according to which the right of the litigant to choose judges as arbitrators is limited to places where there is no permanent court. If there is such a court, a person must appear before it and cannot choose other judges. In other words, the defendant cannot avoid appearing before a permanent court. Relying on various sources, Miron reaches the following conclusion:

> Thus, it transpires that at this time in the Land of Israel, the state rabbinical court and its judges, who are appointed by a committee on behalf of the government, elected by the public in democratic elections, and by virtue of rules and regulations set forth with the consent of the overwhelming majority of the Jewish community, including all the representatives of the organized religious community, have the authority of a permanent court. Moreover, the selection of the judges and the establishment of the rabbinical courts is conducted in collaboration with the Chief Rabbis of Israel and the Chief Rabbinical Council, which are also bodies elected by rabbis, rabbinical judges and the public, and thus this test also helps determine that indeed the official rabbinical court is a permanent court for the entire Jewish population of Israel.[17]

16 Simcha Miron, *Halachic Status of the State Rabbinical Courts*, 22 TORAH SHE-BE'AL-PE 94 (Hebrew; 1981).

17 Miron, *Halachic Status*, 96.

Miron expands on the significance of the authority given by law to the rabbinical court when it was defined as the official court and as such preferred over the private ones. In other words, the second tier has halakhic value. But Miron is aware of the fact that if he relies on the law as the source of authority, a problem can emerge in civil cases, in which the official rabbinical court received no authority under the law, and it acts only as arbitrator. Therefore, he tries to argue that it does not matter:

> The halakha cannot accept the division of the secular legislator, for if we live by it, authority in civil matters is with the civil courts, which the halakha forbids … And if the qualification of the secular legislator is void from the perspective of Jewish law, there is no reason to say that it is void precisely in order to leave an empty space in matters of civil law. For it is the common law that no empty space is left in this area, and even in townships where there are no rabbis who deserve to be judges, or all are uneducated and need rabbinical judges to judge them so they do not appear before the courts of the heathen, they appoint the best and brightest among them (according to city officials), although they do not deserve to be judges, and because the citizens accepted them, they can no longer disqualify them.[18]

Nevertheless, Miron again needs the secular legislator, because it is a key source for the precedence of the official court, in his opinion:

> Second, even the secular legislature does not reject the authority of the rabbinical court to act, from the point of view of religious law, as a competent court in civil affairs, except that the secular legislature did not grant the rabbinical court secular enforcement powers of its jurisdiction in these cases.[19]

As part of the discussion, both in his rulings and in the article, Miron relies on two HCJ rulings, one of them from 1977, which permitted the Petah Tikva Rabbinical Court to issue a writ of refusal (which became the *Katz* HCJ case). Based on this, he states:

> We should regard the district rabbinical court as a permanent court of the city, authorized, in terms of Torah law, for all intents and purposes. The difference in the jurisdiction of the rabbinical court with regard to various matters is only in the ability to enforce its judgments. In this respect, the rabbinical court depends largely on the secular legislature and must ensure that the various judgments it issues are enforceable, whether directly, based on the authority of the secular legislature, or indirectly, through an arbitration agreement, or other means available to the rabbinical court.[20]

18 Miron, *Halachic Status*, 97–98.
19 Miron, *Halachic Status*, 99.
20 Miron, *Halachic Status*, 99. Tal wrote similarly in the *Katz* verdict, 617–18.

The meaning of Miron's words, in principle, is that if there is a request by one of the parties to litigate in the official court, whether plaintiff or defendant, the demand should be honored because the official court has precedence halakhically over the private court, and this precedence tops the halakhic default rule of forum selection in a civil conflict ("the plaintiff follows the defendant"). In other words, when the plaintiff prefers a permanent court and the defendant a different one, we follow the desire of the plaintiff; and all the more so in the reverse case.

Miron makes extensive use of the second tier, i.e., the appointment process of rabbinical judges in Israel, and the powers granted to them by law, as expressed in his opinion and understanding of the HCJ rulings. But what are we to do when the same law and the same court change their position, as, for example, in the *Katz* and subsequent rulings, and in particular the *Amir* ruling in 2006? I suppose that Miron would present a position similar to Tal's: the second tier can add but never detract. It is clear, however, that today he would not have been able to write the article as he did, with such clear reliance on the halakhic significance of the second tier. This illustrates the problem of relying on Israeli law as a halakhic source of authority, as I show later.

Other rabbinical judges have expressed similar opinions to that of Miron in rulings and articles written subsequently. Following is only one example. In 1990, the Great Rabbinical Court, headed by Chief Rabbi Avraham Shapira, dealt with a case in which a defendant asked to litigate in Rabbi Karelitz's court, the largest and most important private court in Bnei Brak.[21] The Tel Aviv District Rabbinical Court, where the original suit was filed, accepted the request of the defendant because "the plaintiff follows the defendant." The plaintiff appealed to the Great Rabbinical Court, which accepted the appeal. It opens with the statement that "the decision of the District Court appears astonishing." Based on that statement, the Tel Aviv rabbinical judges might have thought that they "had been appointed by the public to discuss only matters between husband and wife, domestic peace, alimony, and divorce. But not matters of civil law." The tone of the Great Rabbinical Court is reminiscent of the words of Miron:

> The difference between them is only that the state granted the rabbinical judges of Israel exclusive jurisdiction of coercion through state authorities, but when litigating a court case, they are judges of Israel in every respect, according to the Torah tradition of many generations. It is a commandment to place rabbinical judges in every city and every province so that they may litigate according to Torah law, and we have no other rabbinical judges but those in the district courts. Their litigating and their rulings are based on the legal procedures enacted by

[21] Appeal 384/748 (16.1.90), 7 SHURAT HADIN 463 (2002).

> the Chief Rabbinate, and these regulations are also recognized by the secular law, and these regulations encompass all matters of law and justice, both matters of conflict and law, and matters not contested. There is no doubt that the judges of the district rabbinical courts are the ones about whom the Torah said to place judges in Israel.[22]

In other words, the law gave the rabbinical court coercive jurisdiction only in marriage and divorce laws, but does not prevent it from litigating matters of civil law, where its authority derives from the Torah. (It is easy to imagine the damage that the HCJ ruling in the *Amir* case caused to this argument). What, then, makes the district court preferable to Karelitz's court, as both appear to litigate in matters the civil law only by virtue of the Torah alone? Why are the rabbinical judges of the District Court "the ones about whom the Torah said to place judges in Israel?" The answer is provided directly:

> The judges of the district courts are appointed by the public at large through the appointment committee, which includes all the sectors that represent the citizens of the state, and the public took it upon itself to be judged by them in all matters in which the *Shulchan Aruch* ruled and are included in the procedural regulations, and their status is that of permanent rabbinical judges in that city and province, and R. Moshe Iserlish's ruling applies to them, as noted, and the plaintiff or the defendant cannot say, "I will not litigate before them." … And here the defendant argues that he wants to litigate in the court headed by Rabbi Karelitz … but no one appointed them, not only in the same region, as the rabbinical judges in the district court have been appointed, but in the city of Bnei Brak proper they were not appointed by the public, but litigate for those who choose to come before them, but when the plaintiff asks to litigate in the permanent court, in the district court, the law is with him.[23]

In other words, the precedence of the official court is clear and derives from the additional authority granted to it by law, which includes, among others, the fact that it is intended to serve as a rabbinical court to the general public; in any case, its authority is derived from the appointment committee of rabbinical judges, operating in accordance with the general public, which is not the case of the private courts that were not authorized by the public. However great the Torah scholarship of the judges in the private court may be, the judges of the official court are preferable to them. It follows that the legal status Israeli law confers to the official rabbinical courts and their appointed judges carries substantial halakhic weight.

22 Appeal 384/748, 463–64.
23 Appeal 384/748, 464.

USING THE ISRAELI LAW AS A HALAKHIC ARGUMENT: FALL

The halakhic reliance on Israeli law is most problematic, and I want to illustrate why by referring to another case, on which I will expand because of its current importance: a suit for damages for libel, filed by one rabbi against another. This case shows that reliance on authority by virtue of the law is a double-edged sword.

In 2003, the plaintiff filed his claim in a private court, perhaps the largest in the country based on the volume of its activity, called the Jerusalem Court for Civil Affairs and Clarification of Genealogy (JCCA), which is headed by Rabbi Avraham Dov Levin.[24] At the same time, the defendant demanded to have the case litigated in the official district court. In this case, we have both the ruling of the private court, which naturally claimed that it had jurisdiction, and of the Great Rabbinical Court, to which the plaintiff appealed after the District Court ruled that it had jurisdiction.[25]

The plaintiff argued that the fact that the official court is part of the Israeli legal system is to its detriment. Naturally, he relied on the majority opinion in the *Katz* HCJ ruling. His claim, as formulated by the private civil court, is as follows:

> He also argues that this court, which does not operate under the auspices of the authorities, is not limited by law in issuing writs of refusal, and by contrast, the district rabbinical court, acting under auspices of the authorities, has been restricted by the HCJ from issuing writs of refusal, and based on the HCJ decree, the district court is not authorized by law to litigate civil cases, and it is doubtful whether its civil law activity under the Arbitration Act is permissible.[26] It appears, therefore, that the district court is powerless to enforce by means of writs of refusal, as opposed to this court, which holds the power to do so.[27]

Naturally, the private court accepts this argument. It indeed believes that its authority is at least not less than that of the official court, and even greater. It is interesting that it relies on the same answer by Feinstein that served as the source of the preferred authority of the official court:

> Rabbi Moshe Feinstein wrote … when a certain rabbinical court has legal authority to coerce the defendant to litigate before it and its judgment can be carried out, then this fact grants it, in this matter, priority over a rabbinical court elsewhere that does not have this authority … It follows that the court that has the authority to carry out its judgment with regard to a party that does not obey the law has precedence over a court, however important it may be, that lacks such power. Therefore,

[24] Case no. 423–63, 9 JCCA RULINGS 15 (2005).

[25] Appeal 2971-35-1 (9.11.04) (http://tinyurl.com/nghdvev).

[26] Probably they refer to HCJ 6103/93 Levi v. Rabbinical Court of Appeals, Jerusalem (1994), PD 48(4) 591.

[27] Case no. 423–63, 15.

> refusal to litigate in a court that has coercive power is tantamount to refusing to litigate before a Torah court. Thus, in our case, A is right that this court has priority, for it is not restricted by the HCJ from issuing writs of refusal to parties that do not obey its orders, over a court that operates by virtue of the authorities and is restricted by them from issuing writs of refusal.[28]

In other words, reliance on the added authority that Israeli law grants to the official rabbinical court is problematic: the law giveth, and the law taketh away. It may happen that, precisely by virtue of the law, the private court acquires an excess of power over the official court.

The Great Rabbinical Court discussed this case in late 2004 and was already aware of the ruling of the civil rabbinical court. At this point we are still more than a year before the *Amir* case. The judge, Rabbi Izirer, determined that both private and official courts are at least equal, and in any case, it is necessary to follow the defendant. He nevertheless argued for the priority of the official rabbinical court. His statement is a synthesis of sorts between two arguments we have seen, both the one raised to consolidate the priority of the official courts and the one from Tal and from the judges (in Appeal 5305-24-1) who tried to defend the authority of the court from its attackers in the Supreme Court:

> The district court is accepted by the vast majority of the religiously observant public, which regards it as its court in both family and civil matters. The district rabbinical court litigates every day and has been elected by representatives of the entire public … What has been written about the rabbinical court being elected to litigate only family matters and not civil matters is not accurate. The rabbinical courts are not the creation of the law of the Rabbinical Courts Jurisdiction. The rabbinical courts are the continuation of Knesset Israel and the Jewish community since the days of the British Mandate, and before that, authorized to litigate civil matters as well as family matters … The appellant argues also that the rabbinical court has no authority based on a "doubt" raised by a HCJ justice regarding the authority to engage in arbitration, and therefore their judgments cannot be enforced as arbitration. We have only reality and practice to rely on in the matter of the law. The reality is that tens and hundreds of judgments of rabbinical courts as arbitrators are later approved by the civil court and are granted enforcement authority in practice, certainly not less than those of other rabbinical courts.[29]

It is quite clear that the judges who wrote this judgment in 2004 felt that reliance on the preferential authority of the official court by virtue of the law was problematic. Although the HCJ had already reduced this authority, or at least raised

[28] Case no. 423–63, 17–18.

[29] Appeal 2971-35-1, 3–4.

significant questions about it, which was not convenient for the Great Rabbinical Court, the judges felt the need to explain why it did not harm their authority.

In 2005, Rabbi Eliyahu Schlesinger, who served for several years as a judge in the Jerusalem private court mentioned previously, delivered a lecture that was published later as an article.[30] Most of the comments are aimed at destroying the foundation of the claim that the official rabbinical court is a permanent court by virtue of its acceptance by the general Israeli public, an argument developed by Miron and used by many rabbinical judges later. According to Schlesinger, the rabbinical judges are in practice appointed by the secular entities who do not uphold the halakha, who cannot be relied on to appoint deserving rabbinical judges, and who even require the that rabbinical judges declare their allegiance to the laws of the state, which are the "laws of Gentiles," contradictory to Torah law. Moreover, the official courts are subject to the rulings of the HCJ, which often invalidates their verdicts. By contrast, the private courts can litigate purely according to Torah law, and therefore observant Jews prefer to litigate in private courts.[31] In other words, state laws harm the halakhic status of the official courts. The private courts that are not subject to them and to the "evil" HCJ are preferable.

THE SUPREME COURT MAKES A HALAKHIC PROHIBITION

Schlesinger was not aware of how prophetic his words were when he spoke in 2005 about the subordination of the rabbinical courts to the HCJ. By the time his talk was published, the *Amir* HCJ ruling had been issued, which definitively removed the authority of the district rabbinical courts to litigate matters of civil law.

The HCJ rulings in both the *Katz* and *Amir* cases are reflected in another civil judgment given by the JCCA in 2007.[32] The JCCA refers to the effect of HCJ rulings both on the definition of the official rabbinical court as a permanent court and on the question of enforcement authority. First, contrary to the opinions of Miron and other official rabbinical judges, the official rabbinical court is not a permanent court in the halakhic sense, because, despite what the judges said, it is not appointed by virtue of the public but by governmental authority. This determination is based on references to ten HCJ decisions dealing with "the manner of selection and appointment by law" of the official rabbinical judges. The extensive preoccupation of the Supreme Court with the matter indicates that those who appoint the official judges are not the people of the city, but the government authority, contrary to what Miron

30 Eliyahu Schlesinger, *Halakhic Status of the Official Rabbinical Courts* (Hebrew), 45 TORAH SHE-BE'AL-PE 165 (2006).

31 Schlesinger, *Halakhic Status*, 174–75.

32 Case no. 971-67, 11 JCCA RULINGS 14 (2009). In this case the plaintiff (!) wanted the case to be dealt by the private court, while the defendant asked for an official rabbinical court.

and others say. "And because the authority of the district rabbinical court is not that of a city court but that of a court on behalf of the governing authority, with the HCJ ruling that denies the authority of the district court to litigate in matters of civil law, its status is that of other sages who did not receive the appointment of the many."[33]

The *Amir* case has one more implication:

> A rabbinical court that can enforce its verdicts on parties who do not obey the law has precedence over a court, however important it may be, that does not have such powers. Thus, refusal to litigate in a court that has enforcement power is tantamount to refusal to litigate before a rabbinical court. And … because the verdicts of the district rabbinical court, according to the HCJ ruling, cannot be enforced, and therefore the plaintiff cannot ask to litigate in the district court, and he must appear before the court, and if he does not appear the court will discuss granting permission [to sue in civil court] … and this is how the court of Rabbi Karelitz ruled … regarding defendants who asked to litigate in the district court: "the Tel Aviv district court for now has no jurisdiction by law according to the ruling of the HCJ, and therefore there is an obligation to litigate in a place where it is possible to enforce the verdict legally … if not … the rabbinical court is forced to see it as refusal, with all its implications."[34]

These statements are repeated in several other judgments given by private courts in Jerusalem and Bnei Brak following the HCJ ruling in the Amir case. Moreover, the rulings of JCCA contain a firm halakhic ruling by the person who exerted the greatest influence on the rabbinical courts, both private and official – Rabbi Shalom Yosef Elyashiv.[35] The halakhic ruling also relies on the legal situation in Israel, but it expresses the exact opposite of the long-standing reliance of the official rabbinical courts on Israeli law: "Rabbi Elyashiv has already ordered that the district rabbinical court that litigates in matters of civil law is in violation of the rulings of the HCJ: it commits theft."[36]

What does this mean? Elyashiv was asked whether, given that, according to the main halakhic rules, the official court can rule in civil matters, therefore a *defendant* (and it must be emphasized) in the said court who asks the litigation to be transferred to the official court is not considered to refuse to litigate according to Torah law, or whether, according to the opinion of the said court, it is indeed a refusal to litigate according to Torah law. His answer was that because the "employer" of the official courts (that is, the state, according to the HCJ ruling) determined the rules

33 Case no. 971-67, 16–17.

34 Case no. 971-67, 18.

35 See Avraham Reiner, *R' Yosef Shalom Elyahiv as a Halachic Decisor*, 33 MODERN JUDAISM 260 (2013). Elyashiv was a judge in the official rabbinical courts system from 1950 to 1972.

36 Case no. 971-67, 17.

and boundaries of their work, and according to them, the rabbinical judges must deal strictly with matters of marriage and divorce and not with civil matters:

> This is no longer a minor interdiction. The halakhic rule also states that it is not allowed to litigate in civil matters, and if they violate the order of their employer they are guilty of theft [for receiving their salary]. It follows from his remarks that the defendant cannot choose this option … The court is prohibited from litigating civil matters even if both parties agree.[37]

In other words, the official judges violate the severe halakhic prohibition against theft by simply litigating civil matters.

Therefore, the HCJ ruling in the Amir case has halakhic significance, and based on it, the official rabbinical court no longer has the status of a permanent court in civil matters. Moreover, one of the most prestigious decisors of the generation, even in the opinion of many official rabbinical judges, determined that the official court is not allowed to litigate civil cases. It seems to me that it is difficult to find another place where Elyashiv bestows such high – halakhic – status on the Supreme Court. But the important development is the reversal caused by the HCJ ruling: if, as we have seen, the position of the official courts has been that they have halakhic precedence that overrides the rule whereby "the plaintiff follows the defendant," so that even if the defendant asks to litigate in a private court his request should not be accepted, according to the judges of the private courts, the situation is now been reversed: owing to the HCJ, their court now has precedence over the official court, so that the defendant's demand to litigate in the official court should *not* be accepted!

How did the official courts respond to the HCJ ruling? Many of them decided to ignore the ruling, and there are several rulings in arbitration cases that began after the HCJ ruling in the *Amir* case.[38] Why did they choose to act in this way? It is quite clear that the matter has to do with the straightforward understanding of these rabbinical judges that if they stop litigating civil cases brought before them, they confirm the criticism of the private courts and admit that they are not proper halakhic courts. Anyone who knows the halakhic literature, even superficially, knows that most of the activity of the rabbinical courts over the generations has been in this area of civil law. The official courts in Israel regard themselves as the continuation of these courts, which operated throughout Jewish history, and therefore are not willing to accept the narrow definition that Israeli law ascribed to them, as courts litigating matters for marriage and divorce only. This is not merely a symbolic matter,

37 Private letter from the JCCA to the author (June 16, 2009).

38 According to the ISRAEL STATE COMPTROLLER REPORT 58b 931 (2007), 257 new civil cases opened between May and December 2006, i.e., the seven months after the HCJ *Amir* ruling.

and as we have seen, it has halakhic significance, even if litigating civil matters in practice made up only a very small fraction of the work of these courts.

But then again, the Supreme Court ruled that a rabbinical court cannot deal with monetary cases as an arbitrator.[39] Justice Rubinstein, who is a religious person, noted there:

> Unfortunately, as one who respects the rabbinical courts, this is an unfortunate story not because of the conduct of the parties themselves, but because of the attitude of the rabbinical court ... Whatever the opinion of the rabbinical court may be regarding the Sima Amir ruling, it is binding as far as the rabbinical courts are concerned.

MAY THE LEGISLATOR GIVE WHAT THE COURT TAKETH AWAY

Clearly, the only solution to the problem is to appeal to the legislator.[40] Similarly to the HCJ ruling in the Amir case, the bills submitted to fix the problem that the ruling has created must be viewed through halakhic lenses. These bills are intended to restore to the official court its halakhic status as a permanent court, authorized to discuss both matters of marital law (*even haezer*) and matters of finance (*hoshen mishpat*) by virtue of state law. The various bills are divided into two types: in addition to proposals that suggest the precise restoration of the *status quo ante* (that is, permitting the official court to litigate civil cases as arbitrator[41]), most of the proposals suggest a substantial upgrade that would empower the official courts to litigate by virtue of law (albeit with the consent of the parties), and not only as arbitrator.[42] Why so?

I think the answer can be found in the explanatory notes to a bill introduced in 2001.[43] Similarly to bills introduced after the *Amir* ruling, this proposal suggested that "in civil matters that can be the subject of agreement between the parties, the rabbinical court will have jurisdiction after all parties concerned have agreed in writing." However, in 2001, the official court could still litigate civil matters as arbitrator. Why was it then important to give it such authority by law? The bill indicates why: the Arbitration Law effectively subordinates the rabbinical court to the civil court. The law wants to change this situation:

[39] PCA 4198/10 Ivgi v. Gabbay (http://elyon1.court.gov.il/files/10/980/041/w07/10041980.w07.htm).

[40] Cf. J. Rubinstein, PCA 4198/10.

[41] E.g., Draft Bill Amending Rabbinical Courts Jurisdiction Act (Arbitration in monetary cases) 2006 (http://knesset.gov.il/privatelaw/data/17/142.rtf).

[42] E.g., Draft Bill Amending Rabbinical Courts Jurisdiction Act (Jurisdiction in monetary cases) 2006. (www.knesset.gov.il/privatelaw/data/17/488.rtf).

[43] Draft Bill Amending Rabbinical Courts Jurisdiction Act (Jurisdiction in other cases) (No. 2) 2001, HH 600.

> The purpose of this bill is to grant rabbinical courts similar status to that of the civil courts, with the consent of both parties, and allow the rabbinical court to issue verdicts without the approval of the civil court.

In other words, the goal is to create equality (except for the need for consent of the parties) between the official rabbinical court and the civil court. Both institutions should have authority by law to litigate civil matters.

Such statutory authority has halakhic significance. It would certainly define the official court as a permanent court, with greater certainty than if it was allowed to try civil matters only as arbitrator. Therefore, the superiority of the official court over the private courts, also in civil matters, would be clear to everyone, because whereas the former is almost equal in power with the civil court and acts under direct authorization of the law, the latter operates with the authority of an arbitrator only, and as such is subject to the civil court.

The purpose of these legislative initiatives is to make the legal system of the State of Israel, which is the main support of the official rabbinical court (a support that turned out to be an empty vessel), again come to the aid of the court official and rule decisively which one has precedence over the other in the halakhic argument between the two types of rabbinical courts. In other words, Israeli law should restore the second tier of the official court, which was destroyed by the HCJ ruling in the *Amir* case.

CONCLUSION

As we have seen, the halakhic status of the official rabbinical court is greatly affected by its status under Israeli law. Over the years, it was perceived as having a two-tier structure, with the second tier, granted to it by Israeli law, having halakhic significance. The legal status conferred to it in Israeli law and the official appointment of rabbinical judges raise it above the other rabbinical courts by defining it as a permanent court and thereby denying this definition to other courts.

However, when the position of the Supreme Court changed, from being an asset this status has become a burden. The opinion of the *Amir* and *Katz* rulings is that the official court has only one tier, and this is the one granted to it by law, of which the Supreme Court is the authorized interpreter. The HCJ determined that the official court lacks authorities that over the years it has taken for granted. It was determined, first, that it has no authority to obligate litigants to appear before it (strictly from the legal point of view) as arbitrator; second, that it has no authority to litigate in civil matters. As we have seen, in this matter also there are two sides to the coin: basing the halakhic argument about the foundation of the court on Israeli law carries risks; when this status changes, so does the halakhic status of the court.

The private rabbinical courts, especially the private Court for Civil Affairs in Jerusalem, understood this reality well. In their view as well, the official court, like all other courts, has only one tier, the one created by halakha. But in the case of the official court, this tier is slighter than their own, at least when it comes to litigating civil matters, precisely because of its official status. The official court is no longer a permanent court; this crown now belongs only to certain private courts, and therefore they can obligate defendants who wish to litigate before the official court to appear instead before them. Furthermore, in their opinion, the legal status of official court also has halakhic significance. Thus, among other things, because their "employer" orders that they should not litigate in civil matters, the official judge who does so in defiance of the order is a "thief," and the litigant who approaches him causes him to commit a violation.

The official rabbinical court understands this quite well. Although this is not the first time that it feels the price it is paying for being institutionalized by law, in this case, we speak about a reduction of its jurisdiction that touches on the self-determination of the official court as a halakhic court. That is why it tries to restore its authority to deal with monetary cases by a new legislation.

14

Is Conversion a Human Right?: A Comparative Look at Religious Zionism and Hindu Nationalism

Leora Batnitzky

Freedom of religion, as understood in modern democratic societies and also in contemporary human rights discourse, is most often defined in terms of individual conscience. In this way, the freedom to change one's conscience – that is, the freedom to convert – epitomizes contemporary conceptions of religious freedom.[1] But is religious conversion a human right? I do not purport to provide an answer to this question here, but rather to think about why this question is difficult to answer. I consider and compare the deep anxieties about religious conversion shared by religious Zionists and Hindu nationalists, as well as the ways in which the respective states of Israel and India have institutionalized these anxieties in their legal and political systems.

A comparison of religious Zionist and Hindu nationalist anxieties about conversion allows us to appreciate how religious Zionists and Hindu nationalists continue to use not religious, but rather modern liberal ideals, such as the primacy of the rule of law and the importance of individual conscience in matters of religion, to institutionalize what can be described as illiberal policies on conversion. This complicates attempts to criticize religious Zionist and Hindu nationalist approaches to conversion on liberal grounds. While liberalism, democracy, and the rule of law are often seen as complementing one another, there can also be significant tensions between them. Religious Zionist and Hindu nationalist policies on conversion illustrate some of these tensions. At the same time, in academic discussions, it has become commonplace to point to the theological underpinnings of the modern nation-state. The comparison between religious Zionist and Hindu nationalist approaches to conversion allows us to see the other side of the coin in recognizing some of the ways in which the structures and commitments of the modern nation-state inform modern religious self-understandings.

[1] See Art. 18, Universal Declaration of Human Rights (www.un.org/en/documents/udhr) and Art. 9, European Convention on Human Rights (www.echr.coe.int/NR).

In the first part, I consider some of the broad affinities between religious Zionism and Hindu nationalism as they pertain to religious conversion. The second part shows how ambivalence about conversion informs not just religious Zionism and Hindu nationalism, but also their secular predecessors and counterparts. The third part focuses on the use religious Zionists and Hindu nationalists have made of modern liberal commitments to the rule of law and the priority of individual conscience in institutionalizing their anxieties about religious conversion. Finally, the conclusion considers the implications of this analysis for thinking about whether religious conversion is a human right, as well as for what religious Zionist and Hindu nationalist anxieties about religious conversion might say about contemporary discussions of religious freedom.

BROAD AFFINITIES BETWEEN RELIGIOUS ZIONISM AND HINDU NATIONALISM

Let us begin with preliminary definitions of Hindu nationalism and religious Zionism. As Ashutosh Varshney defines it, "Hindu nationalism has two simultaneous impulses: a commitment to the territorial integrity of India, as well as a political commitment to Hinduism."[2] Religious Zionism might be described in similar terms, with one important caveat: religious Zionism is committed to the territorial integrity of Israel. Religious Zionism is also committed politically to Judaism, but its political commitment is informed by theological presuppositions. These definitions are at best cursory and obviously do not capture the histories and complexities of and within Hindu nationalism and religious Zionism. They do, however, offer us a starting point for noting some parallels, which have been recognized by some Hindu nationalists and Zionists themselves.

Amidst international condemnation of Israel's actions in Gaza in 2014, a rally of 20,000 people supporting Israel took place on August 16. Strikingly, those gathered were not Jews or Christian Zionists, and the rally took place far from the United States. As the *Times of Israel* reported, the gathering was organized by a self-described non-political group, Hindu Samhat, which fights for "Hindu causes" and against "Muslim appeasement."[3] The event's organizer described the rally's rationale: "The destin[ies] of both India and Israel as thriving democracies are intertwined. We both share the same values." And the protesters' banners expressed a sense of a shared Indian and Israeli predicament and destiny: "Hindus and Jews have a right to exist."[4]

2 Ashutosh Varshney, *Contested Meanings: India's National Identity, Hindu Nationalism, and the Politics of Anxiety*, 122:3 DAEDALUS 228 (1993).

3 www.hinduhumanrights.info/interview-with-tapan-ghosh-founder-and-head-of-hindu-samhati.

4 www.timesofisrael.com/20000-march-in-kolkata-in-show-of-support-for-israel.

It would be easy to write these sentiments off as mere political opportunism, that is, as yet another occasion for the Hindu right to express its antipathy toward India's Muslim minority. Yet to do so would be to ignore what is at this point a long history of self-perceived affinities between Hindu nationalism and Zionism.[5] This is not to deny that some, if not many, political players in both India and Israel posit solidarity between Hindu nationalism and Zionism with ulterior motives. But I take as a starting point that at least some of the perceived affinities between Hindu nationalism and Zionism are made in good faith and that these affinities have something to teach us about the self-understanding of significant strands of Hindu nationalist and Zionist thought. The banners from the August 16 rally proclaiming "Hindus and Jews have a right to exist" capture something essential about both Hindu nationalism and Zionism. Despite much of the world's perception that Hindu nationalists and Zionists (and the states of India and Israel more generally) are the powerful parties amongst far less powerful, and often Muslim minorities, Hindu nationalists and Zionists view themselves as beleaguered parties on the world stage who must continue to fight merely to exist. The right to exist for both Hindu nationalists and Zionists is tied not only to the preservation of the states of India and Israel. From the ideological perspectives of Hindu nationalism and Zionism, the right to exist is also the right to maintain exclusively Hindu (or better, Hindutva) and Jewish identities.

The link between the slogan "Hindus and Jews have a right to exist" and current debates about religious freedom is found in the shared ambivalence about religious conversion in India and Israel. Anxieties about religious conversion reflect two significant and perhaps unique overlaps between Indian nationalism and Zionism. First, despite a shared ambivalence about religious conversion, religious freedom, and the right to convert into and out of Hinduism and Judaism are, at least in theory, legally protected in India and Israel. In this way, the modern states of India and Israel differ fundamentally from states such as Saudi Arabia, which view religious conversion out of Islam as corrosive to national identity and, unlike India and Israel, simply outlaw it. Second, anxieties about religious conversion suggest that Hinduism and Judaism, at least from the perspectives of Indian nationalists and Zionists, do not quite fit into the category of religion, if religion is defined largely in terms of individual conviction (or faith). In this connection, while Hindu nationalists and Zionists are committed to their respective views that there is no India without the Hindu people and no Israel without the Jewish people, Hinduism and Judaism are not (despite common misperception to the contrary, especially in the case of Israel)

[5] For an overview of the history of these claims and some of their current expressions, see RAJENDRA ABHYANDKAR, EVOLUTION AND FUTURE OF INDIA–ISRAEL RELATIONS (2012); www.tau.ac.il/humanities/abraham/india-israel.pdf.

established state religions, like Lutheranism (the Church of Sweden) in Sweden or the Anglican Church in England.

These two overlaps point to what is perhaps the most basic convergence between the projects of Indian nationalism and Zionism: At the heart of both projects are unresolved questions about the respective meanings and natures of Hinduism and Judaism. Both projects oppose older formations of their respective traditions. Indian nationalists oppose defining Hinduism in wholly sacral terms, as well as in the form of a modern religion, insisting that the latter was an invention of British colonialism. Zionists reject the theological underpinnings of exilic Judaism, as well as the making of Judaism into a private, modern religion with the advent of the modern nation-state. While in today's world, Hindu nationalism and Zionism are most often understood to be in conflict with various forms of Islamism, the ideological formations of both developed in the context of Christian colonialism and, from the perspectives of Hindu nationalists and Zionists, the remaking of Hinduism and Judaism in the image of Christianity. Just as religious conversion epitomizes religious freedom in contemporary discussions of religious freedom in democratic societies and human rights discourse, so too the notion that religious conversion defines religion as such is a notion associated historically with Christianity, and it is this notion of identity that Indian nationalists and Zionists reject.

These affinities between Hindu nationalism and Zionism are formal ones. As anyone who has spent time in India and Israel knows, the states of India and Israel are very different from each other. And as anyone who knows something about Hinduism and Judaism recognizes, Jewish and Hindu identity and practice are not only very different from each other, but they are also quite varied within themselves. Despite these profound differences, I extend Gary Jeffrey Jacobsohn's claim that the political and religious ideologies that constitute the states of India and Israel are "reverse images" of each other. Jacobson uses this phrase to describe the founding, secular aspirations of each state. As he notes, the modern state of India "was imagined by the principal leaders of the independence movement as a composite culture." In contrast, the founders of the modern state of Israel were committed to a particular ethno-religious group.[6] Yet strikingly, the changing political ideals and ideologies within India and Israel are also reverse images of each other. Within India, Hindu nationalists have shifted the meanings of the composite culture of what had been the pluralist secularism of the Congress Party by broadening Hinduness (Hindutva) to groups that may not necessarily consider themselves Hindu. At the same time, religious Zionists who understand Jewish identity in theological and political terms have eclipsed secularist Zionist conceptions of Jewish identity.

6 GARY JEFFREY JACOBSOHN, WHEEL OF LAW: INDIA'S SECULARISM IN COMPARATIVE CONSTITUTIONAL CONTEXT 253 (2003).

This parallel trajectory suggests another reverse image. Laura Dudley Jenkins has described Hindu nationalism as "exclusive inclusion," because Hindu nationalism can include anyone or any group so long as that person or group relinquishes any claim to a particular identity and assimilates to the cultural practices and ideas of Hindutva.[7] We might term religious Zionism as the inverse of exclusive inclusion, that is, as "inclusive exclusion." Religious Zionists by definition exclude non-Jewish identities, or at the very least relegate them to minority and in many ways inferior status. Yet religious Zionists also eclipse any claims to Jewish pluralism by insisting on the unity of national and religious identity.

Religious Zionist and Hindu nationalist worries about conversion are also reverse images of each other. Religious Zionists worry primarily about who is converting into Judaism, while Hindu nationalists worry about who is converting out of Hinduism (defined broadly to include Buddhism, Sikhism, and Jainism). If conversion is a human right, the ideologies of religious Zionists and Hindu nationalists could both be said to violate this right. By monopolizing the procedures for defining conversion to Judaism, religious Zionists deny anyone who does not subscribe to the authority of the Israeli rabbinate the right to convert to Judaism. In Israel, the Israeli rabbinate's right to define the parameters of membership cannot be defended on the basis of the liberal ideal of freedom of association. When the Israeli rabbinate denies the legitimacy of non-Orthodox and even some Orthodox conversions, this means that those who have converted under the auspices of such authorities are not allowed to marry as Jews in Israel, a ruling that has many practical consequences, not just for the partners in marriage, but also for their offspring. While the Israeli system penalizes Jews, or those who want to identify as Jews, for not converting according to the criteria of the Israeli rabbinate, the Indian system penalizes Hindus (again defined broadly) who have converted to Christianity or Islam by denying them access to the benefits of the reservations system codified in the Indian constitution. Anti-conversion laws in India passed by Hindu nationalists also place a burden on potential converts to Christianity or Islam by making them jump through various bureaucratic hoops. Although the direction of resistance is different, with religious Zionists worrying about who is converting into Judaism and Hindu nationalists worrying about who is converting out of Hinduism, in both Israel and India, state-sponsored definitions of conversion are used to grant or deny benefits to citizens.

One might respond to this state of affairs by simply saying that Israel and India both violate a human right to religious conversion. One might argue that what is needed in both cases is a turn (or return) to more secularist visions of the states, in which freedom of religion, as epitomized by the right to convert, would be instituted.

7 Laura Dudley Jenkins, *Hindu Nationalism and Selective Inclusion*, in IDENTITY AND IDENTIFICATION IN INDIA: DEFINING THE DISADVANTAGED 132 (ed. L. D. Jenkins, 2003).

Yet I'd like to suggest that the matter is more complicated than this. Debates about conversion in Israel and India are tied to unresolved questions about who is a Jew and who is a Hindu. With the rise of religious Zionism and Hindu nationalism, ambivalence about religious conversion has increased in both Israel and India, with major ramifications for the internal politics of both countries. Nevertheless, it is important to recognize that ambivalence about religious conversion was present even in secular forms of Zionism and Indian nationalism. In both cases, defining who is a Jew or who is a Hindu animated early arguments in the histories of the founding of Israel and India.

WANING SECULARISM AND RELIGIOUS CONVERSION

Debates about religious conversion in Israel and India are fundamentally linked to their respective systems of personal law, which each state inherited and self-consciously retained from its colonial past. When David Ben-Gurion, Israel's first prime minister, agreed to allow the religious establishment in Mandate Palestine to continue to have jurisdiction over matters of personal law (including marriage, burial, and conversion) in what would become the state of Israel, he did so in order to preserve Jewish unity. In making what is known as the status quo agreement, Ben-Gurion assumed that Jewish religiosity would dwindle with the founding of the state. And his religious counterparts assumed the opposite: that secular Zionism would fade away.[8] Jawaharlal Nehru, the first prime minister of India, also retained the colonial system that granted religious groups autonomy in matters of personal law. Like Ben-Gurion, Nehru did so as a concession to the quest for Indian unity and also believed that in time the pull of religion would fade away in India.[9]

Yet Ben-Gurion and Nehru had different relations to their own religious traditions. Whereas Ben-Gurion distanced himself from the theological underpinnings of the Jewish tradition, he nevertheless saw Zionism as giving birth to a newer and improved Judaism. This Judaism was cultural and not religious, modern and not traditional, and it was built on a secularized return to the Bible and a rejection of the rabbinic tradition that Ben-Gurion and other secular Zionists opposed not only because of its religious strictures, but also its diasporic politics. As Ben-Gurion famously and concisely put it: "I am not religious, nor were the majority of the early builders of modern Israel believers. Yet their passion for this land stemmed from the Book of Books … though I reject theology, the single most important book in my

[8] For an overview, see Daphne Barak-Erez, *Law and Religion Under the Status Quo Model: Between Past Compromises and Constant Change*, 30 CARDOZO L. REV. 2495–2507 (2009).

[9] JIVANTA SCHOETTLI, VISION AND STRATEGY IN INDIAN POLITICS: JAWAHARLAL NEHRU'S POLICY CHOICES (2011).

life is the Bible."[10] In contrast, Nehru regarded religion, and Hinduism especially, as "superstitious practices and dogmatic beliefs … and uncritical credulousness."[11] Nevertheless, Indian nationalism, like Jewish nationalism, laid claim to a particular land and a particular past. While articulated in different ways, the varieties of Jewish and Indian nationalism were from their beginnings burdened by a creative tension. Both movements, in all their variations, simultaneously strove for radical change and fundamental continuity. In both cases, disagreements about religious conversion continue to embody this tension.

THE ISRAELI CASE

The 1950 Law of Return stated that "every Jew has the right to come to this country as an *oleh* (immigrant)," but the law did not define who counted as a Jew.[12] In the early years of the state, matters of personal status with regard to conversion were not a high priority and were dealt with locally, as they had been in Mandate Palestine. In 1956–57, however, controversy erupted because approximately 10 percent of immigrants to Israel from Poland and Russia were deemed not Jewish by birth. Mafdal, the religious nationalist party, insisted that these immigrants had to have a religious conversion if they were to be registered as Jews. But Ben-Gurion's government maintained that Jewish status was a matter of self-identification: if someone came to the state of Israel and wanted be registered as a Jew, that person should be registered as a Jew.[13]

Ben-Gurion's position did not reflect a commitment to freedom of conscience. Rather, he understood his own claim as adhering to Jewish tradition, which he associated with the Bible (and not with rabbinic Judaism). In his words: "We have one more well-known instance of this in the Bible: Bo'az and Ruth … It doesn't say she [Ruth] immersed herself in a ritual bath."[14] The biblical figure of Ruth works especially well for Ben-Gurion's argument. She was a Moabite who married an Israelite. When her husband, his brother, and his father all died, Ruth's mother-in-law, Naomi, urged Ruth to return to her people. But Ruth pledged her loyalty to Naomi and to Naomi's people, saying. "Entreat me not to leave you, and to return from following after you; for wherever you go, I will go; and where you lodge, I will lodge; your people shall be my people, and your God my God" (Ruth 1:16). For

10 As quoted in ALAN LEVENSON, MAKING OF THE MODERN JEWISH BIBLE: HOW SCHOLARS IN GERMANY, ISRAEL, AND AMERICA TRANSFORMED AN ANCIENT TEXT 117 (2011).

11 JAWAHARLAL NEHRU, DISCOVERY OF INDIA 13 (1004) (1946).

12 www.israellawresourcecenter.org/israellaws/fulltext/lawofreturn.htm.

13 Moshe Samet, *Who Is a Jew 1958–1977*, 36 JERUSALEM QUARTERLY 88–108 (1985).

14 As quoted in Netanel Fisher, *A Jewish State? Controversial Conversions and the Dispute Over Israel's Jewish Character*, 3:33 CONTEMPORARY JEWRY 225 (2013).

Ben-Gurion, people who were not Jewish by birth but wanted to be Jewish and join the Jewish people in the State of Israel were like Ruth. No religious ceremony for conversion was necessary. Political solidarity in the form of self-identification with the Jewish people sufficed.

Ben-Gurion's position on registration held, for the most part, until 1970, when the Law of Return was amended to define who was a Jew: "anyone born of a Jewish mother or who has converted."[15] The catalyst for change was the public outcry after a Supreme Court ruling allowed the child of a Jewish father and non-Jewish mother to be registered as Jewish, in accordance with the father's wishes.[16] While the Law of Return seemingly clarified who counted as a Jew by maintaining, against Ben-Gurion, that formal religious conversion was necessary, it did not specify who had authority to perform such conversion. The matter was further complicated by the fact that the amended Law of Return allows that the rights of Jews as defined by the law "shall be accorded to the child or grandchild of a Jew, to the spouse of a Jew, to the spouse of the child and of the grandchild of a Jew."[17] Contemporary tensions regarding conversion, in both Israel and the diaspora, stem from this change, with the Israeli rabbinic rejecting, nullifying, and maintaining a stranglehold on conversion.

It is important to appreciate what religious Zionists, who advocate this monopoly on conversion, share with Ben-Gurion's secularist vision. Religious Zionists agree with secular Zionists that the establishment of a Jewish state creates a new and different reality for Jews and Judaism. This position pits religious Zionists against ultra-Orthodox Jews, who reject the claim that the State of Israel is a legitimately Jewish state at all. For the ultra-Orthodox, the notion that Israel is a Jewish state violates a basic religious tenet of the Jewish tradition, which holds that the Jewish people will return to the land of Israel with political sovereignty only when the messiah comes. From the perspective of the ultra-Orthodox, Zionists, secular and religious, have taken divine matters into human hands in claiming that Israel is a Jewish state. In contrast to the ultra-Orthodox religious vision, religious Zionists see the establishment of the State of Israel as the first step in a messianic process. Religious Zionists do not claim that secular Zionists are wrong to see Israel as a Jewish state. Instead, they contend that secular Zionists are participating in a messianic process, even if they don't know it.[18]

Religious Zionism is thus not a rejection of secularist Zionism, but a heightening of its premises. This is especially evident when it comes to Rabbi Shlomo

[15] Law of Return (Amend. 2) 5730-1970 S.H. 5730, 34; 24 L.S.I. 28.

[16] H.C. 58/68 Shalit v. Minister of the Interior 23(2) P.D. 477, available in English in Special Volume ISRAEL LAW REPORTS 35–191 (1962–69).

[17] Law of Return (Amend. 2) 5730-1970 Sec. 4A.

[18] For an overview, see AVIEZER RAVITZKY, MESSIANISM, ZIONISM, AND JEWISH RELIGIOUS RADICALISM (trans. Michael Swirsky & Jonathan Chipman, 1996).

Goren's views of conversion. Goren was a religious Zionist who established and then headed the rabbinate for the Israel Defense Forces from 1948–68. He became Chief Rabbi of Israel in 1972 and established what remain today's special training institutes and courts for conversion. Like Ben-Gurion, Goren sought to allow immigrants who came to Israel under the auspices of the Law of Return, but were not Jewish according to Jewish law, to become part of the Jewish people. The ultra-Orthodox would not allow people to convert under these circumstances because, they argued, such people only wanted to convert for nonreligious purposes, such as keeping their families together. Goren concurred with secular Zionists in contending that the state of Israel created a new and unprecedented Jewish reality, and argued for a more lenient policy towards conversion. From a legal point of view, he distinguished between conversions that took place in the state of Israel and conversions that took place in the Diaspora. Since diaspora Jews were subject to the influences of non-Jewish society, he claimed, the stricter approach to conversion advocated by ultra-Orthodox still held outside of Israel. Within Israel, however, immigrants who came to Israel under the Law of Return were allowed to convert. Nevertheless, Goren insisted on converting them according to the strictures of the Israeli rabbinate. As Goren put it to Ben-Gurion, "There is no Jewish nationality without the Jewish religion."[19]

Religious Zionists such as Goren institutionalized a position that is at once expansive and narrow. On the one hand, against their ultra-Orthodox counterparts, religious Zionists sought to expand the conditions under which conversion could be undertaken in the state of Israel. But on the other hand, this approach also narrowed the definition of and path to conversion by granting the Israeli rabbinate control over conversion. The inclusive exclusion of religious Zionist approaches to conversion does not reject but builds on the secularist and pluralist founding of the state of Israel. The religious Zionist view of conversion is an outgrowth (though not necessarily a logical outcome) of the secularist Zionist view of conversion. This means that the religious Zionist view cannot be accounted for simply as a religious issue. Instead, anxieties about conversion are intrinsic to the Zionist project.

THE INDIAN CASE

The Indian constitution, which was heavily influenced by Nehru, emphasizes the rights of individuals, not groups. Article 25 guarantees "freedom of conscience and the right freely to profess, practice and propagate religion." Nehru endorsed a view of religion as a private matter, but decried the politicization of communal forms of

19 ELIEZER BEN RAFAEL, JEWISH IDENTITIES: FIFTY INTELLECTUALS ANSWER BEN-GURION 204 (2002).

religion, which he described as "a narrow group mentality basing itself on a religious community but in reality concerned with political power and patronage for the interested group."[20] Yet, as mentioned previously, Nehru had to adapt to a political reality. He needed to achieve some sort of consensus to govern, and this meant he had to accommodate at least some of the desires of various interest groups, and first and foremost particular religious communities.[21]

Nehru considered the Hindu Marriage Act of 1955 and the Hindu Succession Act of 1956 his greatest political achievements.[22] They reformed Hindu personal law and outlawed polygamy, gave daughters and widows rights of inheritance, and attempted to mitigate restrictions previously based on caste. Nehru believed they were the beginnings of a movement toward the uniform civil code promised by the constitution. The far-right Hindu nationalist group Rashtriya Swayamsevak Sangh (RSS) vehemently opposed the acts, arguing that they were an affront to traditional Hindu values. Yet we find already contained within the Hindu Marriage Act an affirmation of two positions that would become a hallmark of Hindu nationalism – a broad definition of a Hindu, and an aversion to conversion. First, the act defines "Hindu" not only in terms of Hinduism, but also includes Buddhists, Jains, and Sikhs. The act is also clear as to who is not a Hindu – the act extends "to any other person … who is not a Muslim, Christian, Parsi or Jew by religion." Second, the act likens conversion to a non-Hindu religion as akin to adultery, desertion, mental illness, "a virulent and incurable form ofleprosy," and "venereal disease," by citing these as the only legitimate grounds for divorce.[23]

Gandhi died seven years before these acts were passed, but his expansive view of Hinduism and his disdain for conversion were part of his secular nationalism. In an effort to weaken the caste system, Gandhi sought to reform Hinduism from within, and he did so not only by decrying caste distinctions, but also by expanding Hinduism to include Buddhists, Jains, and Sikhs. Many Muslims viewed Gandhi not as a secularist, but as a Hindu nationalist. As Mohammed Ali Jinnah, the leader of India's Muslim League and first president of Pakistan, put it in a 1938 speech to the Muslim League: "I have no hesitation in saying that it is Mr. Gandhi who is destroying the ideal with which Congress was started. He is the one man responsible for turning the Congress into an instrument for the revival of Hinduism."[24] Gandhi was not a Hindu nationalist (indeed, it was a Hindu nationalist who assassinated Gandhi), but debates about who is a Hindu and conversion were part of Indian

[20] NEHRU, DISCOVERY OF INDIA 382.

[21] For analysis, see Subrata Mitra, *Limits of Accommodation: Nehru, Religion and the State in India*, 9:107 SOUTH ASIA RESEARCH 107–27 (1989).

[22] SANKAR GHOSE, JAWAHARLAL NEHRU: A BIOGRAPHY 211 (1993).

[23] http://lawcommissionofindia.nic.in/51-100/report71.pdf.

[24] STANLEY WOLPERT, JINNAH OF PAKISTAN 166 (1984).

nationalism from its beginnings. And though Gandhi may have advocated for religious pluralism, his political secularism was imbued with his expansive understanding of Hinduism.

Gandhi's disdain for conversion was both philosophical and political. He was highly critical of Christian missionary work, called proselytizing "an error, which is perhaps the greatest impediment to the world's progress towards peace,"[25] and associated Christian missionary activity with imperialism: "Christianity in India has been inextricably mixed up for the last one hundred and fifty years with British rule. It appears to us as synonymous with materialistic civilization and imperialistic exploitation by the stronger white races of the weaker races of the world."[26] Philosophically, Gandhi believed in the equality of all religions (*Sarvadharma Samabhava*) and rejected the notion, which he associated with both Christianity and Islam, that there was only one true religion. Since all religions are equal, he rejected the idea of religious conversion: "I believe that there is no such thing as conversion from one faith to another in the accepted sense of the term. It is a highly personal matter for the individual and his God."[27]

But it would be misleading to leave things at this. Gandhi also opposed conversion on nationalist grounds: "Conversion must not mean denationalization. Conversion should mean a definite giving up of the evil of the old, adoption of all the good of the new and a scrupulous avoidance of everything evil in the new. Conversion, therefore, should mean a life of greater dedication to one's country."[28] Gandhi's nationalist anxiety about conversion was directly tied to his far-reaching reformulation of Hinduism. Deeply concerned about the gross injustices of the caste system, he named untouchables "Harijans" (children of Hari, the Hindu name for god). From his perspective, this was an attempt to reform Hinduism by expanding its boundaries to include those who had not previously been included by the oppressive caste system. Gandhi's reform of Hinduism was also protective (as most reform movements are). He sought to safeguard Hinduism by enlarging it, and he was especially incensed by Christian attempts to convert untouchables. As he wrote, "What pains one is their [Christian missionaries'] frantic attempt to exploit the weakness of Harijans … This is no matter for bargain. You must say definitely that this is a matter to be settled by the Hindus themselves."[29]

Gandhi's position also brought him into tension with B. R. Ambedkar, himself an untouchable, over the issue of reservations for depressed classes. The

25 M. K. GANDHI, HINDU DHARMA 232 (ed. Bharatan Kumarappa, 1950).

26 *Young India: Mar 21, 1929, Collected Works of Mohatma Gandhi*, www.gandhiserve.org/cwmg/VOL045.PDF.

27 www.gandhiserve.org/cwmg/VOL051.PDF.

28 www.gandhiserve.org/cwmg/VOL029.PDF.

29 www.gandhiserve.org/cwmg/VOL064.PDF.

reservation system would codify a system of affirmative action meant to address the profound historical discrimination against people of lower castes. Members of lower or "backward" castes would receive allotted educational, occupational, and governmental spots. Gandhi believed that reservations would only create divisions within Hinduism, while Ambedkar embraced reservations as part of his rejection of Hinduism. Gandhi put the matter starkly in a 1931 speech:

> I claim myself, in my own person, to present the vast mass of the "untouchables." … And I would work from one end of India to the other to tell the "untouchables" that separate electorates and separate reservation is not the way to remove this sinister bar … I cannot possibly tolerate what is in store for Hinduism … I will resist it with my life.[30]

Politically, Ambedkar won the day, as special reservations for Scheduled Castes and Scheduled Tribes are included in India's constitution. In 1956, he completely rejected Hinduism and also the attempt to include untouchables (who reject the name Harijans and refer to themselves as Dalits, "oppressed") under the Hindu banner, by leading a mass conversion of Dalits to Buddhism.[31]

There is a deep affinity between the anti-conversion laws instituted by Hindu nationalists in various states in India and Gandhi's concerns about conversion. This is of course not to equate Gandhi's position with these laws, but it is to suggest that there is continuity between them. The 2003 Gujarat Religious Freedom Act, signed into law by Narenda Modi, purports to protect Scheduled Castes and Scheduled Tribes, as well as women and children, from attempts to convert them by means of allurement, force, or fraudulent means.[32] A proposed 2008 amendment to this act attempted to categorize Jainism and Buddhism as subsets of Hinduism; thus, movement between these groups would not be considered conversion. Hindu nationalists share with Gandhi an expansive view of Hinduism coupled with a disdain for conversion. The exclusive inclusion of Hindu nationalism does not reject but builds on the secularist and pluralist founding of the state of India.

Earlier, I argued that we might understand religious Zionist approaches to conversion as an intensification of the premises of secular Zionist views of conversion. Similarly, I have argued that Hindu nationalist approaches to conversion might be understood as an intensification of the premises of secular, Indian nationalist views of conversion. We turn now to the ways in which, in advancing their politics on conversion, religious Zionists and Hindu nationalists have not rejected but rather appropriated some of the basic tenets of the modern nation-state – such as the uniformity

30 As quoted in Jenkins, *Hindu Nationalism*, 131.

31 Ambedkar laid out his arguments for conversion in a 1936 speech, trans. www.columbia.edu/itc/mealac/pritchett/00ambedkar/txt_ambedkar_salvation.html.

32 www.emw-d.de/fix/files/indien-religionsgesetz.pdf.

and sovereignty of law, as well as the importance of personal conviction in matters of religion.

INTERNALIZING THE MODERN NATION-STATE

The respective stances of religious Zionists and Hindu nationalists toward personal law might seem to be another example of reverse images. Religious Zionists jealously guard the political authority granted by the state to the rabbinate to issue and decide on the status of conversions to Judaism. Hindu nationalists want to abolish the personal law system and institute a uniform civil code, promised by the Indian constitution. But this reverse image is misleading. As Alexander Kaye has shown,[33] in the years leading up to the establishment of the Jewish state, the legal philosophy of religious Zionism rejected what had been historically a theological (and not just political) commitment to legal pluralism. Religious Zionists internalized the preference for legal centrism that was also adopted by the state of Israel (and most other modern nation-states). In this way, the legal philosophy and strategy of religious Zionism is formally similar to the legal philosophy and strategy of Hindu nationalists. Both strive for uniformity and centralization. Both reject the traditions of legal pluralism that the states of Israel and India inherited from the British. The difference between the two is that religious Zionists have, at least for the time being, settled for authority over personal status and given up the prospect of a comprehensive law based on the Torah for the state of Israel, whereas Hindu nationalists continue to argue for a uniform civil code.

J. Griffiths has defined legal centralism as the view that "law is an exclusive, systematic and unified hierarchical ordering of normative propositions."[34] This description does not accord with the ways in which Jewish law has been understood historically. From a traditional theological perspective, Jewish law is neither exclusive nor systematic. Instead, the authority of Jewish law exists alongside the authority of the "king" and of elected lay leaders of the community. Jewish law has also historically been highly local and variable. Different communities often had different laws and customs. As Kaye shows, in the decades leading up to the establishment of the state of Israel, many religious Zionists were advocates of legal pluralism.[35] From this perspective, the state of Israel would be analogous to the king. In the words of one thinker, "Every law of a state institution today has the force of the King's Law in its time."[36] In many ways, legal pluralism would have seemed the obvious route to go,

33 Alexander Kaye, *Legal Philosophies of Religious Zionism 1937–1967*, 62–105 (PhD diss., Columbia University, 2013).

34 J. Griffiths, *What Is Legal Pluralism?* 24 J. LEGAL PLURALISM 13 (1985).

35 Kaye, *Legal Philosophies*, 62–105.

36 SHIM'ON FEDERBUSCH, LAW OF KINGSHIP IN ISRAEL (Hebrew; 1952), as cited by Kaye, *Legal Philosophies*, 81.

from a traditionalist perspective. Yet religious Zionism shares with secular Zionism the dual perspective that the establishment of a Jewish state is a break with the past and that there is continuity between the establishment of a Jewish state and the Jewish past. This opened the door for rethinking not just particular Jewish laws, but also what Jewish law as such is and should be.

As Kaye has argued, Rabbi Isaac Herzog, the first Ashkenazic Chief Rabbi of the state of Israel, played a central role in shifting the legal philosophy of religious Zionism away from legal pluralism and toward legal centrism. Before coming to Palestine, Herzog, who was born and raised in England, had been the Chief Rabbi of Ireland. His views on the sovereignty of Jewish law owed as much to European debates about legal positivism as to Jewish sources. In fact, he rejected legal pluralism on the basis of an analogy between Jewish and English law: "it is inconceivable that the laws of the Torah should allow for two parallel authorities – like the courts of law and the courts of equity, the latter stemming from the authority of royal law, that operated in the past in England."[37] Before the state of Israel was established, Herzog advocated for a clause in the constitution guaranteeing that all the laws of the state would be based on the Torah.[38] (He did not advocate for a theocracy; he believed the constitution could be both religious and democratic.[39]) No such clause emerged, and neither did a constitution. Although given jurisdiction only over personal law, religious Zionists continued to centralize their authority by standardizing rabbinic courts and procedures.

But legal centrism and standardization were not the only features of the modern nation-state that religious Zionists adopted for their own purposes. They also elevated the significance of individual conviction in matters of conversion. When Goren became Chief Rabbi in 1972, he was confronted with a complicated case in which the Israeli rabbinate would not let a Jewish man marry a Jewish woman in Israel because the man's mother did not get a Jewish divorce from her first husband before marrying the man's father. According to Jewish law, this made the children of the second marriage *mamzerim* (illegitimate), which meant they could only marry Jews who were themselves *mamzerim*. The case caused a public outcry in which many demanded that civil marriage finally be instituted in Israel. Goren intervened and solved the problem by focusing on the fact that the first husband had converted to Judaism in Europe before coming to Israel. He retroactively annulled the conversion of the woman's first husband. Since the conversion was annulled, this wasn't a Jewish marriage, and a Jewish divorce was not required. Hence, although the

[37] Trans. in MICHAEL WALZER, JEWISH POLITICAL TRADITION, 1: AUTHORITY 475 (2003).
[38] Kaye, *Legal Philosophies*, 98.
[39] Kaye, *Legal Philosophies*, 144–88.

children of the second marriage were born out of Jewish wedlock, they were not *mamzerim* and could marry other Jews.[40]

While this creative decision may have solved the immediate crisis, it also changed the terms by which conversion would be understood in Israel.[41] The ultra-Orthodox condemned Goren and the religious Zionist establishment for this decision. From the perspective of Jewish law, membership trumps theology and even religious practice. For instance, rabbinic sources regard an apostate as simply a bad Jew.[42] At the same time, from the perspective of Jewish law, once someone has converted to Judaism they remain Jewish, even if they revert to their old ways.[43] Ultra-Orthodox critics condemned Goren for stripping a convert of his irreversible status as a Jew. However, in recent years, the ultra-Orthodox have adopted this very strategy of annulling conversions. And the Israeli rabbinate's continued attempt to retroactively determine motives in conversions continues to be one of the greatest sources of divisions among Jews in Israel and the Diaspora.

The Israeli rabbinate's position on conversion only makes sense within the context of the religious Zionist establishment's appropriation of several characteristics of the modern nation-state: the centralization and uniformity of legal authority and law, as well as the elevated significance of individual conscience in matters of religion. Similarly, in attempting to institutionalize their policies on conversion, Hindu nationalists have appropriated the modern nation-state's commitment to legal centrism and uniformity, as well as individual conscience in matters of religion.

Nehru's charge to dissolve personal law and enact a uniform civil code, as promised by Article 44 of the Indian constitution, was the foundation of his secularist ideology. While the far right Hindu nationalist group RSS vehemently objected to the reformation of Hindu personal law in the 1950s, the Bharatiya Janata Party (BJP, Indian People's Party), which is widely regarded as the political arm of the RSS,

40 This, the Langer case, first came before the rabbinical courts in 1956, but was only resolved by Goren in 1972. For a brief overview, see DAVID ELLENSON & DANIEL GORDIS, PLEDGES OF JEWISH ALLEGIANCE: CONVERSION, LAW, AND POLICYMAKING IN NINETEENTH AND TWENTIETH-CENTURY ORTHODOX RESPONSA, esp. 145–48 (2012).

41 Netanel Fisher argues that Goren saw this annulment as only a onetime ruling. It seems to me, however, that Goren's decision in the Langer case set in motion the annulling of conversions by a variety of Orthodox rabbis, including the ultra-Orthodox. See Fisher, *Conversion and the State: Israel's Policy on Conversion to Judaism, 1948–2004* (PhD diss., Hebrew University of Jerusalem; Hebrew; 2011), esp. 179–84.

42 In this connection, in the "Brother Daniel" case (H.C. 72/62 Oswald Rufeisen v. Minister of the Interior 16 P.D. 2428), all of the justices agreed that under Jewish law Brother Daniel should be considered Jewish. Nevertheless, the majority ruled that under secular law (i.e., the laws of the state of Israel), his conversion to Christianity meant that he was not to be considered a Jew under the Law of Return.

43 Classical sources such as Yevamot 47b in the Talmud and Shulhan Arukh, Yoreh Deah 268:12 maintain that a convert who converts for ulterior motives or even retracts his conversion is simply a bad Jew. This is a position Maimonides also endorses.

has made the institution of a uniform civil code a cornerstone of its political vision. Hindu nationalists have adopted Nehru and Gandhi's anti-communalism, arguing that from the Indian state's beginning, the Congress Party has capitulated to minority interests. A uniform civil code would, Hindu nationalists contend, offer equal and uniform treatment of all citizens.

It is on the basis of this reasoning that Hindu nationalists have been critical of the reservations system and even more disapproving of granting reservations to converts to Christianity or Islam. A presidential order of 1950 limited caste reservations to Hindus: "no person who professes a religion different from Hinduism shall be deemed a member of the Scheduled Castes." Amendments in 1956 and 1990 allowed for the inclusion of Sikhs and Buddhists. Many converts to Islam and Christianity over the centuries came from lower caste backgrounds. Indeed, conversion was often a means to rid converts of the caste system. Nevertheless, caste often remained operative within these communities. For this reason, Muslim and Christian groups claim discrimination because they are not eligible for reservations for backward castes.[44]

Hindu nationalists have defined religion in terms of individual conviction in order to exclude Muslims and Christians from reservations, arguing that Muslims and Christians are not eligible for reservations because they are no longer Hindus. As one BJP leader put it in 1990, if "those who embrace these religions believe that they are totally free of social discrimination, why should [they] now seek the benefits of these recommendations?"[45] In 2014, BJP Union social justice minister Thavar Chand Gehlot told the *Times of India*, "Allowing S[cheduled] C[aste] status to converts would provide a fillip to religious conversions. The demand is not constitutional, and we want to work within the parameters of the statute for the welfare of these communities."[46] In many ways, the BJP is just extending the reasoning of India's secular courts on this matter. The Madras Court summarized this reasoning in a 1952 case, *Michael v. Venkataswaran*: "the general rule is [that] conversion operates as an expulsion from caste … a convert ceases to have any caste."[47] As Marc Galanter notes, there seems to be a double standard here: "Non-Hindus cannot be made the recipients of preferences on the basis of purely religious classification in the absence of other evidence of backwardness. One wonders why they can be

[44] SATISH DESHPANDE, DALITS IN THE MUSLIM AND CHRISTIAN COMMUNITIES: A STATUS REPORT ON CURRENT SOCIAL SCIENTIFIC KNOWLEDGE (2010).

[45] As quoted in Thomas Blom Hansen, *BJP and the Politics of Hindutva in Maharashtra*, in COMPULSIONS OF POLITICS: BJP AND COMPETITIVE POLITICS IN INDIA 135, n. 18 (ed. T. B. Hansen & Christophe Jaffrelot, 1998).

[46] http://timesofindia.indiatimes.com/india/Govt-opposed-to-Dalit-status-for-converts/articleshow/44765858.cms.

[47] As quoted in Marc Galanter, *Religious Aspects of Caste: A Legal View*, in TRADITIONAL AND MODERN LEGAL INSTITUTIONS IN ASIA AND AFRICA 112 (ed. David C. Buxbaum, 1968).

excluded from preferences on a purely religious basis in spite of the presence of such evidence."[48]

The most blatant use of liberal principles to advance the claims of Hindu nationalism finds its expression in India's anti-conversion laws. Heiner Bielefeldt, UN Special Rapporteur on freedom of religion or belief, described Hindu nationalist legislation on conversion as "a human rights problem of great concern" and pushed India to "consistently respect, protect and promote the human right to freedom of religion or belief in the area of conversion."[49] Today's anti-conversion laws in India find their basis in the Madhya Pradesh state-government-sponsored 1956 *Report of the Christian Missionary Activities Enquiry Committee*, known also as the Niyogi Report.[50] Protestant groups began to set up missions in the area in 1868, and large numbers of Hindus converted to Christianity at the end of the nineteenth century. By 1956, Madhya Pradesh had thirty-two Protestant missionary organizations set up by foreign missionaries. The report criticized missionaries for using fraudulent and illicit means, as well as force, in converting "illiterate aboriginals and other backward people." It recommended that missionaries with the sole aim of proselytism leave the region. Religious groups who promoted conversion but were also involved in charitable activities were asked to register with the local government. Potential converts had to receive statewide board approval before converting, and medical or other services could not be offered in exchange for conversion.[51]

Leaving aside the obviously large and complex question of whether missionaries were in fact using coercion or other illicit means to convert people, we focus here on the ways in which the recommendations in this report have become the basis for various freedom of religion bills, also known as anti-conversion laws. For instance, the Gujarat Religious Freedom Act of 2003 gives the government the right to "prescribe by rules, the form and time limit within which the person converted is required to give intimation." It does so because the Act's purpose is to "provide freedom of religion by prohibition of conversion from one religion."[52] Here freedom of religion is defined as freedom to preserve one's own religion, and conversion to another religion is seen as potentially threatening the prospective convert's original religion.

[48] Galanter, *Religious Aspects*, 114.

[49] www.christianitytoday.com/gleanings/2012/november/most-troubling-violation-of-human-rights-conversion-says.html?paging=off#bmb.

[50] Gauri Viswanathan, *Literacy and Conversion in the Discourse of Hindu Nationalism*, in CRISIS OF SECULARISM IN INDIA 333–55 (ed. A. D. Needham & R. S. Rajan, 2007). Laura Dudley Jenkins, *Legal Limits on Religious Conversion in India*, 78 LAW & CONTEMPORARY PROBLEMS 109–28 (spring 2008).

[51] Chad M. Bauman, *Postcolonial Anxiety and Anti-conversion Sentiment in the Report of the Christian Missionary Activities Enquiry Committee*, 12.2 INT'L J. HINDU STUDIES 181–213 (2008).

[52] www.emw-d.de/fix/files/indien-religionsgesetz.pdf.

While Christian groups oppose India's anti-conversion laws, some Christian groups in the United States have made similar claims about freedom of religion to argue for religious exemptions in disputes about gay marriage and contraception. "Religious rights bills" in Arizona, Kansas, Tennessee, Idaho, South Dakota, Mississippi, and Oklahoma have all attempted to argue that, on the basis of religious freedom, Christians may choose not to provide services to same-sex couples. Arguments for religious freedom have also been made for religious exemptions for employers who do not wish to pay for contraception for their employees. My aim is not to weigh in on whether these are good arguments or not. Rather, my point is that Hindu nationalist views of conversion are similarly expressed not in the language of religious fundamentalism, but in the modern state's own language of freedom of religion, the sovereignty and uniformity of law, and the importance of individual conviction.

Sumantra Bose has described Hindutva politics as "far more an explicitly modern political interpretation of pan-Indian nationalism than a manifestation of atavistic 'religious fundamentalism.'"[53] As we have seen, this too is the case when it comes to Hindu nationalist approaches to conversion. We have also seen that the politics of religious Zionism are best understood as a modern interpretation of the secular Zionist commitment to legal centrism and individual conscience in matters of religion, rather than as an expression of religious traditionalism or fundamentalism. What does this mean for thinking about whether conversion is a human right?

CONCLUSION

We have seen that religious Zionists and Hindu nationalists share a deep ambivalence about conversion, that their secular counterparts share this anxiety, and that the policies on conversion instituted by religious Zionists and Hindu nationalists have been shaped by the discourse and tools of the modern nation-state, and not by traditionalist or fundamentalist religious arguments. This analysis shows, I believe, that anxieties about conversion in Israel and India are as much political as they are religious. As such, the question to be asked about conversion policies in Israel and India is not about religious freedom, but about political and national identity, and more specifically markers of citizenship.

Goldie Osuri links debates about conversion in India to questions of national sovereignty: "conversion figures not only as a religious matter, but constitutes the fear of divisible sovereignty."[54] I take Osuri's point to be that just as Hindu nationalists attempt to suppress difference with their views of conversion, so too the modern

[53] Sumantra Bose, *Hindu Nationalism and the Crisis of the Indian State: A Theoretical Perspective*, in NATIONALISM, DEMOCRACY AND DEVELOPMENT: STATE AND POLITICS IN INDIA 145 (ed. S. Bose & A. Jalal, 1998).

[54] GOLDIE OSURI, RELIGIOUS FREEDOM IN INDIA: SOVEREIGNTY AND (ANTI-) CONVERSION 29 (2102).

nation-state seeks to suppress difference with its claim to sovereignty. There can be no denying the perniciousness of the suppression of difference. Nevertheless, I would argue against Osuri and many others that the quest for national unity, indeed for sovereignty, can be a good. It is also, I maintain, unavoidable in human affairs. The question to be asked, then, is not whether sovereignty or national solidarity are good things, but rather how a tendency toward erasing differences can be mitigated in a democratic society.

As Bose remarks, "Hindu nationalists … equate 'national culture' with what they call 'Hindu culture,' a 'concept; not necessarily any more dubious than Nehru's dream of a unified, uniform (and 'secular') culture."[55] Seen in this light, we might ask, does the idea of the French Republic differ in kind from the idea of a Jewish or Hindu state? This is a question that many would find ludicrous. Yet I believe that our consideration of religious Zionist and Hindu nationalist anxieties about conversion allows us to see why it might be a question worth considering. The religious Zionist conception of Jewish identity and the Hindu nationalist conception of Hindu identity are closer to notions of French identity than they are to modern conceptions of Christian identity. A Jewish state, a Hindu state, and a French state all share a republican vision of national uniformity based on ancestry, land, and history. Seen in this context, anxieties about conversion in India and Israel are anxieties about citizenship, just as anxieties in France about *laïcité* are anxieties about citizenship. For this reason, concerns, even ambivalence, about conversion in Israel and India can be legitimate, since they are worries about ever-unresolved matters of national identity, which are intrinsic to all sovereign states.

Of course this does not mean that all policies regulating conversion in Israel and India are legitimate. But I suggest that regulation of conversion in Israel and India is not intrinsically illegitimate, so long as conversion is neither mandated nor outright barred. Rather than criticizing Israel and India's conversion policies in terms of a universal human right to conversion, a more apt criticism of religious Zionist and Hindu nationalist policies on conversion would be to point to their resistance to the diversity of their citizenry. The Israeli system does penalize Jews, or those who want to identify as Jews, for not converting according to the arguably narrow criteria of the Israeli rabbinate. The Indian system does penalize Hindus (again defined broadly) who have converted to Christianity or Islam by denying them access to the benefits of the reservations system codified in the Indian constitution. And anti-conversion laws in India passed by Hindu nationalists do place a burden on potential converts to Christianity or Islam by bureaucratizing the conversion process. But the problem in these cases, I would argue, is not one of religious freedom, but of legal centralization

[55] Bose, *Hindu Nationalism*, 159.

and uniformity, which in the context of Israel and India are used to resist political (and not just religious) forms of pluralism.

Ironically, in the context of contemporary discussions of religious freedom and human rights, the states of India and Israel would be more democratic when it comes to matters of conversion by maintaining their historical systems of personal law, not at the expense of but in conjunction with uniform civil systems of law. Here again India and Israel are reverse images of one another. The task for India is to protect its personal law systems for minorities, together with its civil system. And the task for Israel is to finally create a system of civil law to exist side by side with its personal law.[56]

56 I am not suggesting a return to premodern political conditions in either India or Israel, but rather pointing to what Griffiths calls "soft legal pluralism." Griffiths insists that soft legal pluralism implies a necessary movement toward centrism and the necessary inferiority of personal law to state law (Griffiths, *Legal Pluralism*, 41–42). From my perspective, this need not be the case. Instead, personal law and minority status can be better options for freedom of religion for minority groups than a one-law-fits-all system. HANNA LERNER, MAKING CONSTITUTIONS IN DEEPLY DIVIDED SOCIETIES (2011) illustrates this point well.

Index

www.ingramcontent.com/pod-product-compliance
Lightning Source LLC
LaVergne TN
LVHW011523200926
848484LV00001B/134